EDUCATION ACROSS A CENTURY: THE CENTENNIAL VOLUME

EDUCATION ACROSS A CENTURY:
THE CENTENNIAL VOLUME

*One Hundredth Yearbook of the
National Society for the Study of Education*

PART I

Edited by
LYN CORNO

Distributed by THE UNIVERSITY OF CHICAGO PRESS • CHICAGO, ILLINOIS

National Society for the Study of Education

The National Society for the Study of Education was founded in 1901 as successor to the National Herbart Society. It publishes a two-volume Yearbook, each volume dealing with a separate topic of concern to educators. The Society's series of Yearbooks, now in its one hundredth year, contains chapters written by scholars and practitioners noted for their significant work on the topics about which they write.

The Society welcomes as members all individuals who wish to receive its publications. Current membership includes educators in the United States, Canada, and elsewhere throughout the world—professors, researchers, administrators, and graduate students in colleges and universities and teachers, administrators, supervisors, and curriculum specialists in elementary and secondary schools.

Members of the Society elect a Board of Directors. Its responsibilities include reviewing proposals for Yearbooks, authorizing the preparation of Yearbooks based on accepted proposals, and appointing an editor or editors to oversee the preparation of manuscripts.

Current dues (for the year 2001) are a modest $35 ($30 for retired members and for students in their first year of membership). Members whose dues are paid for the current calendar year receive the Society's Yearbook, are eligible for election to the Board of Directors, and are entitled to a 33 percent discount when purchasing past Yearbooks from the Society's distributor, the University of Chicago Press.

Each year the Society arranges for meetings to be held in conjunction with the annual conferences of one or more of the national educational organizations. At these meetings, the current Yearbook is presented and critiqued. All members are urged to attend these meetings. Members are encouraged to submit proposals for future Yearbooks.

Education Across a Century: The Centennial Volume is Part I of the 100th Yearbook. Part II, published simultaneously, is entitled *From the Capitol to the Classroom: Standards-based Reform in the States*.

For further information, write to the Secretary, NSSE, College of Education, University of Illinois at Chicago, 1040 W. Harrison St., Chicago, Illinois 60607-7133.

ISSN: 0077-5762

Published 2001 by the
NATIONAL SOCIETY FOR THE STUDY OF EDUCATION
1040 W. Harrison St., Chicago, Illinois 60607-7133
© 2001 by the National Society for the Study of Education

First Printing
Printed in the United States of America

iv

Dedication

This volume is dedicated to Kenneth J. Rehage,
to honor the portion of the twentieth century
that he devoted tirelessly to NSSE.

Acknowledgments

I inherited the editorship of this volume because of the timing of my appointments to the Board of Directors; I am just one of several Board members who assisted in its preparation. They all deserve thanks from the Society for such a good start on this task. In addition, I must thank Ken Rehage for the background material on NSSE that he provided so generously. Margaret Early was an important calming influence at several junctures in the process; her experience with the full range of requisite editorial tasks served me well. I appreciate fully the work each chapter's authors did to send us their best possible writing, and for their yielding in several cases to an unfamiliar style. Finally, thanks to Liz Sullivan, my dear friend and superior copy editor, for her expertise and generosity.

LYN CORNO
Editor

Editor's Preface

This Yearbook of the National Society for the Study of Education (NSSE) marks the centennial of the Society's founding in 1901, as well as the advent of the twenty-first century. It emphasizes historically important education themes in the context of the present and future.

The full series of NSSE volumes is perhaps best viewed as foundational. Topics range from philosophical issues to educational innovations and include a variety of disciplinary perspectives on curricular change. For example, Part I of the First NSSE Yearbook, which appeared in 1902, was entitled *Some Principles in the Teaching of History*. It was written entirely by Lucy M. Salmon, then a professor of history at Vassar College. Charles A. McMurry, who was the first Secretary-Treasurer of the Society, edited the volume. Part II was entitled *The Progress of Geography in the Schools*, and its main chapter, bearing the same title, was written by Professor W. M. Davis of Harvard University. Part II had one other chapter, "The Relation of Geography to the Sciences," written by Herbert M. Wilson of the U.S. Geological Survey. Ensuing volumes of NSSE Yearbooks began to move away from this format to include multiple authors and several chapters. The annual appearance of two clothbound volumes established the Society's reputation for a balanced and historically rich treatment of broad topics by scholars in education. With the addition of the series, *Contemporary Educational Issues*, beginning in 1971 and terminating in 1995, the Society also addressed more specialized topics, including, for example, urban education and school leadership.

Some NSSE Yearbooks and chapters have been reprinted by request, such as Part II of the Forty-first Yearbook, *Philosophies of Education*, prepared by a committee under the chairmanship of John S. Brubacher. The nineteenth printing of that volume was done in 1966, twenty-four years after it was first published in 1942. As of 1966, 41,600 copies of the volume had been printed. Two NSSE publications have been translated and printed in other countries. One is *Pygmalion Reconsidered*, one of the first volumes (1971) in the Contemporary Educational Issues series. It was edited by Janet D. Elashoff and Richard E. Snow, and was translated into German. More recently, there have been requests to reprint George Madaus's chapter written for the Eighty-seventh Yearbook, Part I, entitled "The Influence of Testing on the Curriculum." This chapter was included, along with others addressing significant issues in curriculum, in the special Ninety-ninth Yearbook, Part II, in which Margaret Early and Kenneth Rehage presented important chapters from past NSSE Yearbooks.

A personal or professional library of the complete collection of NSSE volumes provides an ample research base for an extensive historical analysis of American education in the twentieth century. For scholars in education, NSSE Yearbooks represent a unique record of the history of the field. Although Yearbooks traditionally addressed topics of national import, nothing else like the NSSE collection is available elsewhere in the world.

To commemorate these considerable achievements and to position the Society as it looks forward in the new century, the Board of Directors worked to identify a range of subjects worthy of consideration across one hundred years. Plans for this volume began more than five years ago after the Board of Directors decided that some sort of special publication would be appropriate to celebrate the Society's Centennial Year in 2001. Karen K. Zumwalt, then a member of the Board, volunteered to work with a group of her students to conduct a preliminary review of all the volumes in the Yearbook series. Working only with the *titles* of Yearbooks, this group identified several topics that were addressed frequently in the Yearbooks over the years. They noted specific yearbooks that appeared to be related to these topics.

The next step was to review actual *contents* of the Yearbooks related to the most frequently recurring topics. Various Board members agreed to undertake this review, looking for material in the Yearbooks that could provide the basis for a synthesizing chapter on each of the topics to be included in what came to be called the "Centennial" volume. These reviews resulted in the elimination of some topics as subjects for such a chapter.

There remained aspects of education that will be present perennially for those who struggle to understand and improve children's learning and the nature of schooling. Themes related to these subjects have evolved over the years, and some have been supplanted. Every subject, however, has persistent issues. New problems and resolutions are also reflected in themes that emerged.

Board members volunteered to locate a well-qualified author for each chapter. The authors' charge was to bring their knowledge of the subject forward to the present and, where possible, to look beyond. We asked, in particular, that authors make interpretations against the backdrop of what they found in the Yearbooks. Each author worked closely with a designated member of the Board of Directors to craft the best possible chapter for the Centennial volume.

A stellar cast of chapter authors agreed to analyze what past NSSE volumes have to say about each subject. I am grateful to former and current Board members who, along with myself, provided expert assistance in working with authors. They include Hilda Borko, Robert Calfee, Lilian Katz, Mark Smylie, and Susan Stodolsky.

The chapter authors have done an impressive job in handling the Board's original request. Although each has taken a slightly different approach to the task, there is a consistent appreciation for the material across chapters as each author or team accomplished what at first seemed impossible.

The volume opens with chapters on general substantive areas of education. In this case, a sense of the bigger picture aids consideration of more specific topics.

Curriculum theorist Frances Schoonmaker carefully examines her field in Chapter I, "Curriculum Making, Models, Practices and Issues: A Knowledge Fetish?" The next chapter, written by learning theorist Richard E. Mayer, analyzes NSSE's writing on the psychology of learning in, "Changing Conceptions of Learning: A Century of Progress in the Scientific Study of Education." Chapter III is written by sociologist Elizabeth G. Cohen, who also uses a change metaphor to discuss issues related to equity in "A Shifting Social Context: NSSE Looks at Equity in Schools and Classrooms." In the fourth chapter, educational psychologists Nancy E. Perry and Philip H. Winne address the subject of "Individual Differences and Diversity in Twentieth Century Classrooms."

The next part of the Yearbook presents several chapters written by subject area experts, each addressing more specific concepts and topics. These include, in order of appearance, Stacie G. Goffin's chapter, "Whither Early Childhood Care and Education in the Next Century?" and Richard L. Venezky's "A Century of NSSE Publications on Reading." These two chapters are accompanied by three more on "The Legitimacy of Social Studies in the Curriculum," by Stephen Thornton; "Modern Content and the Enterprise of Science: Science Education in the Twentieth Century," by Joseph Krajcik, Rachel Mamlok, and Barbara Hug; and "Mathematics Education in the Twentieth Century," by Alan Schoenfeld.

The final chapter in the volume presents a critical analysis of NSSE material entitled "The Social Foundations of Education: School and

Society in a Century of NSSE," written by Steve Tozer and Ilhan Avcioglu. Steve and his co-author are in the College of Education at NSSE's new home, the University of Illinois at Chicago. I have located this chapter at the end to close the volume by echoing perhaps the most prominent theme throughout: From the opening of the 20th Century to now, there has been a clear evolution in the way NSSE has explained education issues that mirrors changes in society and social discourse.

Current NSSE Board member, Mark Smylie, has taken over for Ken Rehage as Secretary-Treasurer for the Society until a permanent replacement can be appointed. In 1999, the NSSE Board of Directors celebrated Ken's retirement with him, and said thanks and farewell to the University of Chicago. Interim Secretary-Treasurer Mark Smylie's expansive vision for the Society's future guided NSSE successfully to its new home in 2000.

Although our gratitude to Ken Rehage is beyond bounds, we also wish to recognize the founding members of the Society—John Dewey, Nicholas Murray Butler, and Charles Hubbard Judd. In addition to Ken, who served as Secretary-Treasurer from 1972 until 1999, other Secretary-Treasurers included Guy M. Whipple, who served from 1916-1941; Nelson B. Henry, 1941-1959; and Herman G. Richey, who preceded Ken from 1959-1972.

I speak for the Board in saying we are confident that readers will discover much fresh material within the pages of this Centennial volume, as well as some important perspectives on history. Please join us as we celebrate the past one hundred years of NSSE and anticipate the next!

LYN CORNO

Table of Contents

CHAPTER I

Curriculum Making, Models, Practices and Issues: A Knowledge Fetish?

FRANCES SCHOONMAKER[1]

We are fond of telling each other that this is a period of change, that we are at the parting of the ways. Then we tell each other that people have always said this in every age. Finally, we add that this really does seem rather more of a turning-point than usual, that, in fact, it is a genuine nodal point. Certainly it seems hard to find a time when there were quite so many new educational methods flying about.

> Sir John Adams, Sometime University Professor of
> Education in the University of London, 1927[2]

New educational methods were flying about when Harold Rugg proposed that the National Society for the Study of Education (NSSE) undertake a fundamental look at the curriculum of the schools for its Twenty-sixth Yearbook. The emerging field of curriculum was oriented toward the practical. Schools all across the country were creating new curricula and methods of teaching. Assisting them was a brand-new central-office professional: the curriculum specialist. Most of these specialists were assigned the task of selection and organization of content to be taught. But traditional classroom practices were being challenged by the child-development movement and new advances in what was considered to be the science of education. There were strong divisions among school people over the new educational methods and curriculum development practices. Rugg saw the central issue as a split between those who favored a child-centered approach to the curriculum and those who were future oriented and thought in terms of adult life needs. His idea in proposing the Yearbook was to bring together leading curriculum thinkers with divergent viewpoints and, along the lines of the educational forums of the old Herbart Society,

Frances Schoonmaker is Associate Professor of Education at Teachers College, Columbia University.

get them to talk through their differences and arrive at a synthesis that would strengthen the field.

In looking at the contribution that NSSE Yearbooks have made to our understanding of curriculum making, models, practices, and issues, the Twenty-sixth Yearbook stands as a monument. This is not only due to its monumental two-volume, six-hundred-page size, but for the vision it outlined for the field. Mary Louise Seguel called it "a landmark attempt to draw together all the ideas on curriculum making which had been elaborated upon and tested up to that point."[3] While the vision has been described as being so general as to have little meaning,[4] the vision "came as close to being a statement of curriculum theory as anything set forth up to that time."[5] In later years, Rugg credited the Twenty-sixth Yearbook with beginning a shift in the way curriculum was thought about. "That the report was widely read and discussed is a matter of history."[6] The issues and theoretical positions it delineated were clarified as a result of the Yearbook Committee's efforts, but not put to rest. Indeed, Herbert M. Kliebard marked its contribution to the emergence of still another perspective on the purposes of the curriculum, one that saw the curriculum of the schools as a vehicle for social justice.[7] One would be hard pressed to relate the Twenty-sixth Yearbook's conception of curriculum theory to that of contemporary curriculum discourse. But a great deal of the curriculum theorizing of our day explores the same pivotal issues that concerned the Yearbook Committee, albeit in novel and more complex ways.

While the Twenty-sixth Yearbook is a landmark, it does not stand alone. The titles of NSSE Yearbooks are, in themselves, "a kind of history," reflective of the development of the curriculum field.[8] Prior to the early part of the nineteenth century, educational literature was characterized by a "preoccupation with instructional method," and curriculum was seen primarily as the content or subject matter to be taught.[9] Therefore, it is not surprising to find that more attention has been given to the *subjects* of the curriculum over the hundred years of the Society than to any other topic.

Except in the Fourth Yearbook, *The Place of Vocational Subjects in the High-School Curriculum*, more than two decades passed before the word *curriculum* appeared in a title. Early publications looked at the teaching of history, geography, nature study, and English; vocational, industrial, and health education; and kindergarten. As demands on the schools increased, more and more subjects were added to the curriculum; these were some of the subjects being discussed. While methods of teaching had been the focus of early publications, subject matter specialists began to deal with the rationale for their particular interests to justify these interests in the curriculum. These discussions, beginning with the First Yearbook on teaching of history, contained important curriculum concepts and are deserving of consideration in their own right. This work is not attempted in the present chapter, but remains a pertinent question.

In this chapter, I focus on Yearbooks that seem most related to curriculum as a distinct field of study. This not only includes those volumes with the word "curriculum" in the title—these are few—but those dealing with materials of instruction (including textbooks and technologies), developmental and learning theory, models and methods, and issues connected to curriculum.[10] The Twenty-sixth Yearbook is placed in a positioning point, with contributions before and after viewed in terms of its legacy. Of particular interest is tracing the separation of instruction from curriculum as the curriculum field developed. For many educators and educational researchers "curriculum" came to be seen as a design process, and "instruction" as the implementation of methods and strategies designed to teach a curriculum. The implications of this separation were profound and shaped how we have come to understand curriculum-making, models, issues, and practices, particularly as these affect the role of the teacher.

A Period of Change

The organization of a society for the study of educational issues and problems and the birth of the curriculum field are related to the same sentiments and events. The historical period has been described as one of ferment.[11] Curriculum thinking had outgrown Herbartian theory and the Herbart Society,[12] but the need for a forum for curriculum thinking remained. Schools were being called upon to include more curricula that would serve the interests of the expanding scientific, technological, and industrial complex. In turn, teachers felt the pressure of trying to include more than the school day would hold. Borrowing from business and industry, educators began to talk about efficiency and effectiveness, and look carefully at how to streamline what was now an unwieldy set of school offerings.

What *should* the schools be teaching?[13] Herbert Spencer's question, "What knowledge is of most worth?" had framed the task of curriculum thinking since he first posed it in the mid-1800s. Now it framed the problem that faced the Twenty-sixth Yearbook Committee. The Fourteenth, Seventeenth, and Eighteenth Committees had looked for

answers, reporting on the ongoing work of the Committee on Minimal
Essentials and the Committee on Economy of Time in Education. The
Committee on Minimal Essentials, which included such luminaries as
William Bagley, W. W. Charters, and W. S. Gray, saw the solution to
crowding in the curriculum as a matter of time-efficiency. With appropriate management of the school day and an understanding of "the
social value of the content of the several school subjects," the elementary school educator was thought to be equipped to deal with the pressures of preparing children for life.[14] Inherent in the work of these
committees were questions of worth, but questions of *how much* and
how efficiently eclipsed considerations of purpose and meaning. The
same could be said for the two curriculum-related Yearbooks following.

The Nineteenth and Twentieth Yearbooks reported work of the
Society's Committee on New Materials of Instruction. The Yearbooks
identified a new role for schools in "continuously enriching and revising their materials of instruction."[15] The Committee on New Materials of Instruction argued that the knowledge explosion in every field of
study associated with school curriculum made it impossible to count
on textbooks to present the most current information in any given
field, whether one accepted the prominent place of textbooks in the
curriculum. Curriculum development, despite the "extreme conservatism" of schools, was seen as an essential activity if schools were to
take advantage of the latest research.

The Committee emphasized the role of the teacher in making new
knowledge available to students. It was acknowledged that, unfortunately, not everyone shared this view of the teacher's crucial role. The
Committee had issued a call for activities and materials to be created in
classrooms across the country, and planned to use selected examples in
the Yearbook. Disappointed by the low response by schools, the Committee speculated that "the idea that a teacher may be professionally
productive in a small way has still to be established . . ." and suggested
that publications such as the Yearbook would contribute to understanding the teacher's professionalism.[16] The Society clearly saw these pre-
cursors to the Twenty-sixth Yearbook as "a portion of the contribution
made by this society toward the reorganization of the curriculum."[17]

Extra-Curricular Activities was the topic of the Twenty-fifth Yearbook. The difficult line between what is and is not academic was
acknowledged and re-drawn. The Yearbook Committee apologetically
defined "extra-curricular" as something outside the usual subjects
taught in school or what was considered academic in the traditional

sense. The problem of crowding was relieved, in part, by placing the non-academic outside the boundaries that began and ended the official school day.

Rather More of a Turning-Point Than Usual

The following year, *The Foundations and Technique of Curriculum Construction* appeared, and for the next two decades, it outsold any other Yearbooks produced by the Society.[18] Public opinion regarding the need for curriculum reform in American schools had reached a peak.[19] Curriculum thinkers differed sharply over how to solve the various problems of the schools. In devoting both volumes of its Twenty-sixth Yearbook to "curriculum-making," the Society underscored the gravity of the debate. Its purpose was to show state-of-the-art curriculum (Part I) and to present a consensus perspective that would unify disparate views and could be used as a point of departure for future curriculum initiatives (Part II). Indeed, the "List of Fundamental Questions on Curriculum Making" that preceded the general statement, hammered out by a Committee whose greatest problem was failing to understand one another,[20] formed the basic principles of the emerging field of curriculum inquiry for years to come.

Committee membership "was selected so as to assemble in one working committee the country's outstanding child-centered Progressives (led by Kilpatrick and Bonser) and subject-centered Essentialists (led by Bagley and Judd) for the purpose of trying to achieve a body of agreed-upon theory and proposed curriculum revision."[21] Six professors were included, with twenty associated contributors drawn from administrators and teachers. While no women were on the Committee proper, six of the twenty Associated Contributors were women. Later, Rugg was critical of the Committee's composition:

I wish now that I had known enough in picking the committee to include several of the great leaders on the sociological, psychological, and esthetic frontiers. . . . It might have been difficult, if not impossible, to secure a community of discourse and thought between them and the professors of education for whose scholarship they had little respect. I did the next best thing: I wove into the report the essence of the views of these students of the social frontier. But as for esthetics, that was a blind spot, only to be filled in during the next decade of my own studies.[22]

So, while Rugg clearly saw the need for diversity, he was thinking within the limits of his era. Academic diversity might have enhanced the group's work and, as Rugg speculated, its complexity. Viewed through the present understanding of diversity, one can also ask what might have happened had members of under-represented groups been added to the mix.

Work began with a nationwide survey of current practices in public and private schools to find out whether schools were revising their curricula and, if so, how they were going about doing it. Part I of the Yearbook reported the survey results. It confirmed that curriculum-making was going on across the country. Practice was developing so rapidly that procedures were widely varied; and a concern for standards of practice was commonly expressed.

The experience reported by Stuart A. Courtis was typical. He had found that the evolution of curriculum-making was "the result of the play of chance forces, not of conscious design." Hence, it should be no surprise to the reader to learn that the "outstanding characteristic to be presented by this report is *diversity*."[23] George S. Counts reported that for every subject that had been dropped from the curriculum, three were added in the new curriculum-making efforts, a situation that could not go on indefinitely.[24] Researchers found that teacher committees working with a supervisor or administrator were widely used in curriculum revision. Subject matter content was emphasized. The Yearbook also revealed the extent to which testing was embedded in school practice.[25]

In addition to the surveys, a series of five round tables was planned. These were held for half a day over one or two days for the next two and one-half years. To launch the activity, eight Yearbook Committee members were asked to prepare statements regarding issues and problems in curriculum-making. These were the base of discussion and allowed members to tease out differences in perspective. Rugg hoped the group would arrive at a philosophical position that synthesized these varied perspectives into a more powerful organic whole.

The second volume began with a statement about the foundations of curriculum-making, which was the result of the round-table meetings. It suggested what members could agree to, rather than their differences. "From the beginning of our discussion it was apparent that we did not understand each other," Rugg said.[26] Members identified prejudices and aversions to particular terms, for example, "project method," and found a vocabulary upon which they could agree. The group also discovered that they tended to attack or defend. However, their success was, perhaps, due to the fact that "discussions, beginning almost always with debate, were dominated by a willingness to listen, and eventuated in real roundtable conferences,"[27] which produced the Composite Statement, "The Foundations of Curriculum-Making." The experience was, as Rugg titled the introduction to Part II, "An Adventure in Understanding." The statement began with the "List of Fundamental Questions on Curriculum-Making," followed by the fifty-eight articles of the general statement. The remainder of the book was devoted to statements by Committee members, along with representative quotations from John Dewey, the Herbartians, and their critics.

Each member was given an opportunity to respond to the document. For the most part, responses clarified differing curriculum theories and ranged from W. W. Charters' one-page comment to a lengthy article by William H. Kilpatrick. Herbert M. Kliebard referred to Franklin Bobbitt's statement as the most startling because he affirmed living life in the present, not preparing for adult life, as the central purpose of education. "One can only conclude that Kilpatrick succeeded in completely mesmerizing him."[28] An alternative explanation, given Bobbitt's career over time, is that he was more open to alternative perspectives than he is often given credit for being. In any case, Bobbitt's statement was the only one that showed any real change from his original position.

A Genuine Nodal Point

Over the years, the Twenty-sixth Yearbook has received differing reviews, but those who are seriously interested in the history of education have not ignored it. Ralph W. Tyler credited the Yearbook with providing a critical review of what were current practices, outlining steps for the future, and "clarifying the problems which pioneer curriculum workers were encountering in codifying the conclusions they were reaching regarding the proper perspectives, approaches, and assumptions likely to be helpful in dealing with these problems." He noted, "Rereading these volumes today, one is impressed with the extent to which the proposals made are consistent with contemporary experience."[29]

Robert J. Schaefer criticized the Yearbook for being too school centered and contributing to a pre-empting of education by schools of education. He called Rugg to task for failing to include on the Yearbook Committee scholars from the university disciplines, a criticism that Rugg made of the Committee himself, as noted earlier.[30] However, Rugg did not regret including university professors of education and school-based people, which seemed to be another point of irritation to Schaefer.

Seguel pointed out, "The Committee signed a joint statement, but it was a cautious and limited agreement." While key issues were clarified, "The statement succeeded in clothing the agreements in language general enough to justify a continued academic discussion of the real issues, but, as Rugg himself said, the general statement tended to 'flatten out peaks of emphasis.'"[31] At the same time, it made a significant contribution by illuminating past developments in curriculum and setting the tasks to be undertaken in the future. An array of curriculum workers were identified and the professional role of curriculum specialist legitimized. Perhaps, as Seguel postulated, the Committee essentially made the central argument Rugg had identified, that of child versus society, an irrelevant one by virtue of the thoroughness with which the issue was explored:

By the time the discussions were over, the antagonists knew their differences very well. They did not relinquish them as much as they relinquished their partisan value. The controversy between the claims of the child and society became a permanent one, unsettled, but valuable as a foundational problem and a stimulus to thought. The discussion served to clear the air and enable the profession to move on to equally urgent problems which had not yet been attempted.[32]

Furthermore, the Yearbook enabled Rugg to "subtly infuse curriculum making with the spirit of social criticism."[33]

Kliebard's assessment was not as generous. He referred to the consensus statement as "not so much a reconstruction or reformulation of the different strains of curriculum reform that had emerged since the 1890s as it was a glossing over of the profound differences as to the direction the curriculum should take."[34] George A. Beauchamp held another opinion: "It is a curious thing that efforts of this kind have not been repeated with regularity so that the likenesses and differences of curriculum positions would be kept as clear as they were illuminated by those theorists in 1927."[35]

Decker Walker, too, suggested that the Yearbook was "deserving of more attention and appreciation than it receives."[36] He lauded its focus on curriculum and curriculum-making, acknowledging that it did not arrive at the consensus that it had hoped to achieve. Perhaps, as Daniel Tanner and Laurel Tanner argued, "Whether the committee was cautious or wholehearted in its agreement matters little. The point of importance is that curriculum as a field of professional work emerged from these principles."[37]

Florence B. Stratemeyer's persistent life situations and the "Tyler rationale" may have been linked to ideas that were important to various Committee members. The Twenty-sixth Yearbook definition, for example, underscored the importance of helping the learner control life situations.[38] And the "scientific principles" laid down by the Committee were compatible with Tyler's approach. These principles included the study of American life and individual development as the basis for determining goals and curriculum content. Three "technical tasks of major importance"[39] were: determining long- and short-term objectives of education, experimental discovery of activities and materials of instruction, and finding a process for selecting and organizing learning experiences for each grade level. Through the individual statements, the basic platform of the child-centered approach to education was set forth, ground was laid for the curriculum to focus on society's ills, and the time-honored discipline-based approach was not abandoned. The definition of curriculum and the process of curriculum development were left at a very general level, remaining a source of disagreement within the maturing field of curriculum practice.

The Parting of the Ways

The Committee found it difficult to come up with a definition of curriculum that all members would approve. They agreed in their rejection of curriculum as "formal subject matter (facts, processes, principles), set-out-to-be-learned without adequate relation to life."[40] But it was clear from the supplementary statements that followed the Composite Statement that they held different views as to what this actually meant. Some members seemed to think it was a repudiation of the old discipline-based curriculum, while others seemed to think it meant that the traditional subjects should not be badly taught. Their definition was broad:

The curriculum should be conceived as a succession of experiences and enterprises having a maximum of lifelikeness for the learner. The materials of instruction should be selected and organized with a view to giving the learner that development most helpful in meeting and controlling life situations. Learning takes place most effectively and economically in the matrix of a situation which grips the learner, which is to him vital—worth while. Traits learned in a natural, or lifelike setting, give promise of emerging definitely in appropriate conduct. It is the task of the teacher and the curriculum-maker, therefore, to select and organize materials which will give the learner that development most helpful in meeting and controlling life situations. The method by which the learner works out these experiences, enterprises, exercises, should be such as calls for maximum self-direction, assumption of responsibility, of exercise of choice in terms of life values.[41]

The overall stance taken by the Committee reflected developments in educational psychology, both in its emphasis on the term "learner," and in its emphasis on changed behavior as an outcome of the curriculum.

Curriculum theorists have routinely discussed the matter of definition. Curriculum has been seen as content, or subjects to be learned, while learning of skills and concepts has been viewed as experience. The school's planned program has been considered the vehicle for reconstruction of society and the means of cultural reproduction.[42] Curriculum has been thought about in terms of function, structure, and source. Curriculum has been defined as textbooks, as Arthur W. Foshay pointed out in the Eighty-ninth Yearbook,[43] and as tests, as George F. Madaus suggested in the Eighty-seventh Yearbook.[44]

Numerous questions are related to definition. Among them are 1) Does curriculum encompass both methods and teaching? 2) Is the curriculum the content which can be delivered through any number of instructional methods? 3) Is the role of the teacher to be one of curriculum decision maker or one who implements a program designed off-site? These questions were of interest to the Twenty-sixth Yearbook Committee and to many Yearbook committees thereafter. In following the various definitions of curriculum, we can see "the parting of the ways" as curriculum was defined as a holistic process that included both design and enactment[45] or as a more focused process that involved design, with implementation as a separate process.

By looking at how curriculum has been defined in various Yearbooks, we can begin to follow the splitting of instruction from curriculum. One approach to definition is to focus on function and form of classroom experiences, as could be seen in the Thirty-third Yearbook, *The Activity Movement*. It finessed a definition of curriculum and of activity by failing to define either specifically, due to the many uses of these terms. John Dewey noted that different ideas about the value of activity programs had to do with different ideas about what they mean. But Dewey did not define activity or curriculum; typically, he attempted to clarify oppositions that made definition difficult.[46] Boyd H. Bode was less patient with the lack of definition. Acknowledging that "the Activity Movement is on the trail of a different conception of the learning process," Bode argued, "With a little ingenuity [the critic] might perhaps be able to prove that the Activity Movement on its own showing, includes every form of education, past, present, and future, that the wit of pedagogues is able to devise." This, he continued, was because the Activity Movement failed to define its basic idea and to reflect on its implications,[47] an assertion that seemed to be substantiated by conflicting opinions offered in the remaining chapters of the Yearbook.

Another approach to definition is to provide one broad enough to avoid restricting curriculum to the traditional subjects. The Thirty-fifth Yearbook, *The Grouping of Pupils*, defined curriculum as "all the actual experiences that children have both in and out of school under the guidance of teachers."[48] The student interests and needs were to be taken into account, as well as those of society. In so defining curriculum, the Yearbook Committee seemed to be conscious of the relationship between methods of grouping, their chosen topic, and the curriculum that was to be taught through grouping of students. This awareness may have resulted because three chapters were written by people associated with the curriculum field: Harold B. Alberty, Orville G. Brim, Henry Harap, and L. Thomas Hopkins, all of whom called for curriculum that was much broader than a subject-centered definition would suggest. Along similar lines, in the Thirty-eighth Yearbook, Carleton Washburne suggested, "'Curriculum' is defined broadly enough to include any materials or activities that will affect the learning, development, attitudes, or behavior of the child."[49] The Sixty-first Yearbook Committee drew on the same definition, "all the experiences a child has under the guidance of the school,"[50] and "the planned educational experiences that are provided for the child in school."[51]

The Twenty-sixth Yearbook Committee included representatives with other views about the curriculum, however, which were more specifically focused than its consensus definition implied. Rugg saw one task of the Yearbook Committee as developing a common language that members could use in attempting to understand one another. But common terms agreed to by the Yearbook Committee did not represent common meanings outside the Committee. For most, definition was a matter of emphasis, as was apparent in their individual statements.

For Bobbitt and Charters, emphasis was on preparation for adult life. Charters was willing to trust scientific techniques to verify his points of disagreement with the Committee. Once the members had agreed that "the curriculum should be based entirely upon a study of the needs and interests of the learners," he was satisfied.[52] Bobbitt's position was more conciliatory; the Bobbitt tradition, passed on through Tyler's rational approach to curriculum development, was based on a desire for synthesis of the key elements in curriculum decision making. Its adherents and its detractors recognized that this rational approach to curriculum development has been the predominant model both in the United States and internationally for decades. The Fifty-seventh Yearbook, *The Integration of Educational Experiences*, relied on Tyler's model; his definition of learning as a change in behavior was implicit. While learning is described through the vocabulary of educational psychology, "the interactions of curriculum and instruction,"[53] to use the language of the Forty-ninth Yearbook, are taken for granted. The two are seen as an integrated whole despite the technical language, which defined them as separate processes. This interaction was also implicit in the Sixty-fifth Yearbook, *The Changing American School*. In this Yearbook, John I. Goodlad argued, that "The field of curriculum, although young, has some useful lore"; by this, he referred to the Tylerian approach. A first principle was clarification of educational objectives "for purposes of selecting what to teach and evaluating both pupil performance and program effectiveness."[54] The Ninety-third Yearbook marked the contribution of *Bloom's Taxonomy*; again, the implicit definition of curriculum was Tyler's. While Tyler intended a flexible approach to curriculum development, the rationale, like the Twenty-sixth Yearbook's Composite Statement, was sufficiently general to be useful to people with more narrow perspectives than his.

Kilpatrick argued that the Composite Statement assumed "that the curriculum will be made in advance and handed down from above." He allowed that the sting was somewhat relieved by "various conscience clauses . . . introduced to release dissenters,"[55] who found the top down approach unacceptable. In his view, the curriculum should address the whole of the educative process, which encompasses the student's past, present, and future, as well as unite content, process, and function. "The traditional conception of the function of the curriculum seems on the face of it not to fit either modern psychology or modern social philosophy," he argued.[56] This was in marked contrast to Charles H. Judd's position. Judd feared that Section VI of the Statement, to which Kilpatrick offered no objection, would be accepted "as absolution of their sins, by certain persons whose tendencies are toward happy-go-lucky picnicking as a substitute for study." While he could affirm the new synthesis of knowledge that it set forth, "that knowledge will always have to be systematized and arranged in coherent subjects."[57] Judd, who had taught educational psychology to Bobbitt at the University of Chicago, believed that the future demanded much more rigorous and scientific study of education. He called for a national educational research council to bring together the "scattered efforts which are being made to reconstruct the curriculum," modeled on the natural sciences.[58]

Those who followed Judd's line of thinking became increasingly fascinated by the study of learning and instruction as processes that facilitate learning. This focus resulted in commonly understood terms, "learning" and "instruction," taking on new meaning, and was illustrated in the way the Forty-ninth and Fifty-ninth Yearbooks used these terms. In the Forty-ninth Yearbook, *Learning and Instruction*, the definition of curriculum seemed closely associated with the activity movement:

The curriculum is defined as experience; and it is in terms of experience that pupils learn. Curriculum and instruction are generally understood to be the obverse and reverse of a single educational coin—the means by which learning of pupils is brought about. It is doubtful that the two can ever be separated in function. However, there seem to have been tendencies in these last years to neglect the interactions of curriculum and instruction. But principles for the curriculum are now emerging which are basically the same as those for improved instruction.[59]

The teacher seemed to be in a dynamic role encompassing curriculum and instruction. However, of more significance than the definition of curriculum was acceptance of a behavioral definition of learning, which had the effect of tipping the future balance toward "scientific" approaches. Learning was seen as a "change in behavior correlated with experience" and instruction as the guidance of learning.[60]

The subtlety of "interactions of curriculum and instruction" were lost in the Fifty-ninth Yearbook. Like the Thirty-fifth, it dealt with grouping. But unlike the Thirty-fifth, this Yearbook seemed to have little, if any, curriculum consciousness. Grouping was treated as a social process that could be used as an instructional technique without reference to the curriculum.

A new understanding of learning and instruction required a new definition of curriculum in the Sixty-sixth Yearbook on programmed instruction. Conscious effort was made to separate curriculum and instruction, and was apparent in the definition of instruction drawn from the *Handbook of Research on Teaching*:

Instruction is used as a generic term referring to any specifiable means of controlling or manipulating a series of events to produce modifications of behavior through learning. It is applicable whenever the outcomes of learning can be specified in sufficiently explicit terms to permit their measurement.[61]

It is an empirical process "whereby the behaviors described by those who plan a curriculum are taught."[62] Curriculum development was seen as a process of determining educational ends. Stephen M. Corey cautioned that the separation of means and ends should not be carried to extremes. Instruction could not go on without "curriculum-planning"; the separation of the two was not to suggest that the curriculum was unimportant.[63] Important or not, there was a conspicuous absence of any mention of curriculum in the Seventy-fifth Yearbook, *The Psychology of Teaching Methods*, except as the "something" that was to be delivered by instruction.

By the mid-1970s, the earlier emphasis on method and technique of teaching had resurfaced in a focus on the technologies of teaching. As long as the holistic nature of curriculum was understood, educators studying various curriculum processes did not remove them from the larger curriculum context. However, as the scientific approach advocated by Judd gained momentum, the terms "instructional strategies" and "methods" were used without reference to curriculum. As experimental work on the nature of learning developed, many researchers hoped that generic, *curriculum neutral* methods could be found. This separation of teaching from curriculum has resulted in strikingly different conceptions of curriculum and the role of various curriculum "workers" among educators.

TAKING TEACHING OUT OF CURRICULUM

In early Yearbooks, the separation of curriculum and instruction seemed to be for discussion purposes. Later, the separation was made because they were seen as separate domains of interest. This can be seen in the Sixty-sixth Yearbook, *Programmed Instruction*. The Sixty-sixth Yearbook appeared during a period of extreme optimism about the potential of programmed materials. Many viewed them as the teachers of the future. With rapid changes in knowledge, Yearbook Committee members thought it unrealistic to expect teachers to be involved in higher levels of curriculum-making. "The teacher should concentrate on other teaching tasks—diagnosing learner readiness, guiding learners in their transactions with learning resources and environments, stimulating and enriching learning, and managing learner

involvement."[64] Phil C. Langue cautioned that because so many en-
thusiasts expected programmed materials to replace the teacher, it was
all the more important for education specialists and teachers to have
input into the new materials and media, particularly in making practical suggestions.[65] However, the message from the Yearbook is clear:
"We would like our definition of instruction to suggest a separation
between the instructional process and both administrative and curricular planning."[66] Offering practical suggestions at the planning stage
seemed a narrow role for the teacher in curriculum decision making.

The Seventy-fifth Yearbook, however, marked the extent of the
separation between curriculum and instruction. Robert M. Gagné
called the teaching task one of arranging the environment so learning
could occur, reasoning:

Models of learning thus make possible a conceptual frame of reference within
which learning can be viewed as a set of sequentially ordered processes leading
to the establishment and retention of more or less permanent human capabilities. At the same time, these models provide a conceptualization of what
instruction can and cannot accomplish, when considered as a set of planned
external events designed to influence the ongoing processes of learning.[67]

Chapters on various methods made the assumption that teaching
"acts" may be selected from alternative acts that are applicable to any
subject.

Along similar lines, the Seventy-eighth Yearbook, *Classroom Management*, focused on technical rather than curricular issues related to
student classroom interactions and behavior. Conspicuously missing
was a chapter on the role of the curriculum in creating the kind of environment where student behavior problems are minimized.

The Eighty-second Yearbook, *Individual Differences and the Common
Curriculum*, included one chapter on curriculum practices, written by
Goodlad. Gary D Fenstermacher stated that curriculum encompassed
"knowledge and understanding, the skills and traits that mark a person
as well educated."[68] While it would be hard to argue that most educators are likely to adopt a similar view, it does have the effect of preclud-
ing other approaches without illuminating what is actually meant by
curriculum. The absence of any substantive discussion on curriculum
in a volume devoted to the common curriculum seems curious. At the
same time, however, the Eighty-second Yearbook Committee appeared
to recognize the need for self-critique, and thus included chapters by
Michael W. Kirst and Thomas S. Popkewitz. While these did not focus

on curriculum, both raised important curriculum issues with implications for the teacher's role.

Popkewitz pointed out that pedagogical innovations are situated within complex political, social, and material worlds. His chapter made problematic the assumptions of Yearbook authors who attempted to focus on issues such as the common curriculum, as if they were merely technical activities to be solved by educators. Having raised the possibility of contradictions inherent in attempting to identify a common curriculum base that accounted for individual differences, Popkewitz concluded, "This is not to argue against the task set for this Yearbook, but rather to say that this task involves a philosophical, social, and political complexity that cannot be reduced to behavioral objectives, standardized outcomes, taxonomies of thought, and psychological attributes. Such reduction is to deny what is essential to human identity."[69]

As examination of Yearbooks makes clear, the technical approach, which divided curriculum and instruction, was entrenched in educational thinking by the mid-1970s and part of a broader educational discourse. Perhaps, as Mauritz Johnson, Jr., pointed out in an article that first appeared in *School and Society*, most educators, including scholars, were more interested in improving than understanding the curriculum, and more concerned with action and results than inquiry.[70] Johnson's definition placed him within the camp of those who believed that improvements in curriculum and instruction were separate activities:

> Accepted usage identifies curriculum with "planned learning experiences." This definition is unsatisfactory, however, if "curriculum" is to be distinguished from "instruction." Whether experiences are viewed subjectively in terms of the sensibility of the experiencing individual or objectively in terms of his actions in a particular setting, there is in either case no experience until an interaction between the individual and his environment actually occurs. Clearly, such interaction characterizes *instruction*, not curriculum.[71]

In Johnson's view, the Twenty-sixth Yearbook Committee had accepted a problematic definition of the curriculum. "By considering 'experiences and enterprises' to be the essential elements of curriculum, the Committee obscured the distinction between curriculum and instruction. . . ."[72]

"Experiences and enterprises" had been of special concern to Kilpatrick. His lengthy response to The Foundation of Curriculummaking admittedly focused on "form and function of the curriculum" with "little attention given to content as such." "It is surely not right to make a curriculum out and out before we know how a curriculum can and should function," he argued, relegating "to a distinctly inferior position" much of the scientific approach to curriculum development.[73] But those who separated curriculum and instruction to understand form and function had taken an opposing position. In the end, the teacher was relegated to an inferior position as researchers looked for a generic set of instructional strategies and methods that could be used to ensure learning of any curriculum.

THE ROLE OF THE TEACHER

The Twenty-sixth Yearbook documented the diversity of curriculum-making practices that were going on in the schools. Teachers seemed to be vitally involved in many of these projects. Noting that local school systems should have "adequate central machinery" to study the curriculum continuously, Article 46 of the *Foundations* statement read, "In this work, the cooperation of experienced teachers should be secured, together with that of specialists in curriculum-making."[74]

While the statement is open to a wide array of interpretations, at the very least, the teacher's role in curriculum design was not precluded. This was somewhat confirmed by Johnson's objection to it, noted above. The teacher's role, in his view, was at the "execution stage," in which teachers made final choices based on their own understanding of students, but were "governed by the intended outcomes stipulated by the curriculum and incorporated into the course and unit plans."[75]

The issue of who designed the curriculum was addressed in several Yearbooks subsequent to the Twenty-sixth. The Thirty-fifth spoke of teacher and student involvement in planning and of the importance of preparing materials for teacher adaptation.

In the Forty-fourth Yearbook, Hilda Taba called for a greater role for school people in curriculum-making, though her conception of how this was to be done was locked into her own linear interpretation of the Tyler framework. However, in the same volume, Prudence Cutright offered out a more flexible process with a vital role for the teacher. Assistant Superintendent of the Minneapolis Public Schools, Cutright asserted, "The administrator who complains that teachers are not properly prepared to assume such responsibilities may be overlooking the vital place which in-service training programs ought to hold in every school system or he may be pathetically lacking in confidence in his co-workers." Preparing teachers for this role offered more hope of progress in addressing curriculum problems "than can possibly be made through countless courses of study and syllabi written by experts."[76]

The Forty-ninth Yearbook, *Learning and Instruction*, held out a similarly inclusive role for the teacher, not as an instrument for delivery of learning, but as one who was to be involved in every phase of curriculum and teaching. "In only the most general aspects of the program are these processes of definition of objectives, selection and organization of content, and evaluation carried out by the school apart from the actual instructional processes. Teachers and pupils themselves should be active participants in all these processes."[77] The improvement of instruction was linked to teacher involvement in curriculum construction.[78] However, as noted earlier, the seeds of a much narrower approach to learning and instruction may be found in the behavioral language scattered throughout the Yearbook. It insists that "teaching procedures must be rooted in an experimentally driven psychology of learning," and hopes that a new understanding of "the teaching act . . . gives promise for a new formula for teaching."[79]

The Fifty-ninth Yearbook suggested that the teacher was to learn strategies for use with students, not to raise questions of the worth of what was being delivered. The teacher's role was as narrowly defined in the Sixty-sixth Yearbook on programmed instruction.

In drawing on N. L. Gage's definition of methods, the Seventy-fifth Yearbook precluded the teacher's role in curriculum decision making. David C. Berliner and Gage saw methods as patterns of behavior that recur and may be applied to various subjects, used by more than one teacher, and relevant to learning.[80] The teacher was seen as a decision maker, but "the teacher's job is to find ways, within the framework of classroom teaching, in which the different teaching methods, each with its own advantages for different purposes and different students, can be used."[81] Gagné said the teacher's essential task was "to arrange the conditions of the learner's environment so that the processes of learning will be activated, supported, enhanced, and maintained."[82] In a chapter on teacher decision making, Richard J. Shavelson limited the range of teacher decisions through a model that focused on classroom environment, management, and instructional tasks. Shavelson argued that the training task was to get teachers to integrate smoothly the various facets of decision making into a smooth performance.[83]

By the time the Eighty-second Yearbook appeared, the body of research on learning and instruction was robust. Thomas L. Good and Deborah J. Stipek described teachers as "the most important variable mediating the effect of reward structure or instructional format on low- and high-ability children's learning."[84] Technical language of learning was clearly dominant. Michael W. Kirst referred to the teacher as "a pivotal curriculum screen between external influences and the student, and as a political agent within the classroom in both manifest and latent terms."[85] But he seemed to view the role of teacher as more than the one who implemented educational policy, describing the teacher as "a crucial maker of curriculum policy."[86] This perspective, along with that of Popkewitz (referred to earlier), provided an alternative view of curriculum and teaching.

The idea of teacher as skillful technician who implemented curriculum through wise choices of teaching strategies gained momentum. At the same time, many saw a role for the teacher to play in curriculum decisions through intelligent adaptation, customizing it for a particular context. This was essentially the role that many who followed the Tyler rationale would choose, seeing curriculum design as essentially the work of off-site experts—however, teachers were not being excluded from the role of expert. The classroom role of the teacher was in making intelligent modifications based on the teacher's knowledge of specific students, the local community, and available resources.

This perspective, too, has had a long history in the Society's Yearbooks. It was the primary role of the teacher in *International Understanding and the Curriculum*, the Thirty-sixth Yearbook. The Thirty-eighth Yearbook, *Child Development and the Curriculum*, took a cautious view of what instruments of measurement and development theory could tell us about children. John E. Anderson said, "Every curriculum and every placement of subject matter represents a compromise between the child's abilities and interests and the interests and demands of society."[87] Despite cautions, the Thirty-eighth Yearbook Committee assumed that there was more potential harm in ignoring child development than in making use of it, particularly by the teacher, who guided students and was continuously learning. The final chapter, by Earnest O. Melby, disagreed with the decision to divide the Yearbook into chapters that looked at various subject areas. He accused the Committee of thinking of curriculum before the child, arguing that this was problematic because it assumed the curriculum was already in place, to be mastered by the child. "Perhaps we shall keep on teaching subjects, collecting statistics, and recording the damage done to several bodies of subject matter by unappreciative children."[88] Melby envisioned schools as centers of learning where students, teachers, parents, and the community were all growing together. This implied a delicate role for the teacher as student of children and the curriculum. More in keeping with the perspective of the majority of the Thirty-eighth Yearbook Committee was the Sixty-first Yearbook description of the teacher as "the key to curricular and instructional provisions,"[89] one who implemented and adapted the curriculum.

The particulars of Melby's vision could only be inferred from his critique since he did not spell out details. His idea of schools as centers of mutual growth and learning, where the teacher was engaged in curriculum enactment, that is, making decisions about what is to be taught and how, was the least represented perspective in NSSE Yearbooks. Of all the perspectives on curriculum and teaching, it envisioned the greatest involvement of teachers in the creation of the curriculum in and out of the classroom.

As Karen K. Zumwalt pointed out in the Eighty-seventh Yearbook:

> Whether curriculum and teaching are separate domains has been one of those perennial questions in the field. Semantics and conceptual clarity aside, I think curricular and instructional decisions are intertwined in practice. By assigning curricular decisions elsewhere and relegating teachers to instructional and managerial decisions, one limits the discretionary freedom expected of most professionals and restricts teachers' ability to create effective educational experiences for their students. The current technological orientation with its mandated methods and curriculum strips teachers of their professionalism and undermines the attainment of excellence in the long run.[90]

This separation of curriculum and teaching has not only had an effect on teacher morale, but has limited our understanding of teaching. Donna H. Kerr postulated that an adequate theory of teaching has not been developed, in part, because many have believed a theory of teaching to be reducible to a theory of learning. She argued, "Teaching is more than a nice aid to learning. It has been humankind's way of breaking through the restraints of individuals' commonplace environments of nature, social roles, traditions, language, and survival patterns."[91]

In the Twenty-sixth Yearbook, Rugg argued against a program of curriculum development that built all classroom experiences from the spontaneously expressed interest of children precisely because of what it meant for the teacher's role. "The view that the curriculum should be made only on the spot postulates a genius-like teacher, endowed with intimate and exact knowledge of child life and development, broad vision of alternative lines of growth from childhood to social maturity, grasp of psychology, and rare skill in the management of pupils." He believed such an assumption to be inconsistent with the reality of schools, where mass education is the focus. Nor did the assumption do credit to the complexity of the curriculum development process, one that required expertise beyond what could be expected of any one individual. "The day is past in which a single individual—be he professor, teacher, administrator, psychologist, sociologist, or research specialist of whatever brand—can encompass all of these tasks single-handed."[92] For Rugg, there was a place for the teacher alongside the curriculum expert, but not in place of the curriculum expert.

Over the years, Yearbook Committees have considered the same issues related to what the curriculum should be, who should plan it, and how it should be taught. Differences of opinion have become clearer and more complex, with new branches of inquiry emerging. Researchers engaged in lines of inquiry have seen themselves as separate from the interests of those who continued to call themselves curriculum professionals. Since the Twenty-sixth Yearbook, those devoted specifically to curriculum as a field suggested the extent to which the issues and divisions of the past continue.

People Have Always Said This in Every Age

The Seventieth Yearbook, *The Curriculum: Retrospect and Prospect*, aimed to capture a picture of the "vigorous and rich ideas which permeate our profession . . ." and were available for thinking about the curriculum.[93] While the Twenty-sixth Yearbook offered one definition of curriculum that meant different things to different members of the Committee, no one definition characterized the Seventieth Yearbook. Issues related to goals of education and curriculum development that challenged the Twenty-sixth Yearbook Committee were also apparent in Seventieth Yearbook chapters on social and intellectual systems. Harry S. Broudy argued that several, not always compatible concepts of democracy have shaped the educational goals of schools.[94] James B. Macdonald's chapter, "Curriculum Development in Relation to Social and Intellectual Systems," talked about the complexity of curriculum development as an ethical and political rather than a rational process. He pointed out how efforts to update or revise subject matter and the effective and efficient performance of teachers and instruction failed to recognize the driving force behind what is wanted for schools. This was related to cultural and societal influences, including a growing educational bureaucracy that attempted to maintain its own stability through reform efforts. The technical rationality that objectified everything missed a broader picture of what it is to be a human being. Drawing on Huebner, Macdonald pointed to how school content was "psychologized" through behavioral and cognitive psychology. He called for rational input into plans, but with room for participation of people at all levels.[95]

In the final section on the future, Ole Sand analyzed forces that supported and those that restrained curriculum change, calling for a new kind of leadership *function* that shared power with rather than assumed power over others. He noted, "If one recalls the 1926 yearbook and other books written since then, with their predictions of amazing changes ahead, and then looks at life in classrooms today, a funny thing happened on the way to the future."[96] A chapter by Bruce R. Joyce underscored the range of ideas represented within the Yearbook. Joyce feared that curriculum workers were being co-opted into a dehumanizing system. At the same time, "generic engineering theories about improving education"[97] were in demand. He argued that room needed to be made for everyone within the "educational spectrum." Joyce envisioned curriculum workers with an array of educational technologies who would be able to offer alternatives, as they are needed. While much of his rhetoric was concerned with the quality of human life in schools, his language was not consistent. Joyce's models approach has been compatible with those who favored technical approaches to classroom teaching and saw the teacher as a technician.

The Seventieth Yearbook's promise to provide an array of diverse opinions was fulfilled. But, with the exception of the first section that provided an historical overview, the remainder of the collection would be difficult for any but the most serious student of curriculum to organize conceptually. This in itself suggested the kind of disarray in which the field of curriculum seemed to be at the end of the 1960s. It may also have, in part, led to Joseph J. Schwab's declaration that the field was moribund. Whether the field was moribund due to over-reliance on theory in a practical profession, as Schwab would have it,[98] or had been "led astray by overdependency upon the category 'learning,'" as Huebner would have it,[99] the field had changed profoundly since the Twenty-sixth Yearbook.

The Twenty-sixth Yearbook had legitimized the role of curriculum worker and confronted issues that were troubling schools. The Eighty-seventh Yearbook attempted to bring together what had become a wide array of curriculum workers and examine some of the issues they faced. By the mid-1980s, there was a proliferation of central office staff, often separating curriculum development and staff development functions. Laurel N. Tanner called for unity and harmony, not a balance, but "a synergy—a joint, mutually enhancing relationship based on the best interests of the individual and society."[100]

Proliferation of subject matter had been one of the primary frustrations of educators in the 1920s. In the Eighty-seventh Yearbook, Kliebard pointed out how difficult exclusion was in curriculum matters. Schools were faced with "a never-ending process of making room for an emerging and presumably urgent kind of activity that needs to be performed."[101]

Purposes of education, of concern to the Twenty-sixth Yearbook Committee, were still of interest in the Eighty-seventh Yearbook. Daniel Tanner argued, "The function of general education in a free society is to foster the development of a common universe of discourse, understanding, and competence for an enlightened citizenry, a task that is not possible with a basic education."[102] Tyler reiterated his basic view that "the most generally accepted goal of American education is to help all young people to learn the attitudes, knowledge, skills, and habits necessary for citizens who are to participate intelligently in the responsibilities of a democratic society."[103]

Definition of curriculum and role of the teacher also appeared as concerns in the Eighty-seventh Yearbook. Henrietta Schwartz drew on several definitions of curriculum, noting, "The curriculum encompasses what is to be taught as well as how it is to be taught, yet for many teachers, their job has absolutely nothing to do with curriculum adaptation or change: they view themselves as an instructional delivery system."[104] Zumwalt pointed out that curriculum reform efforts have been guided by technical conceptions of teaching, leaving a superficial idea about the nature of curriculum:

> Those of us in the curriculum field have failed to portray the more complex visions of curriculum that we have come to take for granted. Distinctions such as the planned, intended, explicit, manifest, enacted, implicit, and hidden curriculum are alien concepts. . . . What operates is an impoverished view of curriculum which has profound educational consequences—policy is mandated, with all good intentions, but its net effect may be one of undermining rather than improving education."[105]

A much richer view of the teacher than the one Zumwalt referred to was found in *The Education of Teachers*, part one of the Ninety-eighth Yearbook. The Yearbook envisioned a broader role for teachers than the technical perspective that separated instruction from curriculum. This involved a preparation of teachers that was much more collaborative than education programs had been in the past, drawing on expertise of school-based, as well as university-based, educators. If the larger message of this Yearbook is to be taken seriously, educators at every level of practice need to give much more attention to the kind of ethical and political dimensions of practice that Macdonald called for in the Seventieth Yearbook.

Most recently, in anticipation of the centennial year of the Society, the Ninety-eighth Yearbook, Part II, is titled *Issues in Curriculum: Selected Chapters from Earlier Yearbooks*. Admittedly, any selection involves exclusion, as well as inclusion, and any student of curriculum might propose another set of chapters or another focus than the one represented by the Ninety-eighth Yearbook. In terms of the long-term contribution of the Society, however, it may be more useful to think about the array of chapters from which the editors could choose. Two groups of curriculum thinkers were strikingly under-represented in NSSE Yearbooks devoted to curriculum: the critical theorists, including those with feminist perspectives on the curriculum, and those who are referred to as the *reconceptualists*. Because Yearbooks are read by a wide array of educators, it is likely that many might not otherwise encounter the curriculum thinking represented by these two groups. It is hoped that future Yearbooks will explore these and other emergent strands of curriculum thinking and thus more fully represent the diversity of ideas available when dealing with significant curriculum challenges.

THE LEGACY

The Twenty-sixth Yearbook attempted to face "serious considerations of curriculum," and, in doing so, left an important legacy that the Society has continued by focusing Yearbooks on an array of curriculum methods, models, issues, and practices. Exploring these Yearbooks offers insight into the present state of curriculum and teaching and future work for the Society. At the same time, it is critical to note that an important contribution waiting to be made by an NSSE volume is what might be referred to as *restorative* or *transformative* curriculum thinking, in which the history of curriculum-making, models, practices, and issues is examined from the perspective of the many cultural, linguistic, gender, and racial groups that form American society. This is the kind of work already begun by such groups as the American Educational Research Association (AERA). AERA committees explored the role and status of minorities and women in educational research and development and AERA Special Interest Groups focused on research issues related to diversity. The history of curriculum as seen through Yearbooks belongs to the dominant culture. Absence of knowledge about curriculum-making, models, practices, and issues within the educational traditions of a wide array of under-represented groups diminishes our understanding of curriculum and of education.

In reviewing the separation of curriculum and instruction through NSSE Yearbooks, it is difficult to identify "a genuine nodal point" in the volumes following the Twenty-sixth Yearbook. Instead, various scholars made visible a series of points. The separation of instruction from curriculum is marked by such points. It did not occur in isolation from the broader events that have occurred in the decades spanned by NSSE. Society's increased fascination with technology; shifts in population that have threatened power arrangements of dominant groups; the ambiguous and wavering commitment of the United States to education for all in a society that has become increasingly multicultural, multiracial, and multilingual; and the perceived failure of public schools—all these have increased the demand for standard products of education.

The effect on teachers has been discussed in the literature on curriculum, staff development, and teaching, as Judi Randi and Lyn Corno pointed out in their examination of teachers in the role of innovators. As the wide array of literature drawn on by Randi and Corno indicated, much more research is needed if the teacher's role in curriculum is to be understood. In fact, as Rugg suggested, it is unlikely that the responsibility of curriculum development either can or should rest entirely on teachers. Teachers who are inclined to engage in curriculum design need to draw on a variety of resources to assist them. And not all teachers are interested in the role of curriculum decision maker. Balance and circumstances are critical. There is an important place for curriculum materials designed off-site, for technical strategies that the teacher may select from a repertoire of proved strategies, and for teacher innovation.[106] Researchers do not agree on how much teacher judgment should be permitted in determining when to create, when to adapt, and when to follow a curriculum. But, as Randi and Corno concluded:

Long before reformers called for fresh practices, long before researchers discovered teachers' practical knowledge, and long before teachers were recognized as innovators, creative teachers were listening to their students, discovering how best to teach them, and inventing fresh practices. Through the lens of implementation, teachers' adaptations are variants from ideal, prescribed practices. Through the lens of *innovation*, teachers' adaptations are responses to the unique and varied contexts of teaching.[107]

In the end, we are back to the question of perspective and find ourselves confronted with the difficulty of imagining a consensus that will unify and move the field of curriculum forward. As the Twenty-sixth Yearbook Committee discovered, even those who sit at the table together and talk about their differences may find it very difficult to relinquish their own positions in favor of collaboration. The playing field is much broader than when Rugg called for the Twenty-sixth Yearbook. Whatever we choose to do with this legacy, it stands to remind us that entertaining the ideas of others, even within our own area of specialization, is an activity that is not easy and unlikely to produce complete agreement, but eminently valuable.

But as interesting as it might be, negotiating conflicting perspectives on curriculum may not be the most critical issue confronting curriculum people. At first look, the issue with which I have been most concerned—separation of curriculum and instruction—seems to suggest strong differences of opinion over how knowledge gets, or ought to get, transmitted to students and by whom. In reality, it may be the result of our failure to understand the nature of knowledge.

A Knowledge Fetish

Teaching is very commonly understood to mean little more than the communication of knowledge. So markedly is this the case that a sort of knowledge fetish has been set up.

As one goes to an ironmonger's for hardware, to a fishmonger's for fish, and to a cheesemonger's for cheese, so we naturally turn to the school for knowledge. It is often regarded as a knowledge-store, and the teacher as a knowledge-monger.

Sir John Adams[108]

For decades, Spencer's question, "What knowledge is of most worth?" has guided curriculum thinkers. Attending to the Spencer question has clarified the task, on one hand, but obscured and perhaps misdirected it on the other. The knowledge question invites discussion of content and access. It sets the curriculum tasks of inclusion and exclusion. But it weights intellectual knowledge above other knowledge. Focusing on knowledge has led to more NSSE Yearbooks on subject matter or academic disciplines than on any other topic in education. Traditional boundaries of subject matter have tended to perpetuate the cycle of curriculum reform and failed reform in schools as the public becomes concerned about deficits in this or that subject. Schools have largely settled the problem by attempting to include everything, essentially by repeatedly replacing one series of curriculum innovations with another, and by treating every new innovation as if it were academic knowledge to be taught and tested in the same manner. Decisions about what ought to be learned are largely meaningless, "without an articulated sense of inquiry into the nature and purposes of schooling."[109]

In the Eightieth Yearbook, Jane R. Martin argued that "Contemporary philosophical investigation of curriculum has for some time been in a rut: it has focused on a very limited range of curricular questions and has endorsed a theory of curriculum that is seriously deficient."[110] She urged that "the received theory of our day—the forms of knowledge theory—be replaced by a more general curricular paradigm" addressed to "the whole of that education which is valuable."[111]

Huebner took a compatible view in his chapter in the Eighty-fourth Yearbook, but with a different perspective on the knowledge question. He suggested that the problem with schooling as we know it, whether in schools or other institutions that educate, is that schools "are not places of knowing, but places of knowledge."[112] This raises what might be a more fruitful question for our day than Spencer's. By re-framing the question and asking, "*What is worth knowing?*" we invite action that includes but is not limited to knowledge. Knowledge suggests being informed, understanding things, having wisdom, and being enlightened. It focuses us on bodies of accumulated information and principles. We are set up for the kind of separation that Martin described in the Eightieth Yearbook. Knowing, on the other hand, suggests intelligent, wise, profound participation in life. Knowing involves both knowing *that* and knowing *how*, as Michael Polanyi suggested.[113] It requires our exploration of diverse ways of being, involving our intellectual, physical, emotional, and spiritual selves. It is a part of our participation in the transcendent. We are never finished with knowing; it is part of a creative process that stands alongside our "not-knowing," and sometimes requires that we wait for inspiration, intuition, insight, or synthesis. Knowing is not time efficient in the sense that logical and linear processes can be efficient. Knowing is not certain in the way educators would have knowledge be certain.

In describing modes of knowing, Huebner suggested that every mode is "a mode of being open, vulnerable, and available to the internal and external world . . . is a mode of waiting—hoping and expectancy"; it requires more than work and preparation. "The various modes of knowing are grounded in the possibility of a different future. To wait actively and expectantly for that different future is a manifestation that modes of knowing are grounded in more than merely present forms of knowing. They are grounded in and depend upon hope." And every mode of knowing is also "participation in the continual creation of the universe—of one's self, of others, of the dwelling places of the world." Every mode of knowing also "witnesses the transcending possibilities of which human life is a part."[114]

"What is worth knowing?" if answered in terms of the knowledge question, takes us back into the knowledge dilemma. If answered in terms of how we enter into and participate in the world, the question places us in relationships between people—between people and their ideas and ways of being, between people and their materials and cultural artifacts, and between people and time and space. The question invites and extends dialogue rather than limiting and closing it. It does not preclude, nor is it limited to, quantification and measurement, but recognizes that there is more to being human than can be measured. It takes us to new questions. Questions remind us of how much is not known, not understood, beyond our reach, and how important it is to keep asking, disagreeing, inviting critique, and thinking of alternative ways to frame and explore the problems of curriculum, teaching, and coming to know. A process or dialectic of knowing and not-knowing recognizes that final answers are only ending points for those who are unable to see beyond the present moment. What would curriculum-making look like if we approached it from such a perspective?

NOTES

1. Thanks to the Department of Teaching and Learning, George Peabody College, Vanderbilt University, for allowing me to be a Visiting Scholar and providing access to the Education Library; to Craig Kridel for comments as I attempted to conceptualize the project; and to Lyn Corno for her editorial comments and encouragement.

2. John Adams, *Educational Theories* (London: Ernest Benn Limited, 1927), p. 64.

3. Mary Louise Seguel, *The Curriculum Field: Its Formative Years* (New York: Teachers College Press, 1966), p. 5.

4. Herbert M. Kliebard, *The Struggle for the American Curriculum 1893-1958*, 2nd ed. (New York, London: Routledge, 1995).

5. George A. Beauchamp, *Curriculum Theory*, 3rd ed. (Wilmette, IL: The Kagg Press, 1975), p. 67.

6. Harold Rugg, *Foundations for American Education* (Yonkers-on-Hudson, NY: World Book Co., 1947), p. 576.

7. Kliebard refers to the *humanists*, who stood for the basic subject matter curriculum found in the traditional humanities; the *child development* advocates, who incorporated the newly developing study of children into their thinking; and the *social efficiency* and *meliorism* advocates.

8. William H. Schubert, *Curriculum: Perspective, Paradigm, and Possibility* (New York: Macmillan, 1986), p. 44.

9. Daniel Tanner and Laurel Tanner, *History of the School Curriculum* (New York: Macmillan, 1990), pp. 89-90.

10. The contribution of NSSE Yearbooks devoted to learning is explored in detail in another chapter.

11. See Lawrence A. Cremin, *The Transformation of the School* (New York: Alfred A. Knopf, 1961); Kliebard (1995); Seguel (1966), and Tanner and Tanner (1990), for descriptions of this period.

12. Cremin notes that the ideas of Herbart came into their own "particularly among university professors seeking to develop a scientific approach to pedagogy" (1961, p. 134). The German philosopher and educator Johann Fredrich Herbart (1776-1841) is known not only for his scientific approach to pedagogy, but also as the father of modern psychology. Philosophies of Immanuel Kant and Georg Wilhelm Friedrich Hegel were a great influence on his work, as well as the educational philosophy and program of Johann Heinrich Pestalozzi. Herbart's principles have been, and still are (often unconsciously), at the heart of many educational programs: *preparation*, in which connections are made from the known to what is about to be learned; *presentation*, or delivery of what is to be learned in a psychologically sound way; *association*, or creating analogies with prior learning; and *application*, or using the newly learned knowledge as the basis for learning more knowledge. Herbart's concept of "concentration" became a kind of slogan for emphasis on unity in the curriculum, usually by focusing on all areas of the curriculum through one subject such as history. Schubert (1986, pp. 67-68) provides a brief overview of Herbart's perspective and contribution.

13. Herbert Spencer, *Education* (New York: Appleton, 1860), p. 32. Schubert (1986) says "In one way or another, this question has been a mainstay of curriculum inquiry throughout history."

14. Guy M. Whipple, ed., *Yearbook Publications*, Twenty-first, Twenty-second Yearbooks of the National Society for the Study of Education. "Bound Volumes of the Yearbooks of the Society, 1-24." (Chicago: University of Chicago Press, 1923), p. 11.

15. Guy M. Whipple, ed., *New Materials of Instruction*, Nineteenth Yearbook of the National Society for the Study of Education, Part I (Bloomington, IL: Public School Publishing Co., 1920), p. 11.

16. Whipple, *New Materials of Instruction*, p. 15.

17. Whipple, "Bound Volumes," p. 14.

18. Rugg, *American Education*.

19. Kliebard, *American Curriculum*.

20. Harold Rugg, "Introduction: An Adventure in Understanding," *The Foundations and Technique of Curriculum-construction*, *The Foundations of Curriculum-making*, Twenty-sixth Yearbook of the National Society for the Study of Education, Part II, ed. Guy M. Whipple (Bloomington, IL: Public School Publishing Co., 1926), p. 4.

21. Rugg, *American Education*, p. 636.

22. Ibid.

23. Stuart A. Courtis, "Current Practices in Curriculum-revision in Public Elementary Schools," *The Foundations and Technique of Curriculum-construction*, p. 120.

24. George S. Counts, "Current Practices in Curriculum-making in Public High Schools," *The Foundations and Technique of Curriculum-construction*, p. 139.

25. Seguel offers a succinct review of the information gathered by the surveys for Part I of the Twenty-sixth Yearbook. See her discussion (1966, pp. 123-134).

26. Harold Rugg, "The School Curriculum and the Drama of American Life," *The Foundations and Technique of Curriculum-construction*, pp. 3-16.

27. Rugg, "Introduction," p. 6.

28. Kliebard, *American Curriculum*, p. 157.

29. Ralph W. Tyler, "Curriculum Development in the Twenties and Thirties," *The Curriculum: Retrospect and Prospect*, Seventieth Yearbook of the National Society for the Study of Education, Part I, ed. R. M. McClure (Chicago: National Society for the Study of Education, 1971), pp. 26-44.

30. Robert J. Schaefer, "Retrospect and Prospect," *The Curriculum: Retrospect and Prospect*, Seventieth Yearbook of the National Society for the Study of Education, Part I, ed. R. M. McClure (Chicago: National Society for the Study of Education, 1971), pp. 15-19.

31. Seguel, *The Curriculum Field*, p. 130.

32. Ibid.

33. Ibid., p. 133. Kliebard also notes the importance of the Yearbook in helping to launch the ideas of Rugg and Counts about the role of schools in issues of social justice, p. 158.

34. Kliebard, *American Curriculum*, p. 156.

35. Beauchamp, *Curriculum Theory*, p. 67.

36. Decker Walker, "The Curriculum Field in Formation," *Curriculum Theory Network* 4, 4 (1975), p. 279.

37. Tanner and Tanner, *History of the School Curriculum*, p. 198.

38. See Florence B. Stratemeyer, Hamden L. Forkner, Margaret G. McKim and A. Harry Passow, *Developing a Curriculum for Modern Living*, 2nd ed. (New York: Bureau of Publications, Teachers College, Columbia University, 1957).

39. Whipple, "The Foundations of Curriculum-making: A Composite Statement by the Members of the Society's Committee on Curriculum-making," *The Foundations of Curriculum-making*, p. 17.

40. Ibid., p. 14.

41. Whipple, "Composite Statement," pp. 18-19.

42. Kliebard discusses various perspectives on the curriculum as they coalesce around interest in the humanities, child development, and society's need to conserve or reconstruct itself. Schubert provides a brief overview of each, in "Images of the Curriculum," including William F. Pinar and Madeleine R. Grumet's notion of curriculum as *currere* or the individual's reconstruction of his or her autobiography (pp. 26-34). The issue of definition was of more interest in the late 1960s and early 1970s when Walker and Schaffarzick noted, "Disputes about the proper definition of the term *curriculum* form a literature in their own right." Decker F. Walker and Jon Schaffarzick, "Comparing Curricula," *Curriculum and Evaluation*, eds. A. A. Bellack and H. M. Kliebard (Berkeley, CA: McCutchan, 1977), p. 279.

43. Arthur W. Foshay, "Textbooks and the Curriculum During the Progressive Era, 1930-1950," *Textbooks and Schooling in the United States*, Eighty-ninth Yearbook of the National Society for the Study of Education, Part I, eds. David L. Elliott and Arthur Woodward (Chicago: National Society for the Study of Education, 1990).

44. George F. Madaus, "The Influence of Testing on the Curriculum," *Critical Issues in Curriculum*, Eighty-seventh Yearbook of the National Society for the Study of

Education, Part I, ed. Laurel N. Tanner (Chicago: National Society for the Study of Education, 1988), pp. 83-121.

45. Enactment refers to the curriculum that teachers and students develop within the classroom. See Jon Snyder, Frances Bolin, and Karen Zumwalt, "Curriculum Implementation," In *Handbook of Research on Curriculum*, ed. Philip Jackson (New York: Macmillan, 1992).

46. John Dewey, "Comments and Criticisms by Some Educational Leaders in Our Universities," *The Activity Movement*, Thirty-third Yearbook of the National Society for the Study of Education, Part II, ed. Guy M. Whipple (Bloomington, IL: Public School Publishing Co., 1935), p. 87.

47. Boyd H. Bode, "Comments and Criticisms by Some Educational Leaders in Our Universities," *The Activity Movement*, p. 79.

48. L. Thomas Hopkins, "Differentiation of Curriculum Practices and Teaching Methods in High Schools," *The Grouping of Pupils*, Thirty-fifth Yearbook of the National Society for the Study of Education, Part I, ed. Guy M. Whipple (Bloomington, IL: Public School Publishing Co., 1936), p. 174.

49. Carleton Washburne, "Introduction," *Child Development and the Curriculum*, Thirty-eighth Yearbook of the National Society for the Study of Education, Part I, ed. Guy M. Whipple (Bloomington, IL: Public School Publishing Co., 1939), p. 4.

50. Fred T. Wilhelms, "The Curriculum and Individual Differences," *Individualizing Instruction*, Sixty-first Yearbook of the National Society for the Study of Education, Part I, ed. Nelson B. Henry (Chicago: National Society for the Study of Education, 1962), p. 62.

51. Theodore Clymer and Nolan C. Kearney, "Curricular and Instructional Provisions for Individual Differences," *Individualizing Instruction*, p. 268.

52. Werrett W. Charters, "Statement," *The Foundations of Curriculum-making*, p. 71.

53. G. Lester Anderson, Gertrude Whipple, and Robert Gilchrist, "The School as a Learning Laboratory," *Learning and Instruction*, Forty-ninth Yearbook of the National Society for the Study of Education, Part I, ed. Nelson B. Henry (Chicago: National Society for the Study of Education, 1950), p. 342.

54. John I. Goodlad, "Illustrative Programs and Procedures in Elementary Schools," *The Integration of Educational Experiences*, Fifty-seventh Yearbook of the National Society for the Study of Education, Part III, ed. Nelson B. Henry (Chicago: National Society for the Study of Education, 1958), p. 51.

55. William H. Kilpatrick, "Statement of Position," *The Foundations of Curriculum-making*, p. 146.

56. Ibid., p. 142.

57. Charles H. Judd, "Supplementary Statement," *The Foundations of Curriculum-making*, p. 116.

58. Ibid., p. 117.

59. Anderson, Whipple, and Gilchrist, p. 342.

60. Anderson, "Introduction," *Learning and Instruction*, p. 8.

61. A. A. Lumsdaine, "Instruments and Media of Instruction," *Handbook of Research on Teaching*, ed. N. L. Gage (Chicago: Rand McNally, 1963) cited in Stephen M. Corey, "The Nature of Instruction," *Programmed Instruction*, Sixty-sixth Yearbook of the National Society for the Study of Education, Part II, ed. Phil C. Lange (Chicago: National Society for the Study of Education, 1967), p. 7.

62. Stephen M. Corey, "The Nature of Instruction," p. 10.

63. Ibid., p. 10.

64. Phil C. Lange, "Administrative and Curricular Considerations," *Programmed Instruction*, p. 154.

65. Lange, "Administrative and Curricular Considerations," pp. 175-176.

66. Corey, "The Nature of Instruction," p. 9.

67. Robert M. Gagné, "The Learning Basis of Teaching Methods," *The Psychology of Teaching Methods*, Seventy-fifth Yearbook of the National Society for the Study of Education, Part I, ed. N. L. Gage (Chicago: National Society for the Study of Education, 1976), p. 43.

68. Gary D Fenstermacher, "Introduction," *Individual Differences and the Common Curriculum*, Eighty-second Yearbook of the National Society for the Study of Education, Part I, eds. Gary D Fenstermacher and John I. Goodlad (Chicago: National Society for the Study of Education, 1983), p. 3.

69. Thomas S. Popkewitz, "The Sociological Bases for Individual Differences: The Relation of Solitude to the Crowd," *Individual Differences and the Common Curriculum*, p. 72.

70. Mauritz Johnson, Jr., "Definitions and Models in Curriculum Theory," *Curriculum and Evaluation*, eds. Arno A. Bellack and Herbert M. Kliebard (Berkeley, CA: McCutchan, 1977), p. 4.

71. Ibid., p. 6.

72. Ibid., p. 5.

73. Kilpatrick, "Statement of Position," pp. 141-142.

74. Whipple, *The Foundations of Curriculum Making*, p. 23.

75. Johnson, "Definitions and Models in Curriculum Theory," p. 11.

76. Prudence Cutright, "Practice in Curriculum Development," *American Education in the Postwar Period: Curriculum Reconstruction*, Forty-fourth Yearbook of the National Society for the Study of Education, Part I, ed. Nelson B. Henry (Chicago: National Society for the Study of Education, 1945), p. 275.

77. Anderson, "Introduction," *Learning and Instruction*, p. 2.

78. G. Max Wingo, "Implications for Improving Instruction in the Upper Elementary Grades," *Learning and Instruction*, p. 294.

79. Anderson, "Introduction," *Learning and Instruction*, pp. 4, 7.

80. Berliner and Gage, "The Psychology of Teaching Methods," *The Psychology of Teaching Methods*, p. 5.

81. Ibid., p. 19.

82. Gagné, "The Learning Basis of Teaching Methods," *The Psychology of Teaching Methods*, p. 42.

83. Richard J. Shavelson, "Teachers' Decision Making," *The Psychology of Teaching Methods*, pp. 372-414.

84. Thomas L. Good and Deborah J. Stipek, "Individual Differences in the Classroom: A Psychological Perspective," Fenstermacher and Goodlad, p. 27.

85. Michael W. Kirst, "Policy Implications of Individual Differences and the Common Curriculum," Fenstermacher and Goodlad, p. 285.

86. Ibid., p. 283.

87. J. E. Anderson, "Problems of Method in Maturity and Curricular Studies," *Child Development and the Curriculum*, p. 397.

88. Ernest O. Melby, "A Critique," *Child Development and the Curriculum*, p. 442.

89. Clymer and Kearney, "Curricular and Instructional Provisions for Individual Differences," *Individualizing Instruction*, p. 282.

90. Karen K. Zumwalt, "Are We Improving or Undermining Teaching?" *Critical Issues in Curriculum*, p. 169.

91. Donna H. Kerr, "The Structure of Quality in Teaching," *Philosophy and Education*, Eightieth Yearbook of the National Society for the Study of Education, Part I, ed. Jonas F. Soltis (Chicago: National Society for the Study of Education, 1981), pp. 62-63.

92. Rugg, "Curriculum-making: Points of Emphasis," *Curriculum-making*, pp. 158, 162.

93. Herman G. Richey, "Editor's Preface," *The Curriculum: Retrospect and Prospect*, Seventieth Yearbook of the National Society for the Study of Education, Part I, ed. Robert M. McClure (Chicago: National Society for the Study of Education, 1971), p. vii.

94. Harry S. Broudy, "Democratic Values and Educational Goals," *The Curriculum: Retrospect and Prospect*, p. 113.

95. James B. Macdonald, "Curriculum Development in Relation to Social and Intellectual Systems," *The Curriculum: Retrospect and Prospect*, pp. 95-112.

96. Ole Sand, "Curriculum Change," *The Curriculum: Retrospect and Prospect*, p. 243.

97. Bruce R. Joyce, "The Curriculum Worker of the Future," *The Curriculum: Retrospect and Prospect*, p. 330.

98. Joseph J. Schwab, "The Practical: A Language for Curriculum," Bellack and Kliebard, p. 26.

99. Dwayne Huebner, "Implications of Psychological Thought for the Curriculum," Bellack and Kliebard, p. 68.

100. L. Tanner, "Curriculum Issues in Historical Perspective," *Critical Issues in Curriculum*, p. 3.

101. Kliebard, "Fads, Fashions, and Rituals: The Instability of Curriculum Change," *Critical Issues in Curriculum*, p. 20.

102. D. Tanner, "The Textbook Controversies," Tanner (1988, p. 144).

103. R. W. Tyler, "Progress in Dealing with Curriculum Problems," Tanner (1988, p. 267).

104. Henrietta Schwartz, "Unapplied Curriculum Knowledge," Tanner (1988, p. 42).

105. Zumwalt, in Tanner (1988, p. 154).

106. See Snyder, Bolin, and Zumwalt, "Curriculum Implementation," for further discussion.

107. Judi Randi and Lyn Corno, "Teachers As Innovators," *International Handbook of Teachers and Teaching, Vol. 1*, ed. Bruce J. Biddle, Thomas L. Good, and Ivor F. Goodson (Dordrecht, The Netherlands: Kluwer Academic Publishers, 1997), p. 1213.

108. *Adams, Educational Theories*, p. 15.

109. Kliebard, "Fads, Fashions, and Rituals," p. 32.

110. Jane Roland Martin, "Needed: A Paradigm for Liberal Education," *Philosophy and Education*, pp. 37, 38.

111. Ibid., pp. 57-58.

112. Dwayne E. Huebner, "Spirituality and Knowing," *Learning and Teaching the Ways of Knowing*, Eighty-fourth Yearbook of the National Society for the Study of Education, Part II, ed. Elliot Eisner (Chicago: National Society for the Study of Education, 1985), p. 172.

113. Michael Polanyi and Harry Prosch, *Meaning* (Chicago: University of Chicago Press, 1975).

114. Huebner, "Spirituality and Knowing," pp. 171-172.

CHAPTER II

Changing Conceptions of Learning: A Century of Progress in the Scientific Study of Education

RICHARD E. MAYER

The National Society for the Study of Education (NSSE) has published an edited Yearbook reviewing one or two selected topics in education each year since 1902. With the arrival of the new millennium, this century-long repository of educational study provides an outstanding resource for anyone interested in looking back over the evolution of key ideas in education. There is, perhaps, no more fundamental topic in education than the nature of learning, for at its core, education means the fostering of learning. As an outgrowth of the National Herbart Society in the late 1890s, the NSSE has deep roots in the study of learning, and learning has repeatedly been highlighted in NSSE Yearbooks during the past one hundred years.

The purpose of this chapter is to review changes in the conception of learning in education as discussed in the pages of the NSSE Yearbooks and related NSSE volumes throughout the twentieth century. In particular this chapter explores historical themes concerning changes in the conception of (a) the importance of learning theory in the study of education, (b) the definition of learning, (c) the process of learning, (d) the relation between psychological theory and educational practice, (e) the generality of learning theories, (f) the nature of individual differences in learning, (g) the nature of assessment of learning, (h) the motivational context of learning, (i) the biological context of learning, and (j) the social context of learning. For purposes of analyzing changes in each of these dimensions, I divided the twentieth century into three rough segments—early (consisting of the first few decades), middle (consisting of the middle few decades), and late (consisting of the final few decades).

Table 1 summarizes changes in each of these dimensions over the early, middle, and late segments of the twentieth century; each of

Richard E. Mayer is Professor of Psychology, Department of Psychology, University of California, Santa Barbara.

these changes is discussed respectively in the remaining sections of the chapter. Overall, a century's worth of NSSE book chapters on learning provides insights into the field's struggle to build an educationally relevant theory of learning.

Changing Conceptions of the Importance of Learning: The Rise and Fall of Learning in NSSE Publications

To examine the role of learning in the study of education, I located every NSSE Yearbook or series chapter on learning theory that contained the word "learning" or "learn" in the title—yielding a corpus of more than thirty chapters.[1] The majority came from three NSSE Yearbooks that contained the word "learning" in their titles—*The Psychology of Learning*,[2] *Learning and Instruction*,[3] and *Theories of Learning and Instruction*.[4] I also included a chapter with learning in the title from a NSSE series book entitled *Psychology and Education: The State of the Union*.[5] I did not include chapters from a recent NSSE Yearbook on *Service Learning*[6] because they did not directly address a theory of learning. I did not include chapters from the 1985 Yearbook, *Learning and Teaching the Ways of Knowing*,[7] because none contained the word "learning" or "learn" in the title and because the theme of social constructivism has been explored in depth elsewhere.

An examination of the frequency of NSSE Yearbook chapters on learning reveals that the study of learning has had a roller-coaster ride in the twentieth century, reaching its peak at mid-century. Figure 1 shows by decade the number of chapters about learning theory containing "learning" or "learn" in their titles. "Learning" first appeared in the 1930s, increased in frequency in the 1940s, hit its peak in the 1950s, was still well-represented in the 1960s, declined greatly in the 1970s and 1980s, and has failed to appear since (except for the term "service learning"). Of course, learning was discussed in Yearbook chapters that did not contain the term in their titles, but the pattern shown in Figure 1 provides a general reflection of the rise and fall of "learning" (by that name) in the study of the education.

At first glance, one might conclude that the study of learning has had its day in education, and the field has now moved on to other topics. By the 1960s, for example, Frederick J. McDonald[8] observed that the "forties and early fifties [was] the period when the influence of learning theory on education reached its nadir." Is learning no longer a hot topic in education? This would produce an odd scenario, given the argument that education involves the fostering of learning. Thus,

TABLE 1
CHANGING CONCEPTIONS OF LEARNING

TYPE OF CONCEPTION	EARLY CENTURY	MIDDLE CENTURY	LATE CENTURY
Importance of learning theory	low	high	high—but under different names
Definition of learning	change in behavior	(transition)	change in knowledge
Process of learning	response strengthening	knowledge acquisition	knowledge construction
Relation of learning and education	one-way street	dead-end street	two-way street
Generality of learning theories	no theories	general theories	specific theories
Individual differences in learning	one-size fits all	adapting the pace	cognitive process instruction
Assessment of learning	uniform, basic standards	precise, individual objectives	authentic, diverse goals
Motivational bases of learning	no theories	drive-reduction theories	cognitive theories
Biological bases of learning	inclusion	exclusion	anticipation
Social context of learning	emphasized	de-emphasized	re-emphasized

there is an apparent inconsistency: On the one hand, the study of education is intimately linked to an understanding of how people learn, but on the other hand, the study of learning seems to have dropped off the research agenda in education. The resolution to this apparent paradox is that learning theory is still central to the study of education, but (a) the terminology used to describe learning has been broadened, and (b) teaching and learning are now so closely related that discussions of learning are integrated increasingly into complementary discussions of teaching.

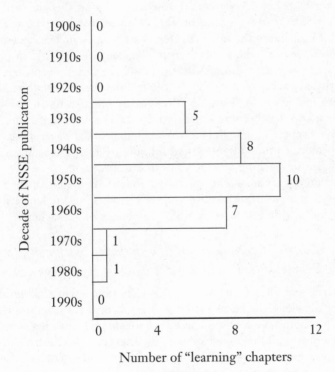

Number of "learning" chapters

FIGURE 1

RENAMING LEARNING

Although classic learning theory is out of favor, learning remains a central theme in NSSE Yearbooks and series books. For many years, a by-product of the cognitive revolution in psychology has been to downplay "learning" (with its connotations of classic behaviorist learning theories) in favor of other terms, such as "memory," "knowledge acquisition," "information processing," and "conceptual change." Instead of talking about learning, scholars focus on changes in knowledge, differences in information processing strategies, or building mental representations in memory. Instead of long discourses on general theories of learning, scholars describe learning within specific subject areas or with respect to specific kinds of learners, thereby adopting the terminology of the subject area or special education.

INTEGRATING TEACHING AND LEARNING

Rather than having chapters devoted to learning theories per se, modern NSSE Yearbooks tend to have chapters that integrate teaching and learning into the same chapter. For example, in *The Psychology of Teaching Methods*,[9] the term "learning" appears in the title of only one chapter, but descriptions of "learning" are heavily represented within the chapters—as indicated by the fact that the Yearbook's index has more references to "learning" than to any other term. In a sense, learning theory has become a victim of its own success. "Learning" is no longer a separate topic to be discussed independent of teaching but rather is more commonly integrated into discussions of teaching specific subjects or teaching specific kinds of learners.

In summary, in answer to questions about whatever happened to "learning," it appears to be alive and well, flourishing under various other names within the pages of NSSE Yearbooks and elsewhere.

Changing Conceptions of the Definition of Learning: From Change in Behavior to Change in Knowledge

What is learning? Learning is a relatively permanent change in a learner's knowledge or behavior that is a result of the learner's experience. This definition contains three components: (a) learning is relatively permanent, (b) learning is due to experience, and (c) learning is a change in a learner's knowledge or behavior. The first component is that learning is a *relatively permanent* change rather than a momentary one. In short, learning lasts over time. The second component is that learning is *caused by experience* rather than by some physical factor, such as recovering from an injury or becoming fatigued. The third component is that learning involves a *change in a learner's knowledge or behavior*.

Even this seemingly basic definition reflects changing conceptions of learning. Although the first two components have remained fairly constant during the course of the twentieth century, the third one has changed dramatically. The third component concerns what is learned, and clarifying this issue has been an ongoing challenge throughout the twentieth century. Behaviorist conceptions focused on learning as a change in behavior, whereas cognitive conceptions focused on learning as a change in knowledge.

CHANGE IN BEHAVIOR

Definitions of learning have appeared repeatedly within NSSE Yearbooks and generally have contained all three definitional components. During the first part of the twentieth century, however, definitions of learning emphasized a change in behavior (as in the third component). In the 1942 Yearbook, *The Psychology of Learning*, for example, E. R. Guthrie[10] stated, "Learning means changes in behavior that are a result of experience," and J. B. Stroud[11] stated, "Learning is a change in performance in the course of practice." Similarly, in the 1950 Yearbook, *Learning and Instruction*, G. Lester Anderson[12] noted that "a change in behavior which results from experience is the generally agreed-upon definition of learning," and in a 1963 chapter entitled "Learning," Sheldon H. White[13] proclaimed, "Learning . . . is a relatively permanent behavior change which is the result of experience."

CHANGE IN KNOWLEDGE

A subtle change in the definition of learning began to appear in the latter part of the twentieth century—instead of seeing learning as a change in behavior, authors recognized learning as a change in knowledge that must be inferred from changes in behavior. Robert M. Gagné[14] defined learning as "the establishment of more or less permanent states within the learner," which could be "inferred from observations of his performance." M. C. Wittrock[15] summarized the new definition by stating that "learning is an effortful constructive process" in which "learners relate relevant memories and schemata to the information they are to learn." Yet, the first stirrings of this shift can be found much earlier among Gestalt psychologists and their associates, such as Kurt Lewin,[16] who viewed "learning as a change in cognitive structure (knowledge)."

Even as the cognitive approach has come to dominate the study of learning, there is debate concerning the nature of the change in knowledge: Does learning involve strengthening and weakening of cognitive connections, adding information to memory, or constructing an organized mental representation? Because changes in how scholars characterize what is learned is perhaps the most significant aspect of

learning theory during the twentieth century, changing conceptions of
the process of learning are examined in the next section.

Changing Conceptions of the Process of Learning: From Response Strengthening to Knowledge Acquisition to Knowledge Construction

How do students learn? The teacher's conception of the learning
process can have a strong influence on what happens in the classroom.
Richard E. Mayer[17] described three metaphors of learning that have
developed during the twentieth century: (a) learning as response
strengthening, (b) learning as knowledge acquisition, and (c) learning
as knowledge construction.

RESPONSE STRENGTHENING

During the early years of the twentieth century, the response
strengthening view came to dominate both psychology and education,
based largely on the pioneering work of E. L. Thorndike.[18] According
to the response-strengthening view, learning occurs when a learner
makes a connection between a stimulus and a response—such as learning to say "4" when the teacher says, "What is 2 + 2?" If the response
is followed by reward—such as a nod from the teacher—the association between the stimulus and response is strengthened. If the response is followed by punishment—such as a reprimand from the
teacher—the association is weakened. This simple principle—called
the "law of effect" by Thorndike, formed the basis for a new, scientifically based psychology of learning and revolutionized educational
practice.

According to the conception of learning as response strengthening
or, more appropriately, as strengthening and weakening of stimulus-
response associations, the learner is a passive recipient of rewards and
punishments, whereas the teacher is a dispenser of rewards and punishments. The implications for instruction are clear: Students need
practice in making responses and consequently receiving rewards and
punishments. A popular instructional method based on the response-
strengthening view is drill and practice with feedback.

The pages of NSSE Yearbooks contain numerous references to the
learning-as-response-strengthening view. For example, McDonald[19]
acknowledged the influence of Thorndike's declaration that "learning
is connecting." Guthrie[20] observed that "the present account is written
chiefly in terms of stimulus and response because these are the two
most observable features . . . in the process of learning." Further,

Guthrie[21] showed how the psychology of learning focused on "associative learning," in which a "response . . . is associated with a new stimulus." Anderson[22] articulated the response-strengthening view in which "the teacher in the school is in the business of assisting children to acquire behavior patterns." Ernest R. Hilgard and David H. Russell[23] characterized this approach as the view that "learning occurs when a child responds . . . and is rewarded for so doing." Even writing in the 1960s, Winifred F. Hill[24] observed that "most of the learning theories in academic psychology have a stimulus-response orientation," and Benton J. Underwood[25] characterized "learning as . . . establishing a new association."

The pages of the NSSE Yearbooks also contain numerous references to the conception of teaching as dispensing rewards and punishments. McDonald[26] shows the influence of Thorndike's view that "teaching is the arrangement of situations which lead to desirable bonds and make them satisfying" and of Thorndike's instructional maxim to "exercise and reward desirable connections, prevent or punish undesirable connections." For example, Anderson[27] described a vision of education in which "the teacher is the . . . dispenser of praise and blame, reward and punishment." In accordance with this view, drill and practice was frequently offered as a useful method of instruction. Stroud[28] argued that "there are intelligent, constructive uses of drill" and showed that "a long list of experiments in psychology has demonstrated the importance of knowledge of results in practice."

Even writing in the 1960s, A. A. Lumsdaine[29] acknowledged that the then-modern instructional technologies of programmed instruction and teaching machines were "pursued in the context of a basically stimulus-response orientation." According to Lumsdaine,[30] by "applying S-R theory and experimental techniques to the practical problems of instruction . . . any educational subject matter could be regarded as an accumulated repertoire of behavior which could be analyzed logically and behaviorally into a number of small steps. . . ."

KNOWLEDGE ACQUISITION

During the mid-1900s, computer technology suggested a fundamentally different conception of learning as information processing.[31] Computers can take in information, operate on it, and store the results in memory. According to the knowledge acquisition view, the same conception can apply to human learning. In this case, learning involves taking information from the outside world, performing some operations on it, and storing the new information in one's memory. In the knowledge acquisition view, information is a commodity that can be transmitted directly from teacher to learner.

According to the knowledge acquisition view, the learner is a recipient of information and the teacher is a dispenser of information. The implications for instruction are clear: Provide as much information as effectively as possible. Favorite instructional methods include lectures and textbooks that efficiently present the to-be-learned material.

In an early statement of the knowledge acquisition view, John G. Rockwell[32] referred to "information collected through the process of learning." In a critical portrayal of the knowledge acquisition view, G. Lester Anderson, Gertrude Whipple, and Robert Gilchrist[33] characterized some classrooms as "lesson-hearing rooms" in which "emphasis is placed on studying lessons and reciting them." Anderson and Arthur I. Gates[34] also critiqued the knowledge acquisition view: "Learning has been too often considered, even by the more sophisticated teacher, as synonymous with memorizing or, at best, as the acquisition of knowledge or skill. While these are legitimately considered forms of learning . . . they are not the most important aspects of it." Lumsdaine[35] critiqued the "conceptions of teaching . . . which concentrate primarily on the stimulus properties of a message which students receive and which tend to assume that what the student is told he then knows." In spite of the largely negative critique of the knowledge acquisition view, cognitive psychologists are quick to point out that domain knowledge is an indispensable part of expertise.[36]

KNOWLEDGE CONSTRUCTION

A third conception—learning as knowledge construction—came to dominate educational psychology during the final portion of the twentieth century. According to the knowledge construction view, learning occurs when a learner builds an organized mental representation that makes sense. Knowledge is not a commodity that can be placed neatly in a learner's head, but rather it is the result of a learner's active sense-making process. For example, Mayer[37] showed how meaningful learning depends on a learner selecting relevant information from what is presented, mentally organizing the material into a coherent representation, and mentally integrating it with existing knowledge.

According to this view, the learner is an active sense maker, and the teacher is a cognitive guide who helps the learner engage in productive cognitive processing on complex academic tasks. The instructional implications include a focus on cognitive activity—including working on challenging, authentic tasks—with support and guidance from more skilled practitioners. Favorite instructional methods include cognitive modeling, in which teacher and learner describe and compare their cognitive processing on a task; guided discovery, in which students explore a challenging problem; and working on projects with others.

The pages of NSSE Yearbooks and series books throughout the twentieth century contain many ways of articulating this cognitive constructivist vision of learning. For example, the move from knowledge acquisition to knowledge construction was foreshadowed by Anderson's[38] critique of mid-century educational theory: "Instead of focusing on the central problem of how to guide the learner wisely . . . they have focused on peripheral problems such as the techniques of presenting information." Similarly, the constructivist view can be seen in Ragsdale's[39] conception of practice as a reflective activity in which a learner "makes trials and uses the perceptions of himself in action as data for guiding later trials" so "his learning includes reflective thinking . . ." (p. 90). Even the earliest NSSE Yearbook entries on learning sometimes foreshadowed the constructivist revolution, such as in the following observation by J. F. Dashiell:[40] "A fundamental assumption of present-day education is that the child is learning in the truest sense when he is achieving new insights."

McDonald[41] showed that the roots of constructivism can be seen in John Dewey's thesis that "learning is . . . problem solving" and in Gestalt psychology's "new conception of the nature of the learning process." McDonald[42] showed how "Gestalt psychology and Dewey's conceptions were highly compatible" and "came to be the preferred psychology of American educators." According to McDonald,[43] because of Gestalt psychology, "the cognitive processes were back in psychology," and "reorganization of perceptions, understanding, and insight became central psychological events." Similarly, Hilgard[44] showed how "in the late 1920s and early 1930s Gestalt psychology . . . came like a breath of fresh air upon the American scene, then dominated by a somewhat stringent behaviorism." Among its contributions, according to Hilgard,[45] are an "emphasis upon . . . organization, . . . meaningfulness, and . . . patterning" rather than "habits." Hilgard[46] argued that the "historian of psychology must recognize [Gestalt psychology's] impact whenever there are references to . . . cognitive processes (insight and understanding) . . . in any discussion of learning."

By the second half of the twentieth century, advances in cognitive psychology led NSSE Yearbook authors to focus more precisely than before on the nature of knowledge construction. As early as 1950,

Anderson and Gates[47] hailed the "increased recognition of the role of cognition in human learning," including "meaning, concept formation, and understanding." Further, Anderson and Gates[48] observed: "During the heyday of behaviorism, psychology neglected or disregarded the intellectual processes and their role in learning," but more recent conceptions of learning focused on "discovery or insight, as opposed to blind, mechanistic reacting." By the 1960s, White[49] recognized a shift in which psychologists were "initially predisposed . . . to view learning in stimulus-response terms," but, he noted, "this viewpoint is beginning to lose ground as mounting evidence begins to show how factors of attention, strategy, and cognitive style within the child help determine his response to stimuli which are presented to him."

A flowchart model of learning—the hallmark of cognitive conceptions of learning—first appeared in an NSSE Yearbook in 1976.[50] Gagné[51] refocused the goal of learning theory on determining "what are the processes involved in learning . . . what is the sequence of transformations brought about by these processes . . . what kinds of outcomes of learning can be inferred from human performance." According to Gagné,[52] "Each act of learning involves the operation of a number of internal processes." Gagné[53] proposed that the outcome of learning was knowledge that could take any of five forms: "verbal information, intellectual skills, cognitive strategies, attitudes, motor skills."

In a full-fledged declaration of modern cognitive constructivism, Wittrock[54] proclaimed: "Today, the study of the learner's cognitive processes in learning and memory is the central focus of research in instruction within educational psychology." According to Wittrock,[55] "Learning is conceived as a result of the learner's active mental processes, rather than as a direct product of environmental conditions or teacher activities." Rather than simply acquire new knowledge, "learners construct their understanding of information."[56] It follows that "we should study what learners do with the information they receive, what mental transformations they perform upon it, what organization they impose on it, and what previous experience they relate to it."[57] In short, Wittrock[58] clearly articulated the view of "learning as a generative process," in which the outcome of learning depends on the "constructivist processes used by the learner."

Similarly, the constructivist vision of teaching as cognitive guidance is also reflected in the pages of NSSE Yearbooks. William A. Brownell and Gordon Hendrickson[59] argued that teaching may be regarded as the "guidance of reorganization"; their rationale was that "learning partakes of the nature of problem solving," so "guidance, not direction is called for." In contrast to response strengthening conceptions of learning, Brownell and Hendrickson[60] claimed that "errors . . . provide fruitful opportunities for constructive teaching."

Even at mid-century, NSSE Yearbook authors challenged educators to adopt constructivist approaches to teaching:

Classrooms should be learning laboratories . . . and should cease to be lesson-hearing rooms. Rather they should be centers where children engage in activities that will lead to learning. . . . The primary task of the teacher is to manipulate the classroom environment so that children will have educative experiences.[61]

At the same time, Anderson and Gates[62] argued that "the teacher can never impose the product directly . . . it is the pupil, not the teacher, who is the active learner." Anderson and Gates[63] saw the role of the teacher as cognitive guide: "Teachers can direct and guide learning" and can "stimulate learning through processes that are meaningful, insightful, or problem-solving in character."

Within the pages of NSSE Yearbooks, Gagné[64] was the first to propose a modern cognitive approach to instruction: "Decisions are based upon the teacher's understanding of what is happening to the student as a learner." It follows that "the essential task of the teacher is to arrange the conditions of the learner's environment so that the processes of learning will be activated, supported, enhanced, and maintained."[65]

Wittrock[66] emphasized the role of teachers in promoting constructivist learning: "Teaching becomes the art of facilitating learners' construction of meaning." He rejected the old role of teachers as dispensers of information or dispensers of rewards: "Learning does not occur automatically when teachers dispense information or reinforcers . . . instead it is a constructive, effortful process influenced by the learner's background of information and cognitive information processing strategies."[67] Wittrock[68] offered suggestions for how teachers could work to guide the cognitive processes of learners: "Teachers facilitate attention by using questions . . . teachers enhance comprehension . . . by stimulating learners to relate relevant memories and schemata to the information they are to learn."

Although cognitive constructivism came to dominate educational psychology by century's end, more radical forms of constructivism also began to sprout—including the idea that direct instruction should be replaced with free exploration by students. Yet even such seemingly contemporary innovations were the subject of warnings posted in NSSE Yearbooks more than sixty years ago: "The philosophy of education that stresses freedom of the learner . . . without regard to the direction in which growth is pointed leads to teaching practices which reduce teacher direction and the guidance of learning to a minimum. The result is that many pupils acquire . . . methods of work and study . . . which are . . . wasteful and inefficient."[69]

More recently, constructivism has been amended to include the idea that learning can be conceived of as guided participation in authentic tasks and that learning emerges from social interaction—themes that can be found in recent NSSE Yearbooks on service learning[70] and on learning ways of knowing.[71] Of course, the idea of contextualizing learning within tasks that students are interested in and of providing scaffolding to students as they work on solving complex problems have their roots in earlier visions of learning, including Dewey's "progressive movement."[72] Future historians will have the perspective to evaluate the contributions of these newly emerging conceptions of learning as a situationally determined and socially constructed process.

Changing Conceptions of the Relation Between Learning and Education: From One-Way Street to Dead-End Street to Two-Way Street

What is the relation between the study of learning and the study of education? Learning and education are so intertwined that it is not possible to study education adequately without having a conception of learning. The study of education is concerned with creating experiences that foster changes in learners—a point made repeatedly in NSSE Yearbooks. For example, J. F. Dashiell[73] observed that "education is guided learning," Anderson[74] noted that "instruction is guidance of learning—a process of bringing about behavioral changes," and Gagné[75] argued that "the central purpose of teaching is the promotion of learning in individuals." In short, education is concerned with how to promote learning.

The study of learning involves understanding how changes in learners occur. To accomplish the goal of promoting learning, it is useful to understand how people learn. This is the rationale for placing an understanding of how people learn on the research agenda for educational studies. Unfortunately, the relation between the study of learning and the study of education has not always been positive during the twentieth century. Mayer[76] has proposed three major phases in navigating the rocky road between psychology and education—one-way street, dead-end street, and two-way street.

ONE-WAY STREET

In the opening decades of the twentieth century, hopes were high that the science of psychology would generate principles from the laboratory that could be applied to improve the practice of education in the classroom. For example, a 1919 Yearbook contained chapters entitled, "Principles of Method in Teaching Reading as Derived from Scientific Investigation" by Gray,[77] "Principles of Method in Teaching Writing as Derived from Scientific Investigation" by Frank M. Freeman,[78] and "Principles of Teaching Arithmetic as Derived from Scientific Investigation" by Walter S. Monroe.[79] In short, the relation between psychology and education was seen as a one-way street: Psychologists developed principles of learning, and educators applied them.

In the case of learning theory, Anderson and Gates[80] characterized the one-way street metaphor that dominated educational psychology during the first third of the twentieth century: "Once it seemed sufficient for the educational psychologist to formulate a set of principles of learning around fairly simple concepts of exercise and effect. The teacher applied these principles through techniques of drill and of reward and punishment." Similarly, from his vantage point in the 1960s, McDonald[81] showed how "early in this century education turned to science as the solution to its problems." Further, McDonald[82] described how, early in the twentieth century, Thorndike "showed convincingly what psychology had to offer education" by "bringing scientific psychology to the attention of the educational profession." Winifred F. Hill[83] acknowledged the "optimistic view that learning theory can make substantial contributions to education." Even at mid-century, Anderson[84] envisioned a system in which teachers would take advantage of "implications for instruction of accumulated knowledge from the field of learning."

DEAD-END STREET

By mid-century, scholars recognized the rift between psychology and education, in which psychologists focused on artificial situations far removed from the classroom and teachers lost interest in pursuing psychological theories. In short, the paths to psychology and education became dead-end streets that failed to meet. McDonald[85] lamented that "psychology had become scientific, but the price was separation from the larger issues and problems facing society." Benton J. Underwood[86] reported "no genuine feeling of satisfaction that the bridges between the schoolroom and the laboratory are substantial." Anderson[87] recognized that "seldom in the education of the teacher is there rapprochement between the psychology of learning and the methodologies of teaching," and Esther J. Swenson[88] observed that "classroom teachers, by and large, are apt to be somewhat impatient of what they often refer to as 'just theory.'" White[89] characterized the lack of interaction between psychologists and educators as follows: "Psychologists and educators, both so interested in learning, have long viewed each other cordially but at some distance. The flow of innovations, problems, and ideas between the two groups has been sparse. . . ."

TWO-WAY STREET

In spite of the problems, there have always been scholars who envisioned the relation between psychology and education as one based on mutual benefit—with education providing realistic learning situations to study and psychology providing methods for understanding how to promote learning in those situations. In short, a third phase is a two-way street based on a mutually beneficial relation between psychology and education. T. R. McConnell[90] recognized the mutual interdependence of psychological theory and educational practice: "What we need most in educational psychology, probably, are carefully designed experiments with double reference: to the fundamental problems in learning theory, on the one hand, and to significant educational problems on the other." Anderson, Whipple, and Gilchrist[91] noted the need to understand theory and practice in terms of each other: "Instructional procedures must be rooted in an understanding of the ways in which children learn." Hilgard[92] argued against the proposition that "once learning theory is in order, the principles of instruction will flow from it." By the last third of the twentieth century, Wittrock[93] was able to document how "knowledge of human learning and memory influences what we know and do about teaching."

This analysis of the relation between education and psychology reveals a complementary progression in the context of research—from methodologically weak classroom research aimed at practical school problems during the one-way street phase, to highly controlled laboratory studies seemingly divorced from practical school issues in the dead-end street phase, to a convergence of laboratory and classroom contexts all aimed at practical school issues in the two-way street phase.

In summary, during the twentieth century, how scholars conceive of the relation between psychology and education has changed—from a one-way street, in which psychology produces principles for education to apply; to a dead-end street, in which psychology and education have little in common; to a two-way street, in which psychology and education mutually contribute to each other by focusing on the nature of learning and how to promote it. Gone are the optimistic days when psychologists dictated how to teach based on their grand theories, and gone are the pessimistic days when psychologists and educators agreed to cease communication. With a new sense of cautious optimism, the twentieth century ends with a third phase in the rocky relation between psychology and education—a phase in which psychologists are challenged to develop learning theories based on realistic situations, and educators recognize that to promote learning, it is useful to understand how learning happens.

Changing Conceptions of the Generality of Learning Theory in Education: From No Theory to General Theories to Specific Theories

The changing relation between psychology and education is reflected in changes in the level of generality of learning theories relevant to education. NSSE Yearbooks have reflected changes in the generality of learning theory in education during the twentieth century—beginning with no theory early in the century, shifting to general theories of learning by mid-century, and ending with specific theories of learning during the latter decades of the century.

NO THEORIES

Early reviews of educational research tended to focus on the practical problems of education, without much reference to underlying theories of how students learn. For example, the Eighteenth Yearbook, Part II, entitled *Fourth Report of the Committee on Economy of Time in Education*,[94] dealt with pragmatic issues such as what to teach and how to teach it. In short, the Committee chosen to write the Yearbook was concerned with "achievement of economy through a better selection of what is taught" and "discovering the most economical methods of teaching it."[95] The issue of what to teach was guided by "acceptance of the point of view of social utility in curriculum making" which holds that "it is uneconomical to teach a child something that he does not need to know."[96] The issue of how to teach was to be guided by a "choice of the scientific method," with instruction decisions based on "experimental data."[97]

The Eighteenth Yearbook, Part II is full of suggestions for how to teach school subjects such as reading, writing, spelling, arithmetic, drawing, and music. In the chapter "Principles of Method of Teaching Reading as Derived from Scientific Investigation," for example, Gray[98] listed several dozen principles, such as "accomplishment in oral reading increases rapidly in the lower grades and steadily, but less rapidly, in the upper grades" (p. 26). However, in summarizing empirical research, little mention was made of any larger conception of how students learn, except for an occasional reference to associationist constructs, such as the "the establishment of habits and associations."[99] Similarly, in Frank N. Freeman's[100] chapter, "Principles of Method in Teaching Writing as Derived from Scientific Investigation," twenty-eight research-based rules were presented, such as, "The writer should face the desk squarely." However, there was no reference to underlying theory. In the chapter entitled "Principles in Teaching Arithmetic as Derived from Scientific Investigation," Walter S. Monroe[101] offered research-based principles, such as, "In learning the tables, the different combinations are not equally difficult and the number of repetitions of the several combinations should correspond to the degree of difficulty, the most difficult receiving the largest number of repetitions." Except for passing references to "associations" and "bonds," the principles for teaching arithmetic were presented as generalizations from empirical data and were not linked to any theory of how students learn. In summary, early in the twentieth century, hopes were high that instructional issues could be settled by empirical research collected using the scientific method.

GENERAL THEORIES

By mid-century, psychologists had developed a general, all-encompassing theory of learning—in fact, several of them. Thorndike had offered educational psychology's first general theory of learning throughout the opening decades of the twentieth century, culminating in his three-volume *Educational Psychology*,[102] but general theories of learning were not widely represented in NSSE Yearbooks until the 1930s, 1940s, and 1950s.

General theories of learning dominated the Forty-first Yearbook, Part II, *The Psychology of Learning*.[103] In the introduction, T. R. McConnell[104] explained that a primary purpose of the Yearbook was "to provide a concise and authoritative statement of three of the most active and influential theories of human learning . . . conditioning, connectionism, and field theory." According to the committee that produced the Yearbook, the "three theories presented are the principal protagonists in the contemporary scene."[105]

Conditioning refers to behaviorist theories of learning and was represented by E. R. Guthrie[106] and Clark L. Hull,[107] two of the era's best-known and most rigorous learning theorists. Guthrie's[108] goal was to "state the rules of learning" in a way that is "understandable and verifiable." For example, one rule was that "a stimulus pattern that is acting at the time of a response will, if it recurs, tend to produce that response," and an instructionally relevant corollary is that "we learn only what we do."[109] Hull[110] built his learning theory upon basic principles, such as his mathematical version of the law of effect:

If the central afferent receptor discharge (s_c) of a stimulus element (S_c) of a stimulus compound is active in the central nervous system at the time that a reaction (r_u) is evoked, and if at about this time there occurs a reinforcing state of affairs, there will result from this conjunction of events an increment to a habit ($_sH_r$).

The underlying mechanism of learning in both theories was a strengthening and weakening of the association between a stimulus and a response—what Hull quantified as "habit strength."[111] As Guthrie[112] noted, a distinguishing feature of conditioning theories of learning was that they were "written chiefly in terms of stimulus and response because these are the two most observable features of the . . . learning process."

Connectionism refers largely to Thorndike's conception of learning, which is based on the same mechanism of learning that Hull and Guthrie described—the strengthening and weakening of S-R associations. The Forty-first Yearbook Committee "had hoped that Thorndike [would] summarize his own point of view . . . but he found it necessary to decline the invitation to do so."[113] Peter Sandiford's[114] chapter defined connectionism as "the doctrine that all mental processes consist of the functioning of . . . connections between situations and responses." In short, "learning is connecting,"[115] and the basic laws of learning are Thorndike's laws of effect, exercise, and readiness. According to

Sandiford,[116] the law of effect is that "a modifiable bond is strengthened or weakened as satisfaction or annoyance attends its exercise"; the law of exercise is that "when a modifiable connection is made between a situation and a response, that connection's strength is, other things being equal, increased," and "when a modifiable connection is not made between a situation and a response over a length of time, that connection's strength is decreased." The law of readiness is that "when a bond is ready to act, to act gives satisfaction and not to act gives annoyance" and "when a bond which is not ready to act is made to act, annoyance is caused." Similarly, Gates[117] reviewed Thorndike's monumental contributions to a connectionist theory of learning, including the crucial role played by rewards in fostering changes in learners.

Field theory refers to Gestalt-like principles of learning, and was represented in the Yearbook by Kurt Lewin[118] and George W. Hartmann.[119] Lewin[120] noted that "psychology is in a dilemma when it tries to develop general concepts and laws" and claimed that conditioning and connectionism theories of learning can mainly address rote learning. In his critique of using the law of effect to explain all learning, Lewin[121] complained that "associationism reached out farther and farther until it prided itself on explaining with one law not only the process of rote learning but any kind of intellectual process." Lewin argued that in addition to examining learning as changes in rote connections, psychology needed to develop theories to explain changes in cognitive structure, motivation, and attitude. Similarly, Hartmann[122] called for broadening the study of learning to include creativity, originality, and transfer. Unfortunately, neither Lewin nor Hartmann presented a theory that came close to the precision and clarity of those offered by Hull or Thorndike.

On the one hand, learning theorists offered a vision of learning as trial and error behavior in which S-R connections are shaped by rewards and punishments. On the other hand, field theorists offered a vision of learning as cognitive construction based on structural understanding, in which insight was the major accomplishment of learning. In reconciling the various general theories of learning available when the Yearbook was written, McConnell[123] showed that "trial and error and insight both roughly describe certain phases of the learning process and fail to describe others," so that "what one emphasizes, the other neglects." In short, the theories did not so much disagree, but rather attempted to explain different kinds of learning. This realization is a major step in the eventual decline of general theories of learning—and in the eventual development of specific theories of learning geared to specific kinds of learning situations. For example, Lewin[124] argued against "attempting to find laws of learning in the broad sense" and set psychology's goal as "develop[ing] more specific laws, each representing the nature of certain types of processes."

During the latter part of the twentieth century, researchers developed more complete psychologies of subject matter. Instead of asking a general question such as, "How do students learn," psychologists of subject matter asked domain-specific questions, such as, "How do students learn to read," "How do students learn to write," or "How do students develop mathematical competence?" For example, domain-specific accounts of learning can be found in several Yearbooks, *Mathematics Education*,[125] *The Teaching of English*,[126] *Becoming Readers in a Complex Society*,[127] *The Teaching of Writing*,[128] and *The Reading-Writing Connection*,[129] or in series books, *Aspects of Reading Education*[130] or *Selected Topics in Mathematics Education*.[131] In comparing the 1942 Yearbook on learning to the 1964 Yearbook on learning, Hilgard[132] noted that "The earlier Yearbook [focused on] theories associated with great names," whereas the newer Yearbook dealt with "concrete problems of educational reform and instruction."

During the early part of the twentieth century, educational researchers focused on teaching of school subjects but lacked a theory of how students learn. During the middle part of the twentieth century, educational researchers developed grand theories of how students learn, but often failed to tie the theories to real school learning in school subjects. During the latter part of the century, educational researchers returned to the study of school subjects but this time had theories that could account for learning in each specific subject. The emergence of theory-based psychologies of subject matter represents one of the major advances in educational psychology during the twentieth century.[133]

Changing Conceptions of Individual Differences in Learning: From One-Size to Adapting the Pace to Cognitive Process Instruction

From the start, scholars have pointed to the challenge of individual differences among students in a given classroom, and, in particular, to the need to address better the needs of low achieving students. The instructional solution has changed from *one size fits all*, in which all students were exposed to the same instruction, to *adapting the pace of instruction*, in which students marched through a hierarchically-arranged curriculum at their own rates, to *cognitive process instruction*, in which at-risk students learned how to process information more productively.

ONE SIZE FITS ALL

During the early twentieth century, schools adopted a *one size fits all* approach that exacerbated the problem of individual differences. For example, Leo S. Brueckner[134] lamented the "failure of the school to recognize the fact of differences in the rate at which pupils learn," which resulted in "the failure of many [students] to make satisfactory progress." The solution, according to Brueckner,[135] was to adapt instructional materials to the needs of the student rather than try to fit all students to the same set of instructional materials: "The time should not be far distant when every classroom will be provided with instructional materials in the skill phases of every subject that will make possible adaptation of instruction to individual differences."

A few years later, Stroud[136] eloquently described the challenge of individual differences: "Approximately a third of the pupils of a given grade equal or exceed the average achievement of pupils one grade above, and about one third equal or exceed that of pupils one grade below." Furthermore, Stroud[137] pointed to the need for an educational solution: "Nor is it to be supposed that individual differences can be reduced by good teaching. In fact, the better the teaching, the greater are such differences."

ADAPTING THE PACE

By mid-century, the solution to the problem of individual differences in learning focused mainly on adapting the pace of instruction. The curriculum could be analyzed hierarchically—so individualization of instruction involved beginning at the child's level of knowledge and working upward at the child's pace. Using a curriculum-based approach, to-be-learned material could be arranged hierarchically, so that the level of content and the pace of presentation could be adapted to the knowledge level of the learner. At mid-century, scholars continued to point to the problems of an inflexible, hierarchical program of instruction. Esther J. Swenson,[138] for example, argued that the "results of instruction cannot be improved by trying to make children do what they are not ready to do at any point in their schooling." In the next decade, McDonald[139] observed that "the problem of individuality in education has not been solved." Lumsdaine[140] proposed using programmed instruction and teaching machines as possible solutions to the problem of adapting instruction to the needs of individual learners. Nevertheless, subsequent events demonstrated that educational technology based on S-R psychology would not solve the problem of individual differences in learning.

A major shift in the conceptualization of individual differences emerged during the final portion of the twentieth century. Instead of viewing the ability to learn as a single monolithic ability, cognitive scientists came to view it as a collection of specific component cognitive processes—such as knowing how to pay attention to appropriate material in a passage, knowing how to plan a solution to a word problem, or knowing how to detect an error in one's essays. Any academic task—from reading a paragraph, to writing an essay, to solving an arithmetic word problem—could be analyzed into a collection of underlying cognitive processes. Although the processes are seldom taught directly to students, successful students learn them. An important instructional implication is that cognitive processing is a teachable skill, so low-achieving students may benefit from cognitive process instruction. R. L. Thorndike's[141] chapter on "how children learn the principles and techniques of problem-solving" foreshadowed the remarkable progress in cognitive process instruction that occurred over the following half-century.

Wittrock[142] summarized the cognitive view in his analysis of "individual differences . . . centered upon cognitive styles and strategies." Earlier, Gagné[143] explained how "cognitive strategies are . . . control processes," that is, how an important part of learning, in addition to knowing verbal information, is to be able to control one's cognitive processes. Metacognition (awareness and control of one's cognitive processing) became a new issue in learning, along with calls to teach metacognitive strategies to students who seemed to lack them. Additional support for cognitive process instruction came from research in cognitive development that pointed to changes in cognitive processing, research in special education that pointed to differences in ways that children processed information, and research in cognitive neuroscience that identified areas in the brain responsible for specific kinds of cognitive processing.

As the curtain fell on the twentieth century, cognitive process instruction remained one of the century's most important new players. Along with the development of psychologies of subject matter, teaching of learning strategies stands as a milestone achievement of learning theory in the twentieth century.

Changing Conceptions of Assessment of Learning: From Uniform and Basic Standards to Precise and Individual Objectives to Authentic and Diverse Goals

The assessment of learning has been a repeated topic in discussions on learning during the twentieth century. Classic complaints about testing sound amazingly contemporary—including the need to broaden assessment beyond rote facts and the destructiveness of holding students to standards they cannot achieve. Assessment of learning has progressed from *uniform and basic standards* to *precise and individual objectives* to *authentic and diverse goals*.

UNIFORM AND BASIC STANDARDS

From the start of the century, a major complaint of educational researchers concerned the focus on low-level rather than high-level skills, that is, on rote learning rather than meaningful learning. For example, Brueckner[144] complained that "most standardized survey tests at the present time deal with relatively narrow outcomes of instruction, such as specific factual knowledge and skills." In addition, Brueckner[145] offered a vision of the solution: "The remedy for this condition is the clear recognition of the use of the whole range of desired objectives of instruction and the use of suitable methods to measure the extent to which all of them are being achieved."

Another major complaint concerned setting standards at levels that are inappropriate for some students. For example, Brueckner[146] noted that "lack of valid standards for achievement to be expected of pupils sometimes results in making excessive and impossible demands on them," while "the opposite is true when standards are too low." David G. Ryans[147] made a similar point by noting that "goals and standards . . . function successfully as incentives only when adapted to pupil ability."

PRECISE AND INDIVIDUAL OBJECTIVES

By mid-century, consensus emerged that the solution to the problem of assessment was to devise precise and individual objectives for learning. Swenson[148] argued that "learners of all ages need to have clear goals" because "a clearly stated objective is, of course, the focus which guides both teacher and pupils." It follows that assessments should be aligned with instructional objectives: "Learning can be properly appraised only in terms of learning goals, those held by the learner and those held by the teacher."[149] Echoing earlier complaints about the need for appropriate goals, Swenson[150] stated that "the expectation that all third-graders must earn standardized test scores at the third-grade national norms must be abandoned." The hallmark of precision became behavioral objectives—statements of exactly which behavior a person should be able to produce under which circumstances. Although "critics pointed out the frequent triviality of objectives stated in terms of student behavior . . . the voices of the critics were drowned out by those advocating the benefits of objectives."[151]

AUTHENTIC AND DIVERSE GOALS

A persistent theme throughout the century was the need to measure a broad array of skills, especially those required for performing complex academic tasks; progress in this area was substantial during the later part of the century. A hallmark achievement in addressing these needs was the publication in 1956 of the *Taxonomy of Educational Objectives*. Known as "Bloom's Taxonomy," it is a guide that emphasized testing of higher-order processing, such as comprehension, application, analysis, synthesis, and evaluation, as well as the ability to remember basic knowledge.[152] Nearly forty years later, the NSSE published a Yearbook devoted to examining the legacy of Bloom's taxonomy—entitled *Bloom's Taxonomy: A Forty-Year Retrospective*.[153]

Perhaps the greatest change in assessment at the end of the twentieth century was the incorporation of higher-level objectives into assessments. In a retrospective analysis of the influence of Bloom's Taxonomy, one of its authors, Benjamin S. Bloom,[154] concluded that "during the past forty years, the ability to use higher mental processes has assumed prime importance." Bloom[155] also noted the intimate relation between assessment and instruction:

For the first time, educators were able to evaluate the learning of students systematically. As they did so, they became aware that too much emphasis was being placed on the lowest level of the Taxonomy—Knowledge. Frequently, as much as 90 percent of the instructional time was spent at this level, with very little time spent on the higher mental processes that would enable students to apply their knowledge creatively. . . . The result of having a more diverse set of educational objectives is an increase in "teaching of higher mental processes."[156]

The *Taxonomy* reflected an important change in focus from simple behaviors in isolation to the cognitive processes underlying complex academic tasks, a shift that came into prominence during the final segment of the twentieth century. For example, Edward S. Furst[157] observed that "The *Taxonomy* may well be a classification of cognitive processes." In spite of being produced during the behaviorist era, "The *Taxonomy* was not built on behaviorist principles."[158] It did not describe learning outcomes in terms of connections between stimuli and responses, but rather described the kinds of cognitive processing students are expected to be able to perform. Similarly, the *Taxonomy* did not describe learning outcomes in terms of the information found in the curriculum. Peter Airasian[159] noted that an important change in the field's conception of assessment was that "achievement testing needed to be based upon more than a list of content topics." Instead, "educational objectives were general statements of transfer-oriented student outcomes."[160]

The *Taxonomy* also codified the growing theme throughout the century that there are many different kinds of learning. William D. Rohwer and Kathryn Sloane[161] observed that the *Taxonomy* authors "rejected the proposition that a single kind of learning accounts for the range of performances humans are capable of attaining." In clearly describing the breadth of cognitive processes involved in meaningful learning, the *Taxonomy* provided a "vision of what constitutes education for productive learning."[162] The *Taxonomy* helped overthrow the "assumption that test items requiring recall of facts were valid surrogates for measuring more complex student behaviors such as reasoning. . . ."[163] Similarly, Lauren A. Sosniak[164] noted that the most influential theme in the *Taxonomy* was that "good education necessarily aims at more than mere recall of factual information." This broader view of learning resulted in "broadening testing from reliance on multiple-choice items to increased reliance on performance or authentic assessments."[165]

Finally, the *Taxonomy* "integrated evaluation into a general model of curriculum development and instructional planning," in which teacher-generated objectives help guide instruction and determine the content of the assessment.[166] Nevertheless, the development of high-stakes testing beginning in the 1980s changed the relation to one in which mandated assessments determined instruction: "The statewide mandated competency tests turn nearly half a century of curriculum and evaluation theory and practice on its head. Instead of testing and measurement being used in the service of educational objectives, curriculum, and instruction, the new tests put objectives, curriculum, and instruction in service of measurement."[167]

In spite of the changing conceptions of assessment popularized by the *Taxonomy*, Anderson[168] pointed to evidence that "forty years after the development of the Taxonomy, teachers . . . construct tests that include a preponderance of knowledge-level items, and ask questions of their students that in the main require them to recall or recognize what they have been taught." Clearly, the emerging vision of assessment taking shape in the late twentieth century has not yet reached its full impact.

Changing Conceptions of the Motivational Bases of Learning: From No Theories to Drive-Reduction Theories to Cognitive Theories

The motivational context of learning has been a consistent theme in the discussion of learning, ranging from discussions based on *no theories* to *drive-reduction theories* to *cognitive theories*. Throughout the twentieth century, motivation was seen as a central force in learning. In a typical statement about the importance of motivation, for example, Dale B. Harris[169] argued that the "problem of motivation to learn is central both to educational psychology and to school practice." Although educators have agreed on the importance of motivation in learning, they have not always agreed on how motivation works in educational settings.

NO THEORY

Early writings in the twentieth century pointed to the importance of motivation without specifying any convincing theory of how motivation works. For example, Willard C. Olson[170] emphasized the "complex psychology of motivation" and offered general suggestions for how teachers could deal with the emotional aspects of education. Although learning to appreciate art was seen as a way to motivate learners, a review of early work revealed that "research in this area is meager and scattering."[171]

DRIVE-REDUCTION THEORIES

By mid-century, Thorndike's classic view of learning by reinforcement was being applied to the psychology of motivation. For example, Ryans[172] declared "motivation [is] one of the conditions upon which learning is dependent." The theoretical mechanism by which motivation worked was an extension of reinforcement theory: "Motivation has a directing effect and . . . a reinforcing effect on learning" through a process of "tension-reduction."[173] An important instructional recommendation is to minimize punishment and emphasize reward: "The least effective devices in classroom motivation are sarcasm, ridicule, low marks, extra work as a penalty, and reprimands before other students."[174] In short, reflecting Thorndike's revision of the law of effect, Ryans[175] proclaimed: "Punishment is probably of limited value in motivating students."

COGNITIVE THEORIES

By the late twentieth century, theories of motivation were couched in cognitive terms, focusing on the learner's attitudes, beliefs, judgments, and interests. Foreshadowing later research, many Yearbook authors acknowledged Dewey's[176] discussions of the role of interest in learning. McDonnell,[177] for example, cited Dewey's claim that "interest had its roots in the core of the person." Ryans[178] suggested that "interests, attitudes, and purposes must sometimes be developed . . . as a first step in learning" because "pupil interests are important sources of motivation."

Anderson[179] acknowledged "interest and motivation as factors in learning" but focused on student beliefs as the mechanism underlying motivation. Foreshadowing cognitive theories of motivation that emerged later in the century, Anderson[180] argued that students "enter learning situations with very definite conceptions of what they should or can do," that persistence in learning depends on the learner's "level of aspiration," and that "the effect of failure and success upon the child" is related to the child's level of aspiration.

Changing Conceptions of the Biological Bases of Learning: From Inclusion to Exclusion to Anticipation

Learning occurs within the human body, so an understanding of the biological bases of learning should be an aid to education. This simple premise has had a disappointing history in educational psychology during the twentieth century. Although cognitive neuroscience was emphasized by educational psychologists such as Thorndike at the start of the century, it lost prominence by mid-century, and its re-emergence has been keenly anticipated ever since.

INCLUSION

The century began with optimism that psychology and neuroscience would together pinpoint the mechanisms of learning and teaching. In establishing educational psychology as a new domain of science at the beginning of the twentieth century, Thorndike emphasized the role of the nervous system in learning—particularly similarities between building syntactic connections between neurons and building bonds between stimuli and responses.[181] A few decades later, field theorists such as Lewin[182] attempted to explain a competing vision of learning also based on the neurological activity in the brain.

A common theme in NSSE Yearbooks, particularly in the first portion of the twentieth century, was the hope that cognitive neuroscience could inform our understanding of learning and teaching. John G. Rockwell[183] noted that "In recent years there has been present a tendency for [psychology and neurology] to approach and reinforce one another." Dashiell[184] observed that "psychologists, it seems, have always had a leaning toward the physiological in their explanations of experimental and behavioral phenomena, and there is today a persistent interest in the neural bases of learning."

EXCLUSION

By the middle of the twentieth century it had become clear that both the connectionists working in Thorndike's tradition and the field theorists working in Lewin's tradition had failed to explain learning in physiological terms. A common theme in NSSE Yearbooks became the failure of cognitive neuroscience to enrich an understanding of learning or teaching. For example, by the 1930s, Rockwell[185] declared, "We know next to nothing about how learning is accomplished in the nervous system." In a direct attack on Thorndike's optimistic emphasis on cell neurology, Rockwell[186] concluded, "There is room for skepticism when the facts of associational psychology are translated into terms of synaptic connections." Dashiell[187] observed that current theories of "processes occurring in the nervous system . . . are as likely to impede as to facilitate a fair understanding of how learning does actually occur," and he further warned, "The less we think of the learner in physiological terms . . . the more profitable will our educational efforts be."

Ryans[188] concluded that "the neurological processes involved [in learning] have not been determined." Guthrie[189] offered a behaviorist rationale for excluding cognitive neuroscience: "We reject explanations of learning based in terms of synaptic resistances or electrical fields in the brain simply because there is at present no way to observe or to know whether laws stated in such terms hold." By mid-century, Anderson and Gates[190] applauded "the emancipation of the psychologist from dependence upon neurophysiology for explanatory principles." Furthermore, they argued that even "Thorndike finally admits

... how little we really know about the neurophysiology of behavior" (p. 13).[191] They concluded that "today we must search elsewhere than in neurophysiology for principles of guidance in directing learning."[192] The attacks continued into the 1960s: "The fundamental difficulty with Thorndike, as with the behaviorists, is that he depends too exclusively for explanation upon the nervous system."[193] Karl H. Pribram[194] noted that educational practice was far removed from neurological science: "Why the hiatus?" he asked. "Most likely because those working with the cerebra produced little of relevance to those working with curricula."

ANTICIPATION

In spite of advances in cognitive neuroscience, discussions of the biological bases of learning and teaching largely disappeared from NSSE chapters during the final third of the twentieth century, with a few notable exceptions. The most important exception is the 1978 Yearbook, *Education and the Brain*.[195] In contrast to "many popular and often oversimplified articles appearing in the general and educational press," the editors wished to provide a scientifically based overview of the potential contribution to education of "understanding of the basic concepts and processes relating to the brain."[196] For example, Wittrock[197] was able to show how recent neuroscience research is consistent with cognitive constructivist views of learning: "One of the most interesting summary findings about the brain is that it actively constructs models of the world."

While many authors in the volume pointed to the potential importance of cognitive neuroscience for understanding academic learning and teaching, that potential can best be characterized as anticipation as the twentieth century came to a close. Jeanne S. Chall and Allan F. Mirsky's[198] summary of the then-current state of the field remains relevant today: "Since the application of the neurosciences to education is still relatively new, it must therefore be approached with caution as well as with the excitement that comes from viewing old problems in a new light."

Changing Conceptions of the Social Bases of Learning: From Being Emphasized to Being De-emphasized to Being Re-emphasized

The social context of learning was widely accepted in pragmatic discussions of education during the early twentieth century. It became neglected during the middle twentieth century in the discussion of theories of learning based on research with laboratory animals in artificial settings, and it re-emerged in the late twentieth century as a theme in research on authentic learning in mentorship situations. Authors writing in NSSE Yearbooks during the twentieth century reflect this pattern of *emphasis, de-emphasis,* and *re-emphasis* on the social context of learning.

EMPHASIS

Willard C. Olson, for example,[199] reminded NSSE Yearbook readers of the "effect of the group on learning." Foreshadowing the cooperative learning movement that developed half a century later, Olson[200] also pointed out an important instructional implication in which "increasing numbers of schools are modifying their practices so as to avoid extreme competitive awards and to promote cooperation and interaction among children." Also consistent with themes that re-emerged later in the century, Paul T. Rankin[201] expanded the notion of social context to include the child's community and home life: "The environment in which children live influences to a marked degree the type and quality of learning in school." Given the importance of the "child's home and his experience outside the school," Rankin[202] recognized the role that community resources, such as libraries and social agencies, play in learning. This recognition of the role of learning outside school sounds remarkably contemporary. Like modern concerns about the negative effects of television, Rankin[203] was concerned that radio and motion pictures emphasized "love . . . crime . . . sex—scarcely a desirable balance for children." Similarly, Anderson[204] expressed the view that "the child does not grow in isolation, but in a community of fellows and elders."

DE-EMPHASIS

By mid-century, learning theory became more narrowly focused on changes in individual learners, with a corresponding decline in discussions of the social context of learning. Of the three major Yearbooks on learning,[205] only one chapter mentioned the word "social" in its title: Carolyn Tryon's and William E. Henry's[206] chapter, "How Children Learn Personal and Social Adjustment." Even this chapter focused on the social development of the individual child rather than on the social context of learning.

RE-EMPHASIS

Although the focus on cognitive changes in individual learners continued under the banner of cognitive constructivism at the end of the twentieth century, there was increasing interest in contextualizing learning within social settings. For example, in an NSSE series chapter, David W. Johnson[207] presented the argument for "education as a social process." In an NSSE Yearbook chapter, Barak Rosenshine[208] reviewed the mushrooming body of research on "classroom instruction," including social issues such as students working in groups. The century came to a close with strong interest in understanding how the process of learning occurs in social settings—including the role of cooperative learning, reciprocal teaching, and cognitive apprenticeship.

Conclusion

Where has our journey through the pages of NSSE chapters taken us? A major task of educational psychology during the twentieth century was the search for an educationally relevant conception of learning. If education is seen as the process of guiding learning, then an educationally relevant conception of learning must be at the core of the study of education. A century's worth of NSSE chapters offers a useful window into the history of educational psychology's search for an educationally relevant conception of learning.

We began with the classic definition of learning as a relatively permanent change in behavior due to experience. But throughout the twentieth century the conception of *what is learned* changed from *behavior* to *knowledge*, that is, from learning as a change in what someone does to learning as a change in what someone knows. This change puts the spotlight on knowledge as the basis of learning, with the educational implication that any educational task can be analyzed into the underlying knowledge that is needed to perform the task. This knowledge may include factual knowledge and simple procedures, but often also includes knowledge of structures and strategies. The most important educational implication is that the goals of learning should be broadened to include all of the kinds of knowledge needed for successful performance on academic tasks.

The evolution of the definition of learning is a by-product of a larger change in the conception of the learning process. The dominant conception of learning at the start of the century was *learning-as-response strengthening*—the idea that learning involves strengthening or weakening of associations between stimuli and responses. The response-strengthening conception was based on the pioneering work of the world's first educational psychologist, E. L. Thorndike, and became a common feature of NSSE chapters on learning. However, by mid-century, the information-processing revolution propelled a new conception of learning into prominence—*learning-as-knowledge acquisition*, in which learning involves storing new information in one's memory. The cycle was completed during the final decades of the twentieth century with the ascendancy of educational psychology's third conception of learning—*learning-as-knowledge construction*, in which learning involves making sense of one's experiences. With its roots in Gestalt psychology's vision of learning by insight (or structural understanding) and Dewey's conception of learning through reflection, the knowledge construction conception provided important implications for instruction. The most important educational implication is that teachers can serve as cognitive guides who provide modeling, coaching, and scaffolding to students as they engage in realistic academic tasks.

Over the century, the rocky relation between psychology and education has progressed from a *one-way street* to a *dead-end street* to a *two-way street*. Early in the twentieth century education sought to apply the research results discovered by psychologists, yielding a one-way street running from psychology to education. By mid-century, the failure of the one-way street approach resulted in an even more dangerous situation, a dead-end street, in which psychologists worked on artificial laboratory problems far removed from school issues, and educators worked in classrooms far removed from research-based theories of how students learn. A promising resolution emerged by century's end, a two-way street, in which psychology and education work together in a mutually beneficial relationship. By providing a realistic context for the study of learning, education saved psychology from its stale theories based on highly artificial tasks and challenged psychology to develop theories that accounted for real human learning. By basing educational practice on educationally relevant theories of how students learn, education could finally begin to fulfill the century-old hope of scientifically based teaching.

The generality of learning theories changed dramatically during the twentieth century—from *no theory* to *general theories* to *specific theories*. In spite of the availability of Thorndike's theory of learning, NSSE chapters published in the early part of the century focused mainly on deriving principles of teaching from empirical research results. By mid-century, general theories emerged that attempted to account for all human and animal learning on a grand scale, so NSSE chapters focused on the grand theories of leading psychologists, such as Thorndike and Hull and Lewin. The failure of general theories to account for all kinds of learning in realistic classroom settings led to the development of specific theories of learning, each aimed at understanding how learning occurs within a more restricted domain. An important result was highly productive strides in the development of psychologies of subject matter, an illusive goal during earlier parts of the century. Instead of studying how people learn in general, educational psychologists at the end of the twentieth century focused on understanding how people learn to read, to write, to think mathematically, to think scientifically, to think historically, and so on.

Changes in the conception of learning had far-reaching effects on the way that educational psychologists viewed the role of individual differences in learning and in the companion issue of the nature of learning assessment. The century opened with a *one-size-fits-all* conception of individual differences in learning, in which all students at a grade level were subjected to the same materials at the same pace. As conceptions of learning came to focus on knowledge acquisition, the conception of individual differences changed to a focus on *adapting the pace* of information presentation. The conception of learning changed to a focus on cognitive construction; this approach highlighted the role of individual differences in the learner's cognitive processing during learning. The result was a focus on *cognitive process instruction*—the idea that students can learn to be more effective in the way they process information. A parallel change occurred in conceptions of learning assessment—from *uniform and basic standards* to *precise and individual objectives* to *authentic and diverse goals*. Overall, the major instructional breakthrough was a focus on teaching and testing of learning and thinking strategies.

Finally, there were also important changes in conceptions of the motivational, biological, and social bases of learning. Conceptions of the motivational bases of learning changed from *no theory*, in which teachers were urged to motivate students on practical grounds; to *drive-reduction theories*, in which motivation was assumed to be based on a form of reinforcement; to *cognitive theories*, in which motivation depended on the beliefs, attitudes, and judgments of the learner. Conceptions of the biological bases of learning changed from *inclusion*, in which neuronal processes were seen as compatible with learning theory; to *exclusion*, in which neuroscience was seen as irrelevant to education; to *anticipation*, in which cognitive neuroscience was seen as a potential source of educationally-relevant insights. Changes in the social bases of learning changed from *emphasis*, in which the social aspects of education were widely acknowledged but without an underlying theory to *de-emphasis*, in which classic learning theories focused rigidly on individual learners, to *re-emphasis*, in which learning theories attempted to incorporate the role of social factors in learning.

From the vantage point of the new millennium, I can see important advances in the one-hundred-year-old struggle for an educationally relevant theory of learning. The most important changes culminated in (a) the definition of learning as a change in knowledge rather than solely as a change in behavior, (b) the vision of learning as a process of knowledge construction rather than solely as knowledge acquisition or response strengthening, (c) the integration of psychological research on learning with the practical challenges of education rather than isolating psychological research solely in laboratories, (d) the conception of individual differences in learning in terms of differences in the ways students process their experiences rather than differences in the rate they can acquire information, (e) the focusing of learning assessments on a broad array of competencies embedded within challenging academic tasks rather than piecemeal assessment of low-level skills, and (f) richer appreciation of the motivational, biological, and social bases of learning.

As it began with a sense of optimism and faith in the power of science, the twentieth century ended with the cautiously optimistic sense that research on learning in school-like tasks will advance both educational practice and psychological theory. What is new, however, is a much richer empirical research base, a better-honed set of research methods for studying school-like learning tasks, and a more productive conception of how learning works. The major contributions of these changes have been (a) the development of psychologies of subject matter, in which learning theories are focused on learning in subject matter domains; (b) the development of cognitive process instruction, in which learning theories are focused on teaching specific strategies for how to learn; and (c) the development of a broader conception of the goals of learning, in which learning theories address the range of kinds of knowledge needed to accomplish academic tasks (ranging from specific facts and procedures to complex structures and strategies). The product of one hundred years of work is a conception of learning that is domain-specific, cognitive-process oriented, and based on analyzing the breadth of underlying kinds of knowledge.

Reviewing the intellectual history of a field is a humbling experience, which demonstrated the risks of predicting where the field will go from here. Perhaps the most surprising lost opportunity of the century was that cognitively oriented learning theorists failed to take full advantage of Gestalt conceptions of structural understanding and instead seem to have opted for a narrower conception of learning based on information processing. A major challenge of the new century, perhaps, then, is to develop a better grasp of the nature of human understanding, which the Gestalt psychologists placed under the banner of *insight*.[209] This branch of the research agenda requires a fuller appreciation of the role of mental models, schemas, conceptual change, and analogical reasoning in learning.

Overall, I come away from this exercise with a firm appreciation of the mutual relation between learning theory and educational practice: If education involves the guiding of learning, then education would be enriched by a better understanding of how students learn. In my opinion, substantial progress already has been made in crafting an educationally relevant conception of learning.[210] Thus, I come away with a sense that continued progress is most likely to be made when psychologists and educators work together to apply scientific methods to understand learning and teaching of authentic academic tasks. In short, what appears to be needed is a mutual focus on understanding how learning works in school-like tasks and a mutual commitment to basing educational research on the methods of science.

NOTES

1. The targeted references consist of chapters in the 1935 Yearbook *Educational Diagnosis*; in the 1938 Yearbook *The Scientific Movement in Education*; in the 1942 Yearbook *The Psychology of Learning*; in the 1950 Yearbook *Learning and Instruction*; in the 1963 Yearbook *Child Psychology*; in the 1964 Yearbook *Theories of Learning and Instruction*; in the 1976 Yearbook *The Psychology of Teaching Methods*; and in the 1981 NSSE Series Book *Psychology and Education*. Full references for each targeted yearbook, as well as references to the chapters used for source material, follow below.

2. Nelson B. Henry, ed., *The Psychology of Learning*, Forty-first Yearbook of the National Society for the Study of Education, Part II (Bloomington, IL: Public School Publishing Company, 1942).

3. Nelson B. Henry, ed., *Learning and Instruction*, Forty-ninth Yearbook of the National Society for the Study of Education, Part I (Chicago: National Society for the Study of Education, 1950).

4. Ernest R. Hilgard, ed., *Theories of Learning and Instruction*, Sixty-third Yearbook of the National Society for the Study of Education, Part I (Chicago: National Society for the Study of Education, 1964).

5. Frank H. Farley and Neal J. Gordon, eds., *Psychology and Education: The State of the Union* (Berkeley, CA: McCutchan, 1981).

6. Joan Schine, ed., *Service Learning*, Ninety-sixth Yearbook of the National Society for the Study of Education, Part 1 (Chicago: National Society for the Study of Education, 1997).

7. Elliot Eisner, ed., *Learning and Teaching the Ways of Knowing*, Eighty-fourth Yearbook of the National Society for the Study of Education, Part II (Chicago: National Society for the Study of Education, 1985).

8. Frederick J. McDonald, "The Influence of Learning Theories in Education," *Theories of Learning and Instruction*, p. 3.

9. N. L. Gage, ed., *The Psychology of Teaching Methods*, Seventy-fifth Yearbook of the National Society for the Study of Education, Part I (Chicago: National Society for the Study of Education, 1976).

10. E. R. Guthrie, "Conditioning: A Theory of Learning in Terms of Stimulus, Response, and Association," *The Psychology of Learning*, p. 17.

11. J. B. Stroud, "The Role of Practice in Learning," *The Psychology of Learning*, p. 356.

12. G. Lester Anderson, "Introduction," *Learning and Instruction*, pp. 1-11.

13. Sheldon H. White, "Learning," *Child Psychology*, Sixty-second Yearbook of the National Society for the Study of Education, Part I, eds. Nelson B. Henry and Herman G. Richey (Chicago: National Society for the Study of Education, 1963), p. 196.

14. Robert M. Gagné, "The Learning Basis of Teaching Methods," *The Psychology of Teaching Methods*, p. 30.

15. M. C. Wittrock, "Learning and Memory," *Psychology and Education: The State of the Union*, p. 261.

16. Kurt Lewin, "Field Theory and Learning," *The Psychology of Learning*, p. 220.

17. Richard E. Mayer, "Cognition and Instruction: On Their Historic Meeting Within Educational Psychology," *Journal of Educational Psychology* 84 (1992), pp. 405-412.

18. Mayer, "E. L. Thorndike's Enduring Contributions to Educational Psychology," *Educational Psychology: A Century of Contributions*, eds. Barry Zimmerman and Dale Schunk (Mahwah, NJ: Erlbaum, in press).

19. McDonald, "The Influence of Learning Theories in Education," *Theories of Learning and Instruction*, p. 11.

20. Guthrie, "Conditioning," p. 19.

21. Ibid., p. 59.

22. Anderson, "Introduction," p. 2.

23. Ernest R. Hilgard and David H. Russell, "Motivation in School Learning," *Learning and Instruction*, p. 46.

24. Winfred F. Hill, "Contemporary Developments Within Stimulus-Response Learning Theory," *Theories of Learning and Instruction*, p. 27.

25. Benton J. Underwood, "Laboratory Studies of Verbal Learning," *Theories of Learning and Instruction*, p. 136.

26. McDonald, "The Influence of Learning Theories in Education," *Theories of Learning and Instruction*, pp. 11-12.

27. Anderson, "Introduction," *Learning and Instruction*, p. 3.

28. Stroud, "The Role of Practice in Learning," *The Psychology of Learning*, p. 362.

29. Lumsdaine, "Educational Technology, Programmed Learning, and Instructional Science," *Theories of Learning and Instruction*, p. 380.

30. Ibid., pp. 382-383.

31. Mayer, "Learners as Information Processors: Legacies and Limitations of Educational Psychology's Second Metaphor," *Educational Psychologist* 31 (1996), pp. 151-161.

32. John G. Rockwell, "Physical Conditioning Factors in Learning," *Educational Diagnosis*, Thirty-fourth Yearbook of the National Society for the Study of Education, ed. Guy Montrose Whipple (Bloomington, IL: Public School Publishing Company, 1935), p. 18.

33. Anderson, Whipple, and Gilchrist, "School as a Learning Laboratory," *Learning and Instruction*, p. 348.

34. G. Lester Anderson and Arthur I. Gates, "The General Nature of Learning," *Learning and Instruction*, p. 15.

35. Lumsdaine, "Educational Technology, Programmed Learning, and Instructional Science," *Theories of Learning and Instruction*, p. 390.

36. Mayer, *The Promise of Educational Psychology* (Upper Saddle River, NJ: Prentice-Hall, 1999).

37. Ibid.

38. Anderson and Gates, "The General Nature of Learning," *Learning and Instruction*, p. 33.

39. C. E. Ragsdale, "How Children Learn the Motor Types of Activities," *Learning and Instruction*, p. 90.

40. J. F. Dashiell, "Contributions to Education of Scientific Knowledge About the Psychology of Learning," *The Scientific Movement in Education*, Thirty-seventh Yearbook of the National Society for the Study of Education, Part II, ed. Guy Montrose Whipple (Bloomington, IL: Public School Publishing Company, 1938), p. 396.

41. McDonald, "The Influence of Learning Theories in Education," *Theories of Learning and Instruction*, pp. 13, 18.

42. Ibid., pp. 19-20.

43. Ibid., p. 20.

44. Hilgard, "The Place of Gestalt Psychology and Field Theories in Contemporary Learning Theory," *Theories of Learning and Instruction*, p. 54.

45. Ibid., p. 62.

46. Ibid., p. 77.

47. Anderson and Gates, "The General Nature of Learning," pp. 13-14.

48. Ibid., pp. 14-15.

49. White, "Learning," *Child Psychology*, p. 197.

50. Gagné, "The Learning Basis of Teaching Methods," *The Psychology of Teaching Methods*, pp. 21-43.

51. Ibid., p. 22.

52. Ibid., p. 42.

53. Ibid., p. 31.

54. Wittrock, "Learning and Memory," *Psychology and Education*, p. 246.

55. Ibid., p. 247.

56. Ibid.

57. Ibid., p. 248.

58. Ibid., pp. 249, 250.

59. William A. Brownell and Gordon Hendrickson, "How Children Learn Information, Concepts, and Generalizations," p. 113.

60. Ibid., p. 115.

61. Anderson, Whipple, and Gilchrist, "School as a Learning Laboratory," *Learning and Instruction*, p. 337.

62. Anderson and Gates, "The General Nature of Learning," *Learning and Instruction*, p. 30.

63. Ibid., p. 26.

64. Gagné, "The Learning Basis of Teaching Methods," *The Psychology of Teaching Methods*, p. 21.

65. Ibid., p. 26.

66. Wittrock, "Learning and Memory," *Psychology and Education*, p. 260.

67. Ibid.

68. Ibid., p. 261.

69. Leo J. Brueckner, "Pedagogical Factors Associated with Learning Difficulties," *Educational Diagnosis*, pp. 49-62.

70. Schine, *Service Learning*.

71. Eisner, *Learning and Teaching the Ways of Knowing*.

72. McDonald, "The Influence of Learning Theories in Education," *Theories of Learning and Instruction*, p. 14.

73. Dashiell "Contributions to Education of Scientific Knowledge about the Psychology of Learning," *The Scientific Movement in Education*, p. 393.

74. Anderson, "Introduction," *Learning and Instruction*, p. 8.

75. Gagné, "The Learning Basis of Teaching Methods," *The Psychology of Teaching Methods*, p. 21.

76. Mayer, "Cognition and Instruction: On Their Historic Meeting within Educational Psychology," *Journal of Educational Psychology* 84, 1992, 405-412.

77. William S. Gray, "Principles of Method in Teaching Reading as Derived from Scientific Investigation," *Fourth Report of the Committee on the Economy of Time in Education*, Eighteenth Yearbook of the National Society for the Study of Education, Part I, ed. Guy Montrose Whipple (Bloomington, IL: Public Schools Publishing Co., 1919), pp. 26-51.

78. Frank N. Freeman, "Principles of Method in Teaching Writing as Derived from Scientific Investigation," *Fourth Report of the Committee on the Economy of Time in Education*, pp. 11-25.

79. Walter S. Monroe, "Principles of Method in Teaching Arithmetic as Derived from Scientific Investigation," *Fourth Report of the Committee on the Economy of Time in Education*, pp. 78-95.

80. Anderson and Gates, "The General Nature of Learning," *Learning and Instruction*, p. 18.

81. McDonald, "The Influence of Learning Theories in Education," *Theories of Learning and Instruction*, p. 24.

82. Ibid., pp. 10, 3.

83. Hill, "Contemporary Developments within Stimulus-Response Learning Theory," *Theories of Learning and Instruction*, p. 51.

84. Anderson, "Introduction," *Learning and Instruction*, p. 1.

85. McDonald, "The Influence of Learning Theories in Education," *Theories of Learning and Instruction*, p. 16.

86. Underwood, "Laboratory Studies of Verbal Learning," *Theories of Learning and Instruction*, p. 136.

87. Anderson, "Introduction," *Learning and Instruction*, p. 5.

88. Esther J. Swenson, "Applications of Learning Principles to the Improvement of Teaching in the Early Elementary Grades," *Learning and Instruction*, p. 256.

89. White, "Learning," *Child Psychology*, p. 222.

90. T. R. McConnell, "The Purpose and Scope of the Yearbook," *Learning and Instruction*, p. 12.

91. Anderson, Whipple, and Gilchrist, "School as a Learning Laboratory," *Learning and Instruction*, p. 348.

92. Hilgard, "A Perspective on the Relationship Between Learning Theory and Educational Practices," *Theories of Learning and Instruction*, p. 403.

93. Wittrock, "Learning and Memory," *Psychology and Education*, p. 244.

94. Whipple, *Fourth Report of the Committee on the Economy of Time in Education*, p. 8.

95. Ibid.

96. Ibid.

97. Ibid.

98. Gray, "Principles of Method in Teaching Reading as Derived from Scientific Investigation," *Fourth Report of the Committee on the Economy of Time in Education*, pp. 26-51.

99. Ibid., p. 27.

100. Freeman, "Principles of Method in Teaching Writing, *Fourth Report of the Committee on the Economy of Time in Education*, p. 11.

101. Monroe, "Principles of Method in Teaching Arithmetic, *Fourth Report of the Committee on the Economy of Time in Education*, p. 80.

102. Edward L. Thorndike, *Educational Psychology* (New York: Teachers College, Columbia University, 1926).

103. Henry, *The Psychology of Learning*.

104. McConnell, "The Purpose and Scope of the Yearbook," in *Learning and Instruction*, p. 3.

105. Ibid., p. 4.

106. Guthrie, "Conditioning: A Theory of Learning in Terms of Stimulus, Response, and Association," *The Psychology of Learning*, pp. 17-60.

107. Clark L. Hull, "Conditioning: Outline of a Systematic Theory of Learning," *The Psychology of Learning*, pp. 61-95.

108. Guthrie, "Conditioning: A Theory of Learning in Terms of Stimulus, Response, and Association," *The Psychology of Learning*, pp. 18, 23.

109. Ibid., p. 24.

110. Hull, "Conditioning," *The Psychology of Learning*, p. 74.

111. Ibid.

112. Guthrie, "Conditioning: A Theory of Learning," *The Psychology of Learning*, p. 19.

113. McConnell, "The Purpose and Scope of the Yearbook," *Learning and Instruction*, p. 5.

114. Peter Sandiford, "Connectionism: Its Origin and Major Features," *The Psychology of Learning*, p. 96.

115. Ibid., p. 98.

116. Ibid., pp. 112, 123, 125.

117. Gates, "Connectionism: Present Concepts and Interpretations," *The Psychology of Learning*, pp. 141-164.

118. Lewin, "Field Theory and Learning," *The Psychology of Learning*, pp. 215-242.

119. George W. Hartmann, "The Field Theory of Learning and its Educational Consequences," *The Psychology of Learning*, pp. 165-214.

120. Lewin, "Field Theory and Learning," *The Psychology of Learning*, pp. 221.

121. Ibid.

122. Hartmann, "The Field Theory of Learning and its Educational Consequences," *The Psychology of Learning*, pp. 165-214.

123. McConnell, "Reconciliation of Learning Theories," *The Psychology of Learning*, p. 251.

124. Lewin, "Field Theory and Learning," *The Psychology of Learning*, p. 220.

125. Edward G. Begle, ed., *Mathematics Education*, Sixty-ninth Yearbook of the National Society for the Study of Education, Part I (Chicago: National Society for the Study of Education, 1970).

126. James R. Squire, ed., *The Teaching of English*, Seventy-sixth Yearbook of the National Society for the Study of Education, Part I (Chicago: National Society for the Study of Education, 1977).

127. Alan C. Purves and Olive Niles, eds., *Becoming Readers in a Complex Society*, Eighty-third Yearbook of the National Society for the Study of Education, Part I (Chicago: National Society for the Study of Education, 1984).

128. Anthony R. Petrosky and David Bartholomae, eds., *The Teaching of Writing*, Eighty-fifth Yearbook of the National Society for the Study of Education, Part I (Chicago: National Society for the Study of Education, 1986).

129. Nancy Nelson and Robert C. Calfee, eds., *The Reading-Writing Connection*, Ninety-seventh Yearbook of the National Society for the Study of Education, Part II (Chicago: National Society for the Study of Education, 1998).

130. Susanna Pflaum-Conner, ed., *Aspects of Reading Education* (Berkeley, CA: McCutchan Publishing Corporation, 1978).

131. Mary Montgomery Lindquist, ed., *Selected Topics in Mathematics Education* (Berkeley, CA: McCutchan Publishing Corporation, 1981).

132. Hilgard, "Postscript: Twenty Years of Learning Theory in Relation to Education," *Theories of Learning and Instruction*, p. 416.

133. Mayer, *The Promise of Educational Psychology*.

134. Brueckner, "Pedagogical Factors Associated with Learning Difficulties," *Educational Diagnosis*, p. 55.

135. Ibid., p. 49.

136. Stroud, "The Role of Practice in Learning," *The Psychology of Learning*, p. 357.

137. Ibid., p. 358.

138. Swenson, "Applications of Learning Principles," *Learning and Instruction*, p. 277.

139. McDonald, "The Influence of Learning Theories in Education," *Theories of Learning and Instruction*, p. 25.

140. Lumsdaine, "Educational Technology, Programmed Learning, and Instructional Science," *Theories of Learning and Instruction*, pp. 371-401.

141. Thorndike, "How Children Learn the Principles and Techniques of Problem Solving," *Learning and Instruction*, p. 192.

142. Wittrock, "Learning and Memory," *Psychology and Education*, p. 255.

143. Gagné, "The Learning Basis of Teaching Methods," *The Psychology of Teaching Methods*, p. 42.

144. Brueckner, "Pedagogical Factors," *Educational Diagnosis*, pp. 49-50.

145. Ibid.

146. Ibid., p. 53.

147. David G. Ryans, "Motivation and Learning," *The Psychology of Learning*, p. 324.

148. Swenson, "Applications of Learning Principles," *Learning and Instruction*, p. 262.

149. Ibid., p. 277.

150. Ibid., p. 278.

151. Peter Airasian, "The Impact of the Taxonomy on Testing and Evaluation," *Bloom's Taxonomy: A Forty-Year Retrospective*, Ninety-third Yearbook of the National Society for the Study of Education, Part II, eds., Lorin W. Anderson and Lauren A. Sosniak (Chicago: National Society for the Study of Education, 1994), p. 91.

152. Benjamin S. Bloom, ed., *Taxonomy of Educational Objectives, Book 1: Cognitive Domain* (New York: Longman, 1956).

153. Anderson and Sosniak, *Bloom's Taxonomy*.

154. Bloom, "Reflections on the Development and Use of the Taxonomy," *Bloom's Taxonomy*, p. 1.

155. Ibid.

156. Ibid, p. 8.

157. Edward J. Furst, "Bloom's Taxonomy: Philosophical and Educational Issues," *Bloom's Taxonomy*, p. 32.

158. William D. Rowher and Kathryn Sloane, "Psychological Perspectives," *Bloom's Taxonomy*, p. 51.

159. Airasian, "The Impact of the Taxonomy," *Bloom's Taxonomy*, p. 83.

160. Ibid., p. 98.

161. Rowher and Sloane, "Psychological Perspectives," *Bloom's Taxonomy*, p. 45.

162. Ibid., p. 62.

163. Airasian, "The Impact of the Taxonomy," *Bloom's Taxonomy*, p. 83.

164. Sosniak, "The Taxonomy, Curriculum, and Their Relations," *Bloom's Taxonomy*, pp. 112-113.

165. Airasian, "The Impact of the Taxonomy," *Bloom's Taxonomy*, p. 96.

166. Ibid., p. 82.

167. Ibid., p. 96.

168. Lorin W. Anderson, "Research on Teaching and Teacher Education," *Bloom's Taxonomy*, p. 139.

169. Dale B. Harris, "How Children Learn Interests, Motives, and Attitudes," *Learning and Instruction*, p. 129.

170. Willard C. Olson, "Emotional and Social Factors in Learning," *Educational Diagnosis*, pp. 63-77.

171. James L. Mursell, "How Children Learn Aesthetic Responses," in *Learning and Instruction*, p. 183.

173. Ryans, "Motivation and Learning," *The Psychology of Learning*, p. 289.

174. Ibid., pp. 298, 301.

175. Ibid., p. 326.

176. John Dewey, *Effort and Interest in Education* (Cambridge, MA: Riverside Press, 1913).

177. McDonald, "The Influence of Learning Theories in Education," *Theories of Learning and Instruction*, p. 13.

178. Ryans, "Motivation and Learning," *The Psychology of Learning*, pp. 324-325.

179. John E. Anderson, "The Relation of Emotional Behavior to Learning," *The Psychology of Learning*, p. 340.

180. Ibid., pp. 348-349.

181. Mayer, "E. L. Thorndike's Enduring Contributions," *Educational Psychology* (in press).

183. Rockwell, "Physical Conditioning Factors in Learning," *Educational Diagnosis*, p. 20.

184. Dashiell, "Contributions to Education of Scientific Knowledge," *The Scientific Movement in Education*, p. 401.

185. Rockwell, "Physical Conditioning Factors in Learning," *Educational Diagnosis*, pp. 17-36.

186. Ibid., p. 20.

187. Dashiell, "Contributions to Education of Scientific Knowledge," *The Scientific Movement in Education*, p. 402.

188. Ryans, "Motivation and Learning," *The Psychology of Learning*, pp. 289-331.

189. Guthrie, "Conditioning: A Theory of Learning," *The Psychology of Learning*, p. 18.

190. Anderson and Gates, "The General Nature of Learning," *Learning and Instruction*, p. 12.

191. Ibid., p. 13.

192. Ibid., p. 14.

193. McDonald, "The Influence of Learning Theories in Education," *Theories of Learning and Instruction*, p. 18.

194. Karl H. Pribram, "Neurological Notes on the Art of Educating," *Theories of Learning and Instruction*, p. 79.

195. Jeanne S. Chall and Allan F. Mirsky, eds., *Education and the Brain*, Sixty-seventh Yearbook of the National Society for the Study of Education, Part II (Chicago: National Society for the Study of Education, 1978).

196. Ibid., p. xiii.

197. Ibid., p. 64.

198. Ibid., p. 375.

199. Olson, "Emotional and Social Factors in Learning," *Educational Diagnosis*, p. 71.

200. Ibid.

201. Paul T. Rankin, "Environmental Factors Contributing to Learning," *Educational Diagnosis*, p. 79.

202. Ibid.

203. Ibid., p. 83.

204. J. E. Anderson, "The Relation of Emotional Behavior to Learning," *The Psychology of Learning*, p. 349.

205. N. B. Henry, *The Psychology of Learning*; N. B. Henry, *Learning and Instruction*; Hilgard, *Theories of Learning and Instruction*.

206. Caroline Tryon and William E. Henry, "How Children Learn Personal and Social Adjustment," *Learning and Instruction*, pp. 156-182.

207. David W. Johnson, "Social Psychology," *Psychology and Education*, p. 265.

208. Barak Rosenshine, "Classroom Instruction," *The Psychology of Teaching Methods*, p. 335.

209. Mayer, "The Search for Insight: Grappling with Gestalt Psychology's Unanswered Questions," *The Nature of Insight*, eds. Robert J. Sternberg and Janet E. Davidson (Cambridge, MA: MIT Press, 1995), pp. 3-32.

210. John D. Bransford, Ann L. Brown, and Rodney R. Cocking, eds., *How People Learn.* (Washington, DC: National Academy Press, 1999); Nadine M. Lambert and Barbara L. McCombs, eds., *How Students Learn* (Washington, DC: American Psychological Association, 1998); Mayer, *The Promise of Educational Psychology*.

CHAPTER III

A Shifting Social Context: NSSE Looks at Equity in Schools and Classrooms

ELIZABETH G. COHEN

The issue of equity is an important thread running through a century of Yearbooks of the National Society for the Study of Education (NSSE). Although we tend to think of equity in the schools as a relatively recent issue, it was a major concern as early as 1916. This chapter analyzes how authors of NSSE chapters conceptualized and wrote about equity in U.S. schools.

Equity denotes equality of educational opportunities and outcomes for all students. Although much has been made elsewhere of the difference between equity defined in terms of formal inputs to schools and equity defined in terms of outcomes, a more inclusive definition is a better match for the breadth of the literature surveyed. If schools achieved this ideal state of equity we would find the following relationships: weak or nonexistent correlations of indices of social class (SES), race, and ethnicity and student educational outcomes such as attainment or performance; few schools segregated by poverty in which the quality of teachers and resources is inferior to that of other schools where students come from richer families; no differences in class, race, and ethnicity according to track and ability group membership within schools; and, finally, no correlations between social class background and academic status differences within classrooms so that those children who are seen as good students by the teacher and their classmates are not especially likely to be from middle-class families.

Achieving equity through intervening in the schools alone is difficult because in many ways schools reflect and mirror inequities in the larger society. Some have argued that schools actively reproduce the inequalities of the larger society. In contrast, others have seen the school as receiving students who are unequal in their potential to succeed because of genetic factors or because of home and community

---

Elizabeth G. Cohen is Professor Emerita of Education and Sociology in the School of Education, Stanford University.

conditions. In this view, the school is not actively responsible for unequal educational outcomes. Rather, school people do "the best they can" with the quality of students they receive. Both these views are represented among the NSSE contributors.

A retrospective view must take into account the profound effects of shifts in the social context of American schools and how these shifts have affected educational opportunities and outcomes. Compulsory schooling and the availability of free public secondary schools were new features at the beginning of the century, vastly increasing opportunities for all, while changing the elite character of the schools forever. The process of industrialization in the early part of the century helped to create differentiation of tracks, such as vocational education. Then, as now, many educators stressed that a key function of the schools was to prepare students for different roles in the economy. Within this past century, the U.S. experienced two major waves of immigration that changed the nature of the school population dramatically. During this time, society became increasingly urban (and suburban), with great concentrations of minority populations in central cities. This trend led to segregated, high-poverty schools in central cities with problems that many view as intractable. Finally, no overview of the social context of schools should omit the role of the courts and the struggle for civil rights in the long, drawn-out battle to desegregate the schools.

Because of these major changes, an author writing about equity in an early Yearbook is not talking about the same kind of school and school population as is a more contemporary Yearbook author. These historical shifts have literally changed what the authors are talking about. At the same time that the schools themselves were changing, the perspectives and assumptions of NSSE authors also shifted. Early authors, compared to later authors, drew very different interpretations from objective data showing correlations between socio-economic status (SES) and educational outcomes. There were changes in which features of the school were seen as the source of inequity. This chapter will focus on these fascinating shifts in perspective created by social changes and the changing context of the schools.

Increasing Focus on Equity

Of 99 Yearbooks, 22 have covered issues related to sociology and the context of school, educational politics and policy, and specific analysis of rural and urban school settings. Particular editors took up particular topics and recruited authors who represented a mixture of educators, historians, and social scientists with relevant interests.

An examination of these Yearbooks shows that the editors were responding to the major shifts in the social context of schooling described above. For example, the 1936 Yearbook on the grouping of pupils, edited by Guy Montrose Whipple,[1] included a chapter by Edward Reisner[2] on social class and its effect on school organizations in the U.S. Reisner clearly understood the introduction of grouping and tracking to American schools as a response to newly heterogeneous school populations and to the demands for workers from growing industries. The trend toward urbanization and its associated social problems are featured in several chapters of John Goodlad's 1966 edition, called *The Changing School*,[3] as well as in Robert Havighurst's 1968 Yearbook entitled *Metropolitanism: Its Challenge to Education*.[4] Demographers Eleanor Bernert and Charles B. Nam explicitly discuss the changing nature of school populations in a chapter entitled "Demographic Factors Affecting American Education" in Part II of the 1961 Yearbook, *Social Forces Influencing American Education*,[5] edited by Nelson Henry. More recently (1995), editors Erwin Flaxman and A. Harry Passow devoted an entire volume to diversity in the school population: *Changing Populations/Changing Schools*.[6] With respect to the courts and desegregation, C. Wayne Gordon, in his 1974 Yearbook, *Uses of Sociology of Education*,[7] included a section entitled "Race/Ethnic Desegregation, Integration, and Decentralization."

Yearbook authors wove equity as a concern into their discussions of each major shift in school context. The concern with equity increased over the years and with the participation of sociologists as editors and authors in the Yearbook.

EARLY DOCUMENTATION OF INEQUALITY

In the earliest Yearbooks, no chapters were devoted to issues of equity. Suddenly, in 1916, equity arrived with Charles Elmer Holley writing Part II of the Yearbook in its entirety.[8] Holley carefully reported a number of systematic surveys and statistical analyses of the association of parental status with the educational attainment of sons and daughters. Taking a sociological view, Holley documented the elite character of high schools by showing that parental education, rental or assessed value of property, and number of books in the home were all strongly correlated with years of high school completed. Holley's volume provided systematic documentation of the relationship of the system of social stratification to one's chances to complete high school—and these educational opportunities were far from equal at the time.

CONCERN WITH LACK OF EQUITY

As the years passed, the tone of Yearbook authors shifted from documentation of the effects of social stratification on academic success and educational attainment to one of dissatisfaction (and sometimes anger) with the inequalities in American schools. In 1974,[9] Wilbur Brookover and his co-authors were angry about the use of testing to differentiate students in ways that affected their life course. In 1995, Norton Grubb[10] described continuing inequities aptly and bluntly:

The dominant responses to the various waves of "new students," then, have been changes in purpose and curricula. But evidently these have not been successful. Poor children continue to do much worse than middle-class children on every dimension of education including persistence, test performance, and attainment. The inequalities of the 1960s have been rediscovered in the 1990s, and the "new demographics" of increasing poverty, continued immigration, and ever larger numbers of minority students are as frightening now as they were a century ago.[11]

The growing chorus of unhappiness with the status quo was joined in 1993 by feminist scholars in Part I of the Yearbook, *Gender and Education*, edited by Sari Knopp Biklen and Diane Pollard.[12] Despite the formal equality of the sexes introduced to the schools by Title IX of the 1972 Education Amendments, authors in this volume described how inequalities in power and resources between men and women in society are translated and reinforced within classrooms.

Shifting Discourse on Equity

It is one thing to document a positive relationship between SES and educational outcomes, but it is quite another to explain how this relationship came about. Recommendations for change depend on the explanation chosen. If the "fault" lies in poor families themselves or in community conditions, interventions will be quite different from those based on explanations of factors in school organization, or teacher bias against lower-class children. The explanations offered in the Yearbooks changed over time; they reflected the history of social thought in the 20th century.

THE NATURE-NURTURE CONTROVERSY

Early in the 20th century, it seemed obvious to some scholars that the explanation for inequalities in school performance lay in individual differences in native ability. They explained observed correlations between social class and ability as a product of genetic factors; people with lower ability were poor and their children inherited their limited abilities. Other scholars saw differences in performance as a consequence of the differences in home and community environments experienced by rich and poor children.

This conflict of opinion was a side branch of the nature-nurture controversy which was well represented in Yearbooks in the early part of the 20th century. For example, Holley[13] found a strong correlation between the educational level of adoptive parents and the educational attainment of their adopted children. He concluded that home environment, rather than inherited differences, must account for what happens in the schools. In doing this particular study and in making this interpretation, he believed he addressed the nature-nurture controversy.

Weighing in on the other side was the more sophisticated work of Heilman,[14] who, in 1928, carried out a causal analysis of correlational data from more than 800 school children. He found that IQ had the strongest influence on achievement, while the influence of SES was small. Heilman concluded that the ability factor was so powerful that schools should create a department with the function of classifying children, adapting school tasks to their learning abilities, and determining the probable occupational levels at which they could succeed. Here the linkage between recommended policy and the "explanation" is particularly strong.

The nature-nurture controversy was still alive in 1940 when Nancy Bayley[15] looked at factors influencing growth of intelligence in young children. Finding only modest correlations between parental educational level and children's IQ at age 9, Bayley inferred that the effects of nature are far more powerful in creating individual differences in intellectual ability than are social class factors, which are fundamentally viewed as environmental. In contrast, Jane Loevinger[16] authored a sophisticated, systematic review of studies correlating measures of socioeconomic status with various measures of intelligence. She found a correlation of around .40 in those studies using a purely verbal measure of intelligence and parental education rather than income as a measure of parental status. She concluded:

The data in the section on associations of intelligence and social status with other variables are illustrative rather than conclusive. They may serve, no less, to convince the reader that the nature of the relationship between social status and intelligence cannot be resolved, once and for always, by the use of foster children, identical twins, or any single statistical technique. Undoubtedly, the relation depends on both heredity and environmental influences on development. For reasons stated at length, little confidence is placed on the quantitative estimates of the relative contributions of heredity and environment.[17]

BLAMING THE STUDENT VERSUS BLAMING THE SCHOOL

Despite Loevinger, the controversy was never really resolved; the terms of the debate underwent a subtle shift from nature versus nurture to blaming the students (and their families) versus blaming the school. Aaron Pallas, Gary Natriello, and Edward McDill[18] refer to early educational researchers and policymakers who placed the locus of school failure in the student, not in the school.

Holley's work is evidence of this historical pattern; he interpreted the correlation of family characteristics with educational attainment of offspring as evidence of a family tradition of education. He concluded that indices of retardation and dropout should not be used as a measure of efficiency of schools because these are related to family factors over which the school has little control. He predicted that the influx of a large number of immigrants without family traditions of schooling would have highly undesirable consequences for the school.

In attempting to explain the relationship of social class to educational attainment, Robert J. Havighurst, in 1961,[19] continued to locate the explanation in characteristics of the student. He saw the typical lower-class person as more "present-oriented," with less desire and willingness than a middle-class person to sacrifice present gains for future ones. Therefore, lower-class parents were less likely to encourage and assist their children to go to college. For Havighurst, the lower college attendance rates of lower-class children were a consequence of the value orientations of their parents rather than a result of the failure of the school to encourage college attendance.

A variety of school features are selected as causal by those Yearbook authors for whom the locus of failure is in the school rather than in the student. Robert Green in 1974[20] pointed to segregated education as responsible for the notion of black inferiority held by black students themselves. Green selected poor self-esteem as the pivotal factor in lowered performance. He cited Dorothy K. Jessup's[21] conclusion that improvement in achievement patterns for minority students is directly related to improvement in their self-concepts. Green referred to research showing that the larger the percentage of blacks in a class, the lower the teacher's evaluation of students' academic ability and motivation. He argued that unless the problem of segregation is remedied, it will be impossible to raise self-concepts.

In the same 1974 Yearbook, Brookover et al. pointed to the schools' sorting and selecting process based on testing of individual differences as the fundamental cause of unequal educational opportunities:

The maximization of individual differences and the differentiation of educational programs for different children are commonly advocated without regard to the effect of such education on the social structure or the opportunities for social mobility. These programs and policies do not recognize that equality of opportunity is not facilitated by highly differentiated educational programs based upon the presumed differences between lower-class and middle-class children. One does not achieve equality by enhancing the differences in children and thus allocating them to different social strata."[22]

For Brookover et al., differentiated curricula act as a self-fulfilling prophecy in which those who are not expected to do well are not exposed to the higher-level curricula and will thus have limited educational and occupational opportunities.

Jeannie Oakes[23] also stressed the importance of differentiated curricula in accounting for unequal outcomes. But underlying the tracking is a conception that intelligence is global, that it is fixed quite early, and that learning is primarily the accumulation of a linear sequence of knowledge and skills. These conceptions, in turn, are historically rooted in beliefs about individual and group differences in intelligence and learning. It is because of these assumptions and beliefs that schools frequently conclude that the disproportionate assignment of low-income and minority students to special remedial programs consisting of uninteresting, repetitive skill-and-drill curricula is an appropriate, if regrettable, response.

EMERGENCE OF RACE, ETHNICITY, AND GENDER

As the century of Yearbooks progresses, there is a shift from analysis of equity only in terms of social class to include race, ethnicity, and gender. The diversity of immigrants to the U.S. undoubtedly affected the growth of emphasis on ethnicity and, to a lesser extent, race. In their 1960 review of the school populations, Bernert and Nam cited the continuing flow of new immigrants from Europe between the beginning of the century until the Depression. Following the Depression, immigration was at a much lower level, although the authors noted that a large proportion of the newcomers in 1960 were from Latin America. As these authors stated, "The educational problems involved in dealing with the immigrant of the early 1900s are being faced, in similar form, by the educators whose task it is now to provide schooling for the large numbers of newly arrived Puerto Ricans and Mexicans."[24] However, the major demographic factor having an impact on schools in the 1960s was not the new immigrants but the enormous increase in elementary enrollments caused by the Baby Boom following World War II.

By 1995, Pallas, Natriello, and McDill[25] described the previous two decades as a time of growing diversity in the school population. They expected that over the next 30 years the number and proportion of Hispanic children and youth would more than double. The number of Asian and African-American children would also rise, thereby creating a racial, ethnic, and cultural configuration of the school-aged population that would be distinctly different from that of 1995. With this growth in diversity would come a growth in the proportion of students who would depart from the idealized middle-class student and family. In the authors' words: "Schools are no longer permitted to overlook student diversity, to reduce it, or to use it as an excuse for vast differences in educational performance."[26]

The issue of school desegregation brought to the fore the intersection of race and schooling; the struggle of minorities has remained central to the educational discourse. In 1995, Christine E. Sleeter's hard-hitting chapter described the underlying drive of multicultural education[27] to empower racial and ethnic groups within the curriculum. In the same volume, the chapter by Robert Lowe and Harvey Kantor[28] focused exclusively on African-Americans, tracing the glacial pace of desegregation, the second-generation resegregation that took place through tracking, and the current failure of the goal of social integration.

The issue of gender does not take center stage until 1993 with Part I of the Ninety-second Yearbook.[29] Gender studies in education was a well-developed literature by this time. Having been accused of focusing exclusively on middle-class white women, feminist theorists writing for the Yearbook were well aware of the necessity to consider race, class and gender simultaneously. The volume contains new questions concerning the bias in research on women, supplanting the old questions on sex differences in achievement and outcomes. Many of the authors were well into post-modernist discourse.

ENTRANCE OF POWER AND PRIVILEGE

Over time, a static analysis of social class shifted to the more dynamic analysis of struggle over power and privilege. This shift reflected a parallel change from the functionalist to the conflict view of inequality in society, which also marked sociology over the same period. The functionalist sees inequality in rewards in society as a result of the imperative that if society is to survive, the most important jobs must go to the most talented. Thus, it is essential for schools to sort and select children on the basis of ability. The school should sponsor the talented so that they will acquire the necessary education for their future roles in society.

For conflict theorists, inequalities result when those who command resources and power in society successfully maintain their grip on power and privilege over time. Those without resources and power strive to gain access. Schools, in this view, tend to reproduce society's inequalities. The schools are middle-class institutions designed to insure that lower-class children find it very difficult to succeed there. Upper-status parents are successful in placing their children in gifted programs and in upper tracks so that they can maintain their advantage. Lower-class parents find their children segregated in inferior schools, which makes the struggle for equality especially difficult.

The earlier functionalist view is represented in the Yearbooks by the full discussion of differences in native abilities and the necessity to differentiate programs to meet the "needs" of these different types of students as well as the "needs" of society for well-trained persons in science, mathematics, business, etc. Havighurst, as one of the pioneering sociologists who documented the differences between the social classes in the U.S., represents an intermediate view.

In Havighurst's chapter on social class influences on American education,[30] he saw the present state and structure of society mirrored in the schools. Characteristic of American sociologists studying stratification in the 1930s and 1940s, he explicitly rejected the idea that the dominance of the middle classes in the schools was the result of class warfare. He was rejecting a Marxian concept of struggle as an explicit conflict between a militant class-conscious labor group and an equally militant capitalist group.[31]

Nonetheless, as a careful observer of class behavior, Havighurst could not avoid documenting the overt hostility in his interview with Bernice, a young woman of lower-class background. He presented a transcript as an illustration of the considerable degree of hostility

toward the middle class felt by some of the lower class who are unsuccessful by middle-class standards. For Havighurst, this behavior illustrated personality as much as it did social structure.

I quit two weeks before the end of school a year ago. I was fifteen at the time
but I talked to Mr. McCoy (the principal). He said they wouldn't come get me
because I would be sixteen before fall. I didn't take the exams. I knew I would-
n't pass them anyway because I didn't do any work except in typing. . . . I was
really going to go all the way through Home Ec because I liked it, but then
my schedule was changed so I could be in a different gym class. They said
they wanted to break up a gang of us girls because we were beating all the
other teams and smarting off a lot. Then I got changed to a gym with a lot of
these high-class girls, as we call them. They think they're better than everyone else. They got a lot of money. They don't like us and we don't like them.
When my class was changed, I didn't even come for gym. So I failed that too.[32]

Havighurst summarized his perspective on how change comes
about in the school: Dominant trends and styles in education are
sponsored by the middle class, with the lower class going along, in
general, though occasionally resisting on some issues where lower-
class opportunities appear to be threatened. The upper class takes no
active part in educational decisions for the public and counts on its
prestige and power to guarantee satisfactory educational arrangements
for its own children. Notice here that Havighurst does use the concept
of power for the upper class, but the middle class is not exercising
power in the schools— it is just open to change.

The educational system is run by middle-class people with middle-class standards, tempered by some understanding of the fact that working-class values
and aspirations as well as habits are enough different from those of the middle
class to make educational adaptations desirable. These adaptations take the
form, on the one hand, of encouraging and motivating the brighter lower-
class students to aspire to middle-class status by means of education, and on
the other hand, recognizing that many lower-class students will not profit
from such academic fare and should be treated differently in school with more
emphasis on getting them through school and into a job or into marriage with
or without high-school graduation.[33]

African-Americans began to raise issues of unequal power as the
source of inequity in the educational system in the context of the Civil
Rights movement and the battle over desegregation. For example,
Green attacked the lie behind the neighborhood school concept.
"Americans act in ways to deny equal educational opportunity to

Blacks and other minorities by defining the 'right' of their children to attend neighborhood schools, while minorities are contained in educationally inferior settings from which they cannot escape."[34] Green argued that there is no legal basis for this "right." He furthered this analysis of power and equity by making a plea for African-Americans to recognize that whites clearly control the American political and educational arenas. Whites do not perceive themselves as threatened by black failure in segregated schools because the problem is "ghettoized."[35] Green asserted that only when multiracial schools are created will whites use their powers and resources to improve the quality of education offered blacks, because then it will be in their own interest.

Twenty years later, Lowe and Kantor took up this analysis of power in their chapter, "Creating Educational Opportunity for African Americans Without Upsetting the Status Quo."[36] The driving forces of educational change after World War II were not simply the demands and protests of those denied equality of educational opportunity, but the "dialectic between those demands and governmental response that tried to address them without infringing on the privileges of whites.[37] On the one hand, these policies did open possibilities of higher education to many African-Americans. On the other hand, many practices have sustained inequalities between blacks and whites. Further, resistance to inequality has been compromised by blacks' limited political power and erosion of resources in urban areas.

Even as courts finally picked up the pace of dealing directly with *de jure* segregation, measures to overcome segregation had limited benefits for African-Americans because they could not control the context in which desegregation took place. Considerable resegregation within desegregated schools occurred through the mechanisms of tracking and placement in special education. Lowe and Kantor argued that this was done to allay the fears of white parents that academic standards would decline or that much mixing of the races would take place.

By fall 1968, militant African-Americans demanded greater representation on governing boards, the hiring of more minority teachers and counselors, the abolition of tracking, and the inclusion of subject matter that reflected the students' cultures. By the 1980s African-American representation on school boards in major urban school systems and among administrators and teachers was achieved. But the new African-American leadership has been unable to dismantle inequitable school practices. Cities with African-American leadership have faced accelerating poverty, which has profoundly undermined equality of educational opportunity. Lowe and Kantor summed up their historical review: "As African Americans have sought entry to the public schools on equal terms, whites have resisted these efforts by trying to bar their entry, by establishing preserves of privilege within public schools, and by removing their children and money from the schools that black children attend in large numbers."[38]

In the same Yearbook, Sleeter[39] traced the origin of multicultural education to protests from the civil rights movement of the 1960s. For example, parents and educators protested the exclusion of people of color from curricula and decision-making in desegregated schools. They singled out the low academic expectations white educators had for children of color, buttressed by assumptions about cultural deprivation. According to Sleeter, multicultural education is not merely a program that one can adopt, but an attempt to shift power in educational decision-making toward groups of color.

Sleeter saw multicultural education as a reconstruction of the entire educational process. She recommended reorganizing disciplinary content around perspectives of diverse racial and ethnic groups, both sexes, and all social classes. In this view, teachers should work with students to analyze inequality and oppression in society and to develop skills for social action.

Oakes[40] also pointed to the role of power and privilege of white and wealthy parents in her history of the development of differentiated school organization. She showed how school reforms at the turn of the nineteenth century reflected the political struggle for wealth, status, and power in a changing society with a rapidly increasing demand for universal access to a high school education. Bureaucratic, differentiated schools provided white and wealthy parents a means to transfer the privilege of access to their children (by way of school credentials) in the merit-based, modern industrial society. At the same time, schools would train children of poor and non-white parents in technical skills and would socialize them to the work habits and attitudes required if they were to "fit in" as factory workers, such as proper deportment, punctuality, and willingness to be supervised.

In reviewing sources of resistance to the contemporary notion that "all children can learn" and to creating new, more equitable educational communities, Oakes pointed to a number of features of schools that operate as obstacles to change.

One of these is pressure from the old power structure of parents who want their children enrolled in the best classes. White and wealthy parents seem as able as ever to use the structure and practice of schooling to advantage their own children. Special academic magnet schools, programs for gifted and talented, and AP courses provide enclaves for these children. Efforts to tamper with these programs in the name of reform run headlong into vehement resistance from individual parents and organized advocacy groups. Within classrooms, efforts to have students work cooperatively in small learning communities are targeted as exploitation of bright students on behalf of the less able.[41]

Oakes contended that reformers must confront the fact that although American education might have been intended originally to promote community interests by preparing children for participation in democratic governance, the emphasis during the 20th century has been on what individual students can "get out" of schooling in terms of income, power, or status—values of competition. Efforts to create democratic learning communities where all children can be smart launch a critical and unsettling rethinking of the most common and fundamental beliefs and values. Such efforts challenge the moral rightness of entrenched views of what schools are for, how schooling should be conducted, and who should have access to what types of learning experiences.

The Critique of Grouping and Tracking

The theme of grouping and tracking, its origin and its critics, has been unusually well represented in the past 100 years of NSSE, starting in 1936[42] with a whole volume on grouping of pupils. Although the bulk of the volume is taken up with the adaptation of instruction to ability groups, the administration of ability grouping, and early research on evaluation of its effects, attention also is given to the rationale of the period for the introduction of grouping and to theoretical considerations involved in pupil grouping.

Reisner[43] set the historical stage for grouping and provided insight into the rationale and motivations of educators of this period. Greater population density, demands from an increasingly industrialized and commercial society for better educated workers, demands from parents for educational advantages for their children, waves of immigrants from Europe, and laws for compulsory school attendance were social factors underlying this particular change. In response to these social changes and to the development of testing, schools differentiated the classical secondary curriculum according to the "needs" of the newly heterogeneous school population. Reisner took the classic functionalist position: "The needs of our heterogeneous school population will be met only as we succeed more and more completely in getting the right children together to follow those school experiences that are adapted to their abilities and economic future."[44] Because Reisner believed that intelligence testing could predict an individual's economic future and that tests provide a true measure of ability, he maintained that tracking and grouping were not only a way for schools to adapt to the challenges they faced, but were in the best interests of the students who were sorted and selected.

FAILURE TO CREATE TRUE GROUPS

Stuart Chapin, a prominent sociologist of the period, along with his co-author Margaret Conway,[45] raised fundamental issues regarding the practice of grouping based on intelligence tests that were absolutely prescient of some of today's work on intelligence as multidimensional. Chapin and Conway started with the simple and profound statement that aggregations of school children at any grade level do not constitute a group in the sociological sense. Interaction and mutual stimulation based upon common interest, the essence of group life, are lacking. True groups have the potential to motivate students to carry out school activities. More cohesive and organic groups would fulfill the task of the educator in training the children in the skills and techniques requisite to adequate social living in a changing world.

LIMITATIONS OF TESTING AS A SORTING DEVICE

Chapin and Conway did not find it surprising that groups created on the basis of a variety of mental and achievement test scores, yielding averages of "doubtful significance," failed to provide the significant common experiences that are the basis of bonds in true group relations. They criticized the adequacy of a composite score as a general criterion in screening pupils because it cannot capture the broad nature of human abilities. For them, the available evidence supported the conception that patterns of different abilities characterize each child regardless of intellectual level. They also raised the issue of stigmatization of "slow" children—certain children will find themselves labeled "slow" in practically all formally recognized activities because a majority of these are centered on subjects that place a premium on the ability to acquire verbal knowledge. "In contrast, if mechanical ability and artistic aptitudes, the ability to inspire and direct others, and similarly unique traits were so recognized that a child who had proved slow in some field might find himself rated 'average' in another group and 'superior' in the field of his special interest, that child might devote a relatively large share of his time and attention to the latter."[46] This chapter clearly foreshadowed contemporary notions of multiple intelligences, as well as the critique of the curriculum as overly centered on verbal knowledge and lacking the basis for adequate motivation for many students.

At the time they wrote, Chapin and Conway were voices in the wilderness; tracking became a standard feature of American secondary schools. It was not until 1974 that Brookover et al. seriously criticized the use of testing to sort and select students. As described in the previous section, the critique became more radical.

The contemporary concern for the education of lower-class whites and minority groups in American society emerges primarily from the practice of identification, classification, and labeling of such students as slow or inferior. Contemporary testing devices are commonly used to objectify the process through which most lower-class and minority students are allocated to educational programs that reduce the possibility of high achievement and social mobility in American society.[47]

Equity and Instruction

Until 1995, Yearbook authors were silent on the topic of equity and classroom instruction. Aside from the above-mentioned critique of differentiated curriculum and grouping, no one discussed the nature of instruction of children from different social backgrounds. At last, Norton Grubb[48] wrote that issues of equity will not be solved without paying much more attention to the inequitable nature of instruction according to social class. He urged serious reform in approaches to teaching because the dominant forms of instruction contain special problems for low-income students. Teaching methods, he noted, had been relatively impervious to change and consisted of routine drills, teacher-centered instruction, skills development, and passive learning. The teacher's main responsibility was to implement the curriculum that was embodied in textbooks or computer programs. School was a long process of discovering a student's deficiencies and overcoming them. Given that uninteresting and relatively meaningless drills were not a source of motivation for students, motivation for schoolwork was simply assumed to arise from other sources.

According to Grubb, this pattern of instruction does not work for lower-class children for a number of reasons. First, given that a threat of a low grade does not have the same motivational power that it does for middle-class students, lower-class students have less motivation for these uninteresting tasks. Second, parents of lower-class students are less able to provide the missing context for decontextualized instruction. Third, the tasks in school are very different from tasks in life and therefore seem meaningless to many children. Fourth, the conventional treatment of student errors leads to a sense of failure and shame; lower-class children have fewer family resources with which to avoid errors.

Grubb acknowledged real differences in the preparation of children for school according to social class.

It is important to understand that deficiencies and inadequacies are defined by the nature of conventional instruction. The differences among students of different class and racial backgrounds have such profound effects largely in the context of instruction based solely on skills and drills which assumes the kinds of motivation background, knowledge, value, and personal relations which lower-class children are likely to lack.[49]

MAKING INSTRUCTION MORE EQUITABLE

In the companion Yearbook for 1995, Jeannie Oakes and Karen Hunter Quartz[50] gathered a number of practical attempts at reforming instruction to make it more equitable. Many of these programs attack sources of inequity described by previous Yearbook authors. For example, the AVID program (Advancement Via Individual Determination)[51] reduces the relationship between social class and college attendance by preparing cadres of working-class youth to succeed in college-track courses in high school. Steinberg and Rosenstock[52] redefined vocational education from a low-status program preparing students for manual labor to a broad program with appeal across social classes.

Robert E. Slavin and Nancy A. Madden's *Success for All* program[53] attacks early failure to learn to read, the strongest predictor of school dropout among lower-class and minority youth. They argue that in order to create schools where all children can be smart, schools in which all students can read must first be created. *Success for All* has been widely disseminated and evaluated, with program schools showing significantly better performance in reading compared to control schools. This program is fairly expensive and requires a full-time facilitator and tutors who can provide one-on-one instruction to supplement the classroom reading program. Small classes are rearranged for reading lessons according to ongoing assessment. Teachers work from scripts during reading instruction. As the students progress, they experience cooperative learning groups.

Still another program described in this NSSE volume by Gene Chasin and Henry M. Levin is *Accelerated Schools*,[54] which works with inner-city schools to transform working conditions, aspirations of the staff, and the decision-making process. Instead of remedial education for low-performing, high-poverty schools, the program prescribes accelerated, active learning for all students. Much of this program centers on reorganizing staff and parents around a new vision of what might be accomplished by playing to students' strengths. Cadres of teachers and parents study the nature of the problems that the school is experiencing and carefully develop possible solutions. The process is democratic, with final decisions resting with the school as a whole. *Accelerated Schools* contrasts with *Success for All* in its emphasis on democratic decision-making and local control of evaluation of instruction. *Success for All* requires a "buy-in" by 80 per cent of the faculty before the training process begins. Once a commitment is made to the program, the materials and approach, as well as the methods of instruction, are a "given" and are not open to a constructivist approach to the staff and parents advocated for *Accelerated Schools*.

TREATING STATUS PROBLEMS IN THE CLASSROOM

Throughout the chapters I have reviewed, there runs a theme concerning educators' and society's view of what it is to be "smart." Starting with Chapin in 1936, sociological writers for the Yearbooks saw this cultural feature as central to the way that schools reproduce the status order of society at large. In the Yearbook devoted to creating educational communities, edited by Oakes and Quartz, two chapters (one by Cohen, Kepner, and Swanson and the other by Krechefsky, Hoerr, and Gardner) focused on the necessary reformulation of the concepts of intelligence and ability as a condition for all students becoming successful learners. As Kepner, Swanson and I phrased this issue:

These same beliefs constitute a major barrier to educational reform. A key part of this belief system is the assumption that intelligence is unidimensional and that there is only one way to be intelligent. Thus it makes sense to talk about people in terms of their placement along a continuum of "smartness." Furthermore, where a person stands on this dimension predicts competence on an infinite set of intellectual tasks. These beliefs about the nature of intelligence are linked to status orders that form within the classroom. High-status students are believed by their teachers and peers to be very intelligent; low-status students are seen to be intellectually incompetent.[55]

The formation of status orders within the classroom leads to differential participation and learning on the part of high- and low-status students. Students from a lower social-class background are especially likely to rank low on academic status. Using a sociological theory, my colleagues and I have shown that when students work together in cooperative groups, students with high academic and peer status talk more and learn more. This theory and research pins down one nexus in which social stratification of the outer society infects the interrelationships and the learning of small groups of students.

To dismantle these status hierarchies, we found it necessary to alter the way that teachers and students look at intellectual ability. We accomplish this goal by creating multiple-ability curricula for small groups that reflect the variety of ways that adults use their intellects, and permit different students to make different kinds of intellectual contributions to the group. In our program, teachers learn how to alter the expectations for competence that students hold for themselves and for one another. Rachel Lotan and I[56] have found that the more frequently teachers use these interventions, the higher the rate of participation of low-status students. Moreover, the more that low-status students participate, the more they learn.

Working to bring equity to the classroom is counter-cultural and requires change in unconsciously held beliefs and assumptions.[57] It is not a simple matter for teachers to treat status problems in the classroom, even when they intellectually understand and philosophically embrace the concepts. Putting that knowledge into practice requires a series of changes in perceptions that can be difficult to achieve and may take considerable time to acquire. For example, recognizing that a quiet, well-behaved student is not just shy but is actually excluded by the others in her group because of her low status is such a perceptual shift.

PRODUCING EQUITABLE CLASSROOMS

The definition of an equitable classroom follows from the definition of equity introduced at the beginning of this chapter. In such a classroom, the relationship between social class, race, and academic performance is weak or non-existent. We should not see an academic status order that is closely related to these societal differences and that influences students' participation in small groups. All students should have equal access to the process of talking and working together. Finally, the distribution of learning outcomes should be changed so that few students fall to the very lowest portion of the performance distribution. Rather, they should be much closer to the average performance.

To achieve this ideal of an equitable classroom, it is necessary to change the nature of the curriculum, as well as the teacher's role. It is also critically important to prevent status problems from allowing some students to dominate while others are excluded from participation. Of the various programs designed to attack problems of inequity, the approach called "complex instruction" is the only one that simultaneously changes all three classroom features.[58] Complex instruction offers an intellectually advanced and challenging multiple-ability curriculum. Students use one another as resources in cooperative groups, with different students able to make different kinds of contributions because of the multiple-ability nature of the open-ended group tasks. Teachers learn to foster interaction in groups and to delegate authority in a way that holds both groups and individuals accountable for their performance. Teachers also learn how to equalize participation in groups by treating expectations for competence so that each student is expected to be competent in some important intellectual abilities required by the task.[59] Evaluations of achievement in classrooms using these strategies have documented significant gains in basic skills, as well as higher-order thinking compared to more conventional classrooms.[60] Moreover, classrooms where more students are talking and working together on multiple-ability tasks are classrooms where the distribution of learning outcomes is more equitable.[61]

CHOOSING AN INSTRUCTIONAL PROGRAM TO INCREASE EQUITY

The programs described as examples of practicable models designed to increase equity are very different from one another. Selection of a particular program depends upon the school or district setting and on which inequities are most pressing (and depressing). For example, the problem of failure by so many students to master reading by the third grade is front and center on the political, as well as educational, stage in many cities and states. Such failure condemns students to continued poor performance and a high probability of early dropout. Thus, it is not surprising that *Success for All* is the logical choice of many schools and districts today. On the other hand, this program does nothing to enable faculty and parents to take control of education in their school, and to make it conform to a well-thought-out vision. One of the most serious criticisms of the approach is not widely understood—teachers must follow a script and have almost no professional autonomy.

If the central focus of inequity is the inner-city school where the staff acts as if the children are incapable of academic excellence and where poor parents are isolated from the operation of the school, then Levin's model of the accelerated school may be ideal. Here is an opportunity to change the school governance in a profoundly democratic manner, allowing parents, teachers, and students to have a hand in their own instructional fate. Here is an opportunity to change the view of inner-city children as being so far below grade level that they should have a program that is primarily made up of drill and practice in the basic skills.

If the issues of inequity center on heterogeneous classrooms with a wide range of academic and linguistic skills, such as in schools without tracking or ability groups, then complex instruction is a suitable model. Like *Success for All*, complex instruction focuses on classroom instruction, but totally unlike Slavin and Madden's program, the teacher has a powerful, professional role to play. Unique to this approach is the central role of creating equitable classrooms. Complex instruction recognizes that creating an equitable classroom using a basis in sociological theory and research is unlikely to evolve from the collaboration of teachers trying to solve problems in their school. Rather, it is a set of ideas that teachers must understand at such a deep level that they will be able to make decisions that will change the fundamental social system of the classroom. This understanding allows teachers to provide access for all students to intellectually challenging materials while ensuring equal-status interaction within cooperative groups.

All three approaches make connections between the nature of instruction and the organizational arrangements of the school. *Success for All* mandates an elaborate system of organizational support for reading instruction, while *Accelerated Schools* is concerned with how schools make decisions concerning instruction. Complex instruction has a model of organizational support for the recommended changes in classroom instruction that includes increased teacher collaboration and support from the principal. As with any successful practicable model for change, all three programs require substantial training, coaching, professional development, and follow-up in schools.

Conclusion

The NSSE yearbooks have, by and large, reflected the "cutting edge" of thought in the area of equity. As the critique of current practices in schools grew, so did the nature of the criticism of the "way schools are" in the yearbooks. As the view of social classes shifted from a static to a more dynamic position, so did NSSE authors. As the field moved beyond the controversy of blaming students and their families versus blaming teachers, the NSSE authors were pointing the way to hidden assumptions about intelligence and, finally, to key differences in instruction that help to construct a different and depressed future for students who enter school without extensive pre-school training by parents and nursery schools.

What are the implications of this extensive critique of the schools for those who are striving to make schools more equitable today? The fundamental inequalities in resources and the maldistribution of well-prepared teachers must be addressed first. As Katie Haycock[62] put it:

American school districts differ considerably in the quality of the education they provide. The differences, however, do not occur willy-nilly. Rather there is a clear pattern: affluent communities, especially those with substantial property values, tend to invest the most and can therefore offer the most to their students; poor communities, by contrast, can provide much less to their children.[63]

The inequities in school finance are so severe that a number of state courts have ruled their own state systems of education to be unconstitutional. And yet, discussion of uniform standards and testing in current school reform remains curiously minimal on this key issue.

Providing equal if not superior resources to schools that poor children attend is a necessary but not a sufficient condition for the achievement of equity. The rationale for differentiating curriculum for poor children so that they receive a substandard education has been thoroughly outgrown and discredited. Nevertheless, as Oakes correctly pointed out, doing away with this type of tracking will meet substantial resistance from parents who are counting on the advantages of an accelerated curriculum to help their children get into the best universities. One solution to this dilemma lies in reform at the classroom level. Changing the nature of instruction so lower-class children can actively contribute their intellectual abilities to their group, maintaining a high level of intellectual challenge in the curriculum, combining traditional academic skills with other skills representing a wider range of human intelligence, demanding a high level of effort and accountability from all learners, and providing the extra support that struggling students require—these are the elements for equitable classrooms that are more likely to be acceptable to middle-class parents. Finding an effective way to work with the concerns of middle-class parents without sacrificing the educational futures of lower-class students is a critical area for future research and development.

The current obsession with high-stakes testing and standards-driven education will only make inequities more severe. Yes, it is very important to have high standards, but if we still have inequitable resources, segregated high-poverty schools, grouping and curriculum differentiation, and classroom instruction that reinforces status differences among students, the result will be outcomes that are more strongly correlated than ever with race and social class. To meet high standards, educators will have to stand on the shoulders of those pioneers in research, development, and practice who have moved ahead to make schools simultaneously more equitable and more successful in academic achievement. The current discourse of school reform must grow and change, taking on the added challenge of increasing equity. Therefore, in addition to continuing the needed research, staff development, and implementation, those who are committed to equity must also struggle to improve public understanding of the consequences of inequity and the possibilities of successful change.

Notes

1. Guy Montrose Whipple, ed., *The Grouping of Pupils*, Thirty-fifth Yearbook of the National Society for the Study of Education, Part I (Bloomington, IL: Public School Publishing Co., 1936).

2. Edward H. Reisner, "Social Change and Its Effect on School Organization in the United States," *The Grouping of Pupils*, pp. 31-38.

3. C. Wayne Gordon, ed., *Uses of the Sociology of Education*, Seventy-third Yearbook of the National Society for the Study of Education, Part II (Chicago: National Society for the Study of Education, 1974).

4. Robert J. Havighurst, ed., *Metropolitanism: Its Challenge to Education*, Sixty-seventh Yearbook of the National Society for the Study of Education, Part I (Chicago: National Society for the Study of Education, 1968).

5. Eleanor Bernert and Charles B. Nam, "Demographic Factors Affecting American Education," *Social Forces Influencing American Education*, Sixtieth Yearbook of the National Society for the Study of Education, Part II, ed. Nelson B. Henry (Chicago: National Society for the Study of Education, 1961), pp. 89-121.

6. Edward Flaxman and A. Harry Passow, eds., *Changing Populations/Changing Schools*, Ninety-fourth Yearbook of the National Society for the Study of Education, Part II (Chicago: National Society for the Study of Education, 1995).

7. Gordon, pp. 213-408.

8. Charles Elmer Holley, ed., *The Relationship Between Persistence in School and Home Conditions*, Fifteenth Yearbook of the National Society for the Study of Education, Part II (Chicago: The University of Chicago Press, 1916).

9. Wilbur B. Brookover, Richard J. Gigliatti, Ronald D. Henderson, Bradley E. Niles, and Jeffrey Schneider, "Quality of Educational Attainment, Standardized Testing, Assessment and Accountability," *Uses of the Sociology of Education*, pp. 161-191.

10. W. Norton Grubb, "The Old Problem of 'New Students': Purpose, Content and Pedagogy," *Changing Populations/Changing Schools*, pp. 4-29.

11. Ibid., p. 15.

12. Sari Knopp Biklen and Diane Pollard, eds., *Gender and Education*. Ninety-second Yearbook of the National Society for the Study of Education, Part I (Chicago: National Society for the Study of Education, 1993).

13. Holley, *Persistence in Home and Social Conditions*, pp. 87-95.

14. J. D. Heilman, "The Relative Influence Upon Educational Achievement of Some Hereditary and Environmental Factors," *Nature and Nurture: Their Influence on Achievement*, Twenty-seventh Yearbook of the National Society for the Study of Education, Part II, ed. Guy Montrose Whipple (Bloomington, IL: Public School Publishing Co., 1928), pp. 35-6.

15. Nancy Bayley, "Factors Influencing the Growth of Intelligence in Young Children," *Intelligence: Its Nature and Nurture: Original Studies and Experiments*, Thirty-ninth Yearbook of The National Society for the Study of Education, Part II, ed. Guy Montrose Whipple (Bloomington, IL: Public School Publishing Co., 1940), pp. 49-79.

16. Jane Loevinger, "Intelligence as Related to Socio-Economic Factors," *Intelligence: Its Nature and Nurture*, pp. 159-210.

17. Ibid., p. 203.

18. Aaron M. Pallas, Gary Natriello, and Edward L. McDill, "Changing Students/ Changing Needs," *Changing Populations/Changing Schools*, pp. 30-58.

19. Robert J. Havighurst, "Social-Class Influences on American Education," *Social Forces Influencing American Education*, pp. 120-143.

20. Robert L. Green, "Northern School Desegregation: Educational, Legal, and Political Issues," *Uses of the Sociology of Education*, pp. 213-273.

21. Dorothy K. Jessup, "School Integration and Minority Group Achievement," *The Urban R's: Race Relations as the Program in Urban Education*, eds. Robert A. Dentler, Bernard Mackier, and Mary E. Washauer (New York: Frederick A. Praeger, 1967), p. 96.

22. Brookover, Gigliotti, Henderson, Niles, and Schneider, p. 162.

23. Jeannie Oakes, "Normative, Technical, and Political Dimensions of Creating New Educational Communities," *Creating New Educational Communities*, Ninety-fourth Yearbook of the National Society for the Study of Education, Part I, eds. Jeannie Oakes and Karen Hunter Quartz (Chicago: National Society for the Study of Education, 1995), pp. 1-15.

24. Bernert and Nam, p. 98.

25. Pallas, Natriello, and McDill, p. 31.

26. Ibid., p. 32.

27. Christine E. Sleeter, "Curriculum Controversies in Multicultural Education," *Changing Populations/Changing Schools*, pp. 162-185.

28. Robert Lowe and Harvey Kantor, "Creating Educational Opportunity for African Americans Without Upsetting the Status Quo," *Changing Populations/Changing Schools*, pp. 186-208.

29. Biklen and Pollard, *Gender and Education*.

30. Havighurst, pp. 120-143.

31. Ibid., pp. 126-127.

32. Ibid., p. 127.

33. Ibid., p. 143.

34. Green, p. 265.

35. Ibid., p. 270.

36. Lowe and Kantor, pp. 186-208.

37. Ibid., p. 186.

38. Ibid., p. 204.

39. Sleeter, pp. 162-185.

40. Oakes, p. 3.

41. Ibid., p. 6.

42. Whipple, *The Grouping of Pupils*.

43. Reisner, pp. 33-36.

44. Ibid., p. 28.

45. F. Stuart Chapin and Margaret L. Conway, "The Social Group in Education," *The Grouping of Pupils*, pp. 57-79.

46. Ibid., p. 76.

47. Brookover et al., p. 162.

48. W. Norton Grubb, pp. 18-24.

49. Ibid., p. 22.

50. Oakes and Quartz, *Creating New Educational Communities*.

51. Mary Catherine Swanson, Hugh Mehan, and Lea Hubbard, "The AVID Classroom: Academic and Social Support for Low-Achieving Students," *Creating New Educational Communities*, pp. 53-69.

52. Adria Steinberg and Larry Rosenstock, "CityWorks: Redefining Vocational Education," *Creating New Educational Communities*, pp. 147-165.

53. Robert E. Slavin and Nancy A. Madden, "Success for All: Creating Schools and Classrooms Where All Children Can Read," *Creating New Educational Communities*, pp. 70-86.

54. Gene Chasin and Henry M. Levin, "Thomas Edison Accelerated Elementary School," *Creating New Educational Communities*, pp. 130-146.

55. Elizabeth G. Cohen, Diane Kepner, and Patricia Swanson, "Dismantling Status Hierarchies in Heterogeneous Classrooms," *Creating New Educational Communities*, pp. 16-17.

56. Elizabeth G. Cohen and Rachel A. Lotan, "Producing Equal-Status Interaction in the Heterogeneous Classroom," *American Educational Research Journal* 32 (1995), pp. 99-120.

57. Cohen, Kepner, and Swanson, pp. 26-27.

58. Elizabeth G. Cohen and Rachel A. Lotan, eds., *Working for Equity in Heterogeneous Classrooms: Sociological Theory in Practice* (New York: Teachers College Press, 1997).

59. Elizabeth G. Cohen, *Designing Groupwork: Strategies for Heterogeneous Classrooms* (New York: Teachers College Press, 1994).

60. Cohen and Lotan, pp. 137-165.

61. Elizabeth G. Cohen, Rachel A. Lotan, and Chaub Leechor, "Can Classrooms Learn?" *Sociology of Education* 62 (1989), pp. 75-94.

62. Katie Haycock, "Creating New Educational Communities: Implications for Policy." *Creating New Educational Communities*, pp. 224-239.

63. Ibid., p. 227.

CHAPTER IV

Individual Differences and Diversity in Twentieth-century Classrooms

NANCY E. PERRY AND PHILIP H. WINNE

Alongside whatever we all may share because we are human is a seemingly innumerable list of differences. Some of us are female, others male. Some of us are typically calm while others excite often and quickly. Some of us wear a hearing aid or glasses but others do not. Some of us can still do algebra while others failed to learn it. Some of us are musically talented, and some cannot carry a tune in a bucket. Some of us speak English at home while others speak a variety of other languages. These individual differences express our diversity.

Careful study of discourses about students and education reveals that the vast proportion attend to individual differences and diversity. Terms such as "normal," "typical," and "average" are abundant. Whether they refer to quality or quantity, such descriptions implicitly refer to individual differences by abstracting or averaging them. Frequent and, we hold, essential supplements to these descriptions are modifiers such as "except," "situated," and statistics characterizing variance such as the range and standard deviation. Such modifiers explicitly mark variation that unmodified labels abstract or average out.

How has education responded to this spectrum of individual differences? This is our topic. We examine it as portrayed in the Yearbooks published by the National Society for the Study of Education throughout the twentieth century. Because even this domain is voluminous, we narrow our focus to elementary and secondary classroom

Nancy E. Perry is Assistant Professor in the Department of Educational and Counselling Psychology and Special Education at the University of British Columbia, Vancouver, British Columbia, Canada. Philip H. Winne is Professor of Education at Simon Fraser University, Burnaby, British Columbia, Canada. He is also Director of Graduate Programs and Research Coordinator in the Faculty of Education.

This chapter is dedicated to the memory of father, William Perry, and mentor, Richard E. Snow. Thanks to Louise Mercer for exceptional help in preparing this chapter.

settings; to trends in public education regarding the inclusion of immigrant, minority, disadvantaged, and disabled students; and to the differentiation of programming, curricula, and instructional methods.

We beg indulgence in beginning our chronicle. Topics concerning individual differences and diversity are complexly historical and contextual. They reach back at least to Plato's *Dialogues* and *The Republic* and afield to such practices as China's program for testing prospective civil servants instituted circa 1000 AD. We recognize these roots but lack space to examine them. So, we set our stage by sketching three seminal developments during the nineteenth century. Each strongly influenced twentieth-century research, practices, and politics concerning individual differences and diversity. Then, we characterize differences among children who populate our classrooms and ways in which our schools have responded to them.

Harbingers and Twentieth-Century Views of Individual Differences

During the 1800s, our culture strove to cope with, profit from, and understand the Industrial Revolution, as well as a surfeit of momentous scientific advances. The debate, excitement, agitation, and misunderstanding these changes engendered in society and government were reflected in education as well as new, scientific approaches to studies of society and its institutions. Within this general foment, developments in three areas—theories about measurement and human abilities, changes in classroom groupings to accommodate individual differences, and a drift away from a common curriculum—gave rise to issues regarding individual differences that twentieth-century education would confront.

MEASUREMENT AND THEORIES ABOUT HUMAN ABILITIES

Studies of individual differences in human abilities in the nineteenth century had tremendous influences on education. Two main facets of work stand out in this broad domain: the invention of educational measurement, and the linking of ability with heredity.

The Planning Committee for the Twenty-first Yearbook, *Intelligence Tests and Their Use*, wrote in its introduction:

The most significant and important movement in the field of education during the past decades has been the rapid development and the constantly increasing use of scientific measurements . . . measurements to ascertain the native ability of the pupil, and measurements to determine his school attainment.[1]

Leonard P. Ayres, writing in the earlier Seventeenth Yearbook, *The Measurement of Educational Products*,[2] credited E. L. Thorndike "for having discovered what is apparently the earliest record of work in the field of educational measurements as we now use that term." In 1864, the Rev. George Fisher, an English school master, invented the "scale book" for assigning levels of proficiency to students' work in school subjects such as arithmetic, spelling, and writing. Subsequently, Fisher's tool was called a specimen; today, it is a rubric. Two significant consequences followed. First, individual differences among students gained objectivity because standards by which students' work was judged now were not the private purview of a subjective judge; they were recorded in the scale book for all to see. On the heels of this change, facets of individual differences became reified.

Ayres went on to recount how surveys, initially intended to inform the public about what schools were accomplishing, evolved into a subservience of education to tests, inventories, and other measurement practices.[3] Nearly eight decades later, in the Ninety-fifth Yearbook, *Performance-Based Student Assessment: Challenges and Possibilities*, editors Joan Baron and Dennie Wolf revisited Ayres's issue:

Significantly, in both the dire and the hopeful accounts of American public education, diversified forms of student assessment . . . have been nominated as a major force. No matter who is telling the narrative, there is an urgent demand to create assessments which will inform us about what American students "know and are able to do . . ."[4]

Throughout the twentieth century, it is clear that the measurement literati understood scores to be incomplete and somewhat pale reflections of individual differences. Questions and cautions about measurements and their uses populate the Yearbooks. But educators, parents, and government officers, naïve about tests and measurements, grew to depend on tests. The earlier reification of constructs was extended. Measurements came to be respected as tools for classifying students and justification for a continual stream of new programs, each intended to remedy failings of its predecessor in accommodating or erasing individual differences. Though the century was not yet two decades old, Charles H. Judd offered this conclusion in the Seventeenth Yearbook, one that might as readily be found in the Ninety-fifth:

The movement toward the development of measurements is both promoted and seriously encumbered by a vague popular demand. Parents have heard that there are methods of finding out whether their children can spell or add or read satisfactorily, and immediately a clamor arises for a measurement of the local school. . . . In the presence of a popular demand for the revelation of imperfections and the absolute certainty that imperfections exist, it is not difficult to understand why there should be a tendency on the part of many school officers to combat the movement toward wide-spread measurement.[5]

A half century prior, Charles Darwin had published his thesis about evolution in *The Origin of Species*. Standing among the greatest, as well as the most vilified, of scientific constructs,[6] this work spurred Darwin's young cousin, Sir Francis Galton, to investigate the heritability of intellectual accomplishments. His 1869 book, *Hereditary Genius*, advanced an empirically grounded interpretation that intellectual capabilities of various kinds were inherited. "So began a long and deeply controversial association between intelligence and heredity that remains with us today."[7]

In exploring his thesis, Galton tried but failed to create useful measures of intellectual capabilities. A few decades later, however, in France, Alfred Binet and his student, Théodore Simon,[8] succeeded. Lewis M. Terman, in the United States, quickly extended their work and published the seminal Stanford-Binet test.[9] In a context where measurements were on the ascendancy in education, the intelligence test rapidly became a common tool for gauging individual differences, particularly a student's potential to learn, and a frequent spark for controversy in educators' discourses about diversity.

In the Eighty-second Yearbook, Thomas L. Good and Deborah J. Stipek judged, "Ability is perhaps the most important and certainly the most controversial individual difference variable related to education"[10] because it constitutes "readiness to profit from a learning experience."[11] Their modern term enfolds two main topics frequently found within the twentieth-century's Yearbooks: achievement and intelligence.

ACHIEVEMENT

Knowledge students gain by participating in instruction or undertaking self-regulated study of subjects—reading, music, algebra, and the like—is what most mean by the term achievement. Attention to this individual difference has been continual, starting with both volumes of the first Yearbooks, *Some Principles in the Teaching of History* and *The Progress of Geography in the Schools*, and carrying through to the most recent subject-focused Yearbook, the Ninety-eighth, *The Reading-Writing Connection*.[12] Individual differences in knowledge-related achievement have also occupied full volumes, such as the Seventeenth Yearbook, *The Measurement of Educational Products*,[13] and the Ninety-fourth, *Performance-Based Student Assessment*.[14] The best-known system for describing differences in knowledge-related achievements was the topic of the Ninety-third Yearbook, *Bloom's Taxonomy: A Forty-year Retrospective*.[15] This taxonomy has rarely been used to characterize intraindividual or interindividual differences, although it is copiously applied to analyses of curricula, and forms a basis for many typologies that describe learning activities, teachers' questions, and test items.

Early views of subject matter achievement as an individual difference were thoroughly quantitative but they were not narrow or simple. One illustration is Edward L. Thorndike's famous characterization of quantification which has too often been misleadingly truncated after the second of these sentences:

Whatever exists at all exists in some amount. To know it thoroughly involves knowing its quantity as well as its quality. Education is concerned with changes in human beings; a change is known to us only by the products produced by it—things made, words spoken, acts performed, and the like. To measure any of these products means to define its amount in some way so that competent persons will know how large it is, better than they would without measurement. . . . Every measurement represents a highly partial and abstract treatment of the product . . . [and] any educational product is a product of ability conditioned by interest.[16]

Individual differences in interest complicate a model of achievement in at least two ways. First, achievement-related becomes an ensemble of "bare knowledge" plus a motivationally linked construct. More significantly, the relations constituting the ensemble can vary over time because, as David G. Ryans noted in the Forty-first Yearbook: "*Interests are themselves learned.*"[17] Four decades later, in the Eighty-second Yearbook, Good and Stipek further elaborated Ryans's point, describing a multifaceted construct of ability and its relation to achievement:

We recognize that individual differences in ability or facility for learning result from a variety of factors, including the quality of previous instruction, social-emotional development, motivation, and so on. Ability is, therefore, considered as both an input variable and an outcome of instruction. The term "input" emphasizes that children bring to each new class an "initial state of competence" and a facility for acquiring new knowledge. Their performance in each class is the consequence of an interaction between these input factors, which we call ability, and characteristics of the learning environment.[18]

In short, today's achievements become tomorrow's abilities. Good and Stipek also are explicit that achievement *cum* ability is multifaceted—it is more than just knowledge of subject matter. We label their view a modern one because attention to kinds of individual differences in achievement, other than knowledge of subject matter, has been relatively rare over the century. For example, no Yearbook has been published about an obviously vital concern, students' motivation. Indeed, only six chapter titles include the term motivation.[19] Similar neglect applies to other individual differences that mediate students' development including the emotions, cognitive styles, dispositions and personality factors, and more.

While many chapter authors of the twentieth-century Yearbooks acknowledged various facets of individual differences in achievement, their response to the challenge presented by this complexity was to divide and conquer. Forms of knowledge were distinguished—Bloom's taxonomy, for example—or subjects per se were differentiated—rhetoric versus mathematics versus vocational skills. As a consequence, today's model of achievement remains simplistic. There is weak coordination of individual differences across the landscape of subject matters. There is practically no articulation of achievement with motivation, interests, personality, and so on. We liken the overall image of achievement at the end of the century to a stained glass window. Hard, sharp borders segregate a panoply of colors of achievement. There is a recognizable scene, achievement *cum* acquired ability, as Good and Stipek termed it, but each element is a separate panel unto itself, fitted next to but barely integrated theoretically with close neighbors or with the larger construct.

INTELLIGENCE

Attention given achievement in the twentieth century is arguably overshadowed by agitation attributable to its counterpart, intelligence. The Society devoted five full volumes to intelligence: Parts I and II of the Twenty-first Yearbook, *Intelligence Tests and Their Use*; the Twenty-Seventh Yearbook, *Nature and Nurture: Their Influence upon Intelligence*; and Parts I and II of the Thirty-ninth Yearbook, *Intelligence: Its Nature and Nurture*. Intelligence also received attention in varying degrees in hosts of individual chapters in other Yearbooks.

In the early twentieth century, universal public schooling brought a burgeoning variety of students into classrooms. Concurrently, schools were enfolded in systemic social changes, the scientific method was brought to bear upon education, and fiscal support declined while costs for materials rose. In this context, cries arose for education to be efficient. As R. R. Breslich put it in the Thirteenth Yearbook:

One of the most pressing problems before the educational public at the present time is to find a means of eliminating the enormous waste of the time of pupils that results from two conditions which prevail in the schools, namely, the failure to provide for the individual differences in capacity found among pupils in the same class, and failure to organize the studying done by pupils so as to avoid the futile efforts which they now put forth to master lessons assigned for home work.[20]

How might this be done? In the Seventeenth Yearbook, Ayres suggested a path that implied a role for intelligence tests:

The center of interest in education has become the child, rather than the teacher, and efforts to improve the quality of instruction begin by finding out what the children can do, rather than by discussing the methods by which the teacher proceeds . . . Knowledge is replacing opinion, and evidence is supplanting guess-work in education as in every other field of human activity.[21]

What children "can do" refers to ability, and ability is inextricably bound up with intelligence. Other leaders were explicit about the role of intelligence and a conception of efficiency. For instance, Edward L. Thorndike wrote in the Twenty-first Yearbook about accomplishment quotients:

When we have measured a pupil in respect to his achievement in a school subject, and his capacity for that subject, the quotient of achievement divided by capacity is an important measure of accomplishment . . . these accomplishment quotients or ratios, familiarly known as A.Q.'s, are recorded year by year for each pupil. The pupils of great natural ability are required to do enough more than the average to keep the A.Q.'s near 1. They are thus protected against habits of idleness and conceit. The pupils of little natural ability are not rebuked or scored for failures in gross achievement. They, too, are required simply to maintain their A. Q.'s near 1 . . . It is surely unwise to give instruction to students in disregard of their capacities to profit by it.[22]

A. A. Sutherland, in the Twenty-fourth Yearbook, went further:

For the comprehension of any particular task or lesson . . . the crucial question is just what amount of general intelligence, or just what amount of the special ability is required . . . Since each individual pupil possesses a larger amount of some one ability than of another, it follows that intelligently directed education demands that he work at one level in subject A (which requires the greater amount of ability) and at a lower level in subject B (which requires a less amount of ability).[23]

As measurement permeated education, not all were sanguine about the whole matter of intelligence and tests of it. Steven S. Colvin, writing in the Twenty-first Yearbook, *Principles Underlying the Construction and Use of Intelligence Tests*, worried that naïve educators might abuse intelligence tests in racing to serve schools' growing diversity: ". . . there is danger at present that the movement in the direction of intelligence testing may grow out of all bounds; that it may be misunderstood in theory and erroneously and even harmfully applied in practice."[24]

FACETS OF INTELLIGENCE

Colvin illuminated a host of features concerning how intelligence was understood at the time.[25] To reveal an oft misunderstood temper of the time, we reproduce select key observations, preserving his italicized emphases.

Intelligence is acquired. Only the capacity is inborn.[26]

Intelligence tests . . . determine an individual's intelligence largely in terms of what he has learned, thus obtaining a measure of his ability to continue learning . . . They measure intelligence only on the assumption that they test ability to learn by discovering what has already been learned.[27]

We never measure inborn intelligence; we always measure acquired intelligence, but we infer from differences in acquired intelligence, differences in native endowment when we compare individuals in a group who have had common experiences and note the differences in the attainment of these individuals.[28]

It cannot be too strongly emphasized that *no test to determine intelligence is valid unless the individual tested has had a reasonable opportunity to learn about the various elements involved in the test and has also been interested in learning.*[29]

It seems probable that all mental tests that are largely linguistic will be unfair to those persons whose training in English either at home or in the schools has been inferior . . . Tests are valid only within a group who have had identical or very similar opportunities for gaining familiarity with the materials of the test, and who have not only the same opportunity to learn, but the same desire to learn.[30]

There are several other factors involved in the ability to perform these [intelligence] tests. Chief of these is the "will to do," the capacity to hold the mind down to a task and keep the attention alert and concentrated in the face of outside interests and distractions . . . A child's success in school is due to his intellectual endowment in part, but only in part. His character and temperament are likewise important factors in his success or failure. Will-to-do a task bulks large in the total school performance. So it would seem that the present so-called intelligence tests are in a measure character tests as well, but of course only in a very small and limited degree.[31]

The construct of intelligence throughout the century has been neither narrow nor simple. Frank N. Freeman, writing the first chapter of the Thirty-ninth Yearbook, *The Meaning of Intelligence*, summarized the mainstream at that time and his preference for a tripartite structure:

Intelligence, then, is the ability to learn acts or to perform new acts that are functionally useful . . . Some would object to making the concept as broad as this. They would confine it to what we ordinarily call the intellectual; that is, to abstract thinking. This, however, seems to be an arbitrary restriction of the term.

In the first place, general intelligence or general intellectual competence is thought of as a composite of a large number of highly particularized abilities . . . In the second place, ability may be thought of as composed of a limited number of primary abilities, each one of which is relatively independent of the others. No one of these may be called intelligence, but intelligence may be thought of as a sum of all . . . The third concept is that ability is made up of a large number of very specialized factors, a limited number of group factors that run through a number of operations, and one factor that is general.[32]

It is fair to say that the scientific outlook was cautious about its findings regarding the form of a construct of intelligence. Harold E. Jones'[33] commentary in the Thirty-ninth Yearbook illustrated this view: "The development of theory has not as yet given a commanding position to the doctrine of a 'general' factor, of 'specific' factors, or of 'groups' factors." Prominent theories at the end of the twentieth century, however, appear to have settled on a multifaceted model. For example, Robert Sternberg's triarchic theory of intelligence differentiated among individuals who excel on conventional measures of intelligence and in traditional academic settings, individuals who excel when presented with novel tasks or situations, and individuals with exceptional practical intelligence who adapt readily to their surroundings and have "street smarts."[34] Howard Gardner's theory of multiple intelligences acknowledges individuals' linguistic, logico-mathematical, musical, interpersonal, intrapersonal, spatial, bodily-kinesthetic, naturalistic, and emotional talents.[35]

THE NATURE-NURTURE CONTROVERSY

It is ironic, though perhaps fitting, that Francis Galton's studies of the heritability of intelligence, which made seminal contributions to statistics and solidified the sense of science within the social sciences, shaped a future of apparently irresolvable controversy about uses of intelligence tests. The Society devoted considerable attention to nature and nurture in the two parts of the Twenty-seventh Yearbook and the entire Thirty-ninth Yearbook. In his introduction to the Twenty-seventh Yearbook, Lewis M. Terman[36] was unequivocal about the potential of education:

Possibly one misconception (now fortunately clarified by recent contributors to the nature-nurture field) has clouded the pertinent issues as much as any single other. This is the notion that a "nature" theory implies a type of "glass bottle" mental development which is quite independent of any stimulation from the environment. No idea could be more misleading, and no phenomenon more impossible. . . . We are interested, not in finding out how he would have developed if he had no environment at all; rather we wish to discover whether or not he can be made a more intelligent individual or a more learned one by improving the conditions of his milieu. . . . More generally, we wish to find the relative potency of all types of human environment to add to, or to detract from, human endowment, and to know the limits placed upon achievement by endowment.[36]

Many agreed, but in a way that reinforced the notion of endowment or native capacity. In the Twenty-seventh Yearbook, Arthur I. Gates wrote in his chapter, "Implications of the Facts for Education:"

A person's ability in any intellectual task depends upon his native capacity and upon the acquired information and skills which may influence his performance . . . the effect of education is not to change directly or to modify the growth of capacity, but only to give the subject useful information, techniques, methods of work, and the like.[37]

In Part II of the Twenty-seventh Yearbook, J. D. Heilman used the new statistical method of path analysis, proposed by the biologist Sewell Wright,[38] to investigate relations among variables including educational age, school achievement measured by the Stanford Achievement Test, and "inborn capacity [represented] by mental age as determined by the Stanford Revision of the Binet Scale." He reported:

. . . probably 50 percent of the variation in educational age was due to such hereditary factors as had been measured . . . In view of the superior potency of intellectual endowment, it is far more important to make classifications in the public schools and in higher institutions of learning upon the basis of intelligence than upon differences in the amount of training.[39]

Authors' general conclusion in the Twenty-seventh Yearbook was that native or endowed ability significantly outweighed almost any typical environmental variation in correlating with, if not determining, school achievement.

A dozen years later, in the Thirty-ninth Yearbook, George D. Stoddard clung to the view that native ability was "a postulate" despite the volume of interpreted data that reified the construct.[40] He opined:

Very likely the importance of the IQ at any age level has been overrated. After school entrance it is clear that mental testing adds little to that knowledge of child ability that could be secured by an analysis of academic records *based on reliable and cumulative measurements in standard school subject matter.*[41]

Stoddard and Beth L. Wellman's chapter, "Environment and the IQ," pressed the importance of environmental factors:

That children inherit not only their organism, but also their dynamic social environment, is obvious . . . One may regard intelligence as emergent from [a multitude of factors—hereditary, constitutional ones specific to an individual but not genetic, and environmental] recognizing that one of these factors may vary from almost negligible to almost crucial strengths.[42]

Other authors in the Thirty-ninth Yearbook spurned Stoddard's view. Summarizing a variety of investigations correlating physiological correlates of intelligence, Leonard Carmichael offered guidance about what society should do to maximize "intelligence in the behavior of its population:"

Society . . . would do well to promote a really scientific understanding of eugenics . . . [so that] society may in time learn to avoid some of those breeding procedures that most often perpetuate unsatisfactory brains and inevitably lead to behavior that is defective . . . Since also many environmental factors, such as nourishment, especially including the appropriate provision or exclusion of the vitamins, oxygen, toxic substances, disease products in the blood stream, and the like, are known to influence the development of the brain . . . such factors should be controlled to the fullest degree possible . . .[43]

The Thirty-ninth Yearbook offered a rare but welcome final section of comments on its overall contents by members of the Yearbook Committee. Florence Goodenough represents well those of the view that nature played a determining role: "Suitable education can aid the individual in realizing his potentialities, but that these potentialities can be materially advanced by training alone has thus far not been demonstrated."[44] Terman, despite views of the Twenty-seventh Yearbook, held that the environment's influence was relatively small and stressed this caveat:

An obtained IQ is not only subject to chance errors . . . but also to numerous constant errors . . . [such that] an obtained IQ, as I have many times pointed out, should never be taken as a final verdict, but only as a point of departure for further investigation of a subject.[45]

Ironically, his caution was directed at studies showing a large environmental influence, implicitly ignoring the obverse, a significant influence of endowment.

GRADES, GROUPS AND DIFFERENTIATION

Although instruction given *en masse* to groups of students had been described at least as early as 1657 by Comenius in his *Great Didactic*,[46] Breslich noted the following in the Thirteenth Yearbook:

The first method of instruction in the earliest schools was entirely individual and not class instruction . . . The teacher remained at his desk and called upon his pupils one at a time to repeat the lesson, giving help or explanation whenever necessary . . . The simultaneous or class method was adopted very slowly.[47]

In the first quarter of the nineteenth century, "introduction of a system of instruction by which all pupils of a group are taught at the same time made it necessary to group children so as to make each group as nearly as possible uniform in ability so that instruction would be best suited to their needs."[48] Grades were created based on an individual difference, or a proxy for individual differences such as age, which was believed to mediate the effectiveness of instruction.

Grades and group instruction were not a panacea, as Breslich recognized in quoting an 1872 paper by Dr. William T. Harris:

The tendency of all classification [placing students into grades] is to unite pupils of widely different attainments. The consequence is that a lesson is too short for some and too long for others. The best pupils in the class are not tried to the extent of their ability . . . The poorest pupils of the class are strained to the utmost.[49]

In Breslich's own words, ". . . mass instruction fails to provide for the very bright and for the very slow."[50]

Educators almost instantly berated what had become necessary to accommodate mass education and grades. A. A. Sutherland's assessment in the Twenty-fourth Yearbook was forceful: "Mass methods are still in use, although they have been shown to be not only unintelligent

. . . but actually brutalizing in their effect upon both pupil and teacher."[51] Plans proliferated for grouping students ever more discerningly according to measured ability or a proxy. They varied such factors as (a) time allocated to learning, (b) material assigned to students, (c) access to special teachers, (d) remedial or augmented instruction, (e) grouping within a single class, (f) grouping by or between classrooms, (g) promotion from group to group or grade to grade, and more.

Progress was slow. Eleven years later, Warren Coxe, chair of the committee for the Thirty-fourth Yearbook, *The Grouping of Pupils*, observed, "Children are everywhere taught in groups. The nature and composition of these groups are matters that demand more attention than they have had in the past."[52] The individual differences upon which each plan was based sparked debate about diversity and education's roles in addressing it. In his Yearbook summary, Coxe observed:

Grouping oftentimes suggests a caste system, determinism, mass instruction, and other terms that for many persons are charged with excessive emotional tone. Furthermore, many of the practices suggested run counter to traditional ways of thinking and that arouses immediate prejudice, if not hostility, in some persons. It seems to be difficult, then, to think about the problem of grouping in a calm, logical, objective manner.

Authors of the Thirty-fourth Yearbook were eclectic in recommending kinds of groups to be formed, and included groups defined by school building, grade, home room, classes for subjects, clubs and extracurricular groups, and temporary groups for activities such as projects. But, without doubt, the distinguishing feature of a group remained ability.

A quarter century later, Harold Shane catalogued "thirty-five plans and proposals, which was by no means comprehensive,"[53] for accommodating individual differences. In proportion, education's lexicon also had expanded to embrace labels, such as creative, gifted, learning deficiency, and more; but ability was still the root discriminating individual difference. A potential re-conceptualizing of ability was offered in his advice that schools ". . . not only encourage but require varied rates of pupil progress."[54] Shane also noted that "Reporting and marking procedures should convey a clear idea of the pupil's rate of progress with respect to his particular developmental characteristics in addition to his progress with respect to assumed norms or standards."[55]

In our view, little of substance had changed by the end of the century. Writing in the Ninety-fourth Yearbook, Aaron Pallas, Gary

Natriello, and Edward McDill[56] recounted five bases for grouping: curriculum tracking; within- and between-class ability grouping; disability grouping in forms of compensatory education, special education, and bilingual education; age grouping; and interest grouping or magnet schools. Except for bilingual grouping and interest grouping, the rest regress to distinctions of ability.

THE PENDULUM OF A COMMON CURRICULUM

In the nineteenth century, massive changes in society and the organization of schools were reflected in correspondingly massive changes to the curriculum. The early part of the century's unwavering focus on moral training transformed into a

patchwork of 'School Subjects,' graded horizontally to fit the chronological grading of boys and girls . . . [with an] emphasis on the study of real things . . . The sheer statistical aspect of what happened . . . is startling. Between 1787 and 1870, no fewer than 149 new titles ('subjects' or 'courses') found their way into the printed program of study of these new secondary schools . . . From science comes a term which aptly describes the school curriculum prior to 1900. It was essentially "morphological." Its designers were interested in classification, in naming parts and describing forms rather than in developing an understanding of function and functioning.[57]

Specialized curricula that accommodated individual differences in abilities and interests were afforded by the textbook. Now more available due to innovations in printing, "the printed word usurped the role of oral expression in the classroom and the textbook domineered over the curriculum of American schools."[58] Textbooks brought specialized authors' erudition to students in a burgeoning variety of new subjects at every grade level. Ironically, the very same textbook that allowed accommodation to diversity ultimately thwarted it. Once purchased, books were too expensive to replace. This unexpected condition was doubly disadvantageous because texts of this era were authored with "a mythical faith in mental discipline [whereby] . . . learning, to be effective, must be hard and disagreeable."[59]

Results were not entirely satisfactory. National committees were struck to facilitate secondary students' transition to university. Beginning with the Committee on Secondary School Subjects, the "Committee of Ten," in 1893 and, in the same year, a parallel Committee of Fifteen on elementary school subjects, the curriculum narrowed and stiffened. "Every subject which is taught at all in a secondary school should be taught in the same way and to the same extent to every pupil as long as he pursues it, no matter what the probable destination of the pupil may be."[60] Ninety years later, in the Eighty-second Yearbook, Gary D Fenstermacher dubbed the result the common curriculum, i.e., that "knowledge and understanding, the skills and traits that mark a person as well educated [and that] should be open to all who can profit from what schools are able to provide."[61] He continued,

Assuming that such a curriculum were available and generally accepted, the point of our inquiries into individual differences would be considerably altered. Instead of studying individual differences to learn how we may most effectively and efficiently teach whatever outcomes we have in mind for different learners, we would seek the means to teach the common curriculum successfully to all students.[62]

Transit toward a common curriculum was turned aside, however. According to W. Norton Grubb, the "common school, with its impulse toward inclusion and its promise of access for all"[63] had to deal with ever broadening individual differences arising from "the invasion of schools by less capable students, or lower-class students, or immigrants."[64] "For these students, the solution was vocational education within the high school . . . for lower-level craft jobs, manual occupations, farming, and the increasing numbers of secretarial and clerical positions of the expanding corporations."[65] Grubb cited the president of the National Education Association who "lamented" in 1897 that "whether agreeable or not, we must recognize the fact that it is the children of the plain people who are crowding our school-rooms today, and these will always be in the majority," a view shared by G. Stanley Hall, who referred to these students as the "great army of incapables."[66]

The pendulum swung back in the 1930s. "While vocational education prepared students for jobs requiring some technical skills, the fact was that many jobs in the economy required virtually no preparation. . . . The solution was [to add] a program of general education"[67] to which another "general" program of life skills was added in mid-century. Adaptations of content to ability flourished in the third quarter of the century. The aggregate result is that all students still have access to schooling, although schooling has become a very different experience for different students. Fenstermacher repeated in his introduction to the Eighty-second Yearbook: "Using individual differences in aptitude, ability, or interest as the basis for curricular variation denies students equal access to the knowledge and understanding available to humankind . . . what Dewey called 'the funded capital of civilization'."[68]

Making Way for Exceptional Learners

Having considered the three constructs that arose during the nine-teenth century to profoundly influence education in the twentieth century (namely, measurement of human abilities, differentiation of instruction and the common curriculum), we now focus our chronicle on students and the ways in which our schools have identified and addressed their individual differences. What will become clear in our story is that students who are exceptional in one way or another—students with disabilities, students with high abilities, students who are socially and economically disadvantaged, and students who come from linguistically and culturally diverse communities—make up the major-ity of students who have attended our schools during the past century.

STUDENTS WITH DISABILITIES

Mara Sapon-Shevin, writing in the Eighty-eighth Yearbook, *Schooling and Disability*, pointed out that, prior to 1900 and before the enact-ment of compulsory education, "many children whose needs could not be met in the regular classroom either did not go to school or dropped out when it seemed clear that the fit between child and school was poor."[69] The turn of the century brought the development of a national (U.S.) special education department (1901)[70] and the creation of special classes in public schools,[71] which included students identified as "slow learners . . . mentally subnormal, epileptics, learning disabled, chronic truants, behavior problem[s] . . . physically handicapped, or immigrant children suffering from language or cultural handicaps."[72]

In 1922, the Council for Exceptional Children (CEC) was formed.[73] Today, it is the largest international organization dedicated to research and advocacy on behalf of exceptional individuals. The CEC and other consumer and advocacy groups, especially parents, have exerted powerful influence on both special education practices and legislation that provide students with disabilities access to public education and appropriate programs once they enroll. The Education of All Handi-capped Children Act (Public Law 94-142), enacted in 1975, revised in 1986, and replaced in 1990 by the Individuals with Disabilities Educa-tion Act (IDEA), entitles all children to free and appropriate public education, even children with the most severe disabilities. These statutes also detail regulations concerning individualized education plans (IEPs), non-discriminatory assessment practices, parent involve-ment and access to information, and guidelines for educating children in the least restrictive environment possible.[74]

Yearbooks devoted to the topic of exceptional students have tended to organize chapters around two broad categories or classes of disabilities that have been distinguished throughout the century: mild or high incidence disabilities, and moderate to severe or low incidence disabilities. The next two sections of our chapter characterize specific disabilities within these broader categories, as identified in and beyond the Yearbooks, and chronicle education's response to them, mainly as interpreted by the authors of the Yearbooks.

MILD DISABILITIES

In the first half of the twentieth century, students with mild forms of mental retardation (educable mental retardation, EMR), emotional disturbances (EDs), speech-language impairments (SIs), and "low vitality" were included in the category of mild disabilities.[75] The latter half of the century, however, saw this category become increasingly differentiated. Today, it also includes students with learning disabilities (LDs), attention deficit/hyperactivity disorders (ADHD), and traumatic brain injuries (TBIs).

Authors of the earliest Yearbooks mentioned "intellectually deficient" or "mentally sub-normal" individuals (see, for example, writings in the Twenty-first Yearbook on intelligence tests, and the Thirty-fourth Yearbook, *Educational Diagnosis*). Those definitions of mental retardation focused exclusively on intellectual functioning, labeling individuals mentally deficient if they performed one standard deviation below average on tests of cognitive abilities. However, in 1973, the American Association for Mental Deficiency proposed a definition of mental retardation that included significant subaverage intellectual functioning (indicated by performance two standard deviations below average on standardized intelligence tests) combined with deficits in adaptive behavior.[76] This was a significant refinement of the earlier definitions because it recognized that many children labeled "mildly retarded" are not identified as such until they enter school. In fact, in 1969, a report by the President's Committee on Mental Retardation, *"The Six-Hour Retarded Child,"*[77] observed that some children who do poorly in school do just fine in family and community activities. Sapon-Shevin claimed this report was "highly significant in illuminating the extent to which mild retardation could be seen as a social construct, [perhaps] the product of rigid and narrow behavioral expectations in public schools."[78] Over time, this notion has been reinforced by critics of the identification-assessment process who argue it is biased against children from culturally and linguistically diverse communities and children from economically disadvantaged communities—groups with a long history of over-representation in classes for EMR children.[79]

Sapon-Shevin placed the birth of learning disabilities in 1963 at the first Association for Children with Learning Disabilities (ACLD) conference.[80] Since then, learning disabilities has been the fastest growing category within special education, today accounting for more than 50 percent of American students supported through special education.[81] Although definitions of learning disabilities vary across states and are highly controversial, most emphasize the following criteria: to have a learning disability, a child must have a measured IQ in the average or above average range, and evidence a significant discrepancy between potential, as measured by the IQ, and actual achievement in school. In addition, the discrepancy must not be primarily due to any other psychological, environmental, or physiological condition, even though these may and often do exist concurrently.[82]

Sapon-Shevin also pointed out that the birth of the LD classification brought with it a reclassification of many children previously identified as mentally retarded, "since this label is generally considered less stigmatizing to children and their parents."[83] As was the case for students labeled mentally retarded, the LD category often has been criticized for being overpopulated by boys, by culturally and linguistically diverse students, and by students from low socio-economic communities. However, LD has been a preferred label for white, middle-, and high-SES groups. Moreover, Sapon-Shevin wrote that special education's newest label, LD/Gifted:

. . . is defined in such a way as to insure its members are almost exclusively members of the dominant culture. They must obtain a high IQ and come from a home environment not characterized by teachers as culturally, socially, or environmentally deprived. Children identified as LD/Gifted are provided with special services (by virtue of their learning disability) and with enrichment and high expectations on the basis of their gifted label. It appears that the category of learning disabilities serves important political functions within public schooling to the extent to which it insures specialized services for only a fraction of those children who are low achievers.[84]

The Yearbooks provide scant coverage of educational problems associated with emotional and behavioral disabilities and, especially, attention deficit/hyperactivity disorder (ADHD). This is particularly true in the second half of the century, even though teachers characterize these students as the most difficult to teach in general education classrooms.[85] Referred to as "social deviants" and "delinquents," children with emotional and behavioral problems appeared in some of the earliest Yearbooks (see, for example, chapters in the Thirty-third and Forty-seventh Yearbooks), but faded from focus during the later half of the twentieth century. Like definitions of learning disabilities, definitions of emotional disturbance vary tremendously. However, common themes include (a) inability to learn, which cannot be explained by intellectual, sensory, or health impairments; (b) inability to build and maintain satisfactory interpersonal relationships with peers and teachers; (c) inappropriate feelings or behaviors under normal circumstances; (d) general pervasive mood of unhappiness or depression; or (e) tendency to develop physical symptoms or fears associated with personal or school problems.[86] Measurement problems, lack of agreement concerning what constitutes good mental health, and a wide variety of theories of emotional disturbance make it difficult to estimate the prevalence of emotional disturbance in the school aged population. A decade ago, the U.S. Department of Education estimated 2 percent of school-aged children were emotionally disturbed. Current estimates (from the Department of Education's web site) suggest these students account for between 9 and 10 percent of the total school enrollment.

Attention deficit/hyperactivity disorder (ADHD) is a relatively new disability—apparently, "there were no hyperactive children 30-40 years ago."[87] We found only one reference to this disorder in our review of the Yearbooks. Willard Olson, writing in the Thirty-fourth Yearbook about the diagnosis of behavior disorders, referred to "overactive" children, saying they are "restless, irritable, fidgety, highstrung, and often appear to be wound up."[88] Today, experts estimate children with ADHD account for approximately 5 percent of the elementary-school population.[89]

The most common intervention for students with ADHD is a controversial one, administering psychostimulant drugs. Although this intervention has met with much controversy in the media and reluctance on the part of parents, hundreds of well-designed research studies demonstrate the effectiveness of drug therapy for 70-80% of individuals identified as having ADHD.[90] Of course, all drugs need to be carefully administered and their effects carefully monitored. Also, it is important to note that drug therapy per se will not improve students' learning and achievement in school. More effective interventions combine drug therapy with cognitive and behavioral interventions that help students acquire the social and academic skills they need to be successful in school and beyond. Given the prevalence of ADHD

and other behavior problems in school-aged children, and the problems these disabilities cause for the broader teaching-learning community, we would like to see them receive more attention in future
NSSE publications.

One other category of mild disability has received little attention
in the field of special education generally, and no mention that we
could pinpoint in the Yearbooks. Traumatic brain injury (TBI) was
included as a class of exceptionality when IDEA was enacted in 1990.
James Salvia and James E. Ysseldyke defined TBI as an acquired injury
to the brain resulting from external physical force.[91] It can cause total
or partial functional disability and/or psychological impairment that
adversely affects cognition, language, memory, attention, reasoning,
abstract thinking, judgment, problem solving, sensory, perceptual, or
motor abilities, psychosocial behavior, physical functions, information
processing, or speech. TBIs typically result from accidents (e.g., an
automobile accident or falling off a swing), physical abuse, or intentional harm. They vary in severity and their impact on daily living.
Many brain injuries go unreported, undiagnosed, and untreated if
caused by common events such as a fall down the stairs or a minor
concussion. Often, problems in school are not linked to such "minor"
accidents, and much more research is needed to understand how best
to support students with TBI in school.

Accompanying continuous expansion of categories of mild disabilities since the turn of the century has been continuous growth within
the categories. Today, more than 90 percent of students who receive
support from special education are characterized as having one or more
of these "mild" disabilities. Sapon-Shevin questioned whether such
growth in special education was a genuine trend toward inclusion or a
wolf in sheep's clothing:

At one level the history of the education of students with mild disabilities
appears to be one of increasing inclusiveness and beneficence. Having moved
beyond viewing handicapped children as unworthy or incapable of education,
schools now include more and more children within their educational purview
. . . However, the growth of special education presents a darker side as well.
Rather than viewing the growth of special education as evidence of an increasing willingness of the schools to attend to individual differences in children,
the proliferation of new categories (particularly the mild disability categories)
can be seen as equally reflecting an *unwillingness* of the regular public school
system to assume responsibility (within regular classrooms) for children who
are not succeeding.[92]

Sapon-Shevin further argued that any historical analysis of the growth of special education in general, and categories of mild disabilities in particular, must consider both "explicit and unspoken motivations for practice and intended and unintended outcomes."[93] She asked if it is possible "that there are no disabled students in any absolute sense; rather, we create disabilities by how we view students, the meanings we create, and the ways we think about people and their differences?"[94] For example, some argue that:

The entire history of the field of mental measurement [has been] an effort to classify people according to a fixed hierarchy, and then to treat people differentially based on these categories . . . others argue that intelligence testing neither constituted the reason for special class assignments nor established the need for special classes . . . these same authors suggest intelligence testing did not become mischievous until later, when the combination of differential funding for special education and the need for a scientific basis to support segregation provided an incentive for classifying as many students as possible.[95]

Certainly, mental measurements have offered "comfortable" but perhaps shallow explanations for why some people are successful and others are not, and they have played a powerful role in shaping our beliefs, policies, and practices.[96] Sapon-Shevin likened the system of classification in education to a game of musical chairs:

. . . our attention becomes focused on who belongs in what chair and what to do with the child who is left out, rather than the conditions which initially established a "shortage" of chairs onto which children must be fit . . . Although the motivations for identifying a population as "learning disabled" or "retarded" and the consequences of so doing may have differed substantially, we need to be very suspicious of the "reality" of any group that did not exist until we had a psychometric test to find its members."[97]

MODERATE AND SEVERE DISABILITIES

Categories of moderate and severe disabilities, the low-incidence disabilities, include individuals who are blind or deaf, have significant physical or health impairments, or have developmental or intellectual disabilities. Although educational opportunities for blind and deaf boys existed in Europe in the eighteenth century,[98] the first "institution" for handicapped children in America, the American School for the Deaf in Hartford, Connecticut, did not open until 1817.[99] In the years that followed, states and school boards recognized their responsibilities to exceptional children and, by the mid-nineteenth century, several state schools had been established. In the Forty-ninth Yearbook, the Yearbook Committee noted: "Today there are few states in the United States that do not have residential institutions for the blind, the deaf, the mentally deficient, and the delinquent."[100] They cited a report commissioned by the U.S. Civil Service during World War II that pointed out that "handicapped" individuals "are excellent workers when they are given the opportunity to produce."[101] Data from that report indicated less absenteeism and turnover, fewer accidents among handicapped workers than among non-handicapped workers, and a production rate better than that of non-handicapped workers. We find it disconcerting that, in the ensuing 60 years, individuals with moderate to severe physical and intellectual disabilities who have skills to work still struggle to find employment that could enable them to lead productive and independent lives.[102]

Kathy Zanella Albright, Lou Brown, Pat VandeVenter, and Jack Jorgensen, writing in the Eighty-eighth Yearbook, echo the goals and mission statements of countless schools and agencies charged with educating and preparing individuals with moderate and severe disabilities for life:

... the purpose of educational programs is to prepare them to function with maximal productivity, individuality, competence, freedom, and integrity in all environments and activities experienced by people without disabilities. That is, they should live and function as productively and efficiently as they possibly can in normalized homes; they should perform real work in real work places next to people without disabilities; they should enjoy the rich and varied recreational and leisure environments and activities experienced by all; and they should function effectively and appropriately in a wide variety of general community environments, such as stores, malls, buses, streets, hospitals, and restaurants.[103]

Albright et al. argued that, unlike normally achieving students without disabilities who typically reach these goals without substantial changes to common school practices, most students with moderate and severe disabilities need explicit and direct skill instruction in "actual domestic, vocational, general community, and recreational/ leisure environments and activities . . . or those skills may never be acquired."[104] Albright et al. were particularly interested in students with severe intellectual disabilities—students with IQ scores below 50 and who may manifest a variety of related difficulties, such as blindness and/or deafness, limited use of extremities, serious maladaptive behaviors, inability to communicate verbally, inability to walk unassisted, extremely low response rates, and severe medical problems. We summarize criteria they offered for judging effective educational programs for these students and suggest they may apply to the larger category of students with low-incidence disabilities.

• As much as possible, integrate students with and without disabilities in the same educational environment, and have them all participate in the same activities.

• Carry out careful "life space" analyses of learning environments and life activities to limit factors that may curtail meaningful participation by students with severe disabilities.

• Focus on teaching functional skills (e.g., cooking, shopping, laundry)—actions that must be performed by someone else, if not by the individual with the disability.

• Apply attitudes and use language, environments, activities, and instructional materials appropriate for students' chronological age versus their developmental age.

• Provide opportunities for students to practice skills learned in instructional settings in a variety of non-instructional settings to support maintenance and transfer of skills.

• Involve parents and guardians in designing and implementing education programs.

• Provide instruction in non-school environments.

• Practice the "principle of partial participation" by adapting activities and environments to minimize exclusion on the basis of behavioral, cognitive, sensory, and motoric difficulties.

• Design comprehensive, longitudinal transition plans to support students as they move from elementary to high-school to post-secondary settings.[105]

Alison Ford and James Black, writing in the Eighty-eighth Yearbook, described how principles like those Albright et al. advocate have been operationalized in community-referenced or community-based curricula that have as their goals direct preparation for life, social integration and interdependence, home-school collaboration, and experiential learning.[106] According to Ford and Black, "the core of community-referenced curricula is devoted to content that directly prepares a student to function in the real world."[107] Such curricula contrast sharply with classroom instruction for students with severe disabilities that, until recently, focused on repeated practice of simple, isolated skills that were non-functional, age-inappropriate, and not generalizable to the world outside of school.[108] Citing Luana H. Meyer,[109] Ford and Black point out that

. . . it is no longer enough to be pleased that we have taught something; we must be able to defend our choice of what we teach by showing that, somehow, the learner's quality of life and the reactions of others to that person are improved as a result of our efforts.[110]

STUDENTS WITH GIFTS AND TALENTS

The Society published volumes focusing entirely on the education of gifted students in 1920, 1924, 1958, and 1979. In other Yearbooks throughout the twentieth century, authors gave substantial attention to issues concerning the education of "rapid learners," "bright children," and students with gifts and talents. The volume of writing in this area does not, however, reflect action. There is a century-long under-appreciation by schools, governments, and agencies that fund research of the needs of learners with gifts and talents. Writing in the Nineteenth Yearbook, Theodore Henry observed:

While no one could object to what has been done to make life less burdensome to those who have entered into it under handicaps so heavy, it cannot be denied that if differentiation of instruction is to be confined to those at the lower end of the scale of mental ability, such differentiation is at best one-sided . . . In order to bring about a proper balance, provision should also be made for those more fortunate individuals, who, by reason of better and larger gifts, stand at the upper end of the scale.[111]

If defective children are entitled to special educational treatment and special study for the purpose of discovering what methods of instruction are best adapted to them, why are not children who are just as far removed from the average, but in the other direction, just as much entitled to special educational opportunity and a special pedagogy?[112]

It's easy to take umbrage at the language Henry used in 1920. However, many educators today will recognize the argument and agree that these exceptional learners, like all learners, are entitled to appropriate education.

Determining what is appropriate education for gifted learners has been controversial, in part because these students are very heterogeneous. Ruth Strang, writing for Fifty-ninth Yearbook, said, "Giftedness is but one feature of the total development of the child . . . Giftedness is many-sided, many-patterned . . . Giftedness is progressive from birth to maturity. It is continually elaborating itself . . .[113] She recognized that learners may be intellectually gifted; may possess particular talents, such as for composing music or poetry, for playing a particular sport, for taking things apart and putting them back together again; or, they may be gifted in social situations.

Strang's broad view of giftedness has been revived in the U.S. Department of Education's 1994 report titled *National Excellence: A Case for Developing America's Talent*, based on the Jacob K. Javits Gifted and Talented Students Education Act of 1988:

Children and youth with outstanding talent perform or show the potential for performing at remarkably high levels of accomplishment when compared with others of their age, experience, or environment . . . These children and youth exhibit high performance capability in intellectual, creative, and/or artistic areas, possess an unusual leadership capacity, or excel in specific academic fields. They require services or activities not ordinarily provided by the schools . . . Outstanding talents are present in children and youth from all cultural groups, across all economic strata, and in all areas of human endeavor.[114]

Recent theories of intelligence, such as Gardner's and Sternberg's, previously mentioned, support these broader, more inclusive definitions of giftedness. They de-emphasize "general intelligence," the quality Terman measured when selecting participants for his now classic study of intellectually gifted individuals across their lifespans.

The Terman studies, begun in 1922 and continuing until 2010, are a unique effort to study the lifespan development of 1,528 individuals scoring in the top one percent (IQ > 140) of the population on the Stanford-Binet test of intelligence.[115] Terman measured these individuals on a wide range of physical, intellectual, and social qualities until his death in 1956,[116] after which his work was continued by colleagues at Stanford University. Pauline Snedden Sears, writing in the Seventy-eighth Yearbook, characterized Terman's work as an effort to debunk myths that "precocious children [are] more prone than the average to insanity . . . weaker physically, undersized, unduly specialized or one-sided in their abilities, and without play interests normal for their age."[117] In fact, the gifted individuals in his sample were larger, stronger, and healthier than the norm and, on average, more emotionally stable and less likely to engage in delinquent activities.[118] Terman has been criticized, however, for his less than random sample of individuals whose parents were better educated than the general population, whose fathers were more likely to hold professional occupations, and the majority of whom were born in the United States into the majority culture. Sears acknowledged that Terman's studies are not very helpful to anyone wanting to "untangle the effects of heredity and environment on child IQ . . . The[se] data are less useful for study of group differences than for examination of the fifty-year development of a group of IQ-talented, environmentally advantaged children."[119]

Since the early twentieth century, debates concerning educational programs for gifted students have seesawed on the relative merits of acceleration versus enrichment—moving students through school or particular subjects quickly versus providing students with additional, more sophisticated, and more thought-provoking work while schooling them with their age-mates. Writing about "flexible promotion schemes" in the Nineteenth Yearbook, Henry cited the superintendent of schools for Evanston, Illinois, who spoke in favor of acceleration:

It is our purpose to give every child an opportunity to progress as rapidly as he is able to go. The great majority of students will keep together. Those who are exceptional, either because they are slow or particularly able, will be limited in their progress only by their own ability to go on.[120]

Expressing a similar view through a critique of the "customary" practice of having students move through school and share a common curriculum with age-mates, Williams wrote in the Fifty-seventh Yearbook, "This tradition is protected by an almost impenetrable wall of fables and feelings which contend that there is a 'right age' for children to meet nearly everything to be done or taught."[121]

Arguments against acceleration and in favor of enrichment typically raise concerns about knowledge gaps that may accrue by covering content too quickly or skipping it entirely—better to develop breadth and depth of knowledge. Although there is fear that acceleration may be socially or emotionally detrimental, most research finds otherwise.[122] Writing in the Seventy-eighth Yearbook, Lyn Fox argued that acceleration and enrichment are complementary, and that gifted learners need both. "By and large, the acceleration of learning . . . leads to higher levels of abstraction, more creative thinking, and more difficult content . . . [Through acceleration], the gifted learner can proceed at a faster pace, to a higher level of content, and to more abstract and evaluative thinking . . ."[123]

Another debate regarding programs for gifted students has been whether to locate their education in regular versus special schools.

Throughout the twentieth century, advocates for gifted learners have tended to view special schools as the ideal placement for gifted learners. In contrast, special schools for gifted learners have been viewed as impractical and elitist by many politicians and members of the public. Henry, writing in 1920, articulated well the concern expressed by many parents and educators today that "segregation of bright children . . . tends to develop priggishness, clannishness, egotism, and vanity . . ."[124]

Alternatives to special schools exist that provide gifted learners with opportunities for enrichment and acceleration without isolating them from the mainstream. Satellite schools specialize in particular domains of study, such as math and science or fine arts. Schools within schools provide gifted students much of their academic instruction together and integrate them with other students for social events and non-academic instruction. Under inclusive programming, gifted students have opportunities for individualized study and to mentor or intern with experts in the school or community. The goal of any program should be to maintain the attention of the gifted student. Strang lamented that "too many of them find school work unrewarding and become disillusioned . . . in too many cases the achievement of gifted children is below their potential ability."[125]

"AT RISK" OR DISADVANTAGED STUDENTS

As the twentieth century aged, an increasing number of learners came to be at risk to fail in school because of their social and/or economic circumstances or cultural and/or linguistic discontinuities between school and their community. Most recently, medical advances have enabled medically fragile children and youth to live and attend school. Ann Lieberman, writing in the Ninety-first Yearbook, noted ". . . some of the problems are so new that they have yet to be described adequately, much less diagnosed for possible solutions."[126] Reflecting laws for compulsory education and the banner of increasing inclusion, Yearbooks throughout the century addressed how best to educate an increasingly heterogeneous student body, notwithstanding exceptionalities, and how best to keep large numbers of dropouts in school (see, especially, Yearbooks for 1966-1968).

The allocation of resources to education has been a persistent focus. For example, Norton Grubb, writing in the Ninety-fourth Yearbook, *Changing Populations Changing Schools*, noted ". . . from the turn of the century . . . low-income students were more likely to be in schools with low levels of resources."[127] Similarly, Aaron Pallas, Gary

Natriello, and Edward McDill, writing in the Ninety-fourth Yearbook, argued that socioeconomic status (SES) is a more direct measure than race or ethnicity of the educational resources and opportunities available for children's schooling.[128] They did acknowledge that nonwhite children are more likely than white children to live in circumstances associated with low SES—to live in poverty; to live with one parent; to have a mother who has not completed high school; and to speak a language other than English. Finally, Cottle, writing in the Seventy-fourth Yearbook, decried that "the conditions of hundreds of thousands of children going to school now, less than thirty years before the year 2000, are so wretched, so inhuman, so unbelievably wrong . . ."[129]

At the turn of the century, schools were already linked to programs addressing the material needs of poor children in the form of settlement houses, which provided children with food and clothing.[130] In the 1960s, school breakfast and lunch programs began, and large-scale compensatory programs, such as Head Start, Title 1, and Chapter 1, were introduced. More recently, health and social services are being offered in schools to students in high-risk circumstances. According to Margaret Wang, Geneva Haertel, and Herbert Walberg, writing in the Ninety-fourth Yearbook,

. . . the placement of these services within the schools, where problems can be seen before they reach crisis proportions, can help to make school-linked services more prevention-oriented than crisis-oriented . . . [and] increase the efficiency and effectiveness with which social and health care services are delivered to students and families who are in adverse circumstances.[131]

According to Pallas et al., differentiated and compensatory programs have been based on assumptions that social and economic liabilities handicap poor and minority children in school and can be compensated for by "enriching" academic experiences.[132] The government adopted this view, funding programs and then monitoring success measured by changes in students' performance on standardized achievement tests aggregated to the school building or higher levels. Decisions concerning grade levels, subject areas, kinds of services, teaching methods, classroom settings, and types of staff have been left to individual school districts. Although this latitude allows for innovation in addressing local problems, Erwin Flaxman, Gary Burnett, and Carol Ascher, writing in the Ninety-fourth Yearbook, note that "there has been relatively little variation or experimentation in Chapter 1 programming at the local level."[133]

Providing services through compensatory education has largely meant segregating low-achieving students for "specialized and individualized supplementary instruction," less euphemistically known as repetitious drill of basic skills.[134] Lieberman criticized this approach:

The view that schooling is mostly about basic skills often sets a ceiling on what teachers come to expect of students and themselves . . . This has all too often limited classroom instruction to clearing away learning deficits; the strengths that students bring to school regardless of their home situations, are then ignored.[135]

Harry Passow's chapter in the Ninety-fourth Yearbook points out that poor children and children from ethnic and racial minority groups traditionally have been under-represented in programs for and writings about individuals who are gifted and talented, while they consistently have been over-represented in special and compensatory education programs.[136]

STUDENTS FROM CULTURALLY AND LINGUISTICALLY DIVERSE COMMUNITIES

As is clear from our writing about other categories of exceptionality, students from culturally and linguistically diverse communities have been present in American schools, and "each wave of arrivals has led to various efforts to cope with them."[137] The Yearbook writings we have already cited have alluded to many of the ways in which these students have been under-served or inappropriately served, mainly through the misuse of measurement data, leading to the misclassification of students, and, often, inappropriate placement in programs. In this section, we focus, specifically, on two programmatic responses to the unique needs of culturally and linguistically diverse learners that have received attention in the Yearbooks: bilingual and multicultural education.

During most of the nineteenth century, children in many immigrant enclaves—Italian, Polish, Czech, French, Dutch, German, and others—could receive school instruction in their native language.[138] Ursula Casanova and Beatriz Arias, writing in the Ninety-second Yearbook, referred to this as the "permissive" period.[139] It lasted until 1917, when, according to Casanova and Arias, along with World War I, the changing nature of immigration, and the advent of common schools, a "cycle of linguistic intolerance and antagonism was ushered in." Through the late 1960s, many states barred languages other than

English in schools. Students were severely punished for speaking other languages in and around school, and language was used as a rationale to segregate Mexican- and Native-American students in the Southwest. The legacy of that period persists, in part because language-minority parents often are ambivalent about bilingual education, believing it could limit their children's social and economic prosperity.[140]

In 1974, the U.S. Supreme Court affirmed rights of language-minority students and assigned responsibility to schools to take "appropriate actions . . . to assure equal educational opportunities for [them]."[141] The Court did not mandate bilingual education, preferring to leave to educators decisions about what constitutes an "instructional remedy." However, Casanova and Arias interpreted that this "purposeful ambiguity has fueled the debate rather than resolving the role of native languages in school."[142]

Proponents of bilingual education interpret the goal of the 1974 Elementary Secondary Education Act (ESEA) Title VII Spanish/English Bilingual Education legislation as one of helping students to function well in two languages, while detractors of the "language maintenance" or "nativist" approach argue that valuable learning time is lost when students are taught in their native languages.[143] They hold that the more students are exposed to English, the faster they will learn it. According to Casanova and Arias, such beliefs have spawned efforts, such as the English Only movement in the 1980s, to scrap bilingual education and standardized test accommodation, making English the official language of the United States.

Of the five states with the largest number of language minority students, three (California, Florida, and Illinois) have passed English Only resolutions. These states have a combined population of over 12 million home speakers of non-English languages and they are also the states most highly affected by waves of immigration in the 1980s . . . It appears, then, that as the numbers of immigrants increase, anti-immigrant sentiment also increases and so does public opinion against bilingual education.[144]

Language is intimately part of culture. Merely acknowledging students' language differences, then teaching them to speak English by adding a program or superficially changing curricula, falls far short of bridging their experiences of cultural discontinuity between home and school. Fully multicultural education, wrote Christine Sleeter in the Ninety-fourth Yearbook, is a "process of school reform that is based on reciprocal dialogue among diverse sociocultural groups and on genuine power-sharing among groups."[145] It requires a transformation of the institution as a whole, including "relations with the community, teaching and learning styles, assessment programs, instructional materials, school policies, and the school staff."[146]

Although many white Euro-American educators presume multicultural education was a response to immigration, its roots are in the 1960s civil rights movement, when African-Americans and other oppressed racial groups demanded rightful access to institutions that had previously excluded them.[147] In her chapter on *Curriculum Controversies in Multicultural Education*, Sleeter explained:

> . . . as schools began to experience desegregation, parents and educators criticized (1) the exclusion of people of color from curricula and from decision making roles and (2) the low academic expectations white educators had for children of color, expectations which were buttressed by assumptions about cultural deprivation.[148]

Over time, multicultural education expanded to embrace issues relating to gender, disability, and other forms of diversity. According to Sleeter, a considerable volume of material produced since the 1970s "articulates . . . changes that should be made in schools to support the strengths and aspirations of diverse groups."[149] Sleeter lamented that what goes on in schools, however, is still largely determined by white middle- and upper-class teachers, administrators, and policy makers who, however well-intentioned, "lack knowledge of a nonwhite American group. In the absence of that knowledge . . . what began in a movement for self-determination . . . very often is reduced to additions to 'business as usual' that do not actually change schooling or shift decision-making power toward oppressed groups."[150]

In frustration, some groups have established minority schools. Charles Glenn, writing in the Ninety-fourth Yearbook, described the "deliberate promotion by government of separate schooling for minority pupils in . . . the interest of those pupils."[151] For example, in 1991, Detroit opened three African-American schools, originally intended to educate African-American males. Under subsequent court order, girls were allowed to attend. Since then, other Afro-centric schools have sprung up around the country. In addition, there is a renewed interest in the efficacy of educating girls apart from boys, there are religious schools, and there are schools for gay and lesbian youths. Proponents of separate schools for minority groups claim that "re-segregation" results in increased self-esteem for minority pupils and a more positive cultural identity, which they believe is associated with higher achievement. Glenn questioned the validity of this argument, citing the paucity of research evidence to support such claims.[152] In addition, he accused minority leaders who call for separate schooling of being "perilously close to the position of white supremacists who argue against racial mixing."[153] Ideally, according to Glenn, we would "create effective integrated schools for a society in which diversity is increasingly a fact of life and . . . a potential source of strength."[154]

Conclusion

Having only a small canvas to represent our views of the twentieth century's landscape of individual differences required us to omit topics investigated throughout the century concerning, for example: "wholesome personalities;"[155] self-confidence, ascendance, submission, introversion, extroversion, and emotionality;[156] motivation, including: wants and needs, traits, attitudes, interests, habits and skills, purposes, and affective and emotional conditions;[157] cognitive styles;[158] and character and its roots in morals, virtues, and values.[159] Nonetheless, we hope our sketch demonstrates that thought, theory, informal observation, controlled experimentation, administrative and organizational reform, and political and legislative mandates concerning individual differences in education have been continual and intense.

H. B. Wilson[160] wrote in the Fourteenth Yearbook ". . . the methods which shall be employed in teaching children are determined by the nature, ability, and interests of the children to be taught." This, indubitably, seems rational. Has the twentieth century's work provided knowledge and tools to apply Wilson's rule?

Regarding the aim to educate everyone about a common curriculum, Fenstermacher wrote in the Eighty-second Yearbook: ". . . one may validly conclude that we do not yet know enough about individual differences to decide whether sufficiently powerful instructional treatments can be devised to offset the effects of human variation on an individual's chances for success in a common curriculum."[161] With respect to differentiating instruction and adapting curricula, Good and Stipek's summary in that same volume was this:

. . . the research suggests that teachers in regular classrooms who attempt to design special programs for the "visually alert" and other programs for the "affectively aware" students are fighting an uphill, and ultimately losing, battle. There are too many individual difference variables within classrooms, and a special program in one area often offsets gains in other areas.[162]

Notwithstanding these conclusions, with which we fundamentally agree, we still suggest that education at the turn of the millennium is not ruined by ignorance about individual differences and diversity. First, considerable progress has been made in identifying and refining typologies, a step without which humane and educative differentiation would be impossible. As Lee Cronbach noted, "The poorer the differential information, the less the teacher should depart from the treatment that works best on average . . . Modifying treatment too much produces a worse result than treating everyone alike."[163] Second, awareness has been greatly elevated about consequences of subtle, as well as explicit and intentional, differentiation of schools' curricula, instructional programs, and special services.

What remains on an agenda for this new century? A first task is to create a genuine theory of individual differences, one that stands on and moves past description, acquiring a capability to forecast reliably how individual differences interact with instructional designs. This is a daunting task. Richard Snow concluded in 1977, "Prescriptive instructional theories of this sort will always be incomplete. They will likely evolve with the locale, and they will not be sufficiently explanatory for scientific tastes."[164] To approximate the ideal, we believe, as did Snow, that theory must evolve beyond descriptions of static individual differences to penetrate and characterize them as "temporally unfolding patterns of engagement with tasks"[165]—what Snow called process theories.

A second task is as formidable. A century and a quarter before the National Society of the Study of Education's first Yearbook, James Boswell[166] chronicled Samuel Johnson's observation about individual differences and education: "He allowed very great influence to education. 'I do not deny, Sir, but there is some original difference in minds; but it is nothing in comparison of what is formed by education.'" Early in the twentieth century, Thorndike[167] concurred:

The task of education is to make changes in human beings. We teachers and learners will spend our time this year to make ourselves and others different, thinking and feeling and acting in new and better ways. These classrooms, laboratories, and libraries are tools to help us change human nature for the better in respect to knowledge and taste and power.

Ralph Tyler echoed both Boswell and Thorndike in the Sixty-first Yearbook: "Are we concerned about individual differences only because they introduce instructional difficulties? We think not. We need to decide what we want to do about variability: what types of behavior do we wish to foster and encourage, what uniformity and what diversity do we desire to promote?"[168]

This enduring question intrinsically couples studies of individual differences with deep issues of humanity, society, government, and education. While one answer, if there is just one, likely will remain elusive, studies of individual differences and educational adaptations to them must proceed to provide tools for constructively critiquing any answer that may be proposed.

Support for this research was provided by grants from the Social Sciences and Humanities Research Council of Canada to Nancy E. Perry (#410-97-1366) and Philip H. Winne (#410-98-0705).

Notes

1. Guy M. Whipple, ed., *Intelligence Tests and Their Use*, Twenty-first Yearbook of the National Society for the Study of Education, Parts I and II (Bloomington, IL: Public School Publishing Company, 1923), p. vii.

2. Leonard P. Ayres, "History and Present Status of Educational Measurements," *The Measurement of Educational Products*, Seventeenth Yearbook of the National Society for the Study of Education, Part II, ed. Guy M. Whipple (Bloomington, IL: Public School Publishing Company, 1918), p. 9.

3. Ibid.

4. Joan Boykoff Baron and Dennie Palmer Wolf, eds. *Performance-Based Student Assessment: Challenges and Possibilities*, Ninety-fifth Yearbook of the National Society for the Study of Education, Part I (Chicago: National Society for the Study of Education, 1996), p. x.

5. Charles H. Judd, "A Look Forward," ed. Guy M. Whipple, *The Measurement of Educational Products, Part I*, pp. 152, 153.

6. Daniel C. Dennett, *Darwin's Dangerous Idea: Evolution and the Meanings of Life* (New York: Simon and Schuster, 1995).

7. Richard J. Herrnstein and Charles Murray, *The Bell Curve* (New York: Free Press Paperbacks, 1996), p. 2.

8. Alfred Binet and Théodore Simon, "Méthodes nouvelles pour le diagnostic du niveau intellectuel des anormaux," *L'Année Psychologique*, 11 (1905), pp. 191-244.

9. Lewis M. Terman, *The Measurement of Intelligence* (Boston: Houghton-Mifflin, 1916).

10. Thomas L. Good and Deborah J. Stipek, "Individual Differences in the Classroom: A Psychological Perspective," *Individual Differences and the Common Curriculum*, Eighty-second Yearbook of the National Society for the Study of Education, Part I, eds. Gary D Fenstermacher and John I. Goodlad (Chicago: National Society for the Study of Education, 1983), p. 17.

11. Ibid.

12. Nancy Nelson and Robert C. Calfee, eds., *The Reading-Writing Connection*, Ninety-seventh Yearbook of the National Society for the Study of Education, Part II (Chicago: National Society for the Study of Education, 1998).

13. Whipple, *Measurement of Educational Products*.

14. Baron and Wolf, *Performance-Based Student Assessment*.

15. Lorin W. Anderson and Lauren A. Sosniak, eds., *Bloom's Taxonomy: A Forty-year Retrospective*, Ninety-third Yearbook of the National Society for the Study of Education, Part II (Chicago: National Society for the Study of Education, 1994).

16. Edward L. Thorndike, "The Nature, Purposes, and General Methods of Measurements in Education," *Measurement of Educational Products*, pp. 16-24.

17. David G. Ryans, "Motivation in Learning," *The Psychology of Learning*, Forty-first Yearbook of the National Society for the Study of Education, Part II, ed. Nelson B. Henry (Chicago: National Society for the Study of Education, 1942), p. 313.

18. Good and Stipek, "Individual Differences," pp. 17-18.

19. Ryans, "Motivation in Learning;" M. L. Goldberg, "Motivation of the Gifted," *Education for the Gifted*, Fifty-seventh Yearbook of the National Society for the Study of Education, Part II, ed. Robert J. Havighurst (Chicago: National Society for the Study of Education, 1958); E. R. Hilgard & D. H. Russell, "Motivation in School Learning," *Learning and Instruction*, Forty-ninth Yearbook, Part I, ed. G. Lester Anderson (Chicago: National Society for the Study of Education, 1950); P. S. Sears & E. R. Hilgard, "The teacher's role in the motivation of the learner," *Theories of Learning and Instruction*, Sixty-third Yearbook, Part I, ed. Ernest R. Hilgard (Chicago: National Society for the Study of Education, 1964); A. I. Gates & F. G. Jennings, "The Role of Motivation," *Development in and through Reading*, Sixtieth Yearbook, Part I, ed. Paul A. Witty (Chicago: National Society for the Study of Education, 1961); H. A. Carroll, "Motivation and Learning: Their Significance in a Mental Health Program for Education," *Mental Health in Modern Education*, Fifty-fourth Yearbook, Part II, ed. Paul A. Witty (Chicago: National Society for the Study of Education, Part II, 1955).

20. E. R. Breslich, "Supervised Study as a Means of Providing Supplementary Individual Instruction," *Some Aspects of High-School Instruction and Administration*, Thirteenth Yearbook of the National Society for the Study of Education, Part I, eds. H. C. Morrison, E. R. Breslich, L. D. Coffman, W. A. Jessup (Bloomington, IL: Public School Publishing Company, 1914), p. 33.

21. Ayres, "History and Present Status of Educational Measurements," pp. 14-15.

22. Thorndike, "Measurement in Education," *Intelligence Tests and Their Use*, p. 5.

23. A. A. Sutherland, "Factors Causing Maladjustment of Schools to Individuals," *Adapting the Schools to Individual Differences*, Twenty-fourth Yearbook of the National Society for the Study of Education, Part I, ed. Guy M. Whipple (Bloomington, IL: Public School Publishing Company, 1925), pp. 9, 10.

24. Steven S. Colvin, "Principles Underlying the Construction and Use of Intelligence Tests." *Intelligence Tests and Their Use*, p. 11.

25. Ibid.

26. Ibid.

27. Ibid., p. 17.

28. Ibid., p. 19.

29. Ibid., p. 20.

30. Ibid., p. 23.

31. Ibid., pp. 38-39.

32. Frank N. Freeman, "The Meaning of Intelligence," *Intelligence: Its Nature and Nurture. Comparative and Critical Exposition*, Thirty-ninth Yearbook of the National Society for the Study of Education, Part I, ed. Guy M. Whipple (Bloomington, IL: Public School Publishing Company, 1940), p. 14.

33. Harold E. Jones, "Personal Reactions of the Yearbook Committee V," *Intelligence: Its Nature and Nurture. Comparative and Critical Exposition*, p. 455.

34. Robert J. Sternberg, *The Triarchic Mind: A New Theory of Human Intelligence* (New York: Penguin Books, 1988).

35. Howard Gardner, *The Unschooled Mind: How Children Think and How Schools Should Teach* (New York: Basic Books, 1991).

36. Lewis M. Terman, "Introduction," *Nature and Nurture. Their Influence upon Intelligence*, Twenty-seventh Yearbook of the National Society for the Study of Education, Part I, ed. Guy M. Whipple (Bloomington, IL: Public School Publishing Company, 1928).

37. Arthur I. Gates "Implications of the Facts for Education." *Nature and Nurture.*

38. Sewell Wright, "Correlation and Causation," *Journal of Agricultural Research* 20, No. 7 (1921), pp. 557-585.

39. J. D. Heilman, "The Relative Influence upon Educational Achievement of some Hereditary and Environmental Factors," *Nature and Nurture. Their Influence upon Achievement*, Twenty-seventh Yearbook of the National Society for the Study of Education, Part II, ed. Louis M. Terman (Bloomington, IL: Public School Publishing Company, 1928), pp. 64-65.

40. George D. Stoddard, "Introduction," *Intelligence: Its Nature and Nurture*, p. 6.

41. Ibid., p. 3.

42. George D. Stoddard and Beth L. Wellman, "Environment and the IQ," *Intelligence: Its Nature and Nurture*, pp. 431, 432.

43. Leonard Carmichael, "The Physiological Correlates of Intelligence," *Intelligence: Its Nature and Nurture*, p. 144.

44. Florence Goodenough, "Personal Reactions of the Yearbook Committee III," *Intelligence: Its Nature and Nurture*, p. 451.

45. Lewis M. Terman, "Personal Reactions of the Yearbook Committee VII," *Intelligence: Its Nature and Nurture*, p. 466.

46. Johann Amos Comenius, *The Great Didactic of Johann Amos Comenius* (London: A. and C. Black, 1896).

47. Breslich, "Supervised Study," pp. 33-34.

48. Ibid., p. 36.

49. Ibid., p. 37.

50. Ibid., p. 48.

51. Sutherland, "Factors Causing Maladjustment," p. 1.

52. Warren W. Coxe, "Introduction," *The Grouping of Pupils*, Thirty-fifth Yearbook of the National Society for the Study of Education, Part I, ed. Guy M. Whipple (Bloomington, IL: Public School Publishing Company, 1936), p. 1.

53. Harold G. Shane, "The School and Individual Differences," *Individualizing Instruction*, Sixty-first Yearbook of the National Society for the Study of Education, Part I, ed. Nelson B. Henry (Chicago: National Society for the Study of Education, 1962), p. 49.

54. Ibid., p. 58.

55. Ibid., p. 59.

56. Aaron M. Pallas, Gary Natriello and Edward L. McDill, "Changing Students/ Changing Needs," *Changing Populations Changing Schools*, Ninety-fourth Yearbook of the National Society for the Study of Education, Part II, eds. Erwin Flaxman and A. Harry Passow (Chicago: National Society for the Study of Education, 1995).

57. Harold Rugg, "The School Curriculum, 1825-1890," *The Foundations and Technique of Curriculum-Construction*, Twenty-sixth Yearbook of the National Society for the Study of Education, Part I, ed. Guy M. Whipple (Bloomington, IL: Public School Publishing Company, 1926), pp. 19-22.

58. Ibid., p. 18.

59. Ibid., p. 24.

60. National Education Association, *Report of the Committee of Ten on Secondary School Studies* (New York: American Book Co., 1894), p. 17.

61. Gary D Fenstermacher, "Introduction," *Individual Differences and the Common Curriculum*, Eighty-second Yearbook of the National Society for the Study of Education, Part I, eds. Gary D Fenstermacher and John I. Goodlad (Chicago: National Society for the Study of Education, 1983), p. 3.

62. Ibid., p. 3.

63. W. Norton Grubb, "The Old Problem of 'New Students': Purpose, Content and Pedagogy," *Changing Populations Changing Schools*, p. 5.

64. Ibid., p. 9.

65. Ibid.

66. Ibid.

67. Ibid., p. 10.

68. Fenstermacher, "Introduction," p. 3.

69. Mara Sapon-Shevin, "Mild Disabilities: In and Out of Special Education," *Schooling and Disability*, Eighty-eighth Yearbook of the National Society for the Study of Education, Part II, eds. Douglas Biklen, Dianne Ferguson, and Alison Ford (Chicago: National Society for the Study of Education, 1989), p. 78.

70. Margaret Winzer, *Children with Exceptionalities in Canadian Classrooms: Fifth Edition* (Scarborough, ON: Prentice Hall Allyn and Bacon Canada, 1999), pp. 3-4.

71. Sapon-Shevin, "Mild Disabilities," p. 78.

72. Seymour B. Sarason and John Doris, *Educational Handicap, Public Policy and Social History: A Broadened Perspective on Mental Retardation* (New York: Free Press, 1979), p. 267.

73. Winzer, *Children with Exceptionalities*, pp. 3-4.

74. John Salvia and James E. Ysseldyke, *Assessment: Sixth Edition* (Boston: Houghton Mifflin Company, 1995), p. 56.

75. Sapon-Shevin, "Mild Disabilities," pp. 83-86; The Yearbook Committee, "Basic Facts and Principles Underlying Special Education," *The Education of Exceptional Children*, Forty-ninth Yearbook of the National Society for the Study of Education, Part II, ed. Nelson B. Henry (Chicago: National Society for the Study of Education, 1950).

76. Ibid., p. 83.

77. President's Committee on Mental Retardation, *The Six Hour Retarded Child: A Report on a Conference on Problems of Education of Children in the Inner City* (Washington, DC: Bureau of Education for the Handicapped, 1969).

78. Sapon-Shevin, "Mild Disabilities," p. 104.

79. Ibid., p. 83.

80. Ibid., p. 81.

81. Anita E. Woolfolk, Philip H. Winne, and Nancy E. Perry, *Educational Psychology: Canadian Edition* (Scarborough, ON: Allyn and Bacon Canada, 2000), p. 134.

82. Sapon-Shevin, "Mild Disabilities," p. 84.

83. Ibid., p. 89.

84. Ibid., p. 91.

85. Woolfolk, Winne, and Perry, *Educational Psychology*, p. 131.

86. Salvia and Ysseldyke, *Assessment*, p. 326. This definition is consistent with the definition provided in PL94-142 and IDEA.

87. Woolfolk, Winne, and Perry, *Educational Psychology*, p. 132.

88. Willard C. Olson, "The Diagnosis and Treatment of Behavior Disorders of Children," *Educational Diagnosis*, Thirty-fourth Yearbook of the National Society for the Study of Education, ed. Guy M. Whipple (Bloomington, IL: Public School Publishing Co., 1935), p. 382.

89. Daniel K. O'Leary, "Pills or Skills for Hyperactive Children," *Journal of Applied Behavior Analysis* 13, 1 (Spring 1980), pp. 119-204.

90. Mark L. Batshaw, *Children with Disabilities*, *4th ed.* (Baltimore: Paul H. Brookes, 1997).

91. Salvia and Ysseldyke, *Assessment*, p. 326.

92. Sapon-Shevin, "Mild Disabilities," p. 86.

93. Ibid., p. 87.

94. Ibid., p. 86.

95. Ibid., p. 87.

96. Ibid., pp. 87-90.

97. Ibid., p. 89.

98. Winzer, *Children with Exceptionalities*.

99. Yearbook Committee, "Basic Facts and Principles Underlying Special Education," p. 8.

100. Ibid., p. 8.

101. Ibid., p. 9.

102. William Healey, "New Employment Opportunities for Individuals with Disabilities," CEC Today 5, 8 (1999), p. 14.

103. Kathy Zanella Albright, Lou Brown, Pat VandeVenter, and Jack Jorgensen, "Characteristics of Educational Programs for Students with Severe Intellectual Disabilities," *Schooling and Disability*, p. 59.

104. Ibid., p. 60.

105. Ibid., p. 74.

106. Alison Ford and James Black, "The Community-Referenced Curriculum for Students with Moderate and Severe Disabilities," *Schooling and Disability*, pp. 142-143.

107. Ibid., p. 143.

108. Ibid.

109. Luanna H. Meyer, "Foreword." Robert J. Gaylord-Ross and Jennifer F. Holvoet, eds., *Strategies for Educating Students with Severe Handicaps* (Boston: Little, Brown, 1985), p. 5-6.

110. Ford and Black, "The Community-Referenced Curriculum," p. 154.

111. Theodore S. Henry, ed., *Classroom Problems in the Education of Gifted Children*, Nineteenth Yearbook of the National Society for the Study of Education, Part II (Bloomington, IL: Public School Publishing Co., 1920), p. 8.

112. Ibid., p. 26.

113. Ruth Strang, "The Nature of Giftedness," *Education for the Gifted*, p. 64.

114. Kirsten R. Stephens and Frances A. Karnes, "State Definitions for the Gifted and Talented Revisited," *Exceptional Children* 66 (Winter 2000), p. 220.

115. Woolfolk, Winne, and Perry, *Educational Psychology*, pp. 118-119.

116. Pauline Snedden Sears, "The Terman Genetic Studies of Genius," *The Gifted and the Talented: Their Education and Development*, Seventy-eighth Yearbook of the National Society for the Study of Education, Part I, ed. A. Harry Passow (Chicago, IL: National Society for the Study of Education, 1979), p. 77.

117. Ibid., p. 75.

118. Woolfolk, Winne, and Perry, *Educational Psychology*, p. 119.

119. Sears, "The Terman Genetic Studies of Genius," p. 76.

120. Henry, *Classroom Problems in the Education of Gifted Children*, p. 20.

121. Clifford W. Williams, "Characteristics and Objectives of a Program for the Gifted," *Education for the Gifted*, Fifty-seventh Yearbook of the National Society for the Study of Education, Part II, ed. Nelson B. Henry (Chicago: National Society for the Study of Education, 1958), p. 149.

122. Winzer, *Children with Exceptionalities*, p. 252.

123. Lynn H. Fox, "Programs for the Gifted and Talented: An Overview," *The Gifted and the Talented*, pp. 106-107.

124. Henry, *Classroom Problems in the Education of Gifted Children*, p. 109.

125. Ruth Strang, "The Nature of Giftedness," p. 78.

126. Ann Lieberman, "Introduction: The Changing Contexts of Education," *The Changing Contexts of Teaching*, Ninety-first Yearbook of the National Society for the Study of Education, Part I, ed. Ann Lieberman (Chicago: National Society for the Study of Education, 1992), p. 3.

127. Grubb, "The Old Problem," p. 7.

128. Pallas, Natriello, and McDill, "Changing Students/Changing Needs," pp. 31-32.

129. Thomas J. Cottle, "Low Income Youth," *Youth*, Seventy-fourth Yearbook of the National Society for the Study of Education, Part I, eds. Robert J. Havighurst and Philip H. Dreyer (Chicago: National Society for the Study of Education, 1975), p. 390.

130. Ibid., p. 11.

131. Margaret C. Wang, Geneva D. Haertel, and Herbert J. Walberg, "The Effectiveness of Collaborative School-Linked Services," *Changing Populations Changing Schools*, p. 258.

132. Pallas, Natriello, and McDill, "Changing Students/Changing Needs," p. 48.

133. Erwin Flaxman, Gary Burnett, and Carol Ascher, "The Unfulfilled Mission of Federal Compensatory Education Programs," *Changing Populations Changing Schools*, pp. 103-105.

134. Ibid., p. 107.

135. Lieberman, "Introduction: The Changing Contexts of Education," p. 4.

136. A. Harry Passow, "Nurturing Potential Talent in a Diverse Population," *Changing Populations Changing Schools*.

137. Grubb, "The Old Problem," p. 3.

138. Ursula Casanova and M. Beatriz Arias, "Contextualizing Bilingual Education," *Bilingual Education: Politics, Practice, and Research*, Ninety-second Yearbook of the National Society for the Study of Education, Part II, eds. M. Beatriz Arias and Ursula Casanova (Chicago: National Society for the Study of Education, 1993), p. 6.

139. Ibid., p. 8.

140. Woolfolk, Winne, and Perry, *Educational Psychology*, p. 175.

141. Casanova and Arias, "Contextualizing Bilingual Education," p. 9.

142. Ibid.

143. Woolfolk, Winne, and Perry, *Educational Psychology*, p. 175.

144. Casanova and Arias, "Contextualizing Bilingual Education," p. 12.

145. Christine E. Sleeter, "Curriculum Controversies in Multicultural Education," *Changing Populations Changing Schools*, p. 164.

146. Ibid.

147. Ibid., p. 163.

148. Ibid.

149. Ibid., p. 164.

150. Ibid., pp. 164-167.

151. Charles L. Glenn, "Minority Schools on Purpose," *Changing Populations Changing Schools*, p. 209.

152. Ibid., p. 213.

153. Ibid., p. 212.

154. Ibid., p. 227.

155. Arthur J. Jones and Harold C. Hand, "Guidance and Purposive Living," *Guidance in Educational Institutions*, Thirty-seventh Yearbook of the National Society for the Study of Education, Part II, ed. Guy M. Whipple (Bloomington, IL: Public School Publishing Company, 1938), p. 3.

156. Ruth Strang, "Guidance in Personality Development," *Guidance in Educational Institutions*.

157. John E. Anderson, "The Relation of Emotional Behavior to Learning," *The Psychology of Learning*; Ryans, "Motivation in Learning," p. 313.

158. Good and Stipek, "Individual Differences."

159. Alex Molnar, ed., *The Construction of Children's Character*, Ninety-sixth Yearbook of the National Society for the Study of Education, Part II (Chicago: National Society for the Study of Education, 1997).

160. H. B. Wilson, "Introduction," *Minimum Essentials in Elementary-School Subjects. Standards and Current Practices*, Fourteenth Yearbook of the National Society for the Study of Education, Part I, ed. S. Chester Parker (Bloomington, IL: Public School Publishing Company, 1915), p. 15.

161. Fenstermacher, "Introduction," p. 5.

162. Good and Stipek, "Individual Differences."

163. Lee J. Cronbach, "How Can Instruction be Adapted to Individual Differences? *Learning and Individual Differences*, ed. Robert Gagné (Columbus, Ohio: C. E. Merrill, 1976), p. 23.

164. Richard E. Snow, "Individual Differences and Instructional Theory," *Educational Researcher* 6, 10 (November 1977), p. 15.

165. Philip H. Winne and Nancy E. Perry, "Measuring Self-Regulated Learning," *Handbook of Self-Regulation*, eds. Monique Boekaerts, Paul R. Pintrich, and Moshe Zeidner (Orlando, FL: Academic Press, 2000), p. 563.

166. James Boswell, "Life of Samuel Johnson, LL.D.," *Great Books of the Western World, vol. 44*, ed. Robert Maynard Hutchins (Chicago: Encyclopedia Britannica, 1952), p. 283.

167. Thorndike, "Measurement in Education."

168. Fred T. Tyler, "Intraindividual Differences," *Individualizing Instruction*, p. 5.

CHAPTER V

Whither Early Childhood Care and Education in the Next Century?

STACIE G. GOFFIN

During its first one hundred years, the National Society for the Study of Education (NSSE) published six volumes devoted to early childhood care and education (ECCE), plus one volume of its Series on Contemporary Educational Issues. In addition, the Thirty-eighth Yearbook on child development and the curriculum, sometimes is identified as being devoted to ECCE. Published in 1939, this volume examined child development as the source of curriculum for the kindergarten through twelve system, but gave limited attention to the education of younger children. However, the volume indicates how child development knowledge, a mainstay for early childhood education, was promoted as an educational anchor for all grades.

As summarized in the Twenty-eighth Yearbook and more deeply chronicled elsewhere,[1] the U.S. history of ECCE extends at least until the early 1800s. The nineteenth century saw the rise and fall of infant schools for poor children ranging in age from eighteen months to four years and, especially relevant for the twentieth century, the emergence of kindergartens. Anticipating issues that NSSE volumes would reflect throughout the 1900s, these programs were characterized by ambivalent relations with public schools, usage determined by social class, and strains generated by a feminine vocation caught in masculine definitions of professionalism.[2]

Then, as now, the way in which these issues were explained and interpreted reflected their social, political, and economic contexts. In contrast to current fascination with recent research on early brain development, for example, concern that overstimulation might cause physical illness or even insanity contributed to the public's loss of interest in infant schools.[3]

This chapter by Stacie Goffin was written while she was Senior Program Officer at the Ewing Marion Kauffman Foundation. In April 2000 she began her new position at the National Association for the Education of Young Children [NAEYC] as Director of the Accreditation Reinvention Project, Washington, DC.

Other contextual factors had more positive consequences for
ECCE programs. Dramatic changes and buoyant optimism for the
future accompanied the arrival of the twentieth century. The growth
of industrialization, urbanization, and immigration in the early 1900s
created fertile soil for the expansion of kindergartens and their ulti-
mate sponsorship by public schools.[4] Authors of the first two NSSE
volumes devoted to ECCE, in 1907 and 1908, sensed an opportunity
to contribute to the outline of that future by focusing on kindergartens and their relationship to public school education. Urging public schools to reform elementary curriculum, the preface to the Sixth
Yearbook, published in 1907, exclaimed, "The problems and conditions involved in this relation have been carefully studied, and the
results are here offered as a contribution to the solution of one of the
most urgent problems in American education."[5]

Still other changes were accepted as a natural backdrop for discussions in the volumes that followed on preschool, parent education,
teacher preparation, and classroom practice. These changes include
most especially the growth in the twentieth century of child development as a domain of scientific study and its status as the primary informant to early childhood curriculum and pedagogy. Consistent with the
growing authority of science, authors confidently presented their conclusions. Not until the 1977 volume of NSSE's Series on Contemporary
Educational Issues did one again sense a tone of uncertainty. This time
the tone was less of anticipation than of disheartenment, conveyed in
response to the federal government's withdrawal from expansive invest-
ments in ECCE programs for low-income children. As expressed by
editors Bernard Spodek and Herbert J. Walberg, "The era of abun-
dance seems to have ended, and we face the years of scarcity."[6] In contrast, the most recent NSSE volume devoted to ECCE, published in
1991, expressed anew the sense of urgent appeal that characterized the
1907 NSSE Yearbook. In response to the nation's burgeoning demand
for ECCE programs—due to increasing numbers of women in the paid
labor force and renewed interest in early education as an effective antidote to the ills of poverty—editor Sharon Lynn Kagan asserted,

Never before has the profession had such opportunity, yet been so divided on
how to capitalize on the attention and support accorded it. Never has the
nation been so torn in coming to grips with its definitions of social responsibility versus private rights. Never have partnerships and collaborations been
more necessary and contention more prevalent. Never have issues, lying dor-
mant for so long, demanded such fresh assessment and re-evaluation.[7]

This chapter reviews these ECCE-related NSSE Yearbooks and assesses them in light of the field's present interests and concerns. I explore two issues in particular: the relationship of early childhood education to public school education and child development knowledge as the source of curriculum for early childhood education. These two issues are as central to the ECCE field at the onset of the twenty-first century as they were at the start of the twentieth.

These two issues both assumed salience during the first quarter of the twentieth century. An examination of the relationship between early childhood education and public school education during this time revealed how increasing demand for preschool and kindergarten education has required modifications to the purposes of reform originally espoused by these programs. Evolution of this relationship has spanned the entire century. In the process of securing a broad, stable base of public and financial support, preschool and kindergarten educators have had to moderate their original intentions and compromise cherished values.

The relationship of child development knowledge to early childhood education has been less evolutionary. After intense debate during the first decade of the 1900s, the science of child development established itself as the primary informant to early childhood curriculum and pedagogy. Its long-held position has only recently been challenged. This challenge reignited discussion of the purposes of early childhood education and has propelled the field to grapple with the relationship between its pedagogy and curriculum.

The Relationship of Early Childhood Education
to Public School Education

CONTROL OF THE KINDERGARTEN CURRICULUM

The first two NSSE volumes that focused on ECCE were published in 1907 and 1908 as a paired set. The first volume documented the tension between proponents of Frederick Froebel's kindergarten, brought to the United States in the 1850s, and those advocating newer, more progressive principles. The second volume focused on needed linkages between kindergartens and the primary grades. The preface to the 1907 volume made clear its desire to promote Progressive views on kindergarten education.

The first American kindergarten opened in 1856. According to Barbara Beatty,[8] kindergartens succeeded where infant schools had not. Kindergartens were not promoted solely as compensatory programs for poor children, thus making them accessible to middle-class children. Further, Froebel's unique, child-centered materials responded to advocates' concerns regarding the academic rigidity of public schools. Finally, his emphasis on combining women's and children's interests helped overcome resistance to the idea of young children being educated outside the home—criteria central, as well, to nursery school education.

By the early 1900s, however, many early childhood educators had begun to question Froebel's philosophy and practice. The result was an intensive, ten-year debate (1903-1913) within the International Kindergarten Union among prominent U.S. leaders of kindergarten education. Leaders such as Susan Blow, Elizabeth Peabody, and others argued for the continued validity of Froebelian tenets and opposing educators asserted that his curriculum was too structured, rigid, and unscientific.

Eventually, the ideas put forth by Progressive early childhood educators, such as Patty Smith Hill (a colleague of philosopher John Dewey and learning theorist Edward Thorndike) prevailed. The culmination of their deliberations was reported in *The Kindergarten*, authored by the Committee of Nineteen.[9] The Sixth and Seventh Yearbooks were published while this debate still was in progress, but without prior knowledge of the Committee of Nineteen and its deliberations, readers of the two volumes would be unaware of the intense debate swirling around the volumes' publication.

Readers surely would be aware of the background dissonance, however. For example, the volumes frequently acknowledged Froebel's "historic" contributions. In exploring the continuity between kindergarten and elementary education in the Seventh Yearbook, Benjamin Gregory, superintendent of schools in Chelsea, MA stated,

Froebel made two bequests. First, he bequeathed us a body of doctrine which is so true, so inspiring, so vitalizing, that it is a priceless possession. Modern psychology has modified some of this doctrine. That was to be expected and the contributions of psychology should be gratefully acknowledged. Surely, a man like Froebel, who looked at truth with such open eyes must have himself expected that this would happen.[10]

Of all the NSSE volumes dedicated to ECCE, the Sixth Yearbook most openly acknowledged the existence of controversy regarding effective practice *within* the early care and education field. In "Some Conservative and Progressive Phases of Kindergarten Education" by Patty Smith Hill, the reader was exposed to the tenor of the debate.

This article is undertaken with the full consciousness of the fact that fairness and justice can only be approximated in any attempt to give an adequate account of the conditions and causes which gave rise to the reactionary movement in kindergarten education. The attempt is made with due humility and a sincere desire to be fair to all parties, in both wings of the kindergarten movement."[11]

With the emergence of progressive principles and child development knowledge as the basis for kindergarten (and later nursery school) practice, curriculum harmony was restored for almost eighty years.

KINDERGARTENS AS AGENTS OF CHANGE

The sense of urgency expressed in the preface to the Sixth Yearbook, noted previously, reflected the authors' beliefs in the importance of kindergarten as a model for public school instruction, as well as the school's role in addressing the dramatic shifts associated with immigration and urbanization. Nursery school curriculum would vary from that of kindergarten. Yet advocates of both saw a child-centered focus on social, emotional, and intellectual development as the basis for: reforming the academic orientation of the primary grades, assisting children in adjusting to society, preparing them for their roles as citizens, and assuring developmental continuity—an argument also presented on behalf of kindergarten through twelve education in 1939 in the Thirty-eighth Yearbook titled *Child Development and the Curriculum*.

In her introduction to the Sixth Yearbook, Ada Van Stone Harris, Assistant Superintendent for Rochester, New York's kindergarten and primary schools, argued:

The correct theory of our educational system should be that the primary and kindergarten are one institution—simply a succession of grades developing naturally. The same spirit should prevail, and to a degree the same methods. As children advance there is a gradual change in the tools used, but the fundamental ideas of all the primary grades are the same—the development of the child.[12]

Kindergartens, therefore, entered public schools as agents of change, and, to some extent, they succeeded. Movable tables and chairs replaced bolted-down desks, group games and play entered the curriculum, and instruction incorporated more use of concrete objects.

Likewise, public school practices influenced kindergartens. Home visits by kindergarten teachers were an early casualty of public sponsorship. Further, teachers adapted the kindergarten's distinctive philosophy and practice to accommodate the academic expectations of the primary grades.[13] Ultimately, public school kindergartens became assimilated into the primary grades,

a departure from the earlier praise of the kindergarten as an antidote to the traditional school. . . . A much more modest bureaucratic rationale became central: that the kindergarten would prepare five-year-olds for first grade in a scientifically determined developmental way.[14]

THE EMERGENCE OF PRESCHOOL EDUCATION

The editor of the Twenty-eighth Yearbook, the second NSSE volume devoted to early childhood education, introduced the volume by noting:

There has arisen a new and different conception of the educational significance of the first half-dozen years of life. Infancy and early childhood are held to be of fundamental and far-reaching importance for the entire development of the individual—of importance, that is to say, not only with respect to his physique, his physical well-being, but even more with respect to his mental well-being, his temperamental and emotional outlook upon life. Adults, and particularly parents, are held responsible, therefore, to an extent and in ways not before deemed possible, for the future success of the child . . ."[15]

The two large volumes, bound as a book of 831 pages, sought to present the status of the new preschool and parent education movement. It documented the diverse purposes set forth by nursery schools: as centers for child development research; sites for child guidance clinics; places for transmitting child development knowledge to mothers; sites for training kindergarten and preschool teachers; and locations for experimental curriculum development. The last of these, especially those experimental sites associated with the Progressive education movement, also had as their intent to reform the public schools.

Proponents of experimental nursery schools advocated for nursery schools as a suitable beginning for children's education and as a lever for basic change in education, "a way of making a breakthrough toward a whole new philosophy of education. This conception of nursery school education was a built-in phase of the progressive education movement with a common body of basic principles and purposes."[16]

In her 1919 chairman's report, Lucy Sprague Mitchell, founder of the Bureau of Educational Experiments, stated, "We think of all our work ultimately in relation to public education."[17] Still, advocates of nursery education were wary of what had happened to kindergartens when they became a part of public schools. As expressed in the

Twenty-eighth Yearbook, "With this advent into the public school-system the kindergarten was confronted with a new problem—it must carry out its own aims and purposes and at the same time adjust itself to existing conditions."[18]

The legitimacy of nursery education as the appropriate starting point for public education was endorsed by George Stoddard and his colleagues at the Iowa Child Welfare Research Station, the first U.S. research institute with the sole purpose of conducting scientific research on the development of normal children. As described by Hamilton Cravens, however,[19] Stoddard's advocacy, and that of his colleagues, was extremely controversial because it challenged mainstream assumptions regarding the immutability of intelligence as promulgated by prominent psychologists, such as Lewis Terman, Florence Goodenough, and John Anderson. Even though Stoddard's research associates contributed frequently to NSSE volumes devoted to ECCE, discussion of this intense controversy is absent from the NSSE volumes under review. Nor is it acknowledged in the Forty-fourth Yearbook, published in 1945, in a chapter that argued for the importance of public school education for two-, three- and four-year-old children[20] that followed the publication in 1940 of two NSSE volumes devoted to the nature and nurture of intelligence.

Ultimately, the findings and conclusions that emerged from the Iowa Child Welfare Research Station were revisited. In conjunction with Benjamin Bloom and J. McVicker Hunt's[21] seminal challenges to the notion of fixed intelligence, they helped position nursery school education as an essential precursor to public school education, especially for low-income children. Modification of once-conventional thought regarding the inflexibility of intelligence, in turn, laid the groundwork for achieving increased alignment between early childhood education and the public school curriculum, albeit not on the terms intended by Progressive early childhood educators in the early 1900s.

Adjusting the Relationship between Nursery Education and Public School Curricula

After the 1965 launch of Head Start and government efforts to identify the most effective curricula for preschoolers, nursery school programs initiated in the 1920s found themselves struggling to defend developmentally focused programs against demands for more academically oriented curricula that promoted school readiness. During the 1970s and 1980s, the struggle between academic and developmental programs was cast as a battle between developmentally appropriate and developmentally inappropriate curricula. The battle's resolution strengthened curricular continuity between programs for three- and four-year-olds and public school education, thus extending advocacy efforts initiated at the start of the century, though in a direction counter to those who had advocated for child development knowledge as the basis for continuity.

The "whole child" focus of experimental nursery schools set the stage for this pivotal skirmish. The nursery school of Harriet Johnson, founded in 1919 (later named the Bank Street School of Education and renowned for the Bank Street Developmental Interaction approach), is among the best known of the experimental nursery schools. It opened under the aegis of the Bureau of Educational Experiments as the science of child development gained momentum. The bureau focused on developing new educational methods and creating ways to connect its research with the public schools. In 1931, the Bureau of Educational Experiments, in response to requests from numerous experimental schools sharing a similar philosophy and in need of teachers, established a teacher education program.[22] This helped its practices become the norm for nursery education—and the dominant voice in NSSE volumes devoted to ECCE.

Until the advent of Head Start, the number of nursery schools remained low, despite dramatic growth through the 1920s. As documented by Bess Goodykoontz, Mary Dabney Davis, and Hazel F. Gabbard in the Forty-sixth Yearbook, only three nursery schools existed in 1920; in 1924, there were records of twenty-five programs, and by 1928, with the expansion of university-based programs, eighty-nine nursery schools were recorded.[23] The launch of Head Start in 1965 dramatically increased the number of nursery school programs. Although organized for a different purpose, Head Start took Bank Street's developmental approach as its prototype.[24] But the story does not end there. This privileged position soon became one of disadvantage.

In a review of Bank Street's history and its evolution from an experimental early childhood program to a prescribed curriculum model, this writer[25] described the defensive stance thrust upon the Bank Street approach and the loss of its experimental character. To compete with academically oriented curriculum models, proponents of the Bank Street approach had to formalize the curriculum and become articulate regarding its contributions to school readiness.

Meanwhile, early childhood advocates continued to believe that a developmental approach might yet serve as a lever to reform public

school curriculum and pedagogy. A formal position statement by the
National Association for the Education of Young Children (NAEYC)
on developmentally appropriate practice was commissioned by its governing board in the mid-1980s. Public school programs for four-year-
olds were increasing, and the concern was that these programs were
didactic in approach. NAEYC hoped its position statement would
thwart the push of the primary curriculum into programs for four-
and five-year-olds. The document later was expanded to address the
education of children aged birth to eight.[26] (Criticisms of that document eventually led to a recently issued revised statement.) A host of
publications followed from prominent organizations in support of
developmentally appropriate practice,[27] shifting support toward developmental practice in public schools.

Yet, just as kindergartens changed once they were incorporated
into elementary schools, developmental practice in preschools has
been subtly, yet fundamentally, revised. Advocacy for developmental
practices has been less frequently couched in terms of achieving holistic educational goals, or even school reform. What now are coined as
traditional (versus Progressive) early childhood practices have been
promoted in terms of their ability to secure school readiness.

Head Start has experienced a comparable transformation. Head
Start was conceptualized not only as an education program, but also as
a catalyst for helping poor people advocate for their own needs. These
political aspirations soon threatened the program's continuing existence, however. It survived by becoming primarily a preschool program,[28] and as a preschool program, it, too, has increasingly emphasized school readiness. Similar to the accommodation required of
kindergartens when they became part of the public schools, the struggle for continuity between preschool and public school curricula has
resulted in curriculum possibilities for young children being narrowed
to achieve more conventional educational outcomes.

SHIFT IN EMPHASIS

Thus history has corroborated the concerns of early childhood
advocates regarding the downward extension of academic goals. (The
positive influence of early childhood programs on public school curriculum and pedagogy, however, rarely seems to be acknowledged.)
Since the onset of the civil rights movement, concerns about equal
treatment for all children also have been expressed.[29] It is perhaps no
wonder, then, that early care and education advocates have tended over
the years to resist public schools as hosts for early childhood programs.

And yet, a shift in attitude can be identified that is, once again, not without historical precedent.

In the early 1900s, private kindergartens successfully approached public schools as program sponsors to accommodate their need for financial resources to support the growing numbers of children aspiring to attend. Confronted by similar demand, early care and education advocates once again are looking to public schools as program sponsors. In contrast to the resistance to public school sponsorship nurtured by NAEYC's position statement on developmentally appropriate practice in the mid-1980s, early care and education advocates, eager for expanded financial support, now welcome the growth of public school prekindergarten programs as a critical finance strategy.[30]

As demand has escalated for more and better early care and education programs, financing and other policy concerns—as reflected in the policy focus of the Ninetieth Yearbook—are displacing debate regarding developmentally appropriate practice in public schools. Several additional factors are aiding this shift: greater acceptance of "school readiness" as a legitimate purpose of ECCE programs; infusion of new resources for publicly supported programs for four-year-olds; acknowledgement that early care and education programs, regardless of auspice, are of uneven quality; and increased attention to the care and education of infants and toddlers.[31]

Kindergartens now are assimilated into elementary schools. Public school education routinely is described as encompassing kindergarten through twelfth grades. Normalization of preschool education as the entry age for public education suggests a similar trajectory for four-year-olds, although the existence of a mixed-delivery system for programs serving children birth through age five mitigates against public schools assuming full responsibility for program delivery. Though in ways contrary to the intent expressed by authors in the first NSSE volumes devoted to ECCE and other Progressive educators, curricular alignment between early childhood education and public school education appears increasingly likely.

In *The Struggle for the American Curriculum*, Herbert M. Kleibard argued that opposing interest groups have been struggling for control of the American public school curriculum since the 1890s.[32] As a result of the growing continuity between ECCE and public school education, early childhood educators now reside with these interest groups. To become persuasive participants, however, early childhood educators will need to consider still another challenge to their historical foundation: the source of early childhood curriculum.

The Source of Curriculum for Early Childhood Care and Education

After intense debate over the source of kindergarten curriculum during the first decade of the 1900s, the science of child development established itself as the primary informant to early childhood curriculum and pedagogy. Recent challenges, however, have reignited discussions about the purposes of early childhood education and the role curriculum performs in the achievement of those purposes.

Current objections to reliance on child development knowledge attempt to re-connect the link between early childhood education and social reform. Suggestive of Progressive advocacy of a century ago, the social, political, and economic context at the dawn of the twenty-first century appears to be less conducive to this line of argument.

ESTABLISHING DEVELOPMENTAL THEORY AS THE SOURCE OF ECCE CURRICULUM

According to historian Cravens,[33] the emergence at the close of the nineteenth century of children as a discrete population group accompanied a new view of the national population and culture as composed of rigidly defined groups or races. As a result, children, like other population groups, were considered legitimate objects of scientific study. By the early 1900s, the new conception of children, child science, and child-oriented public policy had become central elements of the Progressive reform movement.

Cravens divided the period between 1890 and 1930, often characterized as the era of child-saving, into two periods. Between 1890 and 1915, the dominant theme was changing children's circumstances through public policy. For example, the first White House Conference on Children was held in 1909, and in 1912, the Children's Bureau was established. From about 1915 to the 1930s, emphasis shifted to professional activities, i.e., to the use of the human sciences to influence public behavior.

Throughout the entire period, Progressive and professional child-savers believed that science could unlock the secrets of human life, that professional expertise was the highest authority in organized child-saving, and that the many different groups in the American population had to be brought up to national standards of health, nutrition, education, and socialization.[34]

Child development as a scientific domain of study advanced in this context. By 1915, developmental psychology had emerged with an emphasis on both distinctive stages of growth and child psychology.

By the early 1930s, according to Cravens, developmental psychology's intellectual framework and institutional infrastructure were complete.

The insights gleaned from this new science became the primary knowledge base for early childhood education. Jonathan G. Silin called psychology ECCE's primary "supply" discipline.[35] Because developmental and child psychology were so new in 1929, however, the Twenty-eighth Yearbook on preschool and parent education could speak only in general terms about the linkages between child development theory and research and early childhood practice. The relationship was articulated by John Anderson in the Thirty-eighth Yearbook, published in 1939, however, and solidified in his chapter for the Forty-sixth Yearbook, published in 1947.

As the first director of the Minnesota Institute of Child Welfare (established in the 1920s as one of the university-based child research centers), Anderson was a highly credible spokesperson. In 1931, he co-authored with Florence Goodenough *Experimental Child Study*, which stressed the constancy of developmental sequence. Cravens labeled this seminal textbook "one of the most effective statements of mainstream doctrine in child development" and its authors tenacious advocates of biological and psychological determinism based on maturation theory and the notion of fixed IQ.[36]

The Thirty-eighth Yearbook had as its theme the suitability of various parts of the curriculum to different stages of a child's development. Anderson's chapter provided a broad overview of child growth and development to anchor the subject-matter discussions that followed. In his chapter eight years later in the Forty-sixth Yearbook, Anderson specifically addressed the relationship between child development theory and early childhood education: "Insight into the nature of the child as he is and is to be underlies the practical principles of early childhood education."[37]

Highlighting the constancy of the field's thinking on this topic, Anderson in his conclusions uncannily mirrored those presented by Lilian G. Katz in a chapter on pedagogy in the Ninetieth Yearbook, published in 1991.[38] Both authors emphasized that practitioners must coordinate their answers to the questions of "what" (content), "when" (the sequence of content within the development process), and "how" (teaching methods). Their elaborations on these issues were also remarkably similar. Yet their distinctions were critical, for they revealed the gradual unraveling of the pedagogical and curricular consensus forged by Hill and her colleagues after the dismissal of Froebel's tenets.

CHALLENGES TO DEVELOPMENTAL THEORY AS THE PRIMARY
DETERMINANT OF EARLY CHILDHOOD CURRICULUM AND PEDAGOGY

In prefacing her review of the discordance between Froebelian and
Progressive educators regarding kindergarten curriculum, Hill noted,
"History repeats itself in all ages and movements and heresy has
entered the paradise of the kindergarten world, destroying the peaceful
satisfaction and pedagogical egotism of happier days in our early history.[39] After eight decades of widespread acceptance, challenges to child
development knowledge as the field's primary informant have become
increasingly widespread—a development reminiscent of Hill's pronouncement.

In answer to his questions of "what," "when," and "how," Anderson replied, "The answers to all three questions depend upon the level
of maturation of the child and his readiness or previous experience."[40]
He argued that content should be de-emphasized: "Ideally, with young
children, content should be minimized, and stress should be placed on
adjustment and modes of attack on problems. It is not what the child
learns in formal terms which is important but what he gains from
experiences in the way of self-control, emotional balance, initiative,
interest, and enthusiasm for the material in question."[41]

In the NSSE volumes focused on ECCE that follow, Anderson's
answer to the question of "what," "when," and "how" were reiterated,
first by Irving Sigel in the Seventy-first Yearbook published in 1972,
and then by David Elkind in the Ninetieth Yearbook, published in
1991. According to Sigel,

The relationship between developmental theory and preschool programming
is basically the match between theory and practice. Developmental theory ideally describes patterns of growth in cognitive, social, perceptual, and affect
areas. Armed with this knowledge, program builders can proceed to construct
programs that follow the course of growth.[42]

In the Ninetieth Yearbook, Elkind argued for the aims of early childhood education (sounding very much like his NSSE predecessors): "If
the learner is seen as a growing individual with developing abilities, if
learning is regarded as a creative activity, and if knowledge is seen as a
construction, then the aim of education must surely be to facilitate this
growth, this creative activity, and this construction of knowledge."[43]

Concrete answers to the "what" are notably absent from these
responses. And while Katz's response, also found in the Ninetieth
Yearbook, by-passed a direct answer, it acknowledged that children

"must interact *about* something."[44] Katz also recognized that an answer to the question of "what" is complex, subject to proponents' values, ideals, and assumptions about learners' future needs. While seemingly a benign reply, Katz's statement challenged developmental theory as a primary source of early childhood curriculum, thereby questioning what has been a mainstay of NSSE volumes devoted to early childhood education.

Concerns have been mounting about the construction, underlying assumptions, and functions of child development knowledge. As noted by William Kessen in speaking about his fellow developmentalists, "[W]e are all driven, obsessed even, by the *priority of the individual*" and, as a result, developmental psychology has largely ignored the impact of social, economic, cultural, and political forces.[45] Challenging the objectivity of developmental science, Erica Burman concluded, "There is now increasing recognition that behind the mask of detached, disinterested objective research lie interpretative and subjective features that, as is the way of repressed material, exert their influences in forms of which we are not aware."[46] And responding to what they viewed as an ahistorical construction of children, Emily Cahan, Jay Mechling, Brian Sutton-Smith, and Sheldon H. White contended, "The academic disciplines that study the child are increasingly inclined to view the child not as a natural object but as a social object, not as the product of developmental, biological forces alone but as a fiction constructed just as much by social and historical forces located in time and space."[47] Brian Vandenberg and Kessen went so far as to suggest that the concept of development as presently constructed has ceased to be a viable framework for conceptualizing individual change.[48]

As criticisms of child development knowledge have mounted, so have concerns about the application of child development knowledge to practice.[49] For some, the way in which reliance on descriptions of children based on child development knowledge limits teachers' responsiveness to children's individual possibilities is of most concern. As expressed by Valerie Polokow, reliance on child development knowledge remakes children into objects "conditioned, driven, modeled, matured, or staged."[50]

Others asserted there exists a distinction between developmental theory and educational objectives. These challengers contended that reliance on developmental theory as the source of ideas for educational outcomes confuses descriptions of what children can do at various ages and stages with what they ought to be doing. Whereas psychological theories strive to be descriptive and value-free, educational theories are intentionally prescriptive and value-laden. This distinction makes the question of "What should children be learning?" significant as an educational—versus developmental—issue. Thus, as acknowledged by Katz in the Ninetieth Yearbook, answers to the question, "What should be learned" cannot be derived solely from developmental theory or criteria of developmental appropriateness. Educational goals are derived from different sources, including political and moral priorities.

According to Martin Haberman, theories of child development make two assumptions: (a) what can be explained and predicted about child development and behavior by using a theoretical explanation exceeds that portion of growth and behavior that is unpredictable, and (b) regardless of the specific theory, there is a regularity of behavior undergirded by a systematic set of explanations. Consequently,

[t]eachers committed to a theory of development will hold expectations of what is normal and typical which they will inevitably transform into what is desirable. They will then develop and hold expectations for preferred behavior which support their particular theory and make them insensitive to other explanations and understandings.[51]

Haberman focused on the consequences for children of teachers relying on developmental theory. But consequences of this reliance also exist for teachers. By endorsing the notion that what needs to be known about children and teaching exists in an external body of knowledge, teachers become defined more as consumers of knowledge than as its creators.[52]

CHALLENGES TO A UNIVERSAL APPROACH TO APPROPRIATE PRACTICE

In addition to concerns previously noted, changing U.S. demographics and sensitivities intensify the challenge to developmental theory as a basis for determining program content. Most developmental standards are derived from the study of white, middle-class children. Yet by mid-twenty-first century, demographers forecast that Americans of color will represent a majority of the overall population.[53] Katz recently concluded that

the body of knowledge and principles governing the presumed relationships between early experience and mature development that many of us have long taken for granted are based on evidence gathered largely from a relatively limited sample of human experience. Consequently, this body of knowledge of child development no longer seems sufficiently generalizable to serve as a basis for curriculum and pedagogical decisions.[54]

Within the early care and education field, the terms "developmentally appropriate" and "quality programs" tend to be used interchangeably to describe good early childhood programs. This tendency confounds pedagogy with curriculum. With decreasing acceptance of descriptions of child development as prescriptive (versus informative) for practice, a universally accepted definition of program quality appears increasingly unlikely. Cultural variations in definitions of quality are of ascending importance, as are distinctions between the views of parents and professionals.[55] These multiple challenges beg the question of how program quality and content are defined, and by whom.

In the introduction to his monograph on defining program quality from a global perspective, Martin Woodhead confessed that he has

become increasingly convinced that much of what counts as knowledge and expertise about children is deeply problematic, right down to such a fundamental idea as 'early childhood development programme.' While concepts provide welcome tools for organizing thinking they also inadvertently sanction a spurious veneer of coherence on diverse childhood realities.[56]

Challenges to child development knowledge as the primary determinant of ECCE curriculum relaxed the ties that bound early childhood curriculum and pedagogy and opened the way for alternative informants. Shirley Kessler offers the ideal of democracy as a framework. Sally Lubeck argues for a politically driven curriculum that acknowledges cultural differences and the social and economic inequities often associated with them. Jonathan G. Silin advocates for a socially relevant curriculum, and Rebecca S. New argues for an integrated curriculum that simultaneously acknowledges children's interests and teachers' responsibilities to prepare children for participation in their society. Jessica Ball and Alan A. Pence propose that early childhood programs follow a community's vision for its children, incorporating the community's needs and goals for nurturing children.[57]

Common among these postmodern suggestions for early childhood education is a desire to broaden the range of informants and address ethical, cultural, and political issues. These recommendations, however, rarely acknowledge the huge pull being exerted by policy makers on early childhood education to become more academically focused or on growing expectations, spurred by public demands for public accountability, for measurable child outcomes. Proponents of these alternative determinants for ECCE curriculum also seem undeterred by history. As Sue Bredekamp, author of the NAEYC position statement on developmentally appropriate practice, noted, past efforts to reform curriculum and instruction based on notions of holistic education have failed due to fragmented efforts by reform advocates.[58] In addition, the history chronicled in this chapter documents the powerful forces exuded by the institutional structure of public schools.

Whither Early Childhood Education in the Next One Hundred Years?

Developing a different relationship with developmental theory raises the question of what other kinds of knowledge are needed by early childhood teachers. Loss of an agreed upon body of knowledge to inform pedagogical and curricular decisions also raises the specter of relativism. Jerome Bruner suggested, however, that the complex diversity of value commitments inherent in any culture does not have to equate with "an anything goes" relativism. The prevalence of multiple choices need not imply that each is necessarily of equal merit nor eliminate requirements for their justification.[59]

Yet the absence of clearly defined parameters for early childhood curriculum and pedagogy necessitates having insightful, caring practitioners capable of functioning in a complex environment and responding to conflicting demands. As noted by Margret Lambert and Larry Cuban,[60] teaching is characterized by unsolvable problems and management of dilemmas. "Right" answers rarely exist in teaching. Rather, teaching is highly individual, involving teachers' personal definitions of problems and their resolutions, thus explaining recent calls for reforming preparation programs for kindergarten through grade twelve teachers.

The gap between this ideal and the capacity of the early childhood field is particularly immense, however. Few professions are characterized by as much discrepancy between its professional aspirations and empirical descriptions of its performance.[61] Yet calls for stronger teacher preparation programs seldom are inclusive of early childhood teacher preparation. Further, as reflected in the efforts of NAEYC's National Institute for Early Childhood Professional Development to create a cohesive framework for early childhood professional preparation, the field struggles to decide whether a specified knowledge base should be designated a prerequisite for entry into the profession, and, if so, what such a knowledge base should encompass. Questions persist regarding the desirability of out-of-home experiences, the need for "caregivers" to have their own specialized knowledge base, and societal responsibility—a list remarkably similar to one created by Goodykoontz, Davis, and Gabbard for the Forty-sixth Yearbook.[62]

Changing the field's and public's expectations regarding professional preparation is complicated by the fact that ECCE remains a predominantly female field. This is seen not only in the low compensation and stature presently accorded to early childhood teachers, but in the field's acquiescence early in the twentieth century to the values of the new, rising male professional class. The relationship between women's roles and characterizations of early childhood teachers was forged largely by middle- and upper-income women in the late nineteenth and early twentieth centuries as they strove to define new identities for themselves during a rapidly changing time.[63] Barbara Finkelstein concluded:

The pioneers of early childhood education bequeathed an ambiguous professional legacy. On the one hand, they had developed a systematic body of professional knowledge, an effective political coalition, a group of committed professionals, a multiplicity of training institutes, and a new educational institution—the kindergarten. On the other hand, they had passed along an ideology celebrating separate spheres, distinct abilities, and spiritual rather than material rewards for women, and protection rather than rights for children.[64]

Finally, determining the content of professional development is made more complex by changing demographics. The nation's increasing racial and economic diversity challenges the field not only to reconsider the basis of its curriculum and pedagogy but also to expand the conceptualization of the "whole child" beyond social-emotional, intellectual, language, and physical development to include such issues as family support and health care. Such an approach confronts the profession with how to integrate and coordinate its programmatic concerns with those of allied professions. The relationship between early childhood care and education and allied professions is not a new issue for NSSE volumes devoted to ECCE, though. As Millie C. Almy and Agnes Synder stated in the Forty-sixth Yearbook, for example, "Teacher education must abandon its isolation."[65] Given the field's uncertainty regarding its professional knowledge base, however, shifting to cross-professional training will have to be navigated carefully, in order to resist diluting the developmental and educational issues of special concern to ECCE.

These are incredibly complex issues. Yet as the number of women in the labor force escalates, the early care and education field is experiencing increasing demand for its services and, at the same time, the consequences of inadequate training and compensation for its teachers. And as already noted, the field is being challenged to develop a different and updated framework for its practice: to expand the informants to curriculum development; to address issues of cultural and economic diversity; to link with allied professions on behalf of comprehensive services; and to assume accountability for child outcomes. As discussed above, what a new framework for ECCE might embrace has been explored. But discussion has been too sporadic to engender the needed level of dialogue.

Most in the early care and education field would agree that the formal early care and education system should encompass the field's diverse sectors, e.g., center-based child care, Head Start, family child care, and public school- and employer-sponsored programs. (Some would argue for the addition of care provided by kith and kin.) Less consensus exists regarding the age range of children to be served under the heading of early childhood care and education, however. In her chapter on continuity between preschool and formal schooling in the 1991 Yearbook, Bettye M. Caldwell noted, "No matter how much we might want to define early childhood as birth to age eight (as does the National Association for the Education of Young Children), most people envision a fairly sharp segmentation at or around six years."[66] This reality reflects, in part, the fact that children from birth to six years lack a well-developed delivery system for their education, but after age five, one becomes available through the public school system.

This is a timely moment for the field to seek renewed consensus on its purposes and essential elements. The field is in a formative period during which, through its own agency, it can conceptualize its continuing evolution. Whereas other fields in the U.S., such as education and health care, struggle to *reform* themselves—literally to re-form how they conceptualize and implement their work—the U.S. early care and education system still is in the process of *development*. We are not so much reforming a system as creating one.

As documented by these ECCE-related NSSE volumes, during the twentieth century, the early childhood field, after reaching consensus on its pedagogical and curricular foundation, devoted itself to refining and disseminating its child-focused approach to early childhood education. In the context of the field's once-again formative state, conceptualizing the early care and education system as birth through age five presents an opportunity to deliberate the field's distinctive purposes, circumstances, and relationships. Such deliberations could consider ECCE's history of community service, social activism and collaboration, emphasis on nurturing and caring for others, and concern for integrating the intellectual and social-emotional aspects of children's lives. Akin to the efforts of the Committee of Nineteen, extensive discussion is needed to modernize the field's consensus regarding the purposes of ECCE and the elements essential to their achievement.

In the final chapter of the last NSSE volume devoted to ECCE, written in 1991, Kagan predicted that "early childhood education . . . is at the brink of a major shift in how it conceptualizes and defines its mission. Linking care and education, such redefinition affords promising options and opportunities."[67] Almost a decade later, these options and opportunities are materializing. Our appreciation of them would be considerably lessened without knowledge of the extended efforts of our predecessors as traced these last one hundred years by NSSE.

NOTES

1. See, for example, Barbara Beatty, *Preschool Education in America: The Culture of Young Children from the Colonial Era to the Present* (New Haven, CT: Yale University Press, 1995); Sonya Michel, *Children's Interests/Mothers' Rights* (New Haven, CT: Yale University Press, 1999); Emily D. Cahan, *Past Caring: A History of U.S. Preschool Care and Education for the Poor, 1820-1965* (New York: National Center for Children in Poverty, 1989); Sheldon H. White and Stephen Buka, "Early Education: Programs, Traditions, and Policies," *Review of Educational Research*, vol. 14, ed. Ernest Z. Rothkopf (Washington, DC: American Educational Research Association, 1987), pp. 43-91.

2. Barbara Beatty, "A Vocation from on High: Kindergartening as an Occupation for American Women," *Changing Education: Women as Radicals and Conservatives*, eds. Joyce Antler and Sari Knopp Biklen (Albany, NY: State University of New York Press, 1990), pp. 35-50; Beatty, *Preschool Education in America*; Barbara Finkelstein, "The Revolt Against Selfishness: Women and the Dilemmas of Professionalism in Early Childhood Education," *Professionalism and the Early Childhood Practitioner*, ed. Bernard Spodek, Olivia N. Saracho, and Donald L. Peters (New York: Teachers College Press, 1988), pp. 10-28.

3. Beatty, *Preschool Education in America*; Cahan, *Past Caring*.

4. David Tyack and Larry Cuban, *Tinkering Toward Utopia: A Century of School Reform* (Cambridge, MA: Harvard University Press, 1995).

5. M. J. Holmes, "Editor's Preface," *The Kindergarten and Its Relation to Elementary Education*, Sixth Yearbook of the National Society for the Study of Education, Part II, ed. The Society's Committee (Bloomington, IL: Public School Publishing Co., 1907), p. 7.

6. Bernard Spodek and Herbert J. Walberg, "Introduction: From a Time of Plenty," in *Early Childhood Education: Issues and Insights* (Berkeley, CA: McCutchan Publishing Corp., 1977), pp. 1-2.

7. Sharon Lynn Kagan, "Editor's Preface," *The Care and Education of America's Young Children: Obstacles and Opportunities*, Ninetieth Yearbook of the National Society for the Study of Education, Part I, ed. Sharon Lynn Kagan (Chicago: National Society for the Study of Education, 1991), p. xi.

8. Beatty, *Preschool Education in America*. See also Evelyn Weber, *The Kindergarten: Its Encounter with Educational Thought in America* (New York: Teachers College Press, 1969); Elly Singer, *Child Care and the Psychology of Development* (London and New York: Routledge, 1992).

9. See Weber, *The Kindergarten*, for a description of this debate; Committee of Nineteen, *The Kindergarten* (Boston: Houghton Mifflin, 1913).

10. Benjamin C. Gregory, "The Necessity of Continuity Between the Kindergarten and the Elementary School. The Present Status Illogical and Un-Froebelian," *The Coordination of the Kindergarten and the Elementary School*, Seventh Yearbook of the National Society for the Study of Education, Part II, ed. The Society's Committee (Chicago: National Society for the Study of Education, 1908), p. 33.

11. Patty Smith Hill, "Some Conservative and Progressive Phases of Kindergarten Education," in *The Kindergarten and Its Relation to Elementary Education*, p. 61.

12. Ada Van Stone Harris, "Introduction," *The Kindergarten and Its Relation to Elementary Education*, p. 15.

13. Tyack and Cuban, "Tinkering Toward Reform," *Preschool and Parental Education*, Twenty-eighth Yearbook of the National Society for the Study of Education, Parts I and II, ed. The Society's Committee (Bloomington, IL: Public School Publishing Co., 1929).

14. Tyack and Cuban, *Tinkering Toward Utopia: A Century of School Reform*, p. 69.

15. Editor's Preface, *Preschool and Parental Education*, p. ix.

16. Barbara Biber, *Early Education and Psychological Development* (New Haven, CT: Yale University Press, 1984), pp. 13-14.

17. Joyce Antler, *Lucy Sprague Mitchell: The Making of a Modern Woman* (New Haven, CT: Yale University Press, 1987), p. 285.

18. Editor's Preface, *Preschool and Parental Education*, p. 249.

19. Hamilton Cravens, *Before Head Start: The Iowa Station and America's Children* (Chapel Hill, NC: The University of North Carolina, 1993).

20. Ruth Andrus, "Liberalizing the Program for Preschool Children," *American Education in the Postwar Period*, Forty-fourth Yearbook of the National Society for the Study of Education, Part I, ed. The Society's Committee (Chicago: National Society for the Study of Education, 1945).

21. Benjamin S. Bloom, *Stability and Change in Human Characteristics* (New York: John Wiley & Sons, 1964); J. McVicker Hunt, *Intelligence and Experience* (New York: Ronald, 1961).

22. Antler, *Lucy Sprague Mitchell*; Joyce Antler, "Progressive Education and the Scientific Study of the Child: An Analysis of the Bureau of Educational Experiments," *Teachers College Record*, 83 (1982), pp. 559-591.

23. Bess Goodykoontz, Mary Dabney Davis, and Hazel F. Gabbard, "Recent History and Present Status of Education for Young Children," *Early Childhood Education*, Forty-sixth Yearbook of the National Society for the Study of Education, Part II, ed. The Society's Committee (Chicago: National Society for the Study of Education, 1947), pp. 44-69.

24. Barbara Biber, "Introduction to Section III, The Preschool Education Component of Head Start," *Project Head Start: A Legacy of the War on Poverty*, eds. Edward Zigler and J. Valentine (New York: The Free Press, 1979), pp. 155-161; Barbara Biber, *Early Education and Psychological Development* (New Haven, CT: Yale University Press, 1984); Polly Greenberg, "Lucy Sprague Mitchell: A Major Missing Link Between Early Childhood Education in the 1980s and Progressive Education in the 1880s-1930s," *Young Children* 42, no. 5 (1987), pp. 70-84.

25. Stacie G. Goffin, *Curriculum Models and Early Childhood Education: Appraising the Relationship* (New York: Merrill/Macmillan, 1994); Bernard Spodek and Herbert J. Walberg, *Issues and Insights: Early Childhood Education*, 1977, includes chapters by three

authors from the Bank Street College of Education and presents an example of ongoing efforts to inform the debate.

26. Sue Bredekamp, ed. *Developmentally Appropriate Education for Children Birth through Age 8* (Washington, DC: National Association for the Education of Young Children, 1987); Sue Bredekamp, "Redeveloping Early Childhood Education: A Response to Kessler," *Early Childhood Research Quarterly* 48, no.2 (1991), pp. 199-209.

27. See, for example, National Association of Elementary School Principals, *Early Childhood Education and the Elementary School Principal: Standards for Quality Programs for Young Children* (Alexandria, VA: NAESP, 1990); National Association for State Boards of Education, *Right From the Start* (Alexandria, VA: NASBE, 1988); Cynthia Warger, *A Resource Guide to Public School Early Childhood Programs* (Alexandria, VA: Association for Supervision and Curriculum Development, 1988).

28. Polly Greenberg, *The Devil Has Slippery Shoes* (Washington, DC: Youth Policy Institute, 1990); White and Buka, "Early Education."

29. Sharon L. Kagan and Edward F. Zigler, *Early Schooling: The National Debate* (New Haven, CT: Yale University Press, 1987); Goffin, *Curriculum Models*; Evelyn K. Moore and Carol Brunson Phillips, "Early Public Schooling: Is One Solution Right for All Children," *Theory Into Practice* 28, no. 28 (Winter, 1989), pp. 58-63; National Black Child Development Institute, *Child Care in the Public Schools: Incubators of Inequality* (Washington, DC: NBCDI, 1985).

30. Tyack and Cuban, *Tinkering Toward Utopia*; Beatty, *Preschool Education in America*; *Stepping Up Together: Financing Early Care and Education in the 21st Century, Volume II* (Kansas City, MO: The Ewing Marion Kauffman Foundation, 1999). See also Richard M. Clifford, Diane M. Early, and Tynette W. Hills, "Almost a Million Children in School Before Kindergarten: Who Is Responsible for Early Childhood Services? *Young Children* 54, no. 5 (1999), pp. 48-51; Carol. H. Ripple, Walter S. Gilliam, Nina Chanana, and Edward Zigler, "Will Fifty Cooks Spoil the Broth? The Debate Over Entrusting Head Start to the States," *American Psychologist* 54 (1999), pp. 327-343; Anne Mitchell, Carol Ripple, and Nina Chanana, *Prekindergarten Programs Funded by the States: Essential Elements for Policy Makers* (New York: The Families and Work Institute, 1998).

31. See, for example, Carnegie Task Force on Meeting the Needs of Young Children, *Starting Points: Meeting the Needs of Our Youngest Children* (New York: Carnegie Corporation of New York, 1994); Mitchell, Ripple and Chanana, *Prekindergarten Programs Funded by the States*; Ellen Galinsky, Carollee Howes, Susan Kontos, and Marybeth Shinn, *The Study of Children in Family Child Care and Relative Care* (New York: The Families and Work Institute, 1994); The Cost, Quality and Child Outcomes Team, *Cost, Quality and Child Outcomes in Child Care Centers* (Denver: Department of Economics, University of Colorado at Denver, 1995).

32. Herbert M. Kliebard, *The Struggle for the American Curriculum, 1893-1958* (New York: Routledge, 1986).

33. Hamilton Cravens, "Child-Saving in the Age of Professionalism, 1915-1930," *American Childhood: A Research Guide and Historical Handbook*, eds. Joseph M. Hawes and N. Ray Hiner (Westport, CT: Greenwood Press, 1985), pp. 415-488; Hamilton Cravens, *Before Head Start*.

34. Cravens, "Child Saving in the Age of Professionalism," p. 417.

35. Jonathan G. Silin, "On Becoming Knowledgeable Professionals," *Professionalism and the Early Childhood Practitioner*, p. 119.

36. Cravens, *Before Head Start*, p. 170.

37. John E. Anderson, "The Theory of Early Childhood Education," *Early Childhood Education*, Forty-sixth Yearbook of the National Society for the Study of Education, Part II, ed. The Society's Committee (Chicago: National Society for the Study of Education, 1947), p. 74.

38. Lilian G. Katz, "Pedagogical Issues in Early Childhood Education," *The Care and Education of America's Young Children*, pp. 70-100.

39. Hill, "Some Conservative and Progressive Phases of Kindergarten Education," p. 61.

40. Anderson, "The Theory of Child Development," p. 88.

41. Anderson, Ibid., p. 91.

42. Irving E. Sigel, "Developmental Theory and Preschool Education: Issues, Problems and Implications," *Early Childhood Education*, Seventy-first Yearbook of the National Society for the Study of Education, Part II, ed. Ira J. Gordon (Chicago: National Society for the Study of Education, 1972), p. 13.

43. David Elkind, "Developmentally Appropriate Practice: A Case Study of Educational Inertia," *The Care and Education of America's Young Children*, p. 8.

44. Katz, "Pedagogical Issues," p. 61. Italics in original.

45. William Kessen, "A Developmentalist's Reflection," *Children in Time and Place: Developmental and Historical Insights*, eds. Glen H. Elder, Jr., John Modell, and Ross D. Parke (Cambridge, MA: Cambridge University Press, 1993), p. 226.

46. Erica Burman, *Deconstructing Developmental Psychology* (New York: Routledge, 1994), p. 7.

47. Emily Cahan, Jay Mechling, Brian Sutton-Smith and Sheldon H. White, "The Elusive Historical Child: Ways of Knowing the Child of History and Psychology," *Children in Time and Place*, p. 192.

48. Brian Vandenberg, "Is Development an Anachronism?" (paper presented at the biennial meeting of the Society for Research in Child Development, New Orleans, LA, 1993); William Kessen, *The Rise and Fall of Development, 1986 Heinz Werner Lecture Series*, vol. XV (Worcester, MA: Clark University Press, 1990).

49. Similar concerns have surfaced regarding the application of child development knowledge to parent education programs, a topic addressed frequently in the NSSE volumes under review. See, for example, Douglas R. Powell, "Parents, Pluralism, and the NAEYC Statement on Developmentally Appropriate Practice," *Diversity and Developmentally Appropriate Practices: Challenges for Early Childhood Education*, eds. Bruce L. Mallory and Rebecca S. New (New York: Teachers College Press, 1994), pp. 166-182.

50. Valerie Polokov, "Deconstructing Development," *Journal of Education* 171 (1989), p. 78.

51. Martin Haberman, "What Knowledge Is of Most Worth to Teachers of Young Children," *Early Child Development and Care* 38 (1988), p. 37.

52. See Goffin, *Early Childhood Education and Curriculum Models*.

53. Valora Washington and J. D. Andrews, eds. *Children of 2010* (Washington, DC: Children of 2010, 1998).

54. Lilian G. Katz, "Child Development Knowledge and Teacher Preparation: Confronting Assumptions," *Early Childhood Research Quarterly* 11, no.2 (1996), pp. 139-140.

55. For further discussion, see Stacie G. Goffin, ed., "Child Development Knowledge and Early Childhood Teacher Preparation: Assessing the Relationship—A Special Collection," *Early Childhood Research Quarterly* 11, no. 2 (1996), pp. 117-183; Mary Larner, "Parents' Perspectives on Quality Early Care and Education," *Reinventing Early Care and Education: A Vision for a Quality System*, eds. Sharon L. Kagan and Nancy E. Cohen (San Francisco: Jossey-Bass, 1996), pp. 21-42; Bruce L. Mallory and Rebecca S. New, eds., *Diversity and Developmentally Appropriate Practices: Challenges for Early Childhood Education* (New York: Teachers College Press, 1994); Deborah A. Phillips, "Reframing the Quality Issue," *Reinventing Early Care and Education: A Vision for a Quality System*, eds. Sharon L. Kagan and Nancy E. Cohen (San Francisco: Jossey-Bass, 1996), pp. 43-64; Caroline Zinsser, *Over a Barrel: Working Mothers Talk About Child Care* (New York: The Center for Public Policy Research, 1987); Susan D. Holloway and Bruce Fuller,

"Families and Child Care: Divergent Viewpoints," The Silent Crisis in U.S. Child Care." *The Annals of the American Academy of Political and Social Science* 563, ed. Suzanne W. Helburn (May 1999), pp. 98-115.

56. Martin Woodhead, "In Search of a Rainbow: Pathways to Quality in Large-Scale Programmes for Young Disadvantaged Children," *Early Childhood Development: Practice and Reflections* No. 10 (The Hague: Bernard van Leer Foundation, 1996), p. 8; see also Peter Moss, "Defining Quality, Values, Stakeholders and Processes," *Valuing Quality in Early Childhood Services: New Approaches to Defining Quality*, eds. Peter Moss and Alan Pence (New York: Teachers College Press, 1994), pp. 1-9.

57. Shirley Kessler, "Alternative perspectives on early childhood education," *Early Childhood Research Quarterly* 6, no. 2 (1991), pp. 183-197; Sally Lubeck, "The Politics of Developmentally Appropriate Practice: Exploring Issues of Culture, Class, and Curriculum," *Diversity and Developmentally Appropriate Practices*, pp. 17-43; Jonathan G. Silin, *Sex, Death and the Education of Children: Our Passion for Ignorance in the Age of AIDS* (New York: Teachers College Press, 1995); Rebecca S. New, "An Integrated Early Childhood Curriculum: Moving from the What and the How to the Why," *The Early Childhood Curriculum: Current Findings in Theory and Practice*, 3rd ed., ed. Carol Seefeldt (New York: Teachers College Press, 1999), pp. 265-287; Jessica Ball and Alan R. Pence, "Beyond Developmentally Appropriate Practice: Developing Community and Culturally Appropriate Practice," *Young Children* 54, no. 2 (1999), pp. 46-50.

58. Bredekamp, "Redeveloping Early Childhood Education."

59. Jerome Bruner, *Acts of Meaning* (Cambridge, MA: Harvard University Press, 1990); Gordon W. Allport, "The Fruits of Eclecticism—Bitter or Sweet," *Psychologla* 7 (1964), pp. 1-14; Egon G. Guba, "Relativism," *Curriculum Theory* 22, no. 1 (1992), pp. 17-23; Woodhead, *In Search of the Rainbow*.

60. Margret Lampert, "How Do Teachers Manage to Teach: Perspectives on Problems in Practice," *Harvard Educational Review* 62 (1985), pp. 178-194; Larry Cuban, "Managing Dilemmas While Building Professional Communities," *Educational Researcher* 21 (1992), pp. 4-11.

61. See, for example, Galinsky, Howes, Kontos, and Shinn, *The Study of Children in Family Child Care and Relative Care*; The Cost, Quality and Child Outcomes Team, *Cost, Quality and Child Outcomes in Child Care Centers*.

62. Goodykoontz, Davis, and Gabbard, "Recent History and Present Status of Education," pp. 51-54.

63. Beatty, *Preschool Education in America*; Beatty, "Vocation from on High"; Barbara Finkelstein, "Revolt Against Selfishness"; Elly Singer, *Child Care and the Psychology of Development*. For the impact of this relationship on the definition of the mother's role, see Singer, *Child Care and the Psychology of Development*; Nancy Pottishman Weiss, "Mother, the Invention of Necessity: Dr. Benjamin Spock's Baby and Child Care," *Growing Up In America: Children in Historical Perspective*, eds. N. Ray Hiner and Joseph M. Hawes (Urbana, IL and Chicago: University of Illinois Press, 1985), pp. 283-303; Michel, *Children's Interests/Mothers' Rights*.

64. Finkelstein, "The Challenge of Professionalism," p. 20.

65. Millie C. Almy and Agnes Synder, "The Staff and Its Preparation," *Early Childhood Education*, p. 234.

66. Bettye M. Caldwell, "Continuity in the Early Years: Transitions Between Grades and Systems," *The Care and Education of America's Young Children: Obstacles and Opportunities*, ed. Sharon Lynn Kagan, p. 84.

67. Kagan, "Excellence in Early Childhood Education," p. 237.

CHAPTER VI

A Century of NSSE Publications on Reading

RICHARD L. VENEZKY

Across its first century of existence (or nearly that span of time, from 1903 until 2000), the National Society for the Study of Education (NSSE) issued ten complete volumes on reading, nineteen chapters entirely focused on reading in other volumes, and seven additional chapters that at least in part dealt with this same subject. Supplementing this attention to reading were frequent references, descriptions, and explanations that appeared in volumes on curriculum, measurement, textbooks, the high school, and, of course, the language arts. Viewed from one perspective, this assortment of volumes, chapters, and chapter fragments offers an amazing range of issues, treatments, and opinions about reading and reading instruction. Some of these continue to speak imaginatively to issues prominent today and merit republication; others served their time well but have been superseded or outdated. And others are best left in the musty obscurity of university archives and the occasional used book store.

From another perspective, however, these materials can be read as primary source materials for the history of the NSSE, its selection processes, and the people who dominated the reading committees for almost half of the NSSE's existence. This is a more difficult story to compose, given the limited form of evidence, but it is an important one for helping the NSSE select a viable future. This chapter is an attempt to present both of these perspectives, based upon an analysis of the NSSE treatment of reading, from Volume 1 in 1902 until Volume 99, issued at the beginning of the year 2000. Because of the heavy emphasis on reading throughout the history of the NSSE, I have excluded related language arts topics: spelling, writing, and general language arts. These deserve treatment also, but are beyond the capacity of the present chapter. Although this review covers almost one hundred years of publication, the concerns of this chapter are molded more by current

Richard Venezky is Professor of Education Studies in the School of Education, University of Delaware.

issues in research and instruction on reading than by those of the times revisited. This is not to fall into the convenient trap of evaluating the past with the values and attitudes of the present but instead to use the present to select focal points from the vast smorgasbord of ideas that have been explored in almost one-hundred volumes. The primary concerns here are what was said, who did the saying, what was not said, and what this tapestry of inclusion and exclusion reveals about the NSSE, reading research, and reading instruction at different points in time. My intention is to allow the volumes to speak for themselves, not by endless quotations but by a mix of shorter quotations and longer summaries, and then to add reflections to this information.

Writers on the history of schooling, like painters and novelists, are susceptible to the lure of the pastoral dream. Both Europeans and Americans in the nineteenth century viewed the untouched wilderness of North America as an "oasis of harmony and joy,"[1] dappled with "little nooks of still water" that protected us from the swift stream of modern, industrial life.[2] In the same way, writers about our educational past have tended to glorify a time long gone, when teachers were pure and craft-wise, schools small and personal, and students eager to learn and to match their physical growth with intellectual development. For reading, the pastoral dream manifests itself in the glorification of knowledge of the past, a belief that there truly is no new idea under the sun, that our forebears knew everything we know now and perhaps more. The briefest reference to knowledge in the head, for example, is taken as evidence of an early discovery of the importance of background knowledge for comprehension.

Without attempting to examine who knew what when and how well, I will attempt to explain what was known in the past and where it fit into the total scheme of ideas applied to reading research and practice. If this leads to a conclusion that something believed to have been discovered only yesterday was in fact known farther back in time, so be it. I will resist, however, the temptation to assume full knowledge from partial statement.

A second issue is what to attend to across these ten volumes, nineteen chapters, and innumerable fragments. Many topics in the world of reading are visited at least once, and some are treated to repeated visits. My strategy, as explained earlier, is to use the present to filter the past, so I will focus on only a few issues, chief among which will be silent reading, content area reading, phonics, and how reading is defined. These touch upon major areas of current concern and, in addition, illustrate how the NSSE presented reading over the years.

The Evidence

The ten volumes devoted totally to reading span the period 1921 to 1998, beginning with a collection of papers on silent reading (Twentieth, Part II) and ending with the *Reading-Writing Connection* (Ninety-seventh, Part II). In between are several volumes covering the entire field of reading, or nearly so (Twenty-fourth, Part I; Thirty-sixth, Part I; Sixtieth, Part I; Sixty-seventh, Part II; Eighty-third, Part I), and several that focus on specific ages or grades: elementary school (Forty-eighth, Part II), high school and college (Forty-seventh, Part II), and adults (Fifty-fifth, Part II). As with present-day volumes, each of these was developed by a committee, sometimes referred to as The Society's Committee on Reading, but more often labeled according to the content of the specific volume, e.g., The Society's Committee on Adult Reading (Fifty-fifth, Part II). Committees prepared the Year-book proposals, assigned editors, and agreed on chapter outlines. Authorship was then allocated across committee members and often other scholars, who were listed in the volume's introductory pages as "Associated Contributors."

Among the nineteen chapters on reading are an extremely wide variety of topics. The first two were published in 1915 (Fourteenth, Part I) and focused on issues in selecting words for standard vocabulary tests and standards in rates of reading. Both of these chapters appeared in a volume titled *Minimum Essentials in Elementary School Subjects*. The most recent appeared in 1977 (Seventy-sixth, Part I). Chapters on reading were also included in such volumes as *Standards and Tests for the Measurement of the Efficiency of Schools and Schools Systems* (Fifteenth, Part I), *Minimum Essentials in Elementary School Subjects* (Sixteenth, Part I), *New Materials of Instruction* (Nineteenth, Part I; Twentieth, Part I), along with dozens of others.

The Authors and Their Audiences

Attached to Volume 1, Part I, was a Proposed Plan of Work, in which a desire for "strong scientific papers was expressed."[3] The source of such works was also specified. "Age, experience, and ripe study by those who have had opportunity for specialization can alone furnish the best products."[4] These words were probably drafted by Nicholas Murray Butler of Columbia University, president of the NSSE Executive Committee in 1902, with the cooperation of Charles A. McMurry, the Society's secretary-treasurer and yearbook editor for the Herbart

Society, from which the NSSE sprang. For reading, especially if reading practice was the central concern, few researchers prior to the 1930s qualified according to the "age, experience, and ripe study" criteria. One exception was William S. Gray, who studied under Edward Thorndike at Teachers College and who developed one of the first standardized reading tests in the U.S. Gray joined the University of Chicago faculty in 1914 and quickly rose from assistant in education to instructor (1915), to assistant professor and dean of the College of Education (1917), to associate professor (1918), and then to professor (1921). Starting with a single chapter in the Sixteenth Yearbook, Part I, Gray became the dominant specialist in reading for the NSSE for almost forty-five years. He chaired the majority of the Yearbook committees on reading during that period and contributed to at least eleven different volumes.

Gray was thirty-one years old when he wrote his first chapter for an NSSE Yearbook, and he died just before the publication of his last in 1961 (Sixtieth, Part I). According to one of his biographers, Gray published 407 books, book chapters, and articles. In addition, he was president of the American Educational Research Association (1932-33) and first president of the International Reading Association (1956), as well as a co-author of the "Dick and Jane" reading series, which was the most popular in American schooling history except perhaps for the McGuffey Readers.[5] After Gray died, his replacement at the University of Chicago, Helen M. Robinson, became the dominant writer for the NSSE on reading, but her reign was far shorter than Gray's had been. She was a member of the Yearbook Committee for the Sixtieth, Part I, *Development in and through Reading*, and she chaired the Society's Committee on Reading for the Sixty-seventh Yearbook, Part II, *Innovation and Change in Reading Instruction*, but retired from teaching and from most scholarly work in the 1970s.

No other person reached the level of productivity for NSSE that Gray did, yet other nationally renowned scholars in reading were tapped for NSSE chapters, including Gray's University of Chicago colleagues, Guy Thomas Buswell and Charles Hubbard Judd. Among the distinguished scholars of reading who authored NSSE chapters on reading and served on Yearbook committees prior to the last decade were Arthur I. Gates of Teachers College, Ernest Horn of the University of Iowa, David H. Russell of the University of California-Berkeley, and Jeanne Chall of Harvard University. Of this group, Horn was the closest to Gray in involvement in the NSSE. He served on the NSSE Board of Directors in the 1940s, chaired the Yearbook Committee on

Silent Reading (Twentieth, Part II), and served on the National Commission on Reading (Twenty-fourth, Part I), as well as on various other Yearbook committees up to and including the Forty-eighth, Part II, *Reading in the Elementary School*. Horn also contributed at least one chapter on spelling (Eighteenth, Part II).

Gray and Horn were the team captains for reading from the late teens until the late 1940s, with a revolving cast of core team members that included Gerald A. Yoakum and S. A. Courtis in the 1920s, Gates and Yoakum in the 1930s, and Gates and Buswell in the 1940s. With few exceptions, the authors of the reading articles were drawn from schools of education. Psychologists, psychometricians, linguists, and the like were largely ignored by the NSSE reading committees. The exceptions were a few professors of English who also worked in English education and a sprinkling of others, such as Lester E. Asheim, dean of the Graduate Library School at the University of Chicago, who contributed an article "What Do Adults Read?" to the volume *Adult Reading* (Fifty-fifth, Part II).

Totally absent are the best known psychologists who published leading textbooks on reading: Edmund Burke Huey, *The Psychology and Pedagogy of Reading* (1908), Irving H. Anderson and Walter F. Dearborn, *The Psychology of Teaching Reading* (1952), and Eleanor J. Gibson and Harry Levin, *The Psychology of Reading* (1975), to name a few.[6]

Part of the dominance of education faculty authors derived from the practical direction of NSSE reading volumes, at least until *Becoming Readers in a Complex Society* (Eighty-third, Part I). The earlier volumes, directed to teachers and administrators, often contained lesson plans. The desire of the NSSE founders for "strong scientific papers" gave way within a few decades to instructional guides and other practical materials. The Nineteenth Yearbook, Part I, for example, presented "Reading Exercises Based on Children's Experiences," supplied by Miss Abbie A. Atwood, a teacher in Janesville, Wisconsin, as well as exercises for children and adults in non-English speaking families supplied by Miss Clara L. Chitson of School No. 18 in Rochester, NY. The latter exercises were mostly sequences of sentences, such as "Baby sleeps in a large clothes basket," and "I keep the basket clean." Concerns with the "making of English the common language of America" and with Americanization were strongly expressed.[7]

Similarly, the Second Report of the Society's Committee on *New Materials of Instruction*, Twentieth, Part I, was primarily instructional materials, consisting of 285 projects, "based upon the genuine interests of children" and submitted by teachers.[8] The report mentioned no reading skills, and made no attempt to connect the instructional approaches to research results. More materials for teaching reading were offered in the *Report of the Society's Committee on Silent Reading*, Twentieth, Part II and in the *Report of the National Committee on Reading*, Twenty-fourth, Part I, although the latter two were primarily academic reports with a few chapters on materials. The Twenty-fourth Yearbook, although academic in nature, was addressed to teachers and school administrators and was one of the most popular reports issued by the NSSE prior to the last decades. According to the introduction to the Thirty-sixth, Part I, the Society distributed more than 30,000 copies of it by its tenth birthday.[9]

The Thirty-sixth, Part I, lists among its purposes to present information in non-technical terms for teachers and schools officials, as does the Forty-seventh, Part II, *Reading in the High School and College*. The Editor's preface to *Reading in the Elementary School*, Forty-eighth, Part II, described the Yearbook as having an "emphasis on practical principles and procedures which are in harmony with the results of accredited research in recent years."[10] For this reason, the Yearbook was "immediately serviceable to the classroom teacher."[11] Arthur I. Gates, chairman of the Yearbook Committee for the Forty-eighth, Part II, defined the purpose of this Yearbook as follows: "This yearbook has been prepared as a guide to teachers and school officers in their efforts to improve reading in the elementary school."[12]

By the Sixtieth, Part I, *Development in and through Reading*, a slightly more research-oriented audience was addressed: "It was agreed that the primary aim of this yearbook would be to describe well-designed reading programs for all elementary- and secondary-school pupils and to promote the extension of reading instruction in colleges and in organized programs of adult education."[13] The Yearbook discussed materials of instruction, but in a scholarly way, with no exercises given for teachers' direct use, as was done in the earlier reading volumes.

A switch in audiences came with *Innovation and Change in Reading Instruction*, Sixty-seventh, Part II. The audience was no longer defined as teachers and school officials. In fact, this Yearbook did not directly designate an audience but the nature of the chapters made clear that researchers, college- and university-level faculty, and more technical practitioners were the assumed readers. The Chair of the Yearbook Committee, Helen M. Robinson of the University of Chicago, wrote in the Introduction, "Available research has been surveyed, and numerous references are offered to the reader."[14] Chapter 1 summarized theories of reading and current reading models. Another reviewed "the contributions of psychologists, neurologists, and the staff members of medical centers to the understanding of reading disability."[15] Even a chapter on evaluating research was included. The remaining two reading volumes (Eighty-third, Part I; Ninety-seventh, Part II) also were directed at scholars, the latter having a statement by the co-editors, both university faculty, that starts, "For readers, who, like the two of us, claim literacy studies as a specialization. . . ."[16]

The transition from directly addressing teachers with instructional procedures to addressing researchers and teacher trainers came with the rise of cognitive psychology in academia and may have resulted directly from the groundswell of interest that had developed by the middle 1960s in understanding mental processes during reading. Authors as far back as the teens gave lip service to basing practice on research, yet the rapid expansion of public schooling and the lack of significant funding for educational research until the 1950s kept most education faculty busy preparing teachers and administrators, with little time or support for research.

This switch could also indicate a maturing of a field that was by the mid 1960s so large and so broad that a small group of senior scholars could no longer exert effective control over school programs. That is, one working hypothesis is that the men and women who wrote the reading chapters and edited the reading volumes for the NSSE from the late teens until perhaps the 1960s used the NSSE as part of a campaign to control the school reading curriculum. Almost all major writers from this period—Gray, Gates, Durrell, Yoakum, Horn, Betts, et al. —were authors of commercial reading and spelling materials. Each had openly declared a commercial interest in the instructional methods and materials that teachers adopted, and even if they could in their own minds separate their financial interests from their professional ones, they nevertheless spent considerable time and effort preparing reading teachers and school administrators to behave in prescribed ways. Many of the authors of NSSE chapters since the 1960s have also developed reading materials, yet the chapters on reading written by these people have tended to be directed at other scholars and thus less open to criticism of commercial bias.

Reading Defined

How reading is defined reveals something about both the state of research into this process and the focus of instructional practices.

Authors at the beginning of this century viewed reading as a thought-getting process. "The grasp of thought through the written characters is reading," declared a manual for teachers published in 1903.[17] This did not eliminate an emphasis on oral reading at this same time nor did it ensure that strategies for getting meaning from print would be taught. It did, however, show that translation from printed symbols to sound was not sufficient to qualify as reading. The first discussion of reading as a process in the NSSE volumes occurred in the *Report of the National Committee on Reading*, Twenty-fourth, Part I. This report distinguished both intensive and extensive reading and work-type and recreational reading.

Intensive-extensive refers to the difference between deep, careful reading (and rereading) of a small number of texts (intensive) and the more moderate reading of a wide variety of works (extensive). The distinction between work-type reading and recreational reading has even greater importance for instruction, however, because of the overemphasis in most reading programs over the past 150 years on reading of narrative fiction. In discussing the relation of reading to content subjects, the Committee for the Twenty-fourth Yearbook, Part I wrote, "The reading done in the so-called 'reading period' has been largely narrative. Yet studies have demonstrated that the pupil who reads narrative material quite well may read very poorly when the passages tell the condition of an arithmetic problem or give directions to be followed in the study of grammar."[18]

This work-type versus recreational distinction carries implications for instruction of both types in that teaching literature as work-type reading may lead to as negative a result as teaching work-type reading as recreational. A study referenced by the Committee found that students developed negative attitudes toward reading literature as a result of the literature teaching in their schools.[19] The Yearbook authors argued for teaching literature as recreational reading, not as study and work.

Teaching Reading, A Second Report, Thirty-sixth, Part I, defined a good reader as one who "recognizes essential facts or ideas presented, reflects on their significance, evaluates them critically, discovers relationships between them, and clarifies his understanding of the ideas apprehended."[20] Work-type and recreational reading are still recognized as important classifications, but the emphasis in reading shifted from broad classifications of types to more specific classifications of thought processes. A chapter in the Forty-fifth Yearbook, Part I, *The Measurement of Understanding*, adopted a communication perspective and classified reading with listening as receptive skills while writing and speaking were classed as expressive skills. The justification given for this classification is, "Each presents somewhat different problems in the analysis and appraisal of meanings."[21]

This expressive-receptive contrast should be compared to the current effort to connect reading to writing, which was the subject of the Ninety-seventh Yearbook, Part II, *The Reading-Writing Connection*. The expressive-receptive contrast is based upon overlap of skills required for gaining (or generating) meaning, as defined from an information-processing perspective. The reading-writing connection, in contrast, derives more from a literary perspective that focuses on the author-audience connection. For instruction, the connection between reading and listening leads to an emphasis on interpretive skills while that between reading and writing leads more directly to an emphasis on creative processes. From the former come issues of text interpretation; from the latter comes assessment of the intentions of the author (or the author's assessment of an intended audience).

By the Forty-eighth, Part II, *Reading in the Elementary School*, the definition of the Thirty-sixth, Part I, had been recycled, only with a terser vocabulary. Reading was now defined broadly as a "complex organization of patterns of higher mental processes," embracing "all types of thinking, evaluating, judging, imagining, reasoning, and problem-solving."[22] That print was the stimulus for all these processes was assumed from the context, but the print/writing component of reading was of far less concern than were the mental components. Almost twenty years later, defining reading had become problematic. In *Innovation and Change in Reading Instruction*, Sixty-seventh, Part II, Theodore Clymer wrote, "It is the unusual text which devotes much attention to the definition of reading."[23] Clymer also summarized a variety of different definitions and models of reading, varying from a narrow linguistic view that posited reading as "talk written down,"[24] to the Gray model that integrated word perception, comprehension, reaction to what is read, and fusion of new ideas and old.

What is reflected in the various models presented by Clymer is first the important role then assigned to decoding and other word recognition processes—an element rarely present in earlier models—and the skills orientation of the models. Taxonomies of various types of reading skills were common in the research literature by the late 1960s, perhaps influenced by the Benjamin Bloom et al. *Taxonomy of Educational Objectives* (1956).[25] Thomas Barrett, for example, created a taxonomy of both cognitive and affective components of reading comprehension, including literal comprehension, reorganization, inferential comprehension, evaluation, and appreciation.[26]

Attempts at reading definitions from later volumes do not deviate markedly from the ones given by Clymer, whether derived from linguists (Sixty-ninth, Part II) or social constructivist scholarship (Ninety-seventh, Part II). What is missing from the NSSE chapters and volumes is a broader perspective as given in some recent writings on literacy, such as those by Carl Kaestle and Cathy Davidson.[27] Davidson, in particular, argued that true literacy involves active, autonomous engagement with print. *Active* engagement implies an ability to generate messages, as well as to receive them. *Autonomous* engagement implies that the reader not only translates print into a form of language from which he or she can obtain meaning, but also has the propensity and willingness to relate the information to prior knowledge, to compare it to his or her own opinions, and to judge independently the writer's message and intentions. The results of such judgments do not always need to be as momentous as when Martin Luther began to do this with his reading of the Bible, but they should represent a new interpretation with each reading. When Thomas Jefferson said he would prefer newspapers without government over government without newspapers, he assumed the populace was able to read these papers actively and autonomously. [28]

The Subjects Covered

The topics or subjects covered by the chapters and volumes varied across time and across authors. The most extensive coverage was given to instructional methods and materials, as well as to assessment. Remedial reading and disabilities were discussed in at least four Yearbook chapters, beginning with the Thirty-fourth and ending with the Seventy-seventh, Part II. Adult reading has been treated in three Yearbook chapters (Eighteenth, Part I; Thirty-sixth, Part I; and Fifty-fifth, Part II). Much briefer attention has been given to summer gain and loss in reading (Thirty-fourth), library and supplementary reading (Sixteenth, Part I), standard reading rates (Fourteenth, Part I), school survey results (Thirty-seventh, Part II), readiness (Forty-fourth, Part II), teaching reading to non-English speakers (Eighteenth, Part I), research quality (Sixty-seventh, Part II), and time distributions for reading instruction (Fourteenth, Part I). More extensive coverage was given to a few subjects, including similarities and differences between oral and silent reading and content-area reading.

Not covered at all are a group of topics related to research, such as the reading results from the National Assessment of Educational Progress, the National Adult Literacy Survey, and the 1991 International Education Association Reading Survey. No chapter has ever been devoted entirely to methods used for the study of reading, such as explanatory case studies, quasi-experimental methods such as interrupted time series, or hierarchical linear modeling. Speed reading has also been ignored, as have cross-language studies. It is difficult to find even a mention of reading in another country or culture, or in any writing system except English. Other than a few brief sketches (e.g., Forty-seventh, Part II, 28ff), Yearbooks ignored the history of reading instruction, as well as the history of literacy.

SILENT READING

During the first three decades of this century the Yearbooks placed major emphasis on promoting silent reading as a replacement for oral reading. This was a particular campaign of Gray and his University of Chicago colleague, Buswell, and is reflected in numerous chapters devoted to the topic, as well as a full volume, *Report of the Society's Committee on Silent Reading*, Twentieth, Part II. This volume is unusual in that it has a section devoted to submitted research papers, as well as a section containing sample lessons for teaching silent reading. Either due to the success of Gray and his colleague or to changing times and changing attitudes toward reading, silent reading was so enthusiastically embraced that by the Thirty-sixth, Part I, *The Teaching of Reading—A Second Report*, Gray was forced to report, "The large importance attached to silent reading has resulted unfortunately in several related practices and trends that cannot be defended. Among these are the almost exclusive emphasis on silent reading in many schools and a corresponding neglect of oral reading."[29] In the Forty-eighth Yearbook, Part II, *Reading in the Elementary School*, Ernest Horn and James F. Curtis presented an entire chapter on fostering oral reading. Their tracing of the history of silent reading targeted Buswell as the one who over-emphasized the process, claiming that oral reading in the primary grades interferes with the development of silent reading.

Buswell not only did eye-movement studies of oral and silent reading, from which his claims for the superiority of silent reading originated, but also co-authored a series of readers, *The Silent Reading Hour*, for teaching silent reading.[30] In the introduction to the first reader of this series, Buswell reproduced one of his eye-movement charts and explained, "Scientific investigations have shown that only

by silent reading can such rapid and rhythmical control of eye-move-
ments . . . be secured. The superiority of the silent-reading process is
now fully established."[31] The teacher was also warned, "The value of
this book as an instrument for teaching silent reading will be seriously
impaired if the child is allowed to read from it orally."[32]

Buswell did condone the teaching of oral reading in the primary
grades, especially for the initial development of a reading vocabulary,
but others, extending Buswell's argument to its illogical conclusion,
advocated teaching silent reading from the beginning. Two such persons were Emma Watkins, who published *How to Teach Silent Reading
to Beginners*,[33] and James E. McDade, a former school official from
Chicago, who developed and tested a method for teaching beginning
reading silently.[34] Irving H. Anderson and Walter F. Dearborn devote
considerable space to the oral-silent controversy and offer alternative
explanations for Buswell's experimental results.[35] Although NSSE volumes carried the silent-reading crusade into the 1930s, apparently the
enthusiasm among researchers for the issue died by the end of the
1920s. According to Nila B. Smith, "During the early part of the
period [1924-1935] many studies were reported on the subject of silent
reading, but by the latter part, investigators showed little interest in
this subject."[36]

CONTENT-AREA READING

One of the great mysteries of the U.S. school curriculum is why the
teaching of reading is so over-weighted toward literature at the expense
of every other type of reading. In the early Colonial period teaching
reading was bound with religious indoctrination. *The New England
Primer* and even the one-page hornbook contained heavy doses of religion: the Creed, the Lord's Prayer, catechisms, and, where space
allowed, a homily or two. Up to the Civil War the Bible was an ever-
present text for reading instruction once the primer was completed.[37]
By the time the thirteen colonies combined into an independent
nation, nationalism and good character had become the central themes
of the reading texts, particularly for beginners. But over the first three
decades of nationhood, literature, speeches, and poetry became the
fodder of reading development, with British authors far outnumbering
American ones.

By the middle of the nineteenth century American writers were as
evident in the reading texts as British ones were, and by the end of the
century Americans were in the majority. Without question, though, by
1900 learning to read meant learning to read literature, and this biased

interpretation of reading has continued uninterrupted to the present day. The Society's Committee on Reading, in introducing its Forty-seventh Yearbook, Part II, *Reading in the High School and College*, claimed that around 1900 the primary aims of reading instruction were "appreciation and interest in literature" and "cultivating expressive oral reading."[38] "Getting the thought from the printed page" was only then becoming a stated objective of formal reading instruction. It was assumed, however, that general reading habits and interests transferred from one subject to another.

From the 1920s until the late 1940s the NSSE Yearbooks gave significant attention to content-area reading. The Twentieth, Part I, contained strong statements in favor of using non-fiction materials for early lessons in reading, and the *Report of the National Commission on Reading*, Twenty-fourth, Part I, was probably the strongest single report ever issued in this country on the necessity for and the methods of teaching content-area reading. Among other suggestions, the authors offered, "There is an urgent need for more books of the non-literary type, which can be read by pupils of [grades two and three]."[39] Similarly, the Thirty-sixth, Part I, targeted content-area reading as the "greatest opportunity for progress in teaching reading during the next decade."[40] Drawing on the Twenty-fourth, Part I, this Yearbook also described specific ideas for teaching content-area reading. The Forty-seventh, Part II, also stressed content-area reading, devoting a full chapter, plus parts of other chapters, to it.

However, by the 1950s interest in content-area reading was declining. Wilma Longstreet, author of "The School's Curriculum," for the Seventy-second, Part II, *The Elementary School in the United States*, pointed out that in the 1960s there was a push for a kindergarten through twelfth-grade language arts curriculum with literature as the core. And E. Margaret Early, author of "Reading in the Secondary School," for the Seventy-sixth, Part I, stated that the focus of reading at that level was clearly on reading literature. Some relief appeared in the Eighty-third, Part I, *Becoming Readers in a Complex Society*, where a full chapter was devoted to contrasting reading strategies for expository and literary text types. However, the focused attention the Twenty-fourth, Part I, gave to content-area reading has never returned.

The causes of this literary domination have varied over time. In the nineteenth century, when oral reading dominated, the choice of reading selections was as much driven by a desire to have interesting and varied pieces for reading aloud to parents, school inspectors, and visitors as it was by any other cause. By the time silent reading replaced oral reading as the dominant mode of school reading, university-based academics controlled the school curriculum through the Committee of Ten, the Committee of Fifteen, and various professional organizations. Nicholas Murray Butler of Columbia University and Charles Eliot of Harvard were among those committee members who could see no valid content except literature for school readers. Eliot went even further, calling the existing readers "ineffable trash," insisting that all school reading be from full-length novels.[41]

In part, the emphasis on literature was an attempt at cultural development. The United States, by the beginning of the twentieth century, was a dominant world power in finance, trade, military capacity, and industry. Where it was not superior was in cultural spheres: art, music, dance, architecture, and literature. Emphasizing cultural matters in school, it was thought, might lead to a more cultured citizenship that could compete with their European peers for world dominance. At a minimum, literature was viewed as a catalyst for cultural regeneration, "one of the agencies through which culturally accepted images of behavior, social and moral standards of behavior . . . are transmitted to the new generation."[42]

The continued dominance of literature, particularly in the elementary reading curriculum, is reinforced by the integrated kindergarten through twelfth-grade language arts curriculum in which reading at the lower elementary level merges into literature in the middle school. The consequences are that many children, but especially those at risk for reading failure, do not acquire the reading strategies they need for comprehending science, mathematics, and social studies textbooks. They also do not learn to write these genres.

PHONICS

Throughout nearly one-hundred years of Yearbooks, almost every major area of reading instruction has been covered: readiness, introductory reading, children's literature, vocabulary, formal and informal assessment, content-area reading, adult reading, and more. The one topic of importance that has never received significant attention in the Yearbooks is phonics. No chapter ever defined what phonics is or is not, what role it plays in learning to read or in reading failure, or how to teach it. The Yearbooks are conspicuous for their avoidance of any serious treatment of this topic.

Part but not all of the blame for this absence could be attributed to Gray's low opinion of the role that phonics should play in reading instruction. In a chapter entitled "Principles of Method in Teaching

Reading, as Derived from Scientific Investigations," written for the Eighteenth, Part II, Gray claimed, "The word should be accepted as the unit of recognition at the outset and analysis or phonetic training should be introduced later when it is needed to keep the word units clear."[43] What Gray apparently meant was that phonics was useful only when too many words are introduced or when words become complicated. He did note, however, that some progressive schools introduced phonics at the end of the second month of grade one and that any phonics-teaching method could be effective.

Two years later, W. W. Theisen, writing in the *Report of the Society's Committee on Silent Reading*, Twentieth, Part II, found, "The question of phonics or no phonics is perhaps of less importance than those of just what, how much, and for whom."[44] Theisen recommended teaching phonics only to those needing it and then in the skill period, not the regular reading period. According to Theisen, phonics detracted from getting the meaning of a passage. The National Committee on Reading, which Gray chaired, also saw a secondary role for phonics. "If commercial charts are used [for teaching phonics] care must be taken to insure that the phonic training is kept in its proper subordinate place and approached in a truly functional way."[45] Later suggestions in the same volume stressed repeatedly that a sight-word vocabulary should be taught before phonics was introduced; then an analytic approach should be used.

Prior to the 1970s the only chapter in which a knowledge of orthography was suggested for teachers was one on teaching spelling, written by Horn in the Thirty-seventh, Part II. "A knowledge of the principles of orthography, of that part of phonetics that pertains to the relation between sounds and printed symbols, and of the history of the language is especially important."[46] No such statement has ever appeared for reading, however.

Bloomfield, the father of structural linguistics in the U.S., wrote on the teaching of reading, emphasizing letter-sound correspondences. He also drafted a set of materials that he used to teach one of his children to read.[47] For many, Bloomfield represented the most knowledgeable advocate of phonics, particularly in the 1940s, and although he did not write for the Yearbooks, Ernest Horn and James F. Curtis, mentioned him in a chapter in the Forty-eighth, Part II, "Improvement of Oral Reading." In this same yearbook, Hildreth wrote about linguistic maturation, mentioning especially "The delight which children take in rhymes," which she claimed "promotes their discrimination of word sounds."[48] Phonics, however, was not mentioned as a strategy for teaching reading in grade one. "Sounding" was given as one of many word recognition strategies for grades two and three, but with a warning: "Slow children, however, should not have much work in phonics because they are unable to benefit much from it."[49] Even average readers needed to be protected from phonics, according to Hildreth, at least until they reached a mental age of seven.

When Rudolph Flesch's *Why Johnny Can't Read* (1955) appeared, most reading "experts" either attacked it for its extremism or ignored it.[50] The Yearbooks, for the most part, engaged in the same tactics. Paul Witty, for example, writing the opening chapter in the Sixtieth, Part I, *Development in and through Reading*, disposed of Flesch with the accusation, "Some writers have not only alleged a specific cause of reading problems but have also proposed simple panaceas. One of the most frequently recommended correctives is the initiation of a specific form of phonetic instruction."[51] Here, as in other places, there is a hint that, at that time, the mere mention of the word "phonetics" was sufficient to invoke hissing from the reading establishment. A later chapter (Ch. VI) by Emmett A. Betts and Ralph C. Preston in the same volume gave a slightly more even-handed mention of Flesch but cited only objectionable statements from his text.

Also typical of how the reading establishment treated phonics then was the chapter in the Sixtieth, Part I, "The Role of Teacher Education" by Gray, the last yearbook chapter that he would write. (Gray died before the Sixtieth Yearbook went to press.) Gray's presentation of the knowledge and skills that teachers needed for teaching reading was based on the replies he received from thirty-five reading specialists and school leaders. He made no mention of knowledge of orthography, or phonics, or any related topic for either pre-service or in-service education.

However, not all writers of this period ignored or rejected phonics. In total contrast to these treatments was an article by Robert C. Pooley of the University of Wisconsin, also in the Sixtieth, Part I, that asserted, "Not a reputable system of teaching reading exists today that does not give extensive attention to phonetic training throughout the entire primary and middle grades."[52] Pooley, who was identified with language arts teaching but not with the reading establishment, was clearly a lone voice. He went on to say, "Phonics of the old-fashioned type has given way to new phonetic systems that teach sounds but not 'phonetics.'"[53]

To demonstrate how divided on this topic the reading community was by that time, a chapter in the Sixtieth by Donald D. Durrell and

Alice K. Nicholson, "Preschool and Kindergarten Experience," sounded like a page from the recent National Academy of Sciences report on reading. "One of the essentials for progress in reading is that the child be able to notice separate sounds in spoken words. If he cannot do this, he will be unable to relate the sounds to the printed letters."[54] The authors noted that while speech was usually based upon syllables, sounds within syllables defined the units of phonetic writing. According to these authors, most children required direct instruction in letter-sound relations.

By the time of the Sixty-seventh Yearbook, Part II, *Innovation and Change in Reading Instruction*, it was difficult to ignore phonics totally. The opening chapter of this volume, "What Is Reading?," by Theodore Clymer, was mainly concerned with the decoding versus meaning-getting controversy. Extremist views, mostly those by people who favored phonics instruction, were pointed out, but the tone was far more neutral than earlier Yearbooks' treatment of phonics.

The over-reaction to phonics by the reading establishment was not without some justification. Many of those who favored a strong emphasis on phonics knew little about either the reading process or about reading instruction. Typical of this class of writing was a chapter, "Linguistics and Reading," in the Sixty-ninth, Part I, *Linguistics in School Programs*, by Sumner and Josephine Ives. The authors attributed to "persons with linguistic training" this opinion: "The first step in the process of reading is decoding the written message—that is, of reconstructing speech from written symbols. One understands the meaning only after decoding the symbols."[55] With this mistaken view as a base, the writers then continued, "Hence, attention to meaning should be deferred until instruction in this decoding has been well started."[56]

In spite of these linguistic misconceptions, Jeanne S. Chall and Sue S. Conrad were able to report in the Eighty-third, Part I, *Becoming Readers in a Complex Society*, "Basal readers published during the 1970s and 1980s contain stronger phonics programs . . . than in comparable texts published during the 1950s and 1960s."[57] Nevertheless, a serious treatment by the NSSE of phonics remains to appear, and we are left with little understanding of why the reading establishment appears still to be hostile to phonics instruction.

What Does All This Mean?

Reading has played a highly visible role in the NSSE publication programs. Committees were appointed, volumes were developed on the topic, and many extra chapters on reading were written for Year-books on more general schooling topics, such as the elementary school, standards and tests, and the scientific movement in education. So what is there to say about all this? What conclusions of value are there for the future of the NSSE?

An outsider, arriving anew at the door of the NSSE establishment and encountering only the reading volumes and chapters, might be puzzled over the purpose of the organization. The constitution and name point directly toward research, yet the majority of the reading chapters have been on instruction, some of it unrelated to any empirical base. For many years the volumes were motivated by interest in instructional methods and materials. More recently, a wider range of issues has appeared, yet the scientific study of reading still seems to be an interloper, a part of the background noise. Serious discussions of the quality of reading research are exceedingly rare, as are discussions of research needs, research training, research funding, and dissemination of research results. What, then, does the second "S" in NSSE mean?

Equally puzzling is the process by which volumes are commissioned. Why were certain topics on reading selected for the last few volumes, yet equally important issues ignored, e.g., the role of phonemic awareness in reading failure, racial/ethnic differences in reading achievement, research and instructional methodology for adult literacy, staff development, assessment of reading ability, and how to teach decoding. Should the NSSE attend to the most pressing issues in classroom practice or to the topics that academically based researchers prefer to work on? If the former, how will issues be selected? And if the latter, how will the NSSE distinguish itself from such publications as *Review of Research in Education* and *Review of Educational Research*?

Opportunities exist now, as they did in the mid-1920s, to publish major reports on reading issued by other organizations. The National Academy of Sciences report on reading and reading failure is one such report.[58] Another is the recently issued final report of the National Panel on Reading, a joint project of the National Institute of Child Health and Human Development and the Department of Education. This report complements the National Academy report in that it probes the scientific merits of research on reading. Just as the NSSE published the *Report of the National Committee on Reading* in 1925, it could consider republishing the above mentioned reports if the sponsoring agencies would agree.

What about the NSSE authors and editors? Should anyone be allowed to assume the dominant position that William S. Gray held for so many years? What encouragement does NSSE now give to Yearbook committees for selecting authors? Are "age, experience, and ripe study" still required? These are a few of the issues that this chapter has stirred up. As the NSSE moves into its second century, it needs to reflect on what it is, where it has come from, and especially where it wants to go.

NOTES

1. Leo Marx, *The Machine in the Garden* (New York: Oxford University Press, 1964), p. 3.

2. Washington Irving, "The Legend of Sleepy Hollow," 1820; cited in *Machine in the Garden*, p. 3.

3. Lucy M. Salmon, ed., "Proposed Plan of Work," *Some Principles in the Teaching of History*, First Yearbook of the National Society for the Study of Education, Part I (Bloomington, IL: Public School Publishing Co., 1902), p. 63.

4. Ibid.

5. John T. Guthrie, ed., *Reading: William S. Gray. A Research Retrospective, 1881-1941* (Newark, DE: International Reading Association, 1984).

6. Edmund B. Huey, *The Psychology and Pedagogy of Reading* (New York: Macmillan, 1908); Irving H. Anderson and Walter F. Dearborn, *The Psychology of Teaching Reading* (New York: The Ronald Press Co., 1954); Eleanor J. Gibson and Harry Levin, *The Psychology of Reading* (Cambridge, MA: MIT Press, 1975); *New Materials of Instruction*, Nineteenth Yearbook of the National Society for the Study of Education, Part I, ed. The Society's Committee (Bloomington, IL: Public School Publishing Company, 1921).

7. Charles F. Towne, "Reading for Non-English-Speaking Adults," *Materials in Instruction*, p. 41.

8. F. J. Kelly, "Introduction and Second Report of the Committee," *Materials in Instruction*, p. vii.

9. Guy M. Whipple, "Introduction," *The Teaching of Reading*, Thirty-sixth Yearbook of the National Society for the Study of Education, Part I, ed. The Society's Committee (Bloomington, IL: Public School Publishing Co., 1937), p. vii.

10. Nelson B. Henry, "Editor's Preface," *Reading in the Elementary School*, Forty-eighth Yearbook of the National Society for the Study of Education, Part II, ed. The Society's Committee (Chicago: National Society for the Study of Education, 1949), p. vi.

11. Ibid.

12. Gates, "Character and Purposes of the Yearbook," Ibid, p. 1.

13. Paul A. Witty, "Purpose and Scope of the Yearbook," *Development in and through Reading*, Sixtieth Yearbook of the National Society for the Study of Education, Part I, ed. The Society's Committee (Chicago: National Society for the Study of Education, 1961), p. 11.

14. Helen M. Robinson, "Introduction," *Innovation and Change in Reading Instruction*, Sixty-seventh Yearbook of the National Society for the Study of Education, Part II, ed. Helen M. Robinson (Chicago: National Society for the Study of Education), p. 2.

15. Ibid.

16. Nancy Nelson and Robert C. Calfee, "The Reading-Writing Connection," *The Reading-Writing Connection*, Ninety-seventh Yearbook of the National Society for the Study of Education, Part II, ed. Nancy Nelson and Robert Calfee (Chicago: National Society for the Study of Education, 1998), p. 2.

17. Mary E. Laing, *Reading: A Manual for Teachers* (Boston: D. C. Heath, 1903), p. 65.

18. Guy M. Whipple, "The Relation of Reading to Content Subjects and Other School Activities," *Report of the National Committee on Reading*, Twenty-fourth Yearbook of the National Society for the Study of Education, Part I, ed. Guy M. Whipple (Bloomington, IL: Public School Publishing Co., 1925), p. 97.

19. Ibid., p. 141.

20. Gray, "A Decade of Progress," *The Teaching of Reading*, p. 26.

21. Harry A. Greene and W. S. Gray, "The Measurement of Understanding in the Language Arts," *The Measurement of Understanding*, Forty-fifth Yearbook of the National Society for the Study of Education, Part I, The Society's Committee (Chicago: National Society for the Study of Education, 1946), p. 175.

22. Gates, *Reading in the Elementary School*, p. 3.

23. Theodore Clymer, "What Is Reading?: Some Current Concepts," *Innovation and Change in Reading Instruction*, p. 8.

24. Ibid., p. 9.

25. Benjamin S. Bloom, ed., *Taxonomy of Educational Objectives. Book I: Cognitive Domain* (New York: Longman, 1956).

26. Clymer, "What Is Reading?," p. 19ff.

27. See, for example, Carl F. Kaestle et al., *Literacy in the United States: Readers and Reading Since 1880* (New Haven: Yale University Press, 1991), and Cathy N. Davidson, *Revolution and the Word* (New York: Oxford University Press, 1986).

28. Letter to Edward Carrington, 16 January, 1787. Reprinted in Gilbert C. Lee, ed., *Crusade Against Ignorance: Thomas Jefferson on Education* (New York: Teachers College Press, Teachers College, Columbia University, 1961), pp. 101-103.

29. Gray, "Decade of Progress," p. 9.

30. Guy T. Buswell and William H. Wheeler, *The Silent Reading Hour: First Book* (Cambridge, MA: Ryan and Buker, 1923).

31. Ibid., p. iv.

32. Ibid., p. vii.

33. Emma Watkins, *Lippincott's Silent Reading for Beginners* (Philadelphia: J. B. Lippincott, 1925).

34. Mitford M. Mathews, *Teaching to Read, Historically Considered* (Chicago: University of Chicago Press, 1966), p. 194.

35. Anderson and Dearborn, *Psychology of Teaching Reading*, pp. 152-175.

36. Nila B. Smith, *American Reading Instruction* (Newark, DE: International Reading Association, 1965), p. 256.

37. Richard L. Venezky, "From the Indian Primer to Dick and Jane: An Introduction to the UPA American Primers Collection," *American Primers: Guide to the Microfiche Collection*, ed., Richard L. Venezky (Bethesda, MD: United Publications of America, 1990), pp. ix-xxx.

38. The Yearbook Committee, "The Nature and Development of Reading," *Reading in the High School and College*, Forty-seventh Yearbook of the National Society for the Study of Education, Part II, ed. The Society's Committee (Chicago: National Society for the Study of Education, 1948), p. 28.

39. Whipple, "Relation of Reading," p. 103.

40. Gray, "Decade of Progress," p. 19f.

41. This statement was published by Charles W. Eliot in 1891 and is cited in Nila B. Smith, *Reading Instruction*, p. 429.

42. Cited in the Forty-seventh, Part II, p. 11, from an article by Robert J. Havighurst published in 1941.

43. William S. Gray, "Principles of Method in Teaching Reading, as Derived from Scientific Investigations," *Fourth Report of Committee on Economy of Time in Education*, Eighteenth Yearbook of the National Society for the Study of Education, Part II (Bloomington, IL: Public School Publishing Co., 1919), p. 33.

44. W. W. Theisen, "Factors Affecting Results in Primary Reading," *Report of the Society's Committee on Silent Reading*, Twentieth Yearbook of the National Society for the Study of Education, Part II (Bloomington, IL: Public School Publishing Co., 1921), p. 12.

45. Whipple, "Materials," p. 200.

46. Ernest Horn, "Contributions of Research to Special Methods: Spelling," *The Scientific Movement in Education*, Thirty-seventh Yearbook of the National Society for the Study of Education, Part II, ed. The Society's Committee (Bloomington, IL: Public School Publishing Co., 1938), p. 114.

47. Bloomfield's views on teaching reading were expressed in a two-part article that he published during World War II, "Linguistics and Reading," *The Elementary English Review* 19 (1942): 125-130, 183-186. The materials he used to teach his children to read were later edited and published by a close colleague, Clarence Barnhart. See Bloomfield and Barnhart, *Let's Read, a Linguistic Approach* (Detroit: Wayne University Press, 1961).

48. Gertrude Hildreth, "Reading Programs in the Early Primary Period," in *Reading in the Elementary School*, p. 67.

49. Ibid., p. 117.

50. Rudolf Flesch, *Why Johnny Can't Read and What You Can Do About It* (New York: Harper and Brothers, 1955). The reaction of the reading community to Flesch followed the adage, "Whenever anyone points a finger at an educational problem, educators study the finger."

51. Witty, "Purpose and Scope," p. 2f.

52. Robert C. Pooley, "Reading and the Language Arts," *Development in and through Reading*, p. 42.

53. Ibid.

54. Donald D. Durrell and Alice K. Nicholson, "Preschool and Kindergarten Experience," *Development in and Through Reading*, p. 264.

55. Sumner Ives and Josephine Ives, "Linguistics and Reading," *Linguistics in School Programs*, Sixty-ninth Yearbook of the National Society for the Study of Education, Part II, ed. Albert H. Marckwardt (Chicago: National Society for the Study of Education, 1970), p. 255.

56. Ibid.

57. Jeanne S. Chall and Sue S. Conrad, "Resources and Their Use for Reading Instruction," *Becoming Readers in a Complex Society*, Eighty-third Yearbook of the National Society for the Study of Education, Part I, ed. Alan C. Purves and Olive S. Niles (Chicago: National Society for the Study of Education, 1984), p. 211.

58. Catherine E. Snow, M. Susan Burns, and Peg Griffin, eds., *Preventing Reading Difficulties in Young Children* (Washington, DC: National Research Council, 1998).

CHAPTER VII

Legitimacy in the Social Studies Curriculum

STEPHEN J. THORNTON

History, geography, and civics were already established school subjects when the first National Society for the Study of Education (NSSE) Yearbooks were published a century ago. Economics, sociology, anthropology, and sometimes psychology were in the early stages of staking out a place in the curriculum. Other areas of study also emerged that are less directly tied to the traditional academic subjects, including global and environmental education and ethnic and women's studies. Collectively, these subject matters became known as the "social studies."

It remains contested whether the "social studies" denotes that the constituent subjects retain their individual autonomy, or are combined for broader educational purposes, or both. Nevertheless, it is evident that some social studies subject matters have secured greater legitimacy than others. By legitimacy, I mean they came to be broadly considered standard and accepted in American education. This chapter deals with the question of why some subjects acquired legitimacy as they did. The chapter focuses on the treatment of the social studies in a century of NSSE yearbooks, especially the seven volumes devoted to education in the social studies, history, and geography. Three of these volumes incorporated "social studies" in the title and two each addressed "history" and "geography" in their titles.

Accounts of why some conceptions of the social studies have been legitimated usually emphasize the basically conservative social purposes schools serve,[1] or the press of circumstances under which teachers work,[2] or some combination of these two arguments.[3] What these accounts share, as Nel Noddings once put it, is "what cannot be done with general approval" in curriculum innovation.[4] In other words, curriculum innovation cannot be ideologically neutral nor can it avoid the effects of the institutional features of schooling. At the same time,

Stephen J. Thornton is Associate Professor of Social Studies and Education at Teachers College, Columbia University.

however, other factors affecting legitimacy, such as the alignment of content with an academic subject and the relative weight assigned to content or process, have received less systematic scrutiny.

This analysis deals with four conceptions of the social studies. Although they overlap in significant respects, each type is characterized by a distinctive curricular form and implies somewhat different methods and materials of instruction. Moreover, each type features different educational goals, as we shall see. Figure 1 can also represent the legitimacy assigned to the four conceptions. Generally, content has beaten out process; however, the consequences of alignment with an academic subject are less straightforward. I first consider the upper left box.

	Subject Integrity	Integrated
Content	American History Survey	Expanding Communities
Process	History Inquiry	Integrated-Process Approaches

FIGURE 1
Four Conceptions of the Social Studies

The Survey Course in American History

The survey course in American history has been a staple of the curriculum in elementary, middle, and high schools for generations. Judged by criteria such as its ubiquity in schools, state laws mandating its teaching, and its requirement for college admission, this course is the most legitimated of any in the social studies. Its characteristic features include a chronological arrangement of subject matter and an emphasis on a broad, synthetic treatment of selected names, dates, and events in American history. The course has been tied customarily to purposes of citizenship education, and instruction has relied on textbooks. These course features have come to seem natural in American education even though they have not necessarily been characteristic of history instruction in other nations.[5]

The survey course secured an important role in the American curriculum by the beginning of the twentieth century. This was due in no small part to the efforts of the first generation of professional historians. Not only was history a more established subject than the then-nascent social sciences, the historians were first to form a professional association. They were thus well positioned to champion their subject in the emerging modern curriculum. A series of national committees of subject matter specialists and educators in the 1890s and the first decade of the twentieth century declared American history an essential course in both elementary and secondary schools. For example, the influential Committee of Seven of the American Historical Association (AHA) took up the purposes of American history in secondary schools in its 1899 report. The Seven acknowledged the importance of "social and industrial history" for citizenship education (a major theme of the emergent progressive education movement), but declared it an "absolute necessity that a course in American history should aim to give a connected narrative of political events. . . ."[6]

In a sense, the question of what purposes should take precedence in the study of American history was disputed throughout the twentieth century. For example, different answers to this question were strikingly evident in the first two Yearbooks of what was then the National Society for the Scientific Study of Education. Part I of the first Yearbook was written entirely by the historian Lucy Salmon, who was one of the Seven.[7] Salmon argued that the principles underlying the teaching of history rested on "psychological laws." For instance, she believed understanding American history depended on studying its European antecedents. She therefore recommended postponing teaching of the former until students had acquired a thorough grounding in the latter.

In the Society's next Yearbook, education professor Frank McMurry charged that Salmon had matters backward. He challenged Salmon's emphasis on "the nature of the child determin[ing] the selection of subject matter in history." Rather, he said, educators should begin with "topics that bear strongly on the present" and only then select topics "that are best adapted to each age of the child."[8] This suggested to McMurry an emphasis on American history from the outset, tracing events back to their European antecedents only when necessary.

The Salmon-McMurry dispute was but one early indication that determining to teach American history does not resolve what parts of it to teach, how to teach it, and to what ends. Historians figured that their involvement and support of school history entitled them to be its curricular gatekeepers. They believed that the methods and materials of history largely constituted its educational significance. In this view, school history is essentially "the social sciences simplified for pedagogical purposes."[9] In contrast, in the public schools as well as the burgeoning schools of education and normal schools, a movement that would eventually be called the social studies was developing. These educators believed education should be directed at civic improvement by addressing current social problems. The integration of subjects such as sociology and economics were, they thought, well suited to the task. American history was not necessarily excluded from the social studies, but its purpose was to provide a basis for understanding and solving contemporary problems.[10]

To some extent the history and social studies perspectives were reconcilable in the opening decades of the twentieth century because progressivism permeated both historical and educational thought. There was a shared confidence that modern scholarship could be applied to current social problems. For example, the historians Charles and Mary Beard wrote bestseller textbooks with considerable attention to the contemporary problems of American society and decision-making about them.[11]

The National Education Association's Committee on Social Studies report on the secondary grades in 1916 popularized the term "social studies." Despite this committee's apparent commitment to citizenship education over the integrity of the established subjects such as history, they recommended that American history retain its integrity as a separate course. The committee said, however, that the subject matter of American history should be selected based on its proximity in time, current importance in society, and "the present life interests of the pupil."[12] Significantly, the committee failed to provide much guidance on just what such a course should look like. In retrospect, the main significance of the 1916 report for American history may have been its endorsement of its continuation as a separate course. Having survived as a staple of the curriculum, the course was to prove open to interpretations that bore little relationship to the intentions of the 1916 committee.

To Harold Rugg, a leader of the social reconstruction wing of the social studies movement, however, the 1916 report did not go far enough. In the first of the three NSSE Yearbooks that were actually titled "social studies," Rugg mounted a frontal assault on subject-based courses such as American history. He asked if such courses "prepare pupils adequately for life activities."[13] His answer was a resounding, "No." Supremely confident that his purposes could be achieved through modern methods of curriculum making, Rugg designed a detailed, problem-based program of study and accompanying instructional materials, which will be discussed later in this chapter. Although Rugg eschewed the notion of a traditional survey of American history, he included in his materials a great deal of history. How he used history, however, departed from the norm: "Each unit of study is centered on a human 'problem,' institution, social system; that is, on a complex of ways of living rather than on 'subject' catalogues of abstracted facts."[14] Until they were eventually forced out of the schools for their alleged radicalism, the Rugg materials proved the most popular alternative to the traditional survey course ever developed.

Even if Rugg's approach is dismissed as an aberration, it was clearly evident in how American history was taught during the 1920s and 1930s. For example, "problems" approaches to American history were common in the teaching-methods books and schoolbooks of the period. This apparent influence of the social studies movement aroused concern in AHA that social studies educators might supplant historians as curricular gatekeepers. Thus, while AHA provided considerable support to the fledgling National Council for the Social Studies (NCSS) for decades after its founding in 1921, AHA also moved to reassert curriculum leadership by appointing a commission on social studies.

The commission failed to arrive at the conclusions AHA had expected. Dominated by progressive subject matter specialists (most notably Charles Beard) and educators, the commission embraced a conception of social studies purposes akin to those of Rugg. Although the well-funded commission published seventeen authoritative volumes on the social studies, it made no recommendations for scope and sequence, making it hard to know precisely what its recommendations meant for the American history course. The task of interpreting what the commission had intended for American history fell, by default, to NCSS.[15]

Although the social studies had seemingly prevailed on the commission, dissatisfaction with the treatment of American history under the aegis of the social studies continued in some quarters. Matters came to a head at the height of World War II. Writing in the *New York Times*, the prominent historian Allan Nevins charged that at the very time when the national heritage was imperiled, American history was being neglected. The villain, Nevins asserted, was the social studies: The parents of the young may have been "taught history by old-fashioned methods but were nevertheless taught it."[16] For the next couple of years, Nevins and the *Times* waged an unrelenting campaign for state legislatures to mandate increased teaching of the American history course.

Outraged social studies leaders quickly counterattacked. Erling Hunt, editor of NCSS's journal, *Social Education*, firmly pointed out that the central charge—American history was not being taught—was simply untrue.[17] At the heart of matters, Edgar Wesley, a former NCSS president noted, was Nevins's endorsement of a traditional survey course. "The way to teach history," Wesley retorted, "is to select problems whose solutions involve *utilization* of history. The formal, direct, frontal attack [i.e., as in college survey courses] does not seem to be very successful in the case of immature students."[18]

Critics of the *Times* campaign also detected hostility to the progressive purposes of the social studies. As Hunt wrote in a letter to the executive secretary of AHA, the critics of the social studies were after "far more" than "adequate attention to American history." Rather, Hunt believed, "economic and social reactionaries" wanted to prevent treatment of "contemporary problems and controversial issues."[19] Historians, too, sensed the ideological thrust of the campaign. The historian John D. Hicks wrote to a friend: "The opposition to the Social Studies Program out here [in California] comes from people who are utterly uninterested in either content or method." Rather, Hicks observed, they wanted "indoctrination" on the virtues of isolationism and distrust of Great Britain, as well as their own conception of American free enterprise as "sacrosanct."[20]

The *Times* campaign led to a common sense of crisis in NCSS, AHA, and the historians' group whose exclusive focus was American history, the Mississippi Valley Historical Association (later the Organization of American Historians). The three organizations set up a national study of American history in schools and colleges. Wesley was appointed to direct the study and compile its final report. The controversy that had led to the study went unmentioned in the report, although the charge that American history had been neglected was soundly refuted. How American history was taught, not how much of it was taught, was identified as the main problem. Nonetheless, three separate school courses in American history were deemed essential,

Wesley wrote, because "historical-mindedness and the historical method can not be learned from other subjects."[21] Specific themes, persons, dates, and events for study at each grade level were suggested, while making clear the course's overall purpose of citizenship education. The report underscored, however, that faith in the efficacy of history was not intended to disparage other social studies courses, such as civics, economics, geography, and sociology.

The Wesley report, in effect, ratified the legitimacy of American history in terms of its integrity as a separate course and its orientation to citizenship education. It was a rare instance in which the chief concerns of both sides were satisfied. NCSS embraced the report.[22] With the crisis resolved, however, the historical associations retreated from their traditional gatekeeping role over history in the schools. The spirit of the Wesley report was not to prove a dominant influence on school history.

Rather, after World War II, as the historian Bernard Weisberger lamented in his recommendations for teaching American history, content and teaching methods departed from the spirit of progressive education.[23] Progressive history, emphasizing conflict between elites and the "people," was replaced by a Cold War closing of the ranks, i.e., neoconservative history that underscored consensus and the absence of fundamental conflict in American society. Moreover, historians themselves were engaged in a process of growing professional specialization which increasingly removed them from grappling with the pedagogical demands of the broad survey courses taught in schools. The activist overtones of a history aimed at current social problems had been marginalized, as had the methods and materials that facilitated such an approach. The course remained, but few of the purposes laid out for it in 1916 survived.

The survey course in American history aroused relatively little interest again until the 1970s and 1980s, when charges that it was being neglected arose anew. As in the 1940s, critics contended that history was being supplanted by intellectually pallid social studies courses oriented to shallow notions of current relevance. Also as in the 1940s, evidence that American history was widely taught failed to still the criticisms.[24] In the 1990s, however, social studies critics were more successful than they had been in the 1940s. The national standards in United States history were based on the assumption that content was being neglected. The accuracy of this estimation seems unsound because research evidence suggests the opposite.[25] Nevertheless, the "new" social historians mostly contented themselves with arguing with social conservatives over the relative weight assigned to some topics over others.[26]

Inquiry Methods in American History

The legitimacy attached to American history mostly has been confined to its content. Repeated attempts to legitimate courses in the process of historical inquiry (lower left box of Fig. 1) have met with limited success. Thus, American history per se has not been legitimated, but only in its guise as a survey course. At times both historians and social studies educators have proposed programs built on historical inquiry; seldom have they been validated.

Historical inquiry, as I use the term here, includes a variety of methods and materials of instruction that emphasize the process of historical inquiry rather than the knowledge that results from that process. I recognize that survey courses often include inquiry objectives; however, these have generally been less significant than particular themes, periods, names, dates, and events prescribed for study. In contrast, historical inquiry approaches stress the process of "doing" history.

The first major movement in this direction began in the 1880s and proved popular for several decades.[27] Based on the seminar method of the German "scientific" historians, the source method aimed at enabling students to construct their own historical accounts from primary sources. In this scheme, the process of historical inquiry was deemed more important than merely reciting second- and third-hand information that was the product of someone else's inquiry.

The emergence of progressive history and the social studies challenged the premises of the source method. Progressive historians disputed that the positivism of "scientific" history was the purpose of historical study. More specifically, Salmon warned that sources alone were an inadequate basis for a sound curriculum. Immature students or even expert teachers, she said, cannot reconstruct history in the classroom by using sources. Other instructional materials were also required if the full meaning of sources was to be grasped.[28]

Where did the source method fit into social studies education? As noted, some social studies educators were skeptical of the educational worth of history, let alone the methods of the historian. Source method proponents countered by asserting their methods' relevance to broader social and educational concerns, such as current events.[29] Nevertheless, it appears that by the 1920s and 1930s the source method was anachronistic. The social studies were caught up in a more general movement to relate school programs to the problems and activities of contemporary life.[30]

Growing concern for academic rigor during the Cold War in the 1950s fueled a revival of interest in the academic disciplines, particularly the structure and methods of inquiry in mathematics and the sciences. By the early 1960s would-be reformers were drawing parallels with the social sciences, whose structure and methods of inquiry were now also deemed worthy of attention. Although the "structure" of history was harder to specify than that of the social sciences, history joined what became known as the "new" social studies. This participation took the form of inquiry teaching through primary sources. There was scant involvement in the resultant history projects, however, by social studies educators. Rather, the reformers, themselves often historians, looked to the discipline of history as a model for program development. They seemed unaware that teaching history through sources had been tried before.

One of the most ambitious new social studies initiatives was the Amherst project in American history. As with other history projects of the time, the Amherst project was largely a reaction against the American survey course, which the reformers believed had ossified. According to William Kline's thorough study of the Amherst project, it was based on two main assumptions. First, learning is better accomplished if the student becomes an active scholar in the content area, and, second, history is best studied utilizing the methods and purposes of the discipline rather than its factual content, sequentially arranged.[31]

Between 1961 and 1971 the Amherst project staff developed dozens of instructional units on sundry topics. The units featured a strong academic orientation. The complexity of the primary sources included suggests that the units were most suited to academically able high school students. The questions posed were the same as a historian might be concerned with, such as identification of a document's frame of reference and appraisal of its reliability as a source. Over time the topics of the units shifted noticeably from relatively traditional historical topics, such as the Missouri Compromise and the Monroe Doctrine, to topics of more obvious contemporary relevance, such as the Watts riots, youth disenchantment, and wartime dissent. Nonetheless, the goals remained fixed on academic history. For instance, the project staff was especially critical when they believed that the Port Washington, New York, school district was using the project to further civil rights concerns.[32]

The discipline of history, as Kline noted, provided the "intellectual boundary" of the project, for both unit development and teacher education.

Moreover, providing systematic pedagogy, such as questioning and discussion techniques and group processes, was almost always left to chance. In effect, "good history" was equated with "good social learning."[33] The wide range of possible educational purposes for American history was ignored.[34]

As with the rest of the new social studies, the Amherst project faded from view as the 1970s wore on. Although there has been no subsequent history inquiry movement on such a large scale, there have been more modest moves to source-based instruction. Two factors seem to account for these moves. First, both advanced-placement American history and some states with centralized testing, such as New York, have incorporated document-based questions in their tests. These questions require a fuller integration of content from a sequential curriculum with the primary sources than did the Amherst project and the earlier source method. At the time of this writing, the tying of source study to high-stakes tests appears to be legitimating source-based instruction.

Second, the intended audience of the other area of revival—students of color in urban schools—may appear incongruous given the charges of elitism sometimes leveled at source study in the past. For example, David Kobrin argued that through the use of primary sources students can construct their "own" histories of the United States and thus counteract feelings of alienation resulting from studying a narrative with which people of color may find little to identify.[35] Although apparently directed at broader social purposes, Kobrin's approach still relies heavily on the methods of the historian, albeit the "new" social historian concerned with the common people rather than the elite. Whether this approach will be widely implemented in an era of national standards—and whether it will fall prey to the same limitations that undermined earlier history inquiry approaches—remains to be seen.

Expanding Communities in Elementary Education

In 1957 Paul R. Hanna could confidently write that elementary social studies consisted of a series of "expanding communities, commencing in the smallest and most fundamental community (the family group), and moving constantly outward through the school, the neighborhood, the state, the nation, and the world."[36] This program of study (upper right box of Fig. 1) became the most successful example of social subjects integration for instructional purposes. By the middle of the twentieth century, it had become the de facto national curriculum.[37]

Giving such legitimacy to integrating academic subjects has been uncharacteristic of secondary education.

The validation of expanding communities is partly attributable to the fact that professional organizations in the academic subjects seldom take the same interest in elementary education as they do in secondary education. AHA published the first nationally influential recommendations for standardizing the elementary scope and sequence in history and civics in 1909. This program, however, was increasingly supplanted by a more integrated social studies in the inter-war decades,[38] reflecting the influence of progressive educators. As John Dewey said in 1937, for the social studies to be worthy of its name, it should not be "taught simply as information about present society," but must be "taught in connection with things that are done, that need to be done, and how to do them."[39]

The curricular form of the social studies that became standard nationally in elementary education was first recognized in the early 1930s. A then widely copied Virginia curriculum was built on the study of "basic social functions, the functions that must be discharged to meet human needs."[40] Although the program drew on sociology, economics, and so forth, it integrated them in the study of social functions. The scope and sequence of this curriculum eventually evolved into expanding communities, with a present- versus past-oriented scope and a sequence based not on chronology but on moving from the familiar to the unfamiliar. This sequence, its advocates claimed, was a "psychological" rather than a "logical" arrangement of subject matter and, thus, "more learnable for children."[41] The accuracy of this claim, as I shall consider below, has long been disputed. Nevertheless, the expanding-communities approach took hold, albeit with its activist side (of such interest to Dewey and other progressive educators) falling afoul of right-wing censorship by mid-century.[42] Nevertheless, no wholesale return to the academic subjects as the organizational basis for the curriculum developed.

Expanding communities was also to outlive the inquiry-oriented projects of the new social studies era. The elementary-school projects were ambitious attempts to place students at the frontiers of knowledge; learning concepts rather than facts was emphasized. The aims of these projects marked a sharp break with established methods and materials of instruction and generally provided little for their fit with the existing scope and sequence. Perhaps the best-remembered project was developed by the leading curriculum reformer of the era, Jerome Bruner. His *Man: A Course of Study* (*MACOS*),[43] although the most controversial of the projects because it was eventually charged with "secular humanism," was nonetheless characteristic of most other projects in significant respects. For example, its approach was based on teaching concepts rather than providing information; the conventional subject matters were largely ignored; teachers were viewed more as facilitators of student activity with curriculum materials than instructional overseers; and primacy was assigned to developing reasoning. As Wilma Longstreet noted at the end of the era, "Ways of objectifying or somehow coping with one's own personal situations are largely excluded from the objectives of not just *Man: A Course of Study* but most of the new social studies programs."[44]

Indeed, the strongly rationalistic bent of the new social studies projects contrasted with the socialization purposes and child development considerations long since established in the elementary grades. By long habit, elementary teachers, parents, and school boards have come to see such purposes as a key responsibility of the social studies. For example, in the primary grades priority is accorded to instilling norms and values such as politeness, consideration for others, honesty, sharing, punctuality, and the observance of significant holidays. In the upper elementary grades, four through six, this orientation shifts to give more attention to academics: For instance, a basal textbook series usually emphasizes knowledge and skills in subjects such as history, geography, and civics. Even here, however, subject matters such as American history and geography have tended to have a content "not excessively removed from children's own experience" and to deal with "concrete and tangible aspects of history."[45]

While expanding communities has endured, its legitimacy has been periodically challenged. Critics accused it of abandoning the academic subjects for community study lacking in intellectual substance. Further, the critique suggests, expanding communities deals with familiar situations children already know rather than stimulating their natural curiosity for the intriguingly unusual or different in time and space; imagination is sacrificed to the mundane. But the dichotomy drawn between imagination and academic rigor versus connecting with children's experience seems to be false, or at least unnecessary.[46]

Although once it may have been true that expanding communities expends itself with the local, this is no longer the case. The conventional third-grade study of communities, for example, can readily include communities distant in time and space. There are well-documented cases in which elementary social studies draws on children's experience and is also put to wide critical and imaginative purposes.

Indeed, several scholars have persuasively argued that equating elementary social studies with the academic subjects may undercut some of the most valuable educational purposes the social studies serve.[47]

Integrated-Process Approaches

The sheer number of social studies programs that have disregarded the boundaries of academic subjects and embraced process over content (lower right box of Fig. 1) suggests that many educators have seen a great need for such approaches. Generally, although they have varied considerably in specifics, these approaches have been directed at the broad purposes of social studies. They share the view that conventional approaches to the social studies are mired in the mere transmission of information. Among the best known of these innovative programs are the aforementioned Rugg materials and *MACOS*, as well as the Harvard Social Studies Project, which was based on the analysis of public controversy.[48] Few of these many innovations in the social studies have won legitimacy, however.

If for the moment we judge legitimacy by implementation and the fidelity of its instructional materials to announced aims, the Rugg materials were an unparalleled success among integrated-process methods. The program was built on the study of problems with content drawn from the social sciences and contemporary social issues. Whereas the Amherst project largely disdained content, Rugg employed it as a means to an end. Perhaps the legitimacy accorded the Rugg materials, albeit of limited duration, suggests that process objectives need grounding in an appropriate content.

Rugg organized his materials around a persistent emphasis on controversial issues, generalization, and designed recurrence of concepts. These features were intended to facilitate learning. While conceding that all students must learn some essential content, such as key aspects of American political development, Rugg underscored that the learning process itself was the heart of matters. He maintained, for example, that debates about which particular cultures should be included in the curriculum may at times be a distraction because "many other groups . . . could be used with equally good educative effect."[49]

Compared to most social studies materials at the time or since, the conceptual sophistication and reading level of the Rugg materials is remarkably high. They make a mockery of charges that progressive education was anti-intellectual. Moreover, as Murry Nelson noted, the Rugg materials were the first curriculum series to secure a nationwide basis in the social studies. Although the call for integrated social studies was scarcely new in the 1920s, Rugg was the first to produce a systematic body of materials that embodied the idea.[50]

Rugg's frame of reference, the evolution of modern American democracy with a focus on the pervasive problems and issues confronting contemporary society, was attacked as subversive by groups such as the American Legion and National Association of Manufacturers. Whereas it had been by far the leading social studies textbook series in junior and senior high schools during the 1930s and early 1940s, within a few years sales plummeted. Soon after, the Rugg materials were driven from the schools where they had already been used.[51] Significantly, no one appears to have questioned the pedagogical effectiveness of the materials.

The Harvard Social Studies Project arose from the concern that conventional social studies courses provided "students [with] no conceptual model for handling the important issues facing society."[52] Concerned about this and the fragmented character of school social studies programs, the Harvard project was designed to analyze the factual and value dimensions of public issues, thus modeling the decision-making process in which citizens in a democracy should engage. Although the teaching of social science concepts and methods was not excluded, concepts and methods were secondary to the requirements of citizenship education. The Harvard project could be fitted into the slot already assigned American history and geography in junior high school, and evaluation revealed its efficacy for student learning. Nevertheless, it failed to find favor in most schools.

MACOS is the final example of the integrated-process approach to be considered. In many ways this project has become symbolic of the failure of such approaches to find legitimacy, because Bruner directed it and the federal government lavishly funded both its development and implementation. *MACOS* was an inquiry-oriented program in the social and behavioral sciences for the upper-elementary grades. It was assumed that rational inquiry about what it means to be human and attendant value dilemmas constituted a proper focus for social studies. By the mid-1970s *MACOS* was being used by more than 300,000 students in forty-seven states. The program was, however, to be dogged by controversy. Many teachers were uncomfortable with its radical break with the existing scope and sequence, let alone its substance. In Congress *MACOS* was attacked for its "secular humanism."[53] The attack on *MACOS*, in retrospect, proved an opening salvo over value conflicts that roiled the social studies for the remainder of the twentieth century.

Although integrated-process approaches had always faced an uphill battle to secure legitimacy, the conservative wave of recent decades made
that task even more difficult.

Conclusion

Consideration of legitimacy for the social studies in the curriculum
inevitably leads back to the perennial curriculum question, What
knowledge is of most worth? As we have seen, who answers this question goes a long way toward determining what the answer will be. It is
striking that there has never been a shortage of persons who feel entitled to answer with authority on what knowledge is of most worth.
They include school people, subject matter scholars, curriculum and
teaching methods specialists, special interest groups promoting or
opposing the teaching of some particular subject matter, school boards,
parents, the media, and politicians. What each group considers educationally significant, however, often differs. Even matters on which
broad-based consensus exists, such as teaching American history, fails
to resolve what goals it should serve, what content and processes to
include, what methods and materials of instruction should be used, or
how its learning activities and outcomes should be evaluated. On subject matters with less societal consensus, such as treatment of public
controversy, agreement has been even harder to secure.

As noted, the seven NSSE yearbooks devoted to the field include
three titled the "social studies," two "history," and two "geography."[54]
This would seem to suggest that we are left with an unresolved question of the field's proper scope and boundaries: Should the constituent
subjects retain their integrity, or be integrated, or both? Given that the
last Yearbook devoted to a constituent subject (geography) was in 1933,
it may seem reasonable to conclude that an integrated conception of
the social studies has prevailed. This conclusion is reinforced by the
titles adopted by the two self-styled commissions, both of which named
themselves after the social studies. Nevertheless, caution should be
exercised because, in practice, the social studies have remained a compromise between the separate subject and integrated conceptions.
Indeed, the 1990s saw a resurgence of the subject conception in the
production of national standards that included, rather confusingly, separate standards for the constituent subjects, such as history and geography, as well as the social studies. While no authoritative definition of
the social studies has emerged, in practice it continues as a compromise
between subject integration and subject autonomy.

The relative emphasis assigned to content or process also remains disputed. It is clear that the content view has prevailed in practice. Although NSSE has not often singled out the content-process dispute for explicit treatment, the reasons for the predominance of content seem evident. Content can be specified explicitly in advance; it fits with customary teacher-centered instructional arrangements; and it is incorporated in widely used textbook series that avoid controversy. In addition, how much content has been learned can be easily measured. It thus fits comfortably with the milieu of American schooling. In contrast, process demands pedagogical inventiveness; learning activities are less easily managed; and learning outcomes are more likely to be idiosyncratic. The unpredictability of the outcomes in process approaches also opens up possibilities for straying into controversial subject matters. Although unwarranted, persistent conservative criticism apparently has persuaded many observers that process is intrinsically lacking in educational substance.[55]

Will the future of the social studies simply repeat the past? Recent reforms, such as national standards, intend to beef up content, although all indications are that content already dominates the curriculum. Rather, the persistent problem has been that students find how they are taught content to be dull and irrelevant to their lives; moreover, studies through most of the twentieth century expressed disappointment in the learning outcomes of social studies instruction.[56] Although reformers have repeatedly tried to remedy this instructional problem, unorthodox methods have seldom gained legitimacy. In other words, the key problem facing the social studies is method, i.e., the effective direction of subject matter to desired results.[57]

It would be going too far to say that educational practice remained stable in the twentieth century. For example, curriculum content has expanded to incorporate changing perspectives on and greater inclusion of African-Americans and women. Experience suggests, however, that new content will not be seen as more relevant by students unless it is delivered by different methods.[58] Dewey seems never to have been more right than when he insisted that effective teaching must incorporate the learner's participation in forming the purposes of the learning process.[59]

Remarkably, the literature on the relationship between method and content is underdeveloped, and, if anything, the focus of methods textbooks is more diffuse than it was in the 1930s. Without a sound basis in methods suitable for children and adolescents, it is hardly surprising that teachers rely on the content and methods they experienced in their college social science courses and see institutionalized in the schools where they work.[60] Far more attention to the pedagogical demands of subject matter that extends beyond mere simplification of the content and methods taught in college courses is urgently needed.

It is currently hard to be optimistic about the prospects for radical change in established patterns of curriculum and instruction, but this may not mean progressive purposes and methods must await a revolution in American education. The experience of the 1940s dispute over American history may be instructive. A consensus was reached on American history. Historians and conservatives appeared satisfied that the academic purposes and integrity of the subject were preserved while progressives insured that the subject's citizenship orientation was endorsed. It may be that the "new" social history of recent years also enhances the prospects for progressive methods as it more closely approximates Dewey's concern with "social and industrial history" than did the consensus history of the early Cold War era.[61] In the hands of teachers well versed in method, the broader purposes of the social studies do reach students, even in conventional courses such as the American survey.[62]

Finally, the most important battle for legitimacy may not be what courses to offer but how to develop and institutionalize methods that reach students. Judged by the scholarly literature presented in the NSSE Yearbooks reviewed, the history of the social studies has been one long battle, with occasional pauses, over what to teach. This emphasis needs reconsideration. After all, does it really matter what we teach if students fail to learn it?

NOTES

1. See, for example, Jean Anyon, "Elementary Social Studies Textbooks and Legitimating Knowledge," *Theory and Research in Social Education* 6, no. 1 (1978), pp. 40-55.

2. See, for example, Larry Cuban, "History of Teaching in Social Studies," *Handbook of Research on Social Studies Teaching and Learning*, ed. James P. Shaver (New York: Macmillan, 1991).

3. See, for example, Linda M. McNeil, *Contradictions of Control: School Structure and School Knowledge* (New York: Routledge and Kegan Paul, 1986).

4. Nel Noddings, "NIE's National Curriculum Development Conference," in *Value Conflicts and Curriculum Issues*, eds. Jon Schaffarzick and Gary Sykes (Berkeley, CA: McCutchan, 1979), p. 312.

5. See, for example, Ray Allen Billington, *The Historian's Contribution to Anglo-American Misunderstanding* (London: Routledge and Kegan Paul, 1966), pp. 23-28.

6. American Historical Association, *The Study of History in Schools* (New York: Macmillan, 1899), p. 76.

7. Lucy M. Salmon, *Some Principles in the Teaching of History*, First Yearbook of the National Society for the Scientific Study of Education, Part I, ed. Charles A. McMurry (Chicago: National Society for the Study of Education, 1902).

8. Frank M. McMurry, "The Course of Study in History," *The Course of Study in History in the Common School*, Second Yearbook of the National Society for the Scientific Study of Education, Part I, ed. Charles A. McMurry (Chicago: National Society for the Study of Education, 1903), pp. 47-48.

9. "The social sciences" in this usage includes history. See Edgar B. Wesley, *Teaching Social Studies in High Schools*, 3rd ed. (Boston: Heath, 1950), p. 34.

10. Linda S. Levstik, "NCSS and the Teaching of History," *NCSS in Retrospect*, Bulletin No. 92, ed. O. L. Davis, Jr. (Washington, DC: National Council for the Social Studies, 1996), p. 22.

11. See Margaret Smith Crocco, "Forceful Yet Forgotten: Mary Ritter Beard and the Writing of History," *The History Teacher* 31, no. 1 (1997), pp. 9-31.

12. Arthur William Dunn, *The Social Studies in Secondary Education*, ed. Murry R. Nelson (Bloomington, IN: ERIC Clearinghouse for Social Studies/Social Science Education, 1994), p. 41. Original work published 1916.

13. Harold O. Rugg, "Do the Social Studies Prepare Pupils Adequately for Life Activities?" *The Social Studies in the Elementary and Secondary School*. Twenty-second Yearbook of the National Society for the Study of Education, Part II, ed. Guy Montrose Whipple (Bloomington, IL: Public School Publishing Company, 1923).

14. Harold O. Rugg, "Curriculum Design in the Social Sciences: What I Believe," *The Future of the Social Studies: Proposals for an Experimental Social-Studies Curriculum*, ed. James A. Michener (Cambridge, MA: National Council for the Social Studies, 1939), p. 148.

15. Stephen J. Thornton, "NCSS: The Early Years," *NCSS in Retrospect*.

16. Allan Nevins, "American History for Americans," *New York Times*, 3 May 1942, Magazine Section.

17. Erling M. Hunt, "More American History? A Rejoinder to Professor Nevins and The *New York Times* Survey, *Social Education* 6, no. 6 (1942), pp. 250-252.

18. Edgar B. Wesley, "History in the School Curriculum," *Mississippi Valley Historical Review* 29, no. 4 (1943), p. 570.

19. Erling M. Hunt to Guy Stanton Ford, 12 November 1942, Series IVC, Box 10, National Council for the Social Studies Papers, Special Collections, Milbank Memorial Library, Teachers College, Columbia University.

20. Quoted in Peter Novick, *That Noble Dream: The "Objectivity Question" and the American Historical Profession* (Cambridge, England: Cambridge University Press, 1988), p. 369.

21. Edgar B. Wesley, *American History in Schools and Colleges* (New York: Macmillan, 1944), p. 62.

22. See Richard E. Thursfield, ed., *The Study and Teaching of American History*, Seventeenth Yearbook of the National Council for the Social Studies (Washington, DC: National Council for the Social Studies, 1947).

23. Bernard A. Weisberger, "United States History" *High School Social Studies Perspectives*, ed. Erling M. Hunt, *et al.* (Boston: Houghton Mifflin, 1962), p. 130; see also Richard E. Gross, "United States History," *Educating Citizens for Democracy*, eds. Richard E. Gross and Leslie D. Zeleny (New York: Oxford University Press, 1958).

24. Stephen J. Thornton, "The Social Studies Near Century's End: Reconsidering Patterns of Curriculum and Instruction," *Review of Research in Education* 20, ed. Linda Darling-Hammond (Washington, DC: American Educational Research Association, 1994); see also David Jenness, *Making Sense of Social Studies* (New York: Macmillan, 1990), pp. 255-260.

25. See Stephen J. Thornton, "Should We Be Teaching More History?" *Theory and Research in Social Education* 18, no. 1 (1990), pp. 53-60.

26. See Gary B. Nash, Charlotte Crabtree, and Ross E. Dunn, *History on Trial: Culture Wars and the Teaching of the Past* (New York: Knopf, 1997).

27. See Hazel W. Hertzberg, *Historical Parallels for the Sixties and Seventies: Primary Sources and Core Curriculum Revisited* (Boulder, CO: Social Science Education Consortium, 1971).

28. Salmon, *Some Principles in the Teaching of History*, pp. 48-49.

29. Fred Morrow Fling, "The Use of Sources in History Teaching During the Last Decade (1909-1919)," *Historical Outlook* 10, no. 9 (1919), pp. 507-508.

30. See Ralph W. Tyler, "Curriculum Development in the Twenties and Thirties," *The Curriculum: Retrospect and Prospect*, Seventieth Yearbook of the National Society for the Study of Education, Part I, ed. Robert M. McClure (Chicago: National Society for the Study of Education, 1971); see also Arthur W. Foshay, "Textbooks and the Curriculum During the Progressive Era, 1930-1950," *Textbooks and Schooling in the United States*, Eighty-ninth Yearbook of the National Society for the Study of Education, eds. David L. Elliot and Arthur Woodward (Chicago: National Society for the Study of Education, 1990).

31. William Alan Kline, "The 'Amherst Project:' A Case Study of a Federally Sponsored Curriculum Development Project" (Ph.D. diss., Stanford University, 1974.)

32. Ibid., p. 134.

33. Ibid., pp. 188-191.

34. See, for example, Stephen J. Thornton, "Curriculum Consonance in United States History Classrooms," *Journal of Curriculum and Supervision* 3, no. 4 (1988), pp. 308-320; see also Jenness, *Making Sense of Social Studies*, pp. 290-293.

35. David Kobrin, "It's My Country, Too: A Proposal for a Student Historian's History of the United States," *Teachers College Record* 94, no. 2 (1992): pp. 329-342.

36. Paul R. Hanna, "Generalizations and Universal Values: Their Implications for the Social-Studies Program," *Social Studies in the Elementary School*, Fifty-sixth Yearbook of the National Society for the Study of Education, Part II, ed. Nelson B. Henry (Chicago: National Society for the Study of Education, 1957), p. 27.

37. For a detailed discussion of the current status of the expanding communities sequence, see Jere Brophy, Janet Alleman, and Carolyn O'Mahony, "Elementary School Social Studies: Yesterday, Today, and Tomorrow," *American Education: Yesterday, Today, and Tomorrow*, Ninety-ninth Yearbook of the National Society for the Study of Education, ed. Thomas L. Good (Chicago: National Society for the Study of Education, 2000).

38. See Patricia Confrey Thevenet, "The Beginnings of Standardized Social Studies Curriculum in the Elementary Schools" (Ed.D. diss., Teachers College, Columbia University, 1994).

39. John Dewey, *The Later Works, 1925-1953* Vol. 11, ed. Jo Ann Boydston (Carbondale, IL: Southern Illinois University Press, 1991), p. 185.

40. Dorothy McClure Fraser, "The Organization of the Elementary-School Social-Studies Curriculum," *Social Studies in the Elementary School*, p. 137.'

41. Ibid., p. 140.

42. See Daniel Tanner, "The Textbook Controversies," *Critical Issues in Curriculum*, Eighty-seventh Yearbook of the National Society for the Study of Education, Part I, ed. Laurel N. Tanner (Chicago: National Society for the Study of Education, 1988), pp. 130-133.

43. See Jerome S. Bruner, *Toward a Theory of Instruction* (Cambridge, MA: Harvard University Press, 1966), pp. 73-101.

44. Wilma S. Longstreet, "The School's Curriculum," *The Elementary School in the United States*, Seventy-second Yearbook of the National Society for the Study of Education, Part II, eds. John I. Goodlad and Harold G. Shane (Chicago: National Society for the Study of Education, 1973), p. 264.

45. Douglas Adler and Matthew T. Downey, "Problem Areas in the History Curriculum," *History in the Schools*, Bulletin No. 74, ed. Matthew T. Downey (Washington, DC: National Council for the Social Studies, 1985), p. 23.

46. For a sample of the attack on expanding communities, see Kieran Egan, "Social Studies and the Erosion of Education," *Curriculum Inquiry* 13, no. 2 (1983), pp. 195-214; and for a rejoinder, Stephen J. Thornton, "Social Studies Misunderstood: A Reply to Kieran Egan," *Theory and Research in Social Education* 12, no. 1 (1984), pp. 43-47.

47. See, for example, Lauren Sosniak and Susan S. Stodolsky, "Making Connections: Social Studies Education in an Urban Fourth-Grade Classroom," *Advances in Research on Teaching, Volume 4: Case Studies of Teaching and Learning in Social Studies*, ed. Jere Brophy (Greenwich, CT: JAI Press, 1993). See also in the same volume Linda S. Levstik, "Building a Sense of History in a First-Grade Classroom."

48. See James P. Shaver and Donald W. Oliver, "Teaching Students to Analyze Public Controversy: A Curriculum Project Report," *Social Education* 28, no. 4 (1964), pp. 191-194, 248.

49. Rugg, "Curriculum Design in the Social Sciences," p. 153.

50. Murry R. Nelson, "The Development of the Rugg Social Studies Materials," *Theory and Research in Social Education* 5, no. 3 (1977): pp. 64-83.

51. Tanner, "The Textbook Controversies," pp. 130-131.

52. Shaver and Oliver, "Teaching Students to Analyze Public Controversy," p. 191.

53. See Jon Schaffarzick, "Federal Curriculum Reform: A Crucible for Value Conflict," *Value Conflicts and Curriculum Issues*; James P. Shaver, "Citizenship, Values, and Morality in Social Studies," in *The Social Studies*, Eightieth Yearbook of the National Society for the Study of Education, Part II, ed. Howard D. Mehlinger and O. L. Davis, Jr. (Chicago: National Society for the Study of Education, 1981).

54. In addition to the five yearbooks cited above, see Charles A. McMurry, ed., *The Progress of Geography in the Schools*, First Yearbook of the National Society for the Scientific Study of Education, Part II (Chicago: National Society for the Study of Education, 1902) and *The Teaching of Geography*, Thirty-second Yearbook of the National Society for the Study of Education, ed. Guy Montrose Whipple (Bloomington, IL: Public School Publishing Company, 1933).

55. Walter C. Parker, "Process and Content in Social Studies: Beyond the Dichotomy" (Paper presented at the annual meeting of the National Council for the Social Studies, Orlando, FL: 1988).

56. For a longitudinal perspective, see Dale Whittington, "What Have 17-Year-Olds Known in the Past?" *American Educational Research Journal* 28, no. 4 (1991), pp. 759-780.

57. The definition is due to John Dewey. See his *Democracy and Education* (New York: Macmillan, 1916), p. 165.

58. For an illustrative discussion, see Gloria Ladson-Billings, "Crafting a Culturally Relevant Social Studies Approach," *The Social Studies Curriculum: Purposes, Problems, and Possibilities*, ed. E. Wayne Ross (Albany, NY: State University of New York Press, 1997), pp. 123-126.

59. John Dewey, *Experience and Education* (West Lafayette, IN: Kappa Delta Pi, 1998), p. 77. Original work published 1938.

60. See James P. Shaver, "Lessons from the Past: The Future of an Issues-Centered Social Studies Curriculum," *The Social Studies* 80, no. 5 (1989), pp. 192-196; Hazel W. Hertzberg, "Are Method and Content Enemies?" *History in the Schools*, ed. Bernard R. Gifford (New York: Macmillan, 1988).

61. There is some evidence that the content of "new" social history is finding its way into school programs. See Catherine Cornbleth, "An America Curriculum?" *Teachers College Record* 99, no. 4 (1998), pp. 622-646.

62. See, for example, Stephen J. Thornton, "Toward the Desirable in Social Studies Teaching," *Advances in Research on Teaching*.

CHAPTER VIII

Modern Content and the Enterprise of Science: Science Education in the Twentieth Century

JOSEPH KRAJCIK, RACHEL MAMLOK, AND BARBARA HUG[1]

During the twentieth century, scientists and educators have been concerned that school science reflects the actual practice of science, with respect both to content that students learn and to the actual way scientists work. "What is worth learning?" and "How should students learn science?" have been enduring questions. Historically, these concerns have been expressed in the National Society for the Study of Education (NSSE) Yearbooks and elsewhere. The Forty-sixth Yearbook Committee expressed its opinion on how science should be taught.

Since experimenting involves "learning by doing," there can be no substitute for it. Pupil experimentation is an essential part of good science education. In every course of science offered at any level, therefore, opportunities should be provided for the pupils to perform experiments.[2]

Based on dissatisfaction of student performance in science, prominent national organizations such as the American Association for the Advancement of Science (AAAS) and the National Research Council (NRC) have recently produced documents that specify what scientifically literate students should know and be able to do as a result of completing kindergarten through twelfth grade science education.

In this chapter we trace "what and how science should be taught" through the twentieth century. We make reference to a number of NSSE publications, as well as other publications, that have influenced science education. NSSE has devoted four Yearbooks to practices in science education: 1) the Third Yearbook, *Nature Study*, 2) the Thirty-first Yearbook, *A Program for Teaching Science*, 3) the Forty-sixth Yearbook, *Science Education in American Schools*, and 4) the Fifty-ninth Yearbook,

Joseph Krajcik is Professor of Science Education at University of Michigan. Rachel Mamlok is Postdoctoral Research Fellow at Weizmann Institute of Science, Rehovet, Israel. Barbara Hug is Postdoctoral Research Fellow at University of Michigan.

Rethinking Science Education.[3] Since the Fifty-ninth Yearbook, NSSE
has not published a Yearbook on science education; however, a number
of the volumes between 1959 and 2000 have devoted considerable
attention to science education. In particular, the Eighty-ninth Yearbook, *Textbooks and Schooling in the United States*, and the Ninety-ninth
Yearbook, *Constructivism in Education*, are noteworthy.[4] The Eighty-
ninth Yearbook discusses the curriculum projects of the 1960s, and the
Ninety-ninth Yearbook, in its exploration of the construct of "constructivism," has several chapters related to science education. We also
cite *Improving Science Education*, edited by Barry Fraser and Herbert
Walberg.[5] Although technically not a NSSE Yearbook, *Improving Science Education* was sponsored by the International Academy of Education as part of the NSSE series on Contemporary Educational Issues.
We use these NSSE publications to examine "what and how science
should be taught." We also examine a number of other important publications that have had an impact on reform efforts in science education. These include *Project 2061: Science for All Americans, Benchmarks
for Science Literacy*, and *National Science Education Standards.*[6] These
publications have defined the science content expectations at the various levels of kindergarten through twelfth grade science education.
Finally, we make reference to a number of seminal articles that have
impacted science education.

Early Developments in Science Education

The Third Yearbook first discussed science education. Wilbur Jackman, the Yearbook's chairperson, presented a case for nature study to
be part of the elementary science curriculum. He defined nature study
to include the study of the earth, sky, and water. He argued that there
is no true dividing line between natural science and nature study. Both
nature study and natural science allow the student to investigate natural phenomena using similar methods of observation and investigation to determine relationships. Jackman claimed nature study's focus
on macroscopic phenomena was appropriate for the elementary students. This focus was critical because the elementary child's "undevel-
oped imagination must picture in the large—he cannot think in grains
of sand" and because the child's immature manipulation skills would
result in experimental errors.[7] The elementary science class could use
the garden as a "perfect laboratory in which to study the subjects of
temperature, light, moisture, soil, and air that are the fundamental conditions of growth."[8]

Although nature study provided opportunities for students to use investigations and observations to draw relationships, the actual practice of nature study in schools may have been different. The Thirty-first Yearbook Committee criticized nature study for a focus on facts, with an exclusion of principles. They also criticized nature study because of the sharp distinction in intellectual ability made between elementary and secondary students. To the Thirty-first Yearbook Committee, mental ability was seen as a gradual and continuous growth process and not a sharp distinction, as was proposed by Jackman and other advocates of nature study.[9]

The Fourth Yearbook again addressed science education. Ellen Richards in "The Present Status and Future Development of Domestic Science Courses in the High School" argued that domestic science should become part of the high school curriculum to help students attain the goals of social, economic, and individual abilities. She defined domestic science as scientific principles applied to the home and individual. The Yearbook presented an outline for the study of domestic science in high school, with such divergent topics as the study of textiles, hygiene, and physics to be studied the first year. Topics such as sanitation and civics, botany, chemistry, and physics were the suggested sequence for the fourth year. Domestic science, Richards further argued, should allow students to develop their "reasoning power" to solve problems.[10]

A discussion of science next appeared in the Thirty-first Yearbook.[11] The Thirty-first Yearbook Committee focused on designing a program for teaching science, as follows:

The new theory requires a curriculum in which learning experiences shall be arrayed in such a manner that, as the child progresses through successive grades, he will have opportunity for continuous enlargement of his knowledge of the problems, principles, and generalizations that scholarly men find worthy of study. The new interpretation of the process of menial growth has now such general acceptance that it has determined the character of our institution for elementary and secondary education, but it has not yet had full recognition in determining the objectives, content and methods of the subjects of study.[12]

The Thirty-first Yearbook Committee held this view of curriculum structure because they envisioned learning as a gradual and continuous process "that begins with the learning experiences of early childhood and continues throughout the period of life."[13] Unfortunately, no coordinated effort existed to develop such an integrated program of study. The program of science education rested on outdated attitudes of development. Nature study dominated the elementary grades, and more specialized programs existed in the high school. The Thirty-first Yearbook Committee adopted new ideas, in which learning was seen as a gradual and concomitant growth of capabilities, which led to a new, generalized program of study for kindergarten through the twelfth grade science. The Committee pictured the major generalizations of science and the associate scientific attitudes as "so important and so extensive in scope that the student may live with them throughout his life."[14] A list of thirty-eight principles and generalizations was presented to guide the selection of specific objectives for science teaching. For instance, the eleventh generalization stated, "All life has evolved from simple forms." The thirty-first generalization stated "The kinetic energy of the molecules determines the physical states of matter."[15]

The Thirty-first Yearbook Committee addressed students' developing functional understandings and scientific attitudes. Functional knowledge would allow individuals to apply and use ideas to make their lives better. The Thirty-first Yearbook Committee also stressed that scientific attitudes come about through the "doing" of scientific investigations. Because the Committee viewed scientific attitudes as characterized by "respect for truth and by freedom from prejudice and personal bias,"[16] the scientific method was seen as a way of instilling these values. They advocated the selection of subject matter so that students could use the scientific method to solve real problems.

A discussion of science education was absent from the NSSE Yearbooks until the Forty-sixth Yearbook, *Science Education in the American School*.[17] The need for a new yearbook arose because of advances in science that occurred during the 1930s and 1940s, particularly those during World War II. The Forty-sixth Yearbook Committee drafted two overall goals for the Yearbook.

- To present a challenging and workable philosophy which will assist and encourage teachers of science to make the contribution to the welfare of our society which they, through their instruction and professional activities, can make and which society expects them to make.
- New kinds of courses and new methods and devices in science instruction are being developed in many places. It is the purpose here to examine these developments, to appraise them, and to determine, in so far as possible, what their implications for the future seem to be.[18]

One major focus of the Forty-sixth Yearbook Committee was on the teaching of science. The Forty-sixth Committee viewed both deductive and inductive teaching as equally important and essential to every science class. However, they were dismayed at the almost exclusive use of the deductive method. They recommended that in most cases the inductive method should be used to develop understanding of the concept and principle. Although they realized that the inductive method consumed much time, they believed that the resulting student outcomes justified the time investment.[19]

The Forty-sixth Yearbook Committee also spoke strongly on the role of the laboratory in science education.

It is regrettable that, in a majority of science classes in which demonstrations and individual pupil experiments are performed, the chief, if not the sole function served by these activities is to verify facts and principles already learned.[20]

To the Forty-sixth Yearbook Committee, verification activities were rarely justified, and they emphasized the antithesis of science. Rather, the Committee recommended the inductive method, with laboratory work preceding, not following, classroom discussion of a concept or principle. They stressed the importance of students making observations and experiencing phenomena.

The Committee viewed de-emphasis on memorization of isolated facts as critical and called for the teaching of concepts and principles to be functional. More important, the Committee stressed that such functional knowledge needs to go beyond the laboratory and "*function* in the daily activities of young people."[21] Textbooks, to the Committee, contained more material than a teacher could effectively teach and caused too many teachers to try to teach "too much."[22]

The Forty-sixth Yearbook Committee also concerned itself with what content should be taught. For instance, in Chapter XIII, "The Content and Methods of Senior High School Science," the Committee concluded that the physics content had "gone stale through the adherence to a set and largely nonfunctional pattern of organization."[23] The Committee recommended that the physics curriculum focus on central themes, a proposal previously made by the Thirty-first Yearbook Committee. They also made recommendations on the structure of the elementary program. At the elementary level students should be acquainted with broad areas of physical and biological science, including such topics as conditions necessary for life, and physical and chemical phenomena.

The NSSE Yearbooks played an important role in shaping the direction of science education in this country in the first half of the twentieth century. A vision of science education emerged in which memorization of scientific facts was de-emphasized and was replaced by one in which students developed understandings that they could apply throughout their lives. In addition, an emphasis was placed on students developing scientific attitudes through scientific investigations, as well as learning the big principles of science.

Development of Inquiry-based Curriculum

The years 1955-1974 have been called "The Golden Age in Education" because of the prominent position education held in the United States. The Sputnik crises in 1957, in which the United States believed it was losing a competitive edge in science and technology to Russia, and criticisms by scientists levied against science education as not mirroring the nature of science helped to fuel this era. Although the Forty-sixth Yearbook Committee tried to steer how science should be taught in schools by recommending inductive teaching and scientific investigations, many of their suggestions did not take hold. The Fifty-ninth Yearbook stated that "little has changed in the past twenty-five years."[24]

The Fifty-ninth Yearbook brought together scientists and educators at the request of the National Science Teachers Association to reassess the purpose of science education in light of increasing significance of science in American culture and criticisms against science teaching.[25] The Fifty-ninth Yearbook Committee's position as to how science should be carried out in schools reflected the development of the inquiry-based curricula that were produced during the late 1950s and 1960s.

Perhaps the greatest injustice that can be done to science is to regard it merely as a collection of facts, and the practice of science as little more than the routine accumulation of minutiae. It is true that science deals with hard, inflexible facts, but it has also to do with very general ideas and abstract principles; and it is the co-ordination of these ideas and observed facts that is the essence of modern science. Facts alone do not constitute a science.[26]

Paul DeH. Hurd, in "Science Education for Changing Times," presented objectives for science teaching emphasizing this position, and stressed that the Yearbook provide a "model by which the teacher may orient his thinking in developing his own purposes for teaching science."[27] Hurd presented seven objectives:

- Students should acquire a useful command of science concepts and principles.
- Students should acquire the ability to carry out the process of inquiry that involves "careful observing, seeking the most reliable data, and then using rationale process to give order to the data and to suggest possible conclusions for further research."[28]
- Students need to understand how society is dependent on scientific and technological achievements.
- Students need to develop an appreciation of the place of science in the modern world, the methods and procedures involved in scientific discovery, the individuals who pursue science, and an intellectual satisfaction for pursuing science as a career or hobby.
- Students need to develop scientific attitudes, such as open-mindedness and a desire for accurate knowledge.
- Students should be acquainted with various careers associated with an understanding of science.
- Students need to acquire certain abilities that will allow them to continue their own learning. Some of these abilities include:
  - Reading and interpreting science writings
  - Locating authoritative sources of science information
  - Performing suitable experiments
  - Using the tools and techniques of science
  - Making valid inferences and predictions from data
  - Recognizing and evaluating assumptions underlying techniques and processes used in solving problems
  - Expressing ideas qualitatively and quantitatively
  - Using the knowledge of science for responsible social action
  - Seeking new relationships and ideas from known facts and concepts.[29]

Hence, like the Forty-sixth Yearbook Committee, the Fifty-ninth Yearbook Committee was concerned with students "doing" science. This position is clearly stated by the Fifty-ninth Yearbook Committee:

With reference to the acquisition of scientific methods and attitudes, it seems obvious that if students are to develop these abilities they must have practice in them. That is, situations should be designed to allow students to select worth-while problems and attempt to solve them. They should have experience in collecting data, making guesses, devising experiments, and checking for accuracy while cultivating methods and attitudes conducive to effective learning in the field of science.[30]

The Fifty-ninth Yearbook Committee saw science as important for all students in the elementary school. They also suggested that the content of the elementary program should be structured in broad areas, similar to the Forty-sixth Yearbook Committee's recommendations. They mentioned areas of living things, resources for the earth, weather, and changes in the earth.

The Fifty-ninth Yearbook Committee was concerned that general science courses were not offered in junior high school as often as other courses during the mid-fifties. Ideally, these courses, structured so that they were relevant to the lives of the students, would draw upon all scientific disciplines for content. As students progressed through the seventh and eighth grades, they should be exposed to more interpretative theoretical science and less descriptive-based content science. As students developed their abilities to internalize concepts, they were to be exposed to more and more problem-based laboratory work.

In the ninth grade, three different general science courses were thought appropriate, depending on the students' backgrounds. A general biology course was offered for students without a strong background in science. This course would serve as an "orientation to science" through examination of several interconnected content areas related to current problems/issues.[31] For students with a background in science, two general courses were offered: biology and physical science. Both courses were designed to give students a deeper understanding of the current methods of scientific research through problem-solving laboratory activities. Students would study "concepts of life" in the biology course and concepts of matter and energy in the physical science course. In both courses, the application to society was stressed. If students selected a general course of study in science, the general courses would be available. If students chose to specialize in the later school years, this option should be available to them as well. For these students or college-bound students, chemistry, physics and advanced biology courses were often available.

In the late 1950s, the Physical Science Study Committee proposed a redesign of high school chemistry and physics courses. They recommended reducing the number of topics covered in each course, and suggested that each develop the student's understanding of a few fundamental concepts in modern thinking of the scientific discipline. In each course, the laboratory portion was crucial and evolved into a problem-solving experience—unlike the traditional cookbook method. In doing so, the activities were made meaningful and challenging to the high school students. In addition, an advanced biology course was offered, which was structured on current modern biology.[32]

Unlike previous Yearbooks, recommendations for future research in science education were made in the Fifty-ninth Yearbook.[33] Fletcher

Watson and William Cooley, in "Needed Research in Science Education," suggested broad areas of research, including a) the learning process, b) the learner and c) the teacher. Paul DeH. Hurd and Philip Johnson, in "Problems and Issues in Science Education," ended the Fifty-ninth Yearbook by considering problems and issues in science education. Several of the problems and issues discussed in the Yearbook remain important today. These include 1) What criteria should be used to select the content of science courses? 2) What criteria do we use to select the material? 3) How should an articulated kindergarten through twelfth grade program in which material is not repeated be developed? and 4) How should a competent core of science teachers be maintained?[34]

During the Golden Era of Education, the U.S. government invested 117 million dollars in the development of science curricula at the elementary and secondary levels to meet two goals:

1. To enrich the science curricula with up-to-date scientific knowledge.
2. To stress scientific inquiry through laboratory experiments.

Teams of scientists, educators, psychologists, and teachers developed a variety of curricular materials. These materials, developed according to learning theories of Jean Piaget, Jerome Bruner and Joseph Schwab, were adapted to the knowledge of the science disciplines, focused on laboratory activities, and stressed the importance of pure science.[35] Key concepts, based upon the following, were included in the new curriculum:

- Presented basic principles of the discipline
- Explained scientific phenomena
- Illustrated scientific phenomena
- Derived from evidence and data
- Developed cognitive skills
- Stressed the role of science in the human enterprise.[36]

Several major high school curricula were developed, including *Biological Sciences Curricula Study* (BSCS), *Physical Science Study Committee* (PSSC), *Harvard Project Physics* (HPP), *Chemical Bond Approach* (CBA), and *Chemical Education Materials Study* (ChemStudy).[37]

The BSCS curricula stressed the development of scientific knowledge, focused on scientific inquiry, and integrated historical and philosophical aspects of science.[38] The curriculum design allowed students to develop understanding through observations and laboratory experiences in which students collected data and drew conclusions. To accommodate the diversity of content and methods used in life sciences, BSCS created three versions of the same course, each focusing on different aspects of biology.[39] Together with the textbooks, BSCS developed student materials, such as laboratory experiments and films to illustrate experiments that were difficult to perform in the laboratory.[40]

The PSSC curriculum regarded the student as a "young researcher," minimized the use of formulas, and stressed the importance of critical thinking. The curriculum presented aspects of modern physics, and excluded most technological applications and some topics of the traditional physics curricula. The curriculum materials consisted of a textbook, a student's workbook, a detailed laboratory guide, and films. The laboratory guide consisted of fifty-one experiments designed to develop concepts presented in the textbook.[41]

The CBA stressed the importance of theory and experiments in the learning of chemistry and focused on students developing logical thinking skills. The unifying theme was the chemical bond, as reflected in the title, *Chemical Bond Approach*.[42] The curriculum expected students to use theory to explain their observations obtained during laboratory exercises and encouraged discussing mental models, such as atomic structure, kinetic theory, and energy.

CHEMStudy focused on the nature of scientific investigation and the way that scientific knowledge was generated.[43] To promote the learning of chemistry, the curriculum emphasized the discovery approach and the integration of laboratory experiments and classroom work, while encouraging students to understand basic concepts rather than to memorize the definition of terms. CHEMStudy de-emphasized practical uses of chemistry in the home and industry. The curriculum included a textbook, a teacher's guide, laboratory experiments, and equipment.[44]

The 1960s also saw the development of kindergarten through eighth grade and junior high school programs that focused on inquiry or scientific processes. At the elementary level, three major curricula were developed. The *Elementary Science Study* program (ESS) focused on students' exploration of science phenomena through open-ended units.[45] The developers drew from Piaget's developmental theories to develop approximately sixty teacher modules in the life and physical sciences. These modules encouraged students to explore science through a discovery approach and recommended that teachers serve as guides. Some of these modules are still published by Delta. *Science: A Process Approach* (SAPA), developed by AAAS, centered on students developing the processes of observation, measurement, classification, and prediction.[46] Robert Gagne's work on task analysis formed the underlying structure of SAPA.[47] The SAPA materials tightly structured student work and relied extensively on kits.[48] *Science Curriculum Improvement Study* (SCIS) focused on students developing understanding of both the process and product of science.[49] Robert Karplus's learning cycle—exploration, concept-invention, and application—provided the main instructional methodology.[50] The exploration and application phases relied on laboratory activities. The exploration phase also provided experiences and data that the teacher could use to develop concept understanding in the concept-invention phase. During the application phase, students would apply their new understandings to hands-on situations. Although different in their approaches, ESS, SAPA, and SCIS helped bring science instruction to the elementary science classroom on a large scale.

The most widely used junior high science curricula developed during the 1960s included *Introductory Physical Science* (IPS), *Probing the Natural World*, and *Investigating the Earth. Introductory Physical Science* used laboratory activities to help students "discover" fundamental concepts of science.[51] IPS focused on a small set of concepts and principles central to physical science and included very few practical applications. *Probing the Natural World* used a laboratory-based, self-paced, individualized approach to help students learn physical science concepts.[52] *Investigating the Earth* focused on students performing activities, stressed the methods of science, and showed the relationship among the different science areas.[53]

The National Science Foundation (NSF) not only committed funds for the development of kindergarten through twelfth grade curriculum materials, but also committed large sums for in-service education programs to help teachers understand the new materials. By the mid-1960s, teachers attended summer workshops to learn how to use the new curricula.

The curricula of the 1960s stressed inquiry, focusing on the discovery or exploration of key scientific principles. Curriculum materials focused on such ideas as: What is science? How does scientific knowledge accumulate? How do scientists work? and What are the models and theories scientists use to guide their work? In answering these questions through inquiry-directed curricula, it was thought that students would learn key scientific concepts and main principles.

Impact of the Curricula Developed During the 1960s

David Elliott in the Eighty-eighth Yearbook described the science curriculum projects of the 1960s as providing updated content that permitted in-depth study, a rich variety of multimedia materials, emphasis on "doing" science through "hands-on" learning activities, and a focus on using unifying themes.[54] John Keeves and Glen Aikenhead, in *Improving Science Education*, presented a similar view. They stated that curriculum reform movements in the 1960s in the U.S., as well as those in Great Britain, had profound and lasting effects on science teaching throughout the world.[55]

During the 1970s, NSF funded studies to explore the impact of the new science curricula. The results indicated that although the new materials were widely used, criticisms of science education still existed.[56] The new curricula, particularly the high school materials, were seen as 1) too difficult for most high school students, 2) no more popular than the older science curricula, 3) not related to everyday life, and 4) failing to increase the number of students who majored in science. These studies indicated the curricula were appropriate for science-oriented students, but not for heterogeneous groups of students.

Researchers examined the level of inquiry specified in the newly developed materials. Dudley Herron, and Vincent Lunetta and Pinchus Tamir found through the analysis of laboratory manuals that the BSCS, PSSC, and CHEMStudy laboratory exercises represented a very low level of inquiry.[57] Students worked often as technicians following "cookbook" recipes. Work by Avi Hofstein and Vincent Lunetta showed that student performance on practical activities was not assessed, and that students were seldom asked to describe or explain hypotheses, methodologies, or results.[58] Lunetta and Tamir recommended greater consistency between the goals, theories, and practice of the curricula.[59] William Kyle, John Penick, and James Shymansky found that teachers were not familiar with using laboratory investigations as a method of teaching. They recommended professional development courses to prepare teachers to use laboratory investigations.[60]

Studies indicated, however, that the curriculum projects led to greater achievement and positive attitudes toward science than did the more traditional approaches. Shymansky and colleagues completed comprehensive studies comparing student outcomes in the 1960s curricula with those in traditional curricula. Based on two meta-analyses, they concluded that the 1960s curricula had a positive effect on student achievement, attitude, and high-order thinking.[61] Ted Bredderman, based on a meta-analysis of studies of ESS, SAPA, and SCIS, reported similar claims.[62]

Yet, the impact of 1960s science curricula remains unclear. The Seventy-second and Eighty-ninth Yearbooks painted a picture that showed the 1960s curricula failing to take hold in schools.[63] Although an update and expansion of subject matter did occur and a rich array of media resulted, what did not carry over was the stress on inquiry, discovery and student initiative in asking questions and seeking answers. Despite unprecedented funding from the federal government and private agencies, the 1960s curricula failed to eradicate a focus on memorization. Arthur Woodward and David Elliot in the Eighty-ninth Yearbook stated that most science textbooks in the 1980s were compendia of scientific terms in which more and more content was continuously added.[64] Many textbooks required the learning of new and unfamiliar facts. These materials were a far cry from what developers of the 1960s envisioned. Unfortunately, many of the materials never dominated the market. After an initial flurry of use, the 1960s curricula failed to take root in schools. The dominant instructional material continued to be the conventional textbook.

Although studies provided evidence that the1960s curricula led to improved achievement and attitude toward science, research also revealed serious weaknesses in the curricula with respect to promoting inquiry and meeting the needs of all students. Wilma Longstreet in the Seventy-second Yearbook and David Elliot in the Eighty-ninth Yearbook ascribed the failure of the 1960s materials to teachers not adopting the new philosophies advocated by the materials.[65] According to Longstreet, the fact that 1960s curricula brought a

significant shift in program objectives from factual acquisition to process and concept acquisition inevitably meant a profound restructuring of the conception of what was educationally valuable.[66]

Shifts in the role of the student and the teacher needed to occur for the 1960s curricula to be successful. The student had to change from a passive consumer of authoritative knowledge to an active producer of concepts and generalizations. This shift in students' roles necessitated a major change in the role of the teacher: from a dispenser of knowledge to a guide. According to Longstreet and Elliot, these shifts never occurred. Although NSF also provided funding for teacher professional development, these efforts were not intense, focused, or spread over time to support change in teachers who were not ready for discovery/inquiry learning. Teachers' educational experience, teacher preparation programs, and professional development experience did not prepare teachers for the flexibility required for discovery/inquiry learning.[67]

New Reform Movements of the 1980s and 1990s

During the late 1970s and the early 1980s, the concern for preparing future scientists and providing students with a rigorous understanding of the structure of the discipline decreased. The importance of integrating social, humanistic, and cultural aspects in science teaching, as well as providing "scientific literacy" to future citizens, became the main goals of science education. Science and technology for all learners emerged as a slogan that embodied a new challenge for science educators.[68] Norris Harms and Robert Yager claimed that science and technology should be part of the education of all "future citizens."[69] The Science, Technology, and Society (STS) approach emerged as an effort to produce an informed citizenry capable of making crucial decisions about current problems and issues, and taking personal actions as a result of those decisions. The purpose of science education was to develop scientifically literate individuals who understood how science, technology, and society influenced one another.

In the 1990s, the STS objectives merged with new goals in science education to foster scientific literacy for all students. Those favoring scientific literacy argued that all students should be able to apply scientific understanding, critical thinking skills, and problem-solving abilities to everyday experiences. Based upon new ideas in learning theory, science learning was seen as involving students in making connections between their current knowledge of science and new scientific ideas presented to them. Moreover, it was believed that students needed to apply science content to new questions and engage in problem solving, planning, decision making, and group discussions.[70]

The National Research Council's (NRC) *National Science Education Standards* raised inquiry to a new level by advocating that more emphasis be given to the following features:

- Understanding of scientific concepts and developing abilities to do inquiry
- Learning subject matter disciplines in the context of inquiry, science and technology, science from personal and social perspectives, and the history and nature of science

- Integrating all aspects of science content (life science, physical science, and earth science)
- Studying a few fundamental concepts
- Implementing inquiry as an instructional strategy.[71]

The NRC further argued

Inquiry into authentic questions generated from student experience is the central strategy for teaching science. Teachers focus inquiry predominately on real phenomena, in classrooms, outdoors, or in laboratory settings, where students are given investigations or guided toward fashioning investigations that are demanding but within their capacities.[72]

In *Improving Science Education*, Herbert Walberg and Barry Fraser discussed how *Project 2061: Science for All Americans* emphasized the importance of cultivating a scientifically literate society and urged substantial and systematic changes in traditional science curricula.[73] *Benchmarks for Science Literacy* specified how students should progress toward scientific literacy and recommended what they should know and be able to do at certain grade levels. The *National Science Education Standards* gave a coherent vision of what it means to be scientifically literate. The benchmarks and standards specified science content expectations at various levels of kindergarten through twelfth grade education. Both *Benchmarks for Scientific Literacy* and the *National Science Education Standards* focused on limiting the number of concepts and principles students studied, but stressed students developing deeper understandings.[74]

These documents have stimulated much thinking about reform in science education. Science standards have influenced science curriculum frameworks in almost all fifty states. These documents, which set standards for all students, aimed to develop high academic standards for all students.

Current Ideas in Learning Theory

Developments in cognitive and social psychology have led to new ways of understanding human learning and knowledge. For example, research showed that when information is acquired through memorization of discrete facts, the level and kind of understanding that results makes it difficult for students to access this information and apply it to new situations.[75] Alternatively, when students acquire new information in a meaningful context and relate it to what is already known, they connect new information to better, larger, and more linked conceptual networks of understanding.[76]

Current theory holds that understanding does not result from memorization, but from an individual's active construction of meaning based upon his or her experiences and interactions in the world. In a sense, learners make their understanding; understanding does not occur by passively taking in information transmitted from a teacher. Building understanding is a continuous process that requires new experiences where students construct and reconstruct what they know. Knowledge is not revealed but built by exploration of the surrounding world, observation and interaction with phenomena, and discussion and interaction with peers, teachers, and more knowledgeable others.[77] One demonstration, for example, will not suffice for teaching a scientific concept. Although such a demonstration might help students learn new terms and form the beginning of an idea, it does not help learners see how the concept explains various phenomena or how the concept is connected to other ideas. Learners benefit from varied opportunities to express and explore their ideas.

Learning also needs to be contextualized for children to develop understanding that they can apply.[78] Phyllis Blumenfeld and her colleagues reiterated this notion by stating, "Knowing and doing are not separated; knowledge is not an abstract phenomenon that readily can be transferred from how it is learned in the classroom for use in other situations."[79] Blumenfeld and colleagues implied that for learners to develop understandings that they can use in new situations, they need to apply their emerging knowledge in situations that are meaningful and important to them. Moreover, learners need to apply knowledge to different situations for their new understandings to be useful in a variety of situations.

Another principle fundamental to learning is social interaction.[80] It involves shared experiences and understandings among students, teachers, community members, or experts. Learners develop understandings of concepts and construct meaning about ideas through sharing, using, and debating ideas with others. The scientific enterprise involves collaborative work.[81]

A final principle central to the development of integrated understandings is that the use of cognitive tools can amplify and expand what students can learn. Cognitive tools, such as computers and accompanying software programs, should help learners solve complex and challenging problems. These tools can support the learner in 1) accessing and collecting a range of scientific data and information, 2) providing visualization and data analysis tools similar to those used by scientists, 3) allowing for collaboration and sharing of information across sites, and 4) developing multimedia documents that illustrate student understanding.[82] These features expand the range of questions that students can investigate and the multitude of phenomena students can experience. The incorporation of technology tools can help transform the science classroom into an environment in which learners actively construct understanding.[83]

Based upon Dennis C. Phillips' description of constructivism presented in the Ninety-ninth Yearbook, the ideas we have presented regarding student learning would be labeled as an example of "constructivism." The Ninety-ninth Yearbook, *Constructivism in Education*, explored the meaning and value of constructivism as a theory to drive practice.[84] Dennis Phillips and Michael Matthews eloquently described the range of meanings that the term "constructivism" holds. Matthews presented various dimensions of constructivism. On the one extreme, constructivism refers to a position on the nature of public knowledge that has been influenced by social forces. One conclusion that follows from this position is that different fields of study, such as physics or biology, do not give an objective reflection of the external world but rather one that is socially constructed. On the other extreme, constructivism refers to how an individual learns. This second position describes learning as being actively constructed by the individual, similar to the position we describe above. Taken to the extreme, this position holds that people cannot construct the same understandings.[85]

The Ninety-ninth Yearbook brought clarity and bounds to the construct of "constructivism." We found, moreover, the position advocated by Richard Gunstone in the volume refreshing. Gunstone argued that although many science educators view themselves as constructivists with respect to the fundamental position they take toward learning, they are not philosophers of science interested in working through the nuances of constructivist theory. Rather, science educators see their work as improving the teaching and learning of science. As Gunstone stated

These researchers [science educators] are not philosophers of science; they are users of philosophy of science in pursuit of better learning and teaching of science.[86]

Inquiry-Based Curricula of the Late 1980s and 1990s

These new ideas in learning, as well as the positions advocated by AAAS and NRC, led to the development of new curriculum projects.

These curricula focused on students performing authentic tasks, learning in context, engaging students in investigations, collaborating, using cognitive tools, and meeting national standards. Inquiry was seen as a strategy for teaching and learning.[87] Inquiry, a central tenet of science, is defined by scientists as the process of conceiving problems, formulating hypotheses, designing experiments, gathering data, and drawing conclusions about a scientific problem or science phenomena.[88]

The designs of the projects allowed students to link new information to existing ideas, build and justify explanations, and make connections between ideas. Many of the curriculum projects discussed below were supported by NSF. They represent only a sample of the innovative programs resulting from work in the late 1980s and 1990s. We will contrast these new projects to the curriculum efforts of the 1960s in the next section.

Scientists in Action, designed on the principle of anchored instruction, creates anchors or foci that generate interest and focuses students on problem solving.[89] Video-based science units, targeted for fifth and sixth graders, create complex contexts that include real-world problems. *Scientists in Action* emphasizes the development of students' scientific reasoning and problem-solving strategies and on integrating knowledge across subject areas.

Computer as Learning Partner (CLP), a project started in the late 1980s, provides a semester-long integrated curriculum for teaching middle-school students basic physical science concepts.[90] The CLP project, which emphasizes conceptual change, begins with students' naïve exploratory heuristics and concepts, and uses technology tools to guide students through a series of predefined experiments and writing exercises that challenge students' previous beliefs.

Based on research from the CLP program, the *Scaffolded Knowledge Integration* (SKI) framework was developed. It has four interrelated aspects: 1) promoting lifelong science learning, 2) making the thinking of science visible, 3) creating autonomous learners who take responsibility for their own learning, and 4) considering the social context of science learning.[91] The SKI framework has been used to build the *Knowledge Integration Environment* (KIE). KIE uses World Wide Web resources and scaffolds to assist students in finding evidence and building arguments around meaningful questions.[92]

The *One Sky Many Voices* project, designed for middle-school science students to investigate meteorological phenomena, uses Internet resources, real-time and near-time data, visualization resources, peers distributed worldwide, and practicing scientists to promote authentic science teaching.[93] The authentic nature of the activities enables students to communicate directly with individuals who have firsthand experiences with phenomena they are studying and to work directly with professional-quality and real-time data in much the same manner scientists do. The curriculum consists of 1) classroom activities utilizing peer coaching and information exchange worldwide, 2) access to updated science developments, and 3) a curricular shell that allows adaptation to local content needs and technology infrastructure.

Learning through Collaborative Visualization, developed for use with high school earth science classes, emphasizes collaboration and investigation.[94] Students posed questions about weather and climate, such as, "What were the weather conditions like that led to the disastrous wild fires in the Los Angeles area in 1993?" "Why is the altitude lower at the poles than near the equator?" and "What is the impact of volcanoes on weather?" Next, students used National Meteorological Center data to explore their questions individually or in small groups, communicating with students in the classroom and with students in other schools. Students used real data and technology tools that mirror ones used by scientists. The program did not have a fixed structure or curriculum; it left decisions about the content and instructional specifications (e.g., topic, outcome, and duration) to individual classroom teachers. Consequently, the degree of structure and direction varied across classrooms.

Kids Network, developed by TERC in the late 1980s and distributed by the National Geographic Society, was one of the first programs that focused on project-based approaches to learning in which technology, especially telecommunications, played a key role.[95] Designed for elementary and middle-school students, the units focused on such questions as "How does your body get the oxygen it needs?" "What's in our water?" and "Too much trash?" To answer these questions, students planned investigations, and gathered, interpreted, and shared data with others. The unit questions encouraged long-distance collaborative investigations that exploited regional differences. Students worked together in small groups to conduct their investigations and transmit their findings via telecommunication to other classes in their research team. Locally collected data were transmitted to a central point, where it was pooled, summarized, and distributed across sites for comparative analysis by scientists who also answered questions via telecommunications.

Project-based Science (PBS) engages students in sustained inquiry.[96] Educational researchers have identified key features related to PBS: 1) a driving question encompassing worthwhile content that is meaningful and anchored in a real-world problem; 2) investigations and artifact creation that allow students to learn concepts, apply information, and represent knowledge; 3) collaboration among students, teachers, and others in the community; and 4) use of technology tools. Several projects have been created based upon these ideas that support students in long-term investigations.[97]

TinkerTools engages middle-school students learning about and reflecting on scientific inquiry.[98] Using a model called the inquiry cycle, students question, predict, experiment, model, and apply their ideas. Software tools support students in the process.

Common Features of the Programs Developed in the 1990s and Differences between Them and the 1960s Curriculum Materials

The programs developed in the 1990s have common features that differ substantially from those of the 1960s. Both developmental efforts, however, made use of current learning theories of their era. Influential thinkers, such as Jerome Bruner and Joseph Schwab, impacted the curriculum projects of the 1960s. Jean Piaget's theories of development also influenced the curriculum projects, particularly those at the elementary level.[99] In contrast, the 1990s curriculum projects incorporate current theories about learning. Although the 1990s efforts had varied interpretations of the learning principles, the efforts can be classified as a family of enactments.[100] Other differences between the 1960s and 1990s curriculum projects resulted from political and social conditions existing at the time of the developments. Below we discuss the differences with respect to 1) purpose of inquiry, 2) instructional differences, and 3) intended outcomes.

PURPOSE OF INQUIRY

Although both the 1960s and 1990s curricula stress inquiry, the focus of the inquiry differs. In the 1960s curriculum efforts, inquiry focused on students exploring the regularities and patterns in science concepts. The purpose of the inquiry was to discover or illustrate a scientific concept or principle. For example, in ChemStudy students performed inquiries to explore the nature of chemical equilibrium.[101] In the 1990s programs, students apply concepts and principles to explore meaningful questions. For instance, in the *Scientist in Action Series* the exploration of water quality is used to introduce students to a variety of scientific concepts. Students then apply these concepts to further explore water quality. In *One Sky Many Voices*, students learn basic weather concepts needed to predict the weather. Project-based science uses benchmark lessons to introduce students to important concepts and principles central to the question being explored.[102] The teacher can also use benchmark lessons to help students develop thinking strategies and process skills. The 1960s curricula were heavily criticized because they failed to mindfully engage students in the inquiry. The 1990s curricula focus on mindful "activity" that will engage students in the content.

INSTRUCTIONAL DIFFERENCES

A number of instructional differences exist between the curriculum efforts of the 1960s and 1990s. First, because the 1960s curricula stressed exploring scientific principles devoid of application and connection to society, they were considered disconnected from the lives of learners. In contrast, the 1990s programs focus students on exploring questions and problems that learners can potentially find meaningful and related to their lives.

Second, the 1990s programs take advantage of what we know about collaboration and building communities of learners to promote learning. Many of the 1990s programs stress collaboration between peers. Others stress collaborations between peers, the community, and scientists. Nancy Songer's *One Sky Many Voices* project makes use of student-scientist collaboration through the use of World Wide Web resources. In contrast, the 1960s programs focused more on the individual.

Third, the curriculum programs of the 1960s and 1990s also differ in their approach to assessment. The 1960s programs focused mainly on paper and pencil tests as a means of assessing learning. In contrast, the 1990s curriculum projects stress the use of multiple methods for assessing student learning. Programs focus on the products that students develop through their investigations as vehicles for both promoting learning and assessing student understanding.

Fourth, most but not all of the 1990s programs take advantage of new learning technologies to support students in exploring, finding information, and communicating. The power and portability of technology during the 1990s, the ubiquitous presence of technology in society, and the decreasing cost of technology led many of the developers to explore the use of these new resources. In contrast, portable technology was not available in the 1960s.

INTENDED OUTCOMES

The programs developed in the 1960s and 1990s also differ with respect to their intended outcomes. Because the 1960s curricula were developed at a time when policymakers feared the United States lacked scientists and technicians to compete globally, the programs sought to prepare individuals who would pursue the study of science. In contrast, the 1990s programs stress developing scientific literacy for all students. The social and political forces at work helped push the idea that all individuals need to know science to make decisions in their daily lives.

Both the 1960s and 1990s programs stressed student learning. However, the focus of the learning differed. The 1960s programs focused student learning on the structure of the disciplines and on basic concepts. The 1990s programs stressed students applying and using ideas to find solutions to important questions. The 1990s programs are also built on meeting national standards which did not exist in the 1960s.

Challenges Related to Enacting Inquiry-based Curriculum of the 1980s and 1990s

Several studies indicate that reform-based science programs that focus on inquiry pose challenges for both learners and teachers. Learners initially face challenges in carrying out and learning through inquiry. Teachers' background in pedagogy and subject matter knowledge creates challenges for teaching through inquiry. These challenges are similar to the ones Wilma Longstreet described in the Seventy-second Yearbook when explaining why the curricula of the 1960s failed. Hence, the challenges faced by students and teachers should not be surprising.

LEARNERS

Challenges exist for students performing the various phases of inquiry: 1) asking appropriate questions, 2) finding and synthesizing information, 3) monitoring scientific procedures, 4) designing investigations, and 5) drawing valid conclusions.

With respect to question asking, students often ask questions that require little effort to answer and that are primarily factual or require yes/no answers, rather than questions that can extend their understanding of a topic.[103] Joseph Krajcik and colleagues found that seventh graders often used personal interest and preferences as sources for questions.[104] Often the questions they developed were not tied to scientific ideas but rather to an attraction to some aspect of the situation or phenomena.

Students also had difficulty finding and synthesizing information related to their investigation, particularly when they searched for information on the World Wide Web. Raven Wallace and colleagues reported that students do not monitor what they have accomplished and they frequently lose their place if the search continues over a period of time, often repeating what they have done or not using the information they have already gathered.[105] Moreover, they have few strategies for reading or evaluating a considerable amount of material on-line.

Difficulties also exist for setting up experimental procedures. Students frequently design experiments that cannot support valid conclusions.[106] Krajcik and colleagues reported that many middle-school students were careful in setting up experimental procedures and constructing apparatus, following directions precisely.[107] However, students varied considerably in how systematic they were in following through on their plans for collecting and recording data. Students' lack of laboratory skills may also impede their work.[108]

Finally, challenges exist in students analyzing data. Krajcik and colleagues noted that although middle-school students had prepared charts and tables to record and organize their observations, individuals did not draw on these tools in transforming the data or looking for patterns of results when trying to synthesize conclusions.[109] This finding supports the work of Kathleen Metz.[110] She reported that the evidence students accept for support of a hypothesis is frequently inadequate.

Wolff-Michael Roth and Anita Roychoudhury claimed that students face these challenges because they lack experience with learning through inquiry.[111] However, these challenges are accentuated because students often rely on teacher directions, plans, and electronic resources, and do not show enough initiative behaviors during inquiry teaching.[112] Because of these challenges, students often fail to learn through inquiry. Carl Bereiter's work indicated that students tend to complete the work rather than learn about underlying science.[113] Moreover, students often do not understand the relationship between the purpose of the investigation and the design of the experiment they conducted. Students also do not connect the experimental work they are conducting to their previous knowledge or to previous experiments, hindering their formation of new understandings.[114]

TEACHERS

The teacher's background in pedagogy and subject-matter knowledge poses challenges for inquiry teaching.[115] Discrepancies exist in how teachers enact inquiry in the classroom and desired practice.[116]

Teachers reported not being prepared to guide students in inquiry science lessons.[117]

Ronald Marx and colleagues reported that teachers face difficulties in helping students ask thoughtful questions, designing investigations, and drawing conclusions from data.[118] Given the inadequate experience and preparation in inquiry teaching, these findings are not surprising. Most teachers themselves have never experienced science learning through inquiry.[119]

Teachers' limited understanding of collaboration can hinder implementation of inquiry-based curricula.[120] Frequently, student groups do not function well, unless teachers know how to use collaborative learning strategies.[121] Students may not know how to collaborate, may not respect one another, and seldom share information; as a result, less dominant students tend to agree with more dominant students.

Assessment in school science is often restricted to paper and pencil tests that do not examine inquiry skills or understanding of scientific investigation.[122] Inquiry teaching, however, requires a variety of alternative assessment methods, including creating products that represent student understanding. Teachers often do not know how to help students design and create products that represent their understanding of content and process adequately. In addition, teachers have difficulty judging the quality of student products.[123] To promote inquiry teaching, teachers need additional professional development and support in implementing alternative assessment strategies.[124]

Although technology can support students in learning through inquiry, teachers' backgrounds in the use of technology often pose challenges for effective use.[125] Often teachers lack preparation in the use of the technology and in how to support students in using technology. Another challenge faced by teachers is how to integrate technology tools into curriculum. Only recently have a number of good examples emerged.[126] Access to hardware can also pose a challenge to teachers. Often computers are tied up in computer labs not designed for science instruction. Phyllis Blumenfeld and colleagues pointed to policy issues, such as financial resources needed to obtain a sufficient number of computers, software packages, and access to telecommunication capabilities, as hindrances to using technology in the classroom.[127]

Finally, particularly at the elementary and middle-school levels, teachers' subject-matter knowledge hinders teachers' willingness and skills to enact inquiry-based teaching.[128] Lack of subject-matter knowledge prevents teachers from helping students see the connections between the content and the inquiry in which they are engaged.

Concluding Remarks

The analysis of the NSSE Yearbooks and the other documents reviewed reveal four persistent themes with respect to what content students should learn and how students should learn science. First, with respect to content, we see an ongoing push by scientists and the education community to continuously update the content. At the same time, we see a push to make certain the "big ideas" of science are focused upon. As the Thirty-first Yearbook Committee stated, "Major generalizations of science and the associate scientific attitudes are so important and so extensive in scope that the student may live with them throughout his life."[129]

Second, a continual effort persists to limit the number of concepts and principles students study in a year to allow for in-depth learning to occur. During the twentieth century, national organizations, scientists, and educators stressed the importance of creating a curriculum with a limited number of concepts and principles. *Benchmarks for Scientific Literacy* referred to curriculum as "overstuffed" and urged a radical reduction in the amount of material covered in the curriculum.[130] Yet, at the same time, as noted by Arthur Woodward and David Elliot in the Eighty-ninth Yearbook, curriculum publishers continually add more and more content to already stuffed textbooks.[131]

A third theme related to how science should be taught shows the persistent effort to make science teaching resemble the actual enterprise of science. A statement by the Forty-sixth Yearbook Committee amply summarized this position:

If the need for using a certain principle is felt, the gathering of the facts that lead to an understanding of the principle is well motivated. Under these circumstances, information gathered from textbooks, from reference books, from experts, from observations, and from experiments will contribute to the building of the concepts and understandings of the principles which the pupil needs to use. The idea is to start with the problem or difficulty and then seek facts, principles, methods or anything else that seems necessary for solving the problem.[132]

Scientists and educators have continually struggled to make science teaching resemble the practice of science during the twentieth century; yet, at the same time, textbooks and classroom practices persist in providing cookbook style hands-on activities.[133]

A fourth theme focuses on de-emphasizing the memorization of material and focusing on students developing problem-solving skills.

This de-emphasis of memorization of facts was stressed in the Thirty-first Yearbook and persisted in science education through the century.

The beginning of the twenty-first century shows promise in bringing about substantial and lasting change in science education. National support for science education is strong. However, given the failures of the 1960s curricula to bring about lasting change, what hope exists that the new reform movement in science education will succeed? In fact, Elliot and Woodward stated in the Eighty-ninth Yearbook that most attempts at educational reform over the past sixty years have had relatively minor effects on the American public school and the textbooks that have persisted as major structures of school programs.[134]

Although we know much work must be done to accomplish lasting change, we see hope. Despite the challenges posed by reform-based science teaching, strong reasons exist for believing substantial and lasting change will occur. New ideas in learning theory support the use of inquiry teaching. Teaching through inquiry can provide a context for students both to want to know, and to apply concepts and thinking skills. In addition, inquiry teaching reflects what occurs naturally in science. New professional development efforts for teachers and new pre-service programs that prepare teachers for reform-based teaching can help prevent the new emphasis on inquiry from sharing the same fate of other innovations. New models of professional development focus on cycles of conversation, enactment, and reflection to promote a vision of new possibilities, understanding of the basis for the innovation, and the development of strategies to meet the challenges.[135] New models of pre-service education focus on greater synergy between instructional practices in the science disciplines and in education, a greater range of school-based experiences, and more time for reflection on the melding of theory with practice. We also recognize that for lasting change to occur, a focus on the system is required to bring about standard-based reform. Issues of policy, infrastructure, curriculum, assessment, and professional development need consideration.[136]

It is fitting to close this chapter by quoting a prominent science educator of the twentieth century. F. James Rutherford, former Chief Executive Officer of the American Association for the Advancement of Science and previous Director of Project 2061, stated in his 1964 seminal paper the central role inquiry should take in science teaching.

When it comes to the teaching of science it is perfectly clear where we, as science teachers, science educators, or scientists stand: we are unalterably opposed to rote memorization of the mere facts and minutiae of science. By contrast we stand foursquare for the teaching of the scientific method, critical thinking, the scientific attitude, the problem-solving approach, the discovery method, and, of special interest here, the inquiry method. In brief, we appear to agree upon the need to teach science as process or method rather than as content.[137]

Perhaps in the twenty-first century, this vision of science teaching will be realized.

NOTES

1. The authors thank Hilda Borko from University of Colorado for her insightful suggestions and feedback on drafts of the chapter.

2. Nelson B. Henry, ed., *Science Education in American Schools*, Forty-Sixth Yearbook of the National Society for the Study of Education, Part I (Chicago: National Society for the Study of Education, 1947), p. 53.

3. Wilbur S. Jackman, *Nature Study*, Third Yearbook of the National Society for the Scientific Study of Education, Part II, ed. Manfred Holmes (Chicago: National Society for the Study of Education, 1904); Guy Montrose Whipple, ed., *A Program for Teaching Science*, Thirty-first Yearbook of the National Society for the Study of Education, Part I (Bloomington, IL: Public School Publishing Co., 1932); Henry, ed., *Science Education in American Schools*; Nelson B. Henry, ed., *Rethinking Science Education*, Fifty-ninth Yearbook of the National Society for the Study of Education, Part I (Chicago: National Society for the Study of Education, 1960). In 1904 and 1905 when the Third and Fourth Yearbooks were published, NSSE was referred to as the National Society for the Scientific Study of Education and not the National Society for the Study of Education.

4. David L Elliot and Arthur Woodward, eds., *Textbooks and Schooling in the United States*, Eighty-ninth Yearbook of the National Society for the Study of Education, Part I (Chicago: National Society for the Study of Education, 1990); Denis C. Phillips, ed., *Constructivism in Education: Opinions and Second Opinions on Controversial Issues*, Ninety-ninth Yearbook of the National Society for the Study of Education, Part I (Chicago: National Society for the Study of Education, 2000).

5. Barry J. Fraser and Herbert J. Walberg, eds., *Improving Science Education* (Chicago: National Society for the Study of Education, 1995).

6. American Association for the Advancement of Science, *Project 2061: Science for All Americans* (Washington, DC: AAAS, 1989); American Association for the Advancement of Society, *Benchmarks for Science Literacy* (New York: Oxford Press, 1993); National Research Council, *National Science Education Standards* (Washington, DC: National Academy Press, 1996).

7. Jackman, *Nature Study*, p. 13.

8. Ibid., p. 32.

9. Whipple, *A Program for Teaching Science*.

10. Ellen H. Richards, "The Present Status and Future Development of Domestic Science Courses in the High School," *The Place of Vocational Subjects in the High-School Curriculum*, Fourth Yearbook of the National Society for the Scientific Study of Education, Part II, ed. Manfred J. Holmes (Bloomington, IL: Public School Publishing Co., 1905).

11. Whipple, *A Program for Teaching Science*.

12. Ibid., p. 5.

13. Ibid., p. 10.

14. Ibid., p. 10.

15. Ibid., pp. 53-55.

16. Ibid., p. 38.

17. Henry, *Science Education in American Schools.*

18. Ibid., pp. 2-3.

19. Ibid., pp. 41-59. The Forty-sixth Yearbook Committee defined deductive methods as first presenting the principle and then giving students opportunities to illustrate, apply and exemplify the principle. They defined inductive teaching as progressing from the facts to concepts and principles.

20. Ibid., p. 51.

21. Ibid., p. 27. Here again as in the Thirty-first Yearbook, functional refers to an individual's ability to apply and use the concept and principles in a new situation or to solve a problem.

22. Ibid., p. 186.

23. Ibid., p. 209.

24. Paul DeH. Hurd, "Science Education for Changing Times," *Rethinking Science Education*, p. 33.

25. Henry, *Rethinking Science Education.*

26. J. Darrell Barnard, "The Role of Science in Our Culture," *Rethinking Science Education*, p. 5.

27. Hurd, "Science Education for Changing Times," p. 34.

28. Ibid., p. 35.

29. Ibid., pp. 34-37.

30. Paul L. Dressel, Mary Alice Burmester, John M. Mason, and Clarence H. Nelson, "How the Individual Learns Science," *Rethinking Science Education*, p. 48.

31. Robert H. Carleton, J. Darrell Barnard, Lucille Berlin, Ralph E. Keirstead, John J. Kinsella, Richard H. Lape, Margaret J. McKibben, and J. Henry Shutts, "Improving Secondary-School Science," *Rethinking Science Education*, p. 160.

32. Ibid.

33. Fletcher G. Watson and William W. Cooley, "Needed Research in Science Education," *Rethinking Science Education.*

34. Paul DeH. Hurd and Philip G. Johnson, "Problems and Issues in Science Education," *Rethinking Science Education.*

35. Jerome Bruner, *Toward a Theory of Instruction* (Cambridge, MA: Harvard University Press, 1966); Jerome S. Bruner, *The Process of Education* (New York: Vintage, 1960); Jean Piaget, "Advances in Child and Adolescent Psychology," *Science of Education and the Psychology of the Child* (New York: Orion Press, 1970); Jean Piaget, *The Language and Thought of a Child*, 3rd ed. (London: Routledge and K. Paul, 1959); Joseph J. Schwab, "The Teaching of Science as Inquiry," *The Teaching of Science* (Cambridge: Harvard Press, 1962).

36. Paul DeH. Hurd, *New Directions in Teaching Secondary School Science* (Chicago: Rand McNally, 1970).

37. Biological Sciences Curriculum Study, *Biological Science: Molecules to Man, BSCS Blue Version* (Boston: Houghton Mifflin, 1963); Biological Sciences Curriculum Study, *Biological Science: An Inquiry into Life, BSCS Yellow Version* (New York: Harcourt and Brace and World, 1963); Biological Sciences Curriculum Study, *High School Biology, BSCS Green Version* (Chicago: Rand McNally, 1963); Physical Science Study Curriculum, *Physics* (Boston: Heath, 1960); Physical Science Study Curriculum, *Physics, Laboratory Guide* (Boston: Heath, 1960); Harvard Project Physics, *An Introduction to Physics,*

(New York, Holt, Rinehart and Winston, 1968); Chemical Bond Approach, *Chemical Systems* (New York: McGraw-Hill, 1962); Chemical Bond Approach, *Investigating Chemical Systems* (New York: McGraw-Hill, 1962); Chemical Education Material Study, *Chemistry: An Experimental Science* (San Francisco: Freeman, 1963); Chemical Education Material Study, *Laboratory Manual for Chemistry: An Experimental Science* (San Francisco: Freeman, 1963); Chemical Education Material Study, *Teacher's Guide for Chemistry: An Experimental Science* (San Francisco: Freeman, 1963).

38. See, for instance, Schwab, "The Teaching of Science as Inquiry."

39. Biological Sciences Curriculum Study, *Biological Science: Molecules to Man*; Biological Sciences Curriculum Study, *Biological Science: An Inquiry into Life*; Biological Sciences Curriculum Study, *High School Biology*.

40. Hurd, *New Directions in Teaching Secondary School Science.*

41. Physical Science Study Curriculum, *Physics*; Physical Science Study Curriculum, *Physics, Laboratory Guide.*

42. Chemical Bond Approach, *Chemical Systems*; Chemical Bond Approach, *Investigating Chemical Systems.*

43. Richard J. Merrill and David W. Ridgeway, *The Chem Study Story* (San Francisco: Freeman, 1969).

44. Chemical Education Material Study, *Chemistry*; Chemical Education Material Study, *Laboratory Manual for Chemistry*; Chemical Education Material Study, *Teacher's Guide for Chemistry: An Experimental Science.*

45. Educational Developmental Center, *Elementary Science Study* (Manchester, MO: Webster Division, McGraw-Hill, 1969).

46. American Association for the Advancement of Science, *Science: A Process Approach* (New York: Xerox Division, Ginn and Company, 1967).

47. Robert M. Gagné, "The Learning Requirements for Enquiry," *Journal of Research in Science Teaching* 1 (1963).

48. American Association for the Advancement of Science, *Science.*

49. Science Curriculum Improvement Study, *Science Curriculum Improvement Study* (Chicago: Rand McNally, 1970).

50. Robert Karplus, "Science Teaching and the Development of Reasoning," *Journal of Research in Science Teaching* 14 (1977).

51. Uri Haiber-Sham, Judson B. Cross, Gerald L. Abegg, John H. Dodge, and James A. Walter, *Introductory Physical Science* (Englewood Cliffs, NJ: Prentice-Hall, 1972).

52. Intermediate Science Curriculum Study, *Probing the Natural World* (Morrisville, NJ: Silver Burdett, 1972).

53. Earth Science Curriculum Project, *Investigating the Earth* (Boston: Houghton Mifflin, 1967).

54. David L. Elliott, "Textbooks and the Curriculum in the Postwar Era: 1950-1980," *Textbooks and Schooling in the United States.*

55. John Keeves and Glen Aikenhead, "Science Curricula in a Changing World," *Improving Science Education*, eds. Barry J. Fraser and Herbert J. Walberg (Chicago: National Society for the Study of Education, 1995).

56. Hurd, *New Directions in Teaching Secondary School Science.*

57. Dudley Herron, "The Nature of Scientific Inquiry," *School Review* 79 (1971); Vincent N. Lunetta and Pinchas Tamir, "Matching Lab Activities with Teaching Goals," *The Science Teacher* 46 (1979).

58. Avi Hofstein and Vincent N. Lunetta, "The Role of the Laboratory in Science Teaching: Neglected Aspects of Research," *Review of Educational Research* 52 (1982).

59. Lunetta and Tamir, "Matching Lab Activities."

60. William C. Kyle, John E. Penick, and John A. Shymansky, "Assessing and Analyzing the Performance of Students in College Science Laboratories," *Journal of Research in Science Teaching* 16 (1979).

61. William C. Kyle, "What Became of the Curriculum Development Projects of the 1960's? How Effective Were They? What Did We Learn from Them That Will Help Teachers in Today's Classrooms?," *Research within Research: Science Education*, eds. David Holdzkom and Pamela B. Lutz (Washington, DC: National Science Teachers Association, 1989); James A. Shymansky, Larry V. Hedges, and George Woodworth, "A Reassessment of the Effects of Inquiry-Based Science Curricula of the 60's on Student Performance," *Journal of Research in Science Teaching* 27 (1990); James A. Shymansky, William C. Kyle, and Jennifer M. Alport, "The Effects of New Science Curricula on Student Performance," *Journal of Research in Science Teaching* 20 (1983).

62. Ted Bredderman, "Effects of Activity-Based Elementary Science on Student Outcomes: A Quantitative Synthesis," *Review of Educational Research* 53, no. 4 (1983).

63. John Goodlad and Harold Shane, eds., *The Elementary School in the United States*, Seventy-second Yearbook of the Society for the Study of Education, Part II (Chicago: National Society for the Study of Education, 1973); Elliot and Woodward, *Textbooks and Schooling in the United States*.

64. Arthur Woodward and David L. Elliot, "Textbooks: Consensus and Controversy," *Textbooks and Schooling in the United States*.

65. Wilma S. Longstreet, "The School's Curriculum," *The Elementary School in the United States*; Elliott, "Textbooks and the Curriculum in the Postwar Era: 1950-1980."

66. Wilma S. Longstreet, "The School's Curriculum," p. 252.

67. Ibid., p. 254.

68. Avi Hofstein and Robert Yager, "Societal Issues as Organizers for Science: Education in the 80's," *School Science and Mathematics* 82 (1982).

69. Norris C. Harms and Robert E. Yager, eds., *What Research Says to the Science Teacher*, vol. 3 (Washington, DC: National Science Teachers Association, 1981).

70. National Research Council, *National Science Education Standards*.

71. Ibid.

72. Ibid., p. 31.

73. Fraser and Walberg, *Improving Science Education*.

74. National Research Council, *National Science Education Standards*; American Association for the Advancement of Science Project 2061, *Benchmarks for Science Literacy* (New York: Oxford University Press, 1993).

75. John D. Bransford, Ann L. Brown, and Rodney R. Cocking, *How People Learn: Brain, Mind, Experience and School* (Washington, DC: National Academy Press, 1999).

76. Ibid.; Ronald W. Marx, Phyllis Blumenfeld, Joseph S. Krajcik, and Elliot Soloway, "Enacting Project-Based Science," *The Elementary School Journal* 97 (1997); Kate McGilly, "Cognitive Science and Educational Practice: An Introduction," *Classroom Lessons: Integrating Cognitive Theory and Classroom Practice*, ed. Kate McGilly (Cambridge, MA: MIT Press, 1994).

77. Denis C. Phillips, "An Opinionated Account of the Constructivist Landscape," *The Ninety-Ninth Yearbook*.

78. John S. Brown, Allen Collins, and Paul Duguid, "Situated Cognition and the Culture of Learning," *Educational Researcher* 18 (1989).

79. Phyllis C. Blumenfeld, Ronald W. Marx, Helen Patrick, Joseph S. Krajcik and Elliot Soloway, "Teaching for Understanding," *International Handbook of Teachers and Teaching*, eds. Bruce J. Biddle, Thomas L. Good, and Ivor F. Goodson (Dordrecht, The Netherlands: Kluwer, 1998), p. 831.

80. Lev S. Vygotsky, *Mind in Society: The Development of the Higher Psychological Processes* (Cambridge, MA: Harvard University Press, 1978).

81. David Klahr, Ann L. Fay, and Kevin Dunbar, "Heuristics for Scientific Experimentation: A Developmental Study," *Cognitive Psychology* 25 (1993).

82. Gavriel Salomon, David N. Perkins, and Tamar Globerson, "The Development of Science Process Skills in Authentic Contexts," *Journal of Research in Science Teaching* 30 (1991); Vincent N. Lunetta, "The Role of Laboratory in School Science," *International Handbook of Science Education*, eds. Barry J. Fraser and Kenneth G. Tobin (Dordrecht, The Netherlands: Kluwer, 1998); Robert Tinker, "Thinking About Science," [on-line], Available: http://www.concord.org/library/papers.html (Cambridge, MA: Concord Consortium, 1997).

83. Marcia C. Linn, "The Impact of Technology on Science Instruction: Historical Trends and Current Opportunities," *International Handbook of Science Education*; Tinker, "Thinking About Science"; Barbara Y. White and John R. Frederiksen, "Inquiry, Modeling, and Metacognition: Making Science Accessible to All Students," *Cognition and Instruction* 19 (1998).

84. Phillips, *Constructivism in Education*.

85. Michael R. Matthews, "Appraising Constructivism in Science and Mathematics Education," *Constructivism in Education*; Phillips, "An Opinionated Account of the Constructivist Landscape."

86. Richard F. Gunstone, "Constructivism and Learning Research in Science Education," *Constructivism in Education*, p. 269.

87. Joseph S. Krajcik, Phyllis C. Blumenfeld, Ronald W. Marx and Elliot Soloway, "A Collaborative Model for Helping Middle Grade Teachers Learn Project-Based Instruction," *The Elementary School Journal* 94 (1994).

88. Avi Hofstein and Herbert J. Walberg, "Instructional Strategies," *Improving Science Education*.

89. Cognition and Technology Group at Vanderbilt, "The Jasper Series as an Example of Anchored Instruction: Theory, Program Description, and Assessment Data," *Educational Psychologist* 27 (1992).

90. Marcia C. Linn, Nancy B. Songer, Eileen L. Lewis, and Judith L. Stern, "Using Technology to Teach Thermodynamics: Achieving Integrated Understanding," *Advanced Technology in the Teaching of Mathematics and Science*, ed. D. L. Ferguson (Berlin: Springer-Verlag, 1993).

91. Linn, "The Impact of Technology on Science Instruction: Historical Trends and Current Opportunities."

92. James Slotta and Marcia C. Linn, "The Knowledge Integration Environment: Helping Students Use the Internet Effectively," *Innovations in Science and Mathematics Education: Advanced Designs for Technologies of Learning*, eds., Michael J. Jacobson and Robert B. Kozma (Mahwah, New Jersey: Erlbaum, 2000).

93. Nancy B. Songer, "Can Technology Bring Students Closer to Science?" *International Handbook of Science Education*; Nancy B. Songer, "Exploring Learning Opportunities in Coordinated Network-Enhanced Classroom: A Case of Kids as Global Scientists," *The Journal of Learning Sciences* 5 (1996).

94. Daniel C. Edelson, Douglas N. Gordin, and Roy D. Pea, "Addressing the Challenges of Inquiry-Based Learning through Technology and Curriculum Design," *Journal of the Learning Sciences* 8 (1999); Douglas N. Gordin and Roy D. Pea, "Prospects for Scientific Visualization as an Educational Technology," *Journal of the Learning Sciences* 4 (1995); Roy D. Pea and Louis M. Gomez, "Distributed Multimedia Learning Environments: Why and How?" *Interactive Learning Environments* 2 (1992).

95. Ronald W. Marx, Phyllis C. Blumenfeld, Joseph S. Krajcik, and Elliot Soloway, "Enacting Project-Based Science"; National Geographic Kids Network, *Acid Rain* (Washington, DC: National Geographic Society, 1989); National Geographic Kids Network, *Solar Energy* (Washington, DC: National Geographic Society, 1992); National Geographic Kids Network, *Too Much Trash* (Washington, DC: National Geographic Society, 1991); National Geographic Kids Network, *What's in our Water?* (Washington, DC: National Geographic Society, 1991).

96. Krajcik et al., "A Collaborative Model for Helping Middle Grade Teachers Learn Project-Based Instruction"; Tinker, "Thinking About Science."

97. Jonathan Singer, Ronald W. Marx, Joseph S. Krajcik, and Juanita Clay-Chambers, "Constructing Extended Inquiry Projects: Curriculum Materials for Science Education Reform," *Educational Psychologist* 35 (2000), pp. 165-178.

98. White and Frederiksen, "Inquiry, Modeling, and Metacognition."

99. See note 35 for relevant references on Bruner, Schwab, and Piaget.

100. Blumenfeld et al., "Teaching for Understanding."

101. Merrill and Ridgeway, *The ChemStudy Story.*

102. Cognition and Technology Group at Vanderbilt, "The Jasper Series"; Joseph S. Krajcik, Phyllis C. Blumenfeld, Ronald W. Marx, and Elliot Soloway, "Instructional, Curricular, and Technological Supports for Inquiry in Science Classrooms," *Inquiry into Inquiry: Learning and Teaching in Science*, eds. James Minstell and Emily Van Zee (Washington, DC: American Association for the Advancement of Science Press, 2000); Singer et al., "Constructing Extended Inquiry Projects"; Nancy B. Songer, "Learning Science with a Child-Focused Resource: A Case Study of Kids as Global Scientists" (paper presented at the Fifteenth Annual Meeting of the Cognitive Science Society, 1993).

103. Julie Erickson and Richard Lehrer, "The Evolution of Critical Standards as Students Design Hypermedia Documents," *The Journal of Learning Science* 7 (1998); Marlene Scardamelia and Carl Bereiter, "Text-Based and Knowledge-Based Questioning by Children," *Cognition and Instruction* 9 (1992).

104. Joseph S. Krajcik et al., "Inquiry in Project-Based Science Classrooms."

105. Raven M. Wallace, Jeff Kupperman, Joseph S. Krajcik, and Elliot Soloway, "Science on the Web: Students Online in a Sixth-Grade Classroom," *The Journal of the Learning Sciences* 9 (2000).

106. Kathleen E. Metz, "Reassessment of Developmental Constraints on Children's Science Instruction," *Review of Educational Research* 65 (1985); Leona Schauble and Robert Glaser, "Scientific Thinking in Children and Adults," *Human Development* 21 (1990).

107. Krajcik et al., "Inquiry in Project-Based Science Classroom."

108. Warren F. Beasley, "Improving Student Laboratory Performance: How Much Practice Makes Perfect," *Science Education* 69 (1985); Vincent N. Lunetta, "The School Science Laboratory: Historical Perspectives and Contexts for Contemporary Teaching," *International Handbook of Science Education.*

109. Krajcik et al., "Inquiry in Project-Based Science Classrooms."

110. Metz, "Reassessment of Developmental Constraints."

111. Wolf-Michael Roth and Anita Roychoudhury, "The Development of Science Process Skills in Authentic Contexts," *Journal of Research in Science Teaching* 30 (1993).

112. Jeffrey T. Spitulnik, Michele W. Spitulnik, and Elizabeth Finkel, eds., *Activity in Pervasive Computing Project-Based Science Classrooms, Proceedings of the International Conference on the Learning Sciences* (Charlottesville, VA: Association for the Advancement of Computing in Education, 1996).

113. Charles Bereiter, "Aspects of Educational Learning Theory," *Review of Educational Research* 60 (1990).

114. Audrey B. Champagne, Richard F. Gunstone, and Leopold E. Klopfer, "Instructional Consequences of Students' Knowledge about Physical Phenomena," *Cognitive Structure and Conceptual Change*, eds. Leo H. T. West and A. Leon Pines (New York: Academic Press, 1985).

115. Ronald W. Marx, Phyllis C. Blumenfeld, Joseph S. Krajcik, and Elliot Soloway, "New Technologies for Teacher Professional Development," *Teaching and Teacher Education* 14 (1998).

116. Robert E. Stake and Jake A. Easley, *Case Studies in Science Education* (Urbana, IL: Center for Instructional Research and Curriculum Evaluation, University of Illinois, 1978).

117. Kathleen M. Donnellan, *NSTA Elementary Teacher Survey on Preservice Preparation of Teachers of Science at the Elementary, Middle and Junior High School Levels* (Washington, DC: National Science Teachers Association, 1982).

118. Marx et al., "Enacting Project-based Science."

119. Ronald W. Marx, Phyllis C. Blumenfeld, Joseph S. Krajcik, and Elliot Soloway, "Enacting Project-Based Science: Experiences of Four Middle Grade Teachers," *The Elementary School Journal* 94 (1994); Stake and Easley, "Case Studies in Science Education."

120. Lunetta, "The School Science Laboratory."

121. Kyle, Penick, and Shymansky, "Assessing and Analyzing the Performance of Students in College Science Laboratories"; Zhining Quin, David W. Johnson, and Robert T. Johnson, "Cooperative Versus Competitive Efforts and Problem Solving," *Review of Educational Research* 65 (1975).

122. Geoffrey Giddings, Avi Hofstein, and Vincent N. Lunetta, "Assessment and Evaluation in the Science Laboratory," *Practical Science: The Role and Reality of Practical Work in School Science*, ed. Brian E. Woolnough (Milton Keynes, UK: Open University Press, 1991).

123. Blumenfeld et al., "Teaching for Understanding."

124. Jane Harrison and Rvika Globman, "Evaluation of Training Teachers in Active Learning: A Research Report" (Ramat-Gan, Israel: Bar-Ilan University and the Ministry of Education (Hebrew), 1988).

125. Ronald W. Marx, "Integration of Technology in the Schools," Congressional Testimony (Washington, DC: United States Congress, 1993).

126. Cognition and Technology Group at Vanderbilt, "The Jasper Series"; Edelson, Gordin, and Pea, "Addressing the Challenges of Inquiry-Based Learning"; Linn et al., "Using Technology to Teach Thermodynamics"; Songer, "Exploring Learning Opportunities in Coordinated Network-Enhanced Classrooms."

127. Blumenfeld et al., "Teaching for Understanding."

128. Ronald W. Marx, John G. Freeman, Joseph S. Krajcik, and Phyllis C. Blumenfeld, "Professional Development of Science Teachers," *International Handbook of Science Education*; Michael Middleton, Rebecca Schneider, Joseph S. Krajcik, and Ronald W. Marx, "Case Studies of Three Middle School Teachers: What They Tell Us about Developing Project-Based Curriculum Materials." (Paper presented at the National Association for Research in Science, Boston, MA, 1999).

129. Whipple, *A Program for Teaching Science*, p. 10.

130. American Association for the Advancement of Science Project 2061, *Benchmarks for Science Literacy*.

131. Woodward and Elliot, "Textbooks: Consensus and Controversy."

132. Henry, *Science Education in American Schools*, p. 186.

133. See, for instance, Elliott, "Textbooks and the Curriculum in the Postwar Era: 1950-1980."

134. David L. Elliott and Arthur Woodward, "Textbooks, Curriculum, and School Improvement," *Textbooks and Schooling in the United States*.

135. Krajcik et al., "A Collaborative Model for Helping Middle Grade Teachers Learn Project-Based Instruction"; Marx et al., "New Technologies for Teacher Professional Development."

136. Phyllis C. Blumenfeld, Barry Fishman, Joseph S. Krajcik, Ronald W. Marx, and Elliot Soloway, "Creating Usable Innovations in Systemic Reform: Scaling-up Technology-Embedded Project-Based Science in Urban Schools," *Educational Psychologist* 35 (2000), pp. 149-164.

137. F. James Rutherford, "The Role of Inquiry in Science Teaching," *Journal of Research in Science Teaching* 2 (1964), p. 80.

CHAPTER IX

Mathematics Education in the Twentieth Century

ALAN H. SCHOENFELD

The 1930, 1951, and 1970 Yearbooks of the National Society for the Study of Education (NSSE) paint detailed pictures of mathematics education in the United States at roughly the first, second, and third quarters of the twentieth century. The Society did not produce a mathematics education Yearbook in the latter part of the century. However, comprehensive volumes, such as the *Handbook of Research on Mathematics Teaching and Learning*, the twenty-fifth anniversary issue of the *Journal for Research in Mathematics Education*, and the *Handbook of Educational Psychology* pick up where the Society left off.[1] Volumes such as these will be the primary sources of examples as we pursue our assigned task, tracing the development of mathematics education through the twentieth century.

Any synopsis is of necessity selective and impressionistic. This one begins with an introduction, which establishes the context for what follows. Then, of the many stories that might be told about one hundred years of mathematics education, this chapter focuses on two. The first main section of the chapter, "The evolving content(s) of mathematics instruction," discusses changes in the mathematics curriculum over the course of the century. The second main section, "On research: psychological, epistemological, and methodological issues," describes the development of the discipline of research in mathematics education. A concluding discussion, "And next?," discusses some of the evolutionary needs and pressures that may shape mathematics education in the early parts of the twenty-first century.

The two main stories told in this chapter are presented as roughly chronological narratives, with supporting examples drawn mostly from the sources mentioned above. Underlying those narratives is the

Alan H. Schoenfeld is the Elizabeth and Edward Conner Professor of Education in the Graduate School of Education, University of California, Berkeley.

perspective that changes in curriculum and research over this past century have been evolutionary, in the Darwinian sense. The key words are growth, diversity, and, responsiveness and adaptation to the (intellectual and political) environment. To characterize those changes in broad brush strokes, one sees evolution . . .

- from a focus on arithmetic in the early Yearbooks to the consideration of mathematics teaching, thinking, and learning at almost all levels. The 1990s witnessed "calculus reform," for example. There now exists an Association for Research in Undergraduate Mathematics Education and a corpus of work on research on "advanced mathematical thinking."[2] The broadened focus can be seen as a concomitant of the democratization of (mathematics) education in the United States.

- from a rather narrow focus on mathematical procedures as the object of study (the Gestaltists, who focused on understanding in a very different way, were a notable exception) to a much broader conceptualization of what it means to know and do mathematics. Today the study of mathematical competency includes the study of knowledge; problem-solving strategies; aspects of metacognition, such as self-monitoring and self-regulation; beliefs about self and mathematics; and mathematical practices.

- from epistemological stances that were largely behaviorist/associationist to those that are grounded in various forms of constructivism, including perspectives as diverse as cognitive science, radical constructivism, sociocultural theory, and situative theory.

- from methodological approaches derived largely from experimental psychology to a wide range of forms of inquiry, with methods derived from fields as diverse as anthropology, computer science, linguistics, philosophy, psychology, and sociology.

Now, a brief description of context. Alongside and at times serving as an impetus to the intellectual changes just described, there have been significant alterations in the social and political landscapes within which mathematics instruction takes place. First, demographics. In 1890, only 6.7% of the fourteen-year-olds in the United States attended high school, and only 3.5% of the seventeen-year-olds graduated. Mass education thus took place at the elementary level; education for the elite was reserved for high school and beyond. Things did not remain this way for long. There were significant changes in enrollment patterns over the course of the century, and with them pressures to adapt the curriculum to the needs of those enrolled in mathematics courses. By the beginning of World War II, for example, almost three-fourths of the children of age fourteen to seventeen attended high school, and 49% of the seventeen-year-olds graduated.[3] These demographic trends continued through the end of the century. By the year 2000 the expectation that one would enroll in college at some point has become the norm rather than the exception.

Second, politics. Throughout the century, the major forces that shaped American society also shaped schooling. This was increasingly the case as the nation industrialized and as technological national defense needs came to be seen as increasingly important. For example, World War II prompted a revitalization of school mathematics. After war broke out the U. S. Office of Education and the National Council of Teachers of Mathematics (NCTM) jointly characterized the level of mathematical competency that schools needed to provide prior to students' entry into the military.[4] Likewise, the cold war had a significant impact on mathematics education. A series of pendulum swings began in the 1950s and 1960s after the Soviet launch of Sputnik made mathematics education a national security issue. The pendulum swings began with the "New Math" in the 1960s, which was supplanted by the "back to basics" movement in the 1970s, which yielded, in turn, to "problem solving" in the 1980s. A possible return to basics was forestalled by a perception of crisis in the mid-1980s.[5] "Standards" and "reform" took the stage in the 1990s, which concluded with the "math wars" and a push, from some groups, for a return to more skills-based instruction.

Federal attention to mathematics and science education waxed and waned in cycles as well. A number of post-Sputnik efforts in the sciences and social sciences, including the New Math, were supported by the National Science Foundation (NSF). One NSF-funded program, a widely distributed social studies curriculum, made the (political, not scientific) mistake of asserting that evolution was scientifically grounded. In response, members of Congress offended by this stance used the rallying cry of "local autonomy" to shut down federal funding for national curricular efforts in all content areas. It was not until the 1990s, with the emergence of the "standards movement," that the NSF was once again in a position to fund the development of mathematics curricula.

Funding for research in mathematics and science education also waxed and waned. As will be elaborated below, research in mathematics education began to coalesce as a discipline in the 1960s and 1970s. As the field coalesced, NSF support increased until the change of the federal administration in 1980, when funding was cut dramatically. Over the course of the 1980s, with congressional support, there was first a recovery of and then a significant increase in education funding at NSF. In the 1990s, the budget and the portfolio of NSF's education and human resources division expanded significantly. However, much of the funding increase went into implementation—some of it supporting curriculum development, most supporting the implementation of "reform" through programs called systemic initiatives. Thus, despite a significant increase in overall education funding, it can be argued that the amount of funding available for field-initiated basic research (that is, research not aimed at particular NSF programmatic goals) declined substantially over the 1990s.

In 1989, a grass-roots reform effort by the National Council of Teachers of Mathematics initiated a nationwide discussion of national standards for mathematics curricula.[6] This effort, grounded in the research on mathematical thinking and learning of the previous two decades, had a significant impact on mathematics education. It stimulated the national reform of mathematics curricula, discussions of national standards in many subject areas, and even the possibility, before President Bill Clinton's plan for it was killed in Congress, of a national mathematics test. The NCTM's initiative also changed the political landscape. Because of the political attractiveness of "high standards" and societal assumptions that knowledge can be tested simply and objectively, frequent testing has become increasingly common nationwide. Many states have implemented "high stakes" assessments. Failure on such tests can result in students being retained in grade or not allowed to graduate. Increasingly, school funding is contingent upon test scores, and teacher salaries and even teacher certification can depend on student performance. In short, high stakes assessments have significant consequences, and are taken very seriously. Since most such tests are oriented toward basic skills, they have a serious impact on classroom practices—typically orienting them toward basic skills. In view of this unexpected set of consequences, it remains to be seen whether the forces unleashed by discussions of "standards" will ultimately turn out to be progressive or conservative.

The Evolving Content(s) of Mathematics Instruction

Having established some of the relevant context, we turn to the first main narrative of this chapter. This section provides a brief trace of the evolution of mainstream mathematics curricula through the century.

At the dawn of the twentieth century, only a small fraction of the population attended high school. High school mathematics was for the elite and was rather advanced; the small number of students enrolled in high school uniformly took courses in algebra, geometry, and physics. Elementary education was for the masses—and elementary mathematics education meant arithmetic.[7] Thus, it is not surprising that the 1930 NSSE Yearbook, which weighed in at 749 pages and was available for a postpaid price of $3.60, was devoted to arithmetic.[8]

Mass education in the early years of the twentieth century was not uncontroversial; adherents of various perspectives fought for primacy. *Humanists* believed in "mental discipline," the ability to reason, and the cultural value of mathematics. *Developmentalists* focused on the alignment of school curricula with the growing mental capacities of children. *Social efficiency educators* thought of schools as the place to prepare students for their predetermined social roles. At the opposite end of the spectrum, *social meliorists* focused on schools as potential sources of social justice, calling for "equality of opportunity through the fair distribution of extant knowledge."[9] In a sense, the authors of the 1930 NSSE Yearbook sought to put such controversies behind them, using "science" as the guide to their approach. Thus, they wrote,

Some readers may feel that this yearbook is too conservative, that it lacks a bold and daring spirit of progressiveness. There has been a conscious attempt to avoid the urging of any point of view not supported by considerable scientific fact. It has seemed preferable to proceed slowly and on sure ground, to be content with sane and moderate progress, rather than to expound a theory of instruction which, though supported by fine hopes and splendid aspirations, has as yet no basis in objective data.[10]

In the spirit of Beckett and Ionesco, we convey the content of the recommendations (and of elementary school mathematics at that time) via lists. The 1930 NSSE Yearbook had two sections, "Some Aspects of Modern Thought on Arithmetic" and "Research in Arithmetic." In the former we find:

Introduction; The social value of arithmetic; The arithmetic curriculum; Some considerations of [teaching] method; Testing, diagnosis, and remedial work in arithmetic; The training of teachers of arithmetic.

In the latter we find:

The purpose and plan of Part II; The techniques of research employed in arithmetic; A critical survey of previous research in arithmetic; The number abilities of children when they enter grade one; A critical evaluation of methods of analyzing practice in fractions; [the results of] Mixed versus isolated drill organization; The learning of the one hundred multiplication combinations [i.e., "the times tables"]; A measurement of transfer in the learning of number combinations; An experimental study in improving ability to reason in arithmetic; A test in arithmetic for measuring general ability; The effect of awareness of success or failure; A study of errors in percentage; The grade placement of arithmetic topics; A review of experiments on subtraction.

Arithmetic drill was the name of the game, with research to tell the reader which drill was most effective.

The case for arithmetic instruction was made largely on its social value:

Without functional ideas of number the work of the modern world could not go on. Science would be lost for want of appropriate expression. Machinery would go out of use and the civilization of our industrial age would perish. The mind of man would be weakened through the loss of its keenest weapon.[11]

At the same time,

A sense of the value of numbers such as modern life demands is neither innate nor easily acquired. It is certain that a child is not born with this sense, and among primitive people it is equally certain that adults have not possessed it.[12]

Broadly speaking, then, the goals of the curriculum as described in the 1930 Yearbook were utilitarian. The practices of mathematics education were reasonably conservative as well. In taking a "scientific" approach, the authors swept aside the prior debates (and rhetoric) about various social purposes for education. It will be noted that throughout the century, the rhetoric has been charged, but that (with the exception of the implementation of the "New Math," which represented a major curricular shift) changes in practice were not nearly as dramatic as the rhetoric that surrounded them.

TOWARD THE MIDDLE

Regarding the curricular state of the art in mid-century, one might well say *le plus que ça change, le plus que ça reste la même chose*. One indication thereof: chapter five of the 1970 NCTM volume *A History of*

Mathematics Education was entitled "Abortive Reform—Depression and War: 1920–1945."

Part II of the 1951 NSSE Yearbook,[13] the first Yearbook since 1930 devoted to mathematics, weighed in at a mere 297 pages. The Society held costs down, with the volume costing $3.50 postpaid. The social context had changed significantly in twenty-one years. College enrollments had declined during the depression, but high school enrollments had risen. The highly demanding high school mathematics curriculum, inherited from the days when high school mathematics was for the elite, led to "rising failure rates, criticisms of the value and effectiveness of instruction in mathematics, and problems of articulation with the lower schools.[14] The mathematics courses in high school that had once been required instead became elective, and vocational courses became available. High school mathematics enrollments plummeted in percentage terms, although increasing in absolute terms because of the much larger percentage of students enrolled at the secondary level. Amid these demographic changes, however, there were the following curricular constants—conditions that held at the dawn of the century and would remain in place through its final years. By and large, mathematics in elementary school meant arithmetic, and instruction was oriented toward computation. The mathematics in high school that "mattered" was demanding and oriented toward college preparation. There was no connection between the two.

The 1951 NSSE Yearbook, like its 1930 antecedent, was devoted to arithmetic. The most significant changes from the previous mathematics education Yearbook regarded the psychological bases for instruction: the mid-century volume rejected the behaviorist perspective of its predecessor and issued a call for instruction for comprehension and even for the development of problem-solving ability. Once again, however, rhetoric outstripped reality. The substance of the elementary mathematics curriculum—arithmetic and its applications—remained more or less constant. Thus, for example, Van Engen, in writing about arithmetic in junior and senior high school, said:

Criticisms of the high school program usually center around the lack of computational facility of the graduate. However, there is a more fundamental criticism. . . . The failure to get the right sum for a column of numbers or the failure to get the proper result in a percentage situation is merely a symptom of the real difficulty. . . . [The] fundamental reasons: (a) arithmetic is still taught as a series of rules that produce the right answer to isolated number situations (provided the student remembers the rules). . . . (b) Mathematics teachers in general are not yet convinced that education is for all American youth.[15]

THE THIRD QUARTER

What a difference a few wars (including cold ones) can make! The 1970 NSSE Yearbook[16] was still a bargain: $5.50 postpaid brought the reader 467 pages. But this was a very different book than its antecedents. Edward G. Begle, one of the major architects of the "New Math," edited the volume and wrote the introduction. It begins:

Not quite two decades have elapsed since the appearance of the last NSSE Yearbook on mathematics education. During that period a revolution in school mathematics has taken place. . . . The chief difference between the old and the new programs is the point of view toward mathematics. No longer is computational skill the be-all and end-all of mathematics. Now there is an equal emphasis on understanding the basic concepts of mathematics and of their interrelationships, i.e., the structure of mathematics.[17]

Folklore has it that the New Math was a failure. The capsule version of the story is that, inaccessible to parents and teachers alike, the New Math met with societal rejection and spawned a counter-revolution, the "back-to-basics movement," which dominated the 1970s. In fact, the story is more complex, for revolutions always leave their traces. Once again because of the underlying role mathematics plays in military preparedness and the increasing importance of technology to the military, the cold war precipitated the involvement of mathematicians in school mathematics. This time, however, mathematicians played a more direct role than heretofore in curriculum development. Whereas the authors of the earlier NSSE mathematics education yearbooks were almost exclusively educators—professors of education, educational psychology and psychology, teacher educators, and educational administrators—the authors of the Sixty-ninth Yearbook were predominantly mathematicians. All five chapters on curriculum content and pedagogy were written by professors of mathematics (the author of the pedagogy chapter having a joint appointment in mathematics education). They focused on mathematical structure in the prospective curriculum.

Once again, lists tell the story. Where in the past the focus was on arithmetic procedures and their applications in context, the focus here was on abstract mathematical structure. Thus we see the following in the table of contents for arithmetic:

I. NUMBER SYSTEMS OF ARITHMETIC.
Why numbers? Sets. Counting Numbers. Comparison of Sets. Comparison of Numbers. Naming of Numbers. Addition. And Subtraction. Algorithms for

Addition and Subtraction. Multiplication. And Division. Algorithms for Multiplication and Division. Primes. Clock Arithmetic. The Integers (Whole Numbers). The Rational Numbers. Decimals.

and for algebra:

II. ALGEBRAIC SYSTEMS
Groups. Fields. Rational Numbers and Order. The Real Number System. The Fundamental Property of the Real Numbers. The Complex Numbers and Plane Vectors. Vector Spaces. Vector Space Axioms. Dependence. Independence, Basis. Linear Transformations and Matrices. Matrices.

There is more of the same kind. The treatment of geometry in high school is much more formal and axiomatic than heretofore, and the concept of function (a core idea of mathematics, which had not previously received much focused attention) is given a prominent role.

THE FOURTH QUARTER

Thanks to the "back-to-basics" movement formed in reaction to the New Math, much of the formalism and emphasis on structure heralded by the 1970 Yearbook was cleansed from the curriculum within a decade of the Yearbook's appearance. However, the level of secondary school mathematics remained stable. School mathematics in the latter part of the twentieth century (at least in rhetoric and in curricular structure) was still aimed at college. The high school course sequence that had stabilized at ninth grade Algebra, tenth grade Geometry, and eleventh grade Advanced Algebra/Trigonometry was a curricular ladder that students climbed on the way to pre-calculus and then high school or college calculus.

Well, some students climbed the ladder; as in earlier years, most fell off it. The sad statistical fact was that from ninth grade on, there was roughly a fifty percent attrition rate in mathematics each year: only half the students who completed ninth grade mathematics went on to take mathematics in the tenth grade, and so on. When local requirements mandated mathematics through ninth or tenth grade, those who could not succeed on the college-prep track were shunted into dead-end courses such as shop math or business math.[18]

There was, then, stability for some time. But another "crisis" in mathematics education reared its head. The U. S. economy faltered while Japan's grew strong, and national reports, such as *A Nation at Risk* by the National Commission on Excellence in Education in 1983, made the case that, absent a strong technical and mathematical base, the U. S. would no longer remain economically competitive. International comparisons, such as the Second International Mathematics Study, documented the poor mathematical performance of U. S. youth relative to those from other industrialized nations.[19] By the mid-1980s there was national concern about mathematics education, alongside a relatively stable curriculum that (a) was aimed at college but had a very high drop-off rate, and (b) was for the most part procedurally rather than conceptually oriented. It was in this context that the NCTM issued the 1989 *Curriculum and Evaluation Standards for School Mathematics.* That volume was followed in 1991 by the NCTM's *Professional Standards for Teaching Mathematics*, and in 1995 by the *Assessment Standards*.[20] (The three volumes will be referred to collectively as the NCTM Standards.)

Reflecting numerous studies of mathematical thinking and problem solving of the previous decade(s), the Standards emphasized *process* as well as content. The first four standards for school mathematics, common to grade levels Kindergarten through twelve, were problem solving, reasoning, communication, and (making) connections. Equally dramatic was the shift in audience. While the mathematical needs of "college-intending" students were clearly delineated, it was equally clear that the Standards were intended for *all* students.

New societal goals for education include (1) mathematically literate workers, (2) lifelong learning, (3) opportunity for all, and (4) an informed electorate.[21]

These new goals, however, did not imply a return to the skills orientation of the first part of the century. The Standards described a series of desired shifts, as follows:

We need to shift –

- toward classrooms as mathematical communities—away from classrooms as simply a collection of individuals;

- toward logic and mathematical evidence as verification—away from the teacher as the sole authority for right answers;

- toward mathematical reasoning—away from merely memorizing procedures;

- toward conjecturing, inventing, and problem solving—away from an emphasis on mechanistic answer-finding;

- toward connecting mathematics, its ideas, and its applications—away from treating mathematics as a body of isolated concepts and procedures.[22]

The three volumes of Standards, particularly the first, had a strong impact on the following decade. In the 1990s the National Science Foundation provided funding for the development of a number of experimental curricula whose goals were aligned with the Standards. These curricula made the goals of reform tangible. They also gave nascent opposition forces something to shoot at. Their focus on mathematics for literate citizenship led to concerns on the part of some that "equity" and "excellence" might be in tension, and that trying to reach all students might lead to a "dumbing down" of curricula. Similarly, the de-emphasis on procedural skills in the Standards, which had been motivated by the presence of calculators and computers, led traditionalists to believe that hard-core mathematical values were being abandoned. The ensuing fracas, called the "math wars," was played out in the press. At the time of this writing, the outcomes and consequences of the math wars are far from clear.

Toward the end of the century NTCM considered its next steps. Much had changed since the issuance of the original *Curriculum and Evaluation Standards*. The context was different: Whereas calling for the use of graphing calculators in 1989 may have been visionary, students at the turn of the century had relatively easy access to sophisticated computer software programs and to the world wide web. International comparison studies documented the contrast between typical U. S. curricula and teaching approaches and the more focused and more conceptual approaches of some other nations.[23]

A decade's worth of research and practical experience with experimental reform curricula provided the base for a much more refined, coherent, and updated vision of mathematics education. In April 2000 NCTM released *Principles and Standards for School Mathematics*,[24] a document designed to build on previous efforts and to lay the foundation for reform efforts in the decades to come. As in the antecedent documents, this has a dual focus, on content and process. The document offers a set of principles to undergird high-quality mathematics instruction. It focuses on five content standards, whose development it traces from pre-kindergarten through grade twelve: number and operations, algebra, geometry, measurement, and data analysis and probability. (This last standard reflects an evolutionary change from previous curriculum documents. Data analysis had become increasingly important—and feasible, due to technology—in the last years of the twentieth century.) It also highlights five process standards: problem solving, reasoning and proof, communication, connections, and representation. NCTM takes a strong stance regarding the possibility of equity and excellence. It proposes a core curriculum that prepares all students for the workplace, mathematically literate citizenship, *and* the pursuit of mathematics in college. Given the widespread availability of computers and calculators, NCTM presumes they will be available as classroom tools, to be used for mathematical explorations as well as for computations. NCTM's stated goal is to use technology in the service of developing mathematical understanding, not as a replacement for it. Mindful of the "math wars" and of misinterpretations of previous Standards documents, *Principles and Standards for School Mathematics* seeks to emphasize procedural competence alongside conceptual understanding, recommending the use of whichever tools (mental computation, paper and pencil, calculators, or computers) are appropriate for the situations at hand.

Finally, it should be noted that curricular change has visited the college campus as well. For much of the century the changes were gradual. In the early part of the century, college mathematics commenced with the study of solid geometry and college algebra; even in the 1940s calculus was a junior-level course, with relatively small enrollments. The curriculum condensed over time, with some subjects, such as solid geometry, being minimized or eliminated. By the mid-1960s calculus was a first-year course, a rite of passage for all students who planned for mathematically related or scientific careers.

"The" calculus course—there was remarkable homogeneity nationwide—remained more or less unchanged through the 1980s. By then, however, calculus was a source of increasing discontent; the course, which was largely procedural, was of little interest to faculty and had distressingly high failure rates. A 1986 conference and the call it issued[25] served as stimuli to "calculus reform." In the years that followed a number of reform projects of different types were developed. Most required that fewer topics be studied, but studied in greater depth. Some were technologically oriented, approaching calculus as computer-based "laboratory courses." Change has been widespread. In a 1994 nationwide survey of mathematics departments, twenty-two percent indicated that they were engaged in "major" reform efforts; another forty-six percent reported modest efforts.[26] Many of these reform efforts were, in various ways, philosophically compatible with the reform efforts in Kindergarten through twelfth grade mathematics.

In sum, substantial change was made during the closing years of the century, although some of that change may be more rhetorical than real. Technology is starting to be used at all grade levels. Reform in Kindergarten through twelve mathematics has taken the firmest hold at the elementary level, and calculus reform seems to be well established. The secondary mathematics curriculum has not changed as rapidly, and the most prominent NSF-supported secondary mathematics curricula have come under some fire in the "math wars." The impact of high stakes testing in the name of "standards" remains to be seen. That, in turn, will affect whether the mathematics curricular pendulum will stabilize or swing widely once again.

On Research: Psychological, Epistemological, and Methodological Issues

We now embark on our second tour of the century, this time focusing on research. The main focus will be on psychological issues; background issues of epistemology and method will be highlighted or summarized when and where they become salient. The story line is rather straightforward. For much of the century "scientific" approaches to the study of mathematical thinking and learning, grounded in behaviorist and associationist theories of learning, predominated in the United States. Through at least the end of the 1960s, alternative perspectives such as those advocated by the Gestaltists or constructivists (notably Piaget and his followers), were marginalized. In the latter part of the century, multiple perspectives flourished. With the emergence of the cognitive sciences came a redefinition of the scope of what it means to know and think mathematically. Various forms of constructivism challenged the objectivism of earlier times; the idea that what people perceive and understand is a function of what they already "know" (that is, are prepared to perceive and understand) became widely accepted. Advocates of situated cognition argued that knowledge is local, subjective, and socially constructed. As the century came to a close, the resolution of some of these contentious issues related to the nature of knowing was in doubt.

In telling this story, I shall move rapidly through the early part of the century, lingering more on the "knowledge explosion" of the final quarter. Key findings and research directions of the period from 1975–2000 will be described in some detail. But first . . .

It is important to note by way of context that for much of the twentieth century, research in mathematics education was not a separate field, but in essence a sub-field of applied psychology. This was in large measure because mathematical procedures in general, and arithmetic procedures in particular, were seen as unambiguous, clearly right or wrong (as opposed to, say, text interpretation), and learnable in a relatively short time—and, thus, wonderful candidates for psychological study. As a result, mathematical content could serve psychology for purposes of research, theory building, and theory testing. Reciprocally, psychology could serve education by providing content-related learning theories. It is also important to note that mathematical content lends itself readily to a hierarchical analysis. The overly simplistic view of mathematical content that predominated for much of the century is that the mathematical edifice can and should be learned "from the bottom up," with the mastery of simple ideas coming prior to their use in applications or their combination into more complex ideas. It should come as no surprise, then, that the vast majority of mathematics education research in the first half of the century, and the bulk of work done in the second half, focused on elementary content. Only in recent years have significant numbers of members of the mathematical community become involved in educational research, with a corresponding increase in research on more advanced mathematical topics.

IN THE BEGINNING (OF THE CENTURY)

Broadly speaking, mathematics education research over the century reflected trends in psychological research. Early in the century, the behaviorists held sway. As the introduction to the 1930 Yearbook stated,

Theoretically, the main psychological basis is a behavioristic one, viewing skills and habits as fabrics of connections. This is in contrast, on the one hand, to the older structural psychology which still has to make direct contributions to classroom procedure, and on the other hand, to the more recent *Gestalt* psychology, which, though promising, is not yet ready to function as a basis of elementary education.[27]

There is, above and beyond homage to what we would today call "motivation," a kind of spare-the-rod-and-spoil-the-child defense of drill-and-practice:

The assumption that children must be unhappy and will develop frightful personalities if exposed to a pedagogy which uses the principles upon which the older schools were based is a sort of inverted old-oaken-bucket delusion. Many aspects of the old school are, after all, distinctly good psychology; they are based on correct theorems related to human nature. . . .

There must be no retreat from the position that felt needs be utilized, that the tasks be made significant, that the sustaining effects of interest be earnestly sought and capitalized. Further, we must continue to seek both increased knowledge of the psychology of the subject matter taught (a field quite neglected by the left wing) and increased skill in the use of such aspects of learning as are suggested by the phrases: drill, continued effort, ability to withstand distraction, persistence though momentarily bored, effort not sustained by rewards at hand but by confidence in values forthcoming in the future . . . [28]

Methodologically speaking, one sees largely what one would expect in a behaviorist approach toward arithmetic. The approach was intended to be scientific, focusing on the careful construction of learning sequences that would enable students to accumulate knowledge effectively. Given the behaviorists' antipathy to mentalism, it is no surprise that the emphasis was on content analysis and the mastery of mathematical procedures. The overall goal of the applied research was to enable students to master the content, with a minimum of errors. The way to achieve this goal was to perform detailed analyses of content, breaking the content into pieces that were small enough to be "mastered" through practice, and assembling the complex whole out of the well-mastered pieces. Yet, there was some sensitivity to children. Thus, in "Some considerations of [pedagogical] method" we find the following summary injunctions:

The content of instruction and drill should be greatly influenced by both the mathematics of the process and also an appreciation of its various difficulties for children. . . . Drill and application should follow effective learning of the content. Drill undertaken before the ideas are mastered only piles up error, discomfort, and a resistive attitude. . . . As far as possible, processes taught and drilled upon should be carried into those types of applications which children can respond to with understanding. . . . Logical niceties in rules and definitions often run counter to the needs of children and should be reserved for adults. Mathematical proprieties are not to be countenanced, but neither are mathematical pedantries. . . . The use of competence tests after learning, of inventory tests at the beginning of the semester's work, of diagnostic tests when break-downs in skills are noticed, and of remedial work assigned in the light of individual needs are integral parts of effective teaching.[29]

The behaviorist research program provided the underpinnings of the 1930 Yearbook's pedagogical recommendations. The Yearbook offered data regarding student performance on arithmetic tasks at various grade levels, allowing for the "benchmarking" of instruction and the setting of baseline expectations.[30] Research studies examined the role of drill in the learning of multiplication and fractions, as well as on mixed versus isolated drill and organization.[31] The analysis of errors was fine-grained. For example, G. M. Norem and F. B. Knight analyze the patterns found in 5,365 errors made by students practicing their multiplication tables.[32]

In hindsight it is easy to dismiss the scientism of much of this work, but the work should not be caricatured: It offered some baseline data and some insights that are useful today. For example, while the analyses focused on the content and not on the learner, it did focus on the content *as would be apprehensible by the learner*. One sees what might be construed as the antecedents of Lee S. Shulman's concept of "pedagogical content knowledge":[33]

An example of teaching knowledge vs. mathematical knowledge of arithmetic may be found in the case of long division. From the mathematical point of view, the accompanying examples are the same. They are all long division examples, and that is all that is to be said. [A dozen examples, beginning with 8946 divided by 42, are given.] From the standpoint of teaching, however, there are important differences between them. . . . [The examples are discussed, with an eye toward the complexities of carrying out the long division algorithm.] . . .

These examples of long division difficulties are not complete, but sufficient to illustrate a very important point of view. *A mathematical description of an arithmetic process does not yield the kind of information about that process which is an essential basis for its instruction to children.*[34]

Despite the tremendous emphasis on testing in the behaviorist program, one also finds wisdom regarding the limitations of the kinds of information that can be gathered by tests.

It is highly important that the causes [of student errors] be discovered with certainty. One or two concrete illustrations may indicate the difficulty of trying to infer the cause of an error from the answer as given on a test paper. . . .

Another illustration may be drawn from a fifth grade pupil who was subtracting 36 from 42 and gave as his answer 14. Judging simply from his answer on a test paper, one would probably say that in addition to the error in the first combination the student had forgotten to borrow and had for this reason subtracted 3 from 4, getting 1 in the ten's place. What the pupil actually did was this: "Thirty-two to forty-two is ten and four more (32 to 36) is fourteen." In such an example as this, simply observing the answer on a test paper does not help the teacher to understand the difficulty. Nothing short of a detailed individual diagnosis in which the teacher observes the mental processes of the pupil as he works would throw light on the real difficulties that are involved.[35]

Of course, the phrase "mental processes" had a slightly different cast in 1930 than it does in 2000 (and is even somewhat surprising to find in a largely behaviorist tome). Nonetheless, the warning embodied within this message is as important today as it was seventy years ago. To put things simply, information gleaned from any form of data or data analysis can be misleading. It is incumbent upon teachers and researchers alike to seek detailed and compelling evidence (preferably using multiple lines of approach) when making claims regarding individuals' knowledge and mental structures.

TOWARD THE MIDDLE

Perhaps the best way to view the 1951 NSSE Yearbook is to consider it a manifesto, grounded in evidence from emerging psychological theories, in opposition to the behaviorist stance reflected in the 1930 Yearbook.

There are new ideas as to ways to learn arithmetic. The application of memorized rules that are not understood, which characterized the teaching of arithmetic at the time of the American Revolution, has been replaced by an emphasis on understanding which has made the phrase "meaningful arithmetic" a common one in today's schools.[36]

As often seems to be the case in education, this new rhetoric coexisted comfortably with the old reality. The emphasis on "meaningful arithmetic" was largely rhetorical, as indicated by the quotation from Van Engen given in the previous section: "Arithmetic is still taught as a series of rules that produce the right answer to isolated number situations (provided the student remembers the rules)."[37] Two of the Yearbook's chapters do offer insights into the psychological state of the art, however.

Chapter VIII of the Yearbook is titled "The psychology of learning in relation to the teaching of arithmetic." The author takes a distanced view of the current controversies, reviewing two main theories (association and field theories) and discussing their contributions. Association theories, which provided the theoretical grounds for the drill-and-practice approach advocated in the earlier Yearbook, were grounded in Edward Thorndike's research on the ways in which mental connections are reinforced by practice. In contrast,

With the development of "field theories" of learning, of which the Gestalt theory is most familiar to school teachers, the center of interest shifted from what was often, and perhaps unjustly, called an "atomistic" concept of learning to one which emphasized understanding of the number system and number relations and which stressed problem solving more than drill on number facts and processes.[38]

The best known example of the Gestaltists' work is Max Wertheimer's discussion of the "parallelogram problem."[39] But Wertheimer provides examples at the level of arithmetic as well:

When I asked children, $\frac{274 + 274 + 274 + 274 + 274}{5} = ?$ or $\frac{272 + 272 + 272}{3} = ?$

or $\frac{273 + 273}{2} = ?$ I got clear-cut results with some bright subjects. . . . Division

by five was understood in its structural meaning. . . . To add or really to multiply in order to divide later corresponds here to the doing and undoing of what we had before . . .

Thinking of certain school attitudes I had so often experienced, I continued to ask such questions. Quite a surprise was in store for me—I had not imagined how extreme the situation often was. A number of children who were especially good in arithmetic in their school were entirely blind, started at once with tedious figuring or begged to be excused from the cumbersome task—they did not look at the situation as a whole at all.[40]

Guy Buswell negotiated the tension between association theories and field theories, arguing that Thorndike had himself written about the need for students to understand the "related and systematic character of arithmetic"[41] and that drill can play a meaningful role in field theories. It is ironic that such words of wisdom are unattended fifty years later: On one side of the "math wars" the advocates of the basics decry "fuzzy math," while on the other side reformers decry "drill-and-kill." (Such polarization is not limited to mathematics, of course: consider the "language wars," in which advocates of "phonics" and "whole language" are at one another's throats.)

In reflecting on this kind of conflict at the metatheoretical level, Buswell's introduction to the two conflicting theories is every bit as wise (and applicable) today as it was when it was written:

The very reason that there are conflicting theories of learning is that some theories seem to afford a better explanation of certain aspects or types of learning, while other theories stress the application of pertinent evidence or accepted principles to other aspects and types of learning. It should be remembered that the factual data on which all theories must be based are the same and equally accessible to all psychologists. Theories grow and are popularized because of their particular value in explaining the facts, but they are not always applied with equal emphasis to the whole range of facts.[42]

The second chapter of psychological/educational interest in the 1951 Yearbook is Chapter XV, "Needed research on arithmetic." Following an introduction written by Buswell, the chapter offers brief research proposals from twenty-one different scholars. Each proposal describes a promising arena for research related to the teaching and learning of arithmetic. These include, it is sad to say, many proposals that could have been written fifty years later. Problems addressed include determining the effectiveness of manipulative materials in teaching arithmetic, students' attitudes, the relative effects of the early and late introduction of students to computational algorithms, and establishing methods to evaluate students' use of arithmetic in functional situations. Perhaps most prescient was the following proposal by Harold Fawcett:

Problem. A study of how children think about number, how concepts are developed, and how meanings are established.

Significance. Present knowledge does not provide us with information as to what goes on in the mind of the child when confronted with situations involving number concepts and number sense. . . .

Sources of Data. Actual classroom situations under the direction of teachers interested in organizing their program in such a manner as to learn and record the thought processes of their students as their number concepts become enriched through guided experience.

Methods of Study. Teachers concerned with this study should be provided with competent help essential to the securing and recording of data accurately reflecting the thinking processes of the students. . . . If a child could be encouraged to talk as he works, to "think out loud," and if a recording could be made, the results would be helpful.[43]

Alas, such studies were not to be—perhaps because they were swept aside by the scientism of the next few decades. From the 1950s through the 1970s, only "objective, quantifiable" data would count in the mathematics education mainstream; not until the late 1970s did "think aloud" methods, classroom observations, and a range of qualitative and interpretive methods make their way into mainstream educational research. While Buswell rightfully did his best to open up the field for a wide range inquiry into mathematical thinking and learning, such attempts, by and large, were unsuccessful. As a coda to this observation, it is also worth mentioning that the name Jean Piaget does not appear even once in the 1951 Yearbook.

THE THIRD QUARTER

As noted in the first main section of this paper, the 1970 NSSE Yearbook represented a sharp break with its two mathematics education antecedents. The Yearbook covered all Kindergarten through twelve mathematics, not merely arithmetic, and the authors of the chapters of the Yearbook's chapters covering curriculum content were all mathematicians. Psychology, epistemology, and research methods were all relegated to one chapter, "Psychology and mathematics education," by Lee Shulman.

In contrast to his predecessors, Shulman gave Piaget his due. Piaget's views of cognitive development are fundamentally important, for they focus attention on what the student "brings to the table" in learning interactions, and on mechanisms of cognitive development. Such considerations are essential if one is to develop detailed and meaningful theories of learning. Equally important are *values*—what one believes it is important for students to learn. Shulman's discussion of such issues served as "deep background" for his discussion of the more applied work of scholars such as Jerome Bruner, David Ausubel, and Robert Gagné, whose ideas had significant impact on educational theory and practice in the 1960s and 1970s. Equally important, Shulman raises underlying epistemological issues:

When theorists differ so systematically over issues of learning and teaching, it is not surprising to find that their differences are rooted deeply in far more fundamental issues. Although the field of psychology ostensibly achieved emancipation from philosophy some eighty years ago, contemporary psychologists continue to fight the same battles that bloodied their philosophical forbears. Thus, the clamor over the relative merits of expository and discovery teaching . . . can best be understood in terms of certain basic controversies relating to the manner in which *anything* becomes known [i.e., epistemology].[44]

Shulman then went on to trace the positions of Gagné and Bruner to the philosophical stances of Aristotle and Plato, respectively, reminding the reader in the process of the importance of one's (often times tacit) assumptions about the nature of knowledge. Whether one is at bottom an empiricist or a rationalist *does* make a difference.

Broadly speaking, Shulman's chapter was about the relevance of psychology to education, writ large. He was not yet concerned with the direct applications of experimental psychology to education—the time was not ripe for such applications, he noted—but with the potential contributions of psychology. What *can* psychology offer? he asked. How must issues be framed in order for the contributions to be meaningful and effective?

His answers were, in essence, an extension of Buswell's discussion of conflicting theories of learning. As Buswell noted, different instructional approaches are likely to be effective at different things and under different conditions. If experimental psychology is to help, Shulman noted, the experiments conducted must reflect that complexity: One must specify learner variables, instructional treatments and variables, content variables, and desired outcomes. Once this is done, questions of "which approach works best" are no longer philosophical issues or issues of common sense. "These are empirical questions demanding empirical answers. Once well put in terms of psychologically meaningful variables rather than in terms of stirring slogans, these issues are amenable to systematic scientific investigation."[45]

Shulman's chapter provided a reflection of the state of affairs in psychology and education in 1970. There is great subtlety in the analyses of theorists' work, accompanied by a deep appreciation of the importance of epistemological issues and of the complexity of learning. There is the recognition that experimental methods have not produced powerful educational results because the complexity of the phenomena being studied had not yet been recognized. And there is the faith that once suitably designed experimentation was undertaken, those results would be forthcoming.

Shulman was right about all but the last.

Faith in the scientific method was a core value of educational and psychological research in the third quarter of the twentieth century. After all, it was science that provided the weapons that put an end to World War II. It was science that provided cures for deadly diseases. It was science that promised to revolutionize and modernize our lives. And it was science that served as the model for research in all the social sciences, so named for obvious reasons.

Beyond the attractions of science (not to mention the prestige of being a scientist!), the shortcomings of other approaches had become clear. The Gestaltists, for example, had relied heavily on post hoc introspective reports to explain the mental processes used while working on problems. However, different theoretical camps had reported different processes—and since all the data came from "within the head," there was no objective way to resolve such conflicts. The behaviorists argued strongly against such mentalism, claiming that research must deal with observable (and thus quantifiable) behaviors only. This was entirely consistent with the spirit of the times, which demanded rigorous, scientific (read: experimental, quantifiable) work.

Alas, much of the educational research conducted at the time was more scientistic than scientific. In "treatment A versus treatment B" or "experimental versus control" comparison studies, the treatments were often ill defined. As a result, individual studies could not be replicated, and the lack of consistent definition led to contradictory results: Typically, some studies showed that a particular (ill-defined) approach "worked," while others did not. For example, David Ausubel's writings motivated more than a hundred studies of "advanced organizers" during the third quarter-century. The cumulative findings were completely inconclusive. A close look reveals that the concept of advanced organizer (a narrative description intended to orient students to the major ideas in a body of text) was sufficiently broad that different researchers could create very different advanced organizers for the same body of text. That is what happened; some worked, and some didn't.

Broadly speaking, any number of methodological difficulties went unrecognized in the rush to reduce complex educational interventions to simple "experiments." For example, if different teachers taught the experimental and control treatments in a comparison study, differences were attributed to the treatments, although the major instructional difference (and an unspecified variable in the experiment) may well have been the teachers. If the same teacher taught the experimental and control treatments, then the most significant (again unrecognized) variable in the different treatments may have been the teacher's enthusiasm for one treatment over the other. The bottom line is that the complexities of instruction were such that their reduction to strict experimental formats was (to say the least!) problematic and ultimately not productive.[46]

During the 1960s and 1970s, mainstream U. S. journals in psychology and education tended to restrict themselves to quantitative studies, which were reported in stereotypically constrained formats. The very notion of *explanation* seemed suspect; authors seemed to shy away from saying, "This is why I think X is taking place," instead reporting, "There is evidence that Y happened. Here is the experimental hypothesis (that Y will or will not happen); here are the methods used; here are the data." (See, for example, the first few volumes of the *Journal for Research in Mathematics Education*. My goal is not to single out any particular studies for comment, but to indicate the spirit of the times.)

The cumulative effect of such narrowness was stultifying, a fact that ultimately caused concern. In a 1978 article, Jeremy Kilpatrick noted that experimenters spent large amounts of time testing students to determine their problem solving abilities, when it would have been much simpler to observe the students while they solved problems. He also observed that many Soviet studies,[47] while lacking the rigor of experimental studies in vogue in the U. S., more than made up for that fact by being interesting and suggestive. Sounding themes similar to those raised by Kilpatrick and Shulman,[48] I wrote the following in a review of a collection of dissertation studies undertaken between 1968 and 1977:

1. There is an absence, if not a neglect, of theory. I find a kind of ad hoc empiricism about all of the studies, which are designed to answer questions like 'Can one do this or that?' or 'Are there relationships between this or that?' One needs to think about how and why things work (or don't work) and to pose the questions in individual studies so that they cast light on the larger questions.

2. The community suffers from its isolationism. Five of the nine studies in this book deal with students in the fourth through seventh grades. Yet developmental psychology is all but ignored: The name Piaget is not to be found once in a set of references that is 31 pages long! There are any number of areas in problem solving in which it is difficult if not impossible to do good research unless one is familiar with related research in the 'cognitive sciences.' There is, for example, an extensive literature on the effects of 'think aloud' instructions. . . . Modeling techniques in artificial intelligence and information-processing psychology are more advanced than our own. Others may not directly address our most important questions, but they can provide us help along the way.

3. There is too great a reliance on statistics, and a deep look at process is avoided. . . . Statistics are valuable in their place. They can suggest hypotheses in preliminary studies and help to test them in well-designed experimental studies. But if we want to understand what goes on in people's heads when they solve problems (and I assume we do!), we have to watch them solving problems.[49]

In sum, the yield from the third quarter-century was rather slim; the net effect of attempts at scientific "rigor" was rigor mortis. However, the work of Piaget and Lev Vygotsky, the "teaching experiments" of the Soviet psychologists,[50] and the emergence of cognitive science planted the seeds for progress.

What follows describes the extraordinary flowering of research in mathematics education over the last quarter of the twentieth century. Before moving to that discussion, however, it must be noted that research in mathematics education only coalesced as a discipline in the latter part of the twentieth century! Perhaps the most tangible sign of its coalescence was the publication, in January 1970, of the first issue of the *Journal for Research in Mathematics Education*. David C. Johnson, Thomas A. Romberg, and Joseph M. Scandura described the history of its emergence as follows:

By the mid-1960s there was a growing number of scholars conducting research on the teaching and learning of mathematics. . . . However, research in the field lacked coherence, and investigators lacked professional identity. . . . If scholars were to flourish, they needed to be able to share their ideas and the results of their investigations. . . . No organized meetings on research were regularly held. . . . many members of NCTM's Board of Directors felt that research papers . . . were not appropriate for its journals. . . . Although many persons felt that NCTM was the obvious organization [to publish a journal in mathematics education] . . . many leaders in the Council were unsure that the organization should sponsor activities for a 'special interest' group of its members.[51]

The story continues as follows. In 1965, NCTM formed the Committee on Research in Mathematics Education. This committee sponsored a number of research-related activities, among them developing a prototype journal issue and conducting a marketing analysis regarding the viability of a research journal. Ultimately the NCTM Board was convinced such a journal would be viable, and it worked toward its creation. As noted above, the first issue of the *Journal for Research in Mathematics Education* (Vol. 1, No. 1) appeared in January 1970. The expansion of the discipline from its humble beginnings in the 1960s into a robust intellectual enterprise at the end of the century was nothing short of extraordinary.

AND IN THE FOURTH QUARTER, A THOUSAND FLOWERS BLOOMED

There are myriad indicators of the growth of the discipline from 1975 to 2000. One is the number of people and organizations that identify themselves as devoted to research in mathematics education. Johnson et al., quoted above, documented the state of affairs as of the mid-1960s. As of 1975, there were few mathematics education research organizations in the U. S., and they were small. Twenty-five years later, both the Special Interest Group for Research in Mathematics Education of the American Educational Research Association and the North American chapter of the International Group for Psychology and Mathematics Education numbered about 300 researchers each (with significant overlap, of course).

To get a sense of substantive change during that time period, one can compare the two research volumes considered to be definitive when they were published: the 1980 *Research in Mathematics Education* and the 1992 *Handbook for Research on Mathematics Teaching and Learning*.[52] *Research in Mathematics Education*, a rather slight volume by contemporary handbook standards, reflected the scientistic spirit of the times. It contains two articles by David C. Johnson that focus on types and methods of research. In "Types of Research," Johnson listed five basic categories of educational research:

The survey ("to establish norms and baseline data. . . ."), the experiment ("It involves the careful control of variables in an experimental situation. . . ."), the case study (". . . involves the intensive study of individuals or situations. . . . It is dangerous to state generalizations . . . since the samples are usually limited"), evaluation (which, "unlike those types considered up to this point, is primarily concerned with changes that occur over time"), and philosophical or historical research.[53]

In "The Research Process,"[54] Johnson provided a description of research methods—but he focused almost exclusively on how to use the right "instruments" to measure particular "variables" when doing statistical analyses. In neither chapter focusing on research is there any mention of the study of mental processes.

The contrast with the *Handbook for Research on Mathematics Teaching and Learning* is dramatic. The *Handbook* itself is massive, the chapters much more diverse in coverage. And the story regarding methods is very different. Thomas Romberg's chapter, "Perspectives on scholarship and research methods," invoked Thomas Kuhn's notions of "normal science" and paradigm shifts.[55] Romberg described research as a social construct, the activity of a scholarly community; he pointed to shifts in paradigms and methods. Indeed, the entire *Handbook* is a study in methodological pluralism—and, in contrast to the 1980 volume, it takes the study of mental constructs as a primary focus of educational research.

One more data point regarding the general expansion of educational research methods over the latter part of the twentieth century is the following. Another handbook that appeared in 1992, The *Handbook of Qualitative Research in Education*[56] is devoted entirely to methodological issues that were not even touched upon in *Research in Mathematics Education*—which was published only twelve years earlier. The two volumes are roughly the same size.

Having pointed to the rapid expansion of the field during the final quarter of the twentieth century, I will now characterize the main dimensions of the research itself. The three key words that serve as leitmotifs for the description are *mind*, *mechanism*, and *culture*. Within that frame, some of the main findings of research in mathematics education are also described. Examples related to both the learning and teaching of mathematics are given.

First, *mind*. The most important fact concerning educational research in the last quarter of the twentieth century is that the study of *mind* came back into fashion, as the central component of the "cognitive revolution." This came about in a particularly ironic way, in which the behaviorists were hoist by their own philosophical/methodological petard. As has been noted, the behaviorists insisted that psychological theorizing must be restricted to the explanation of objectively observable and quantifiable data. A case in point is B. F. Skinner, describing a view he called "operationism":

Operationism may be defined as the practice of talking about (1) one's observations, (2) the manipulational and calculational procedures involved in making them, (3) the logical and mathematical steps which intervene between earlier and later statements, and (4) nothing else.[57]

Needless to say, this kind of approach rules out mentalism and the use of post hoc introspective reports, such as those used by the Gestaltists; reporting on "what went on in my head" stands in clear violation of those rules. But, an insistence on observable results opened the back door for a radically different approach to cognition. The Trojan horse was mechanical: The study of mind was legitimized by the study of machines.

Artificial intelligence (AI) is the field of "machines that think." The goal of much research in AI is to write computer programs that perform various intellectual tasks, e.g., playing chess, solving problems in symbolic logic, or solving mathematical problems. One of the most famous AI programs is the "General Problem Solver," called GPS. GPS played a respectable game of chess. It solved complex "cryptarithmetic" problems, such as the following:

Replace each of the letters A, B, D, E, G, L, N, O, R, and T with a different digit from 0 through 9, so that when the letters are replaced by the digits, the following sum is correct:

$$
\begin{array}{ccccccc}
 & D & O & N & A & L & D \\
+ & G & E & R & A & L & D \\
\hline
 & R & O & B & E & R & T
\end{array}
$$

Finally, given the axioms of set theory as a starting point, GPS managed to prove 51 of the first 53 theorems in Bertrand Russell and Alfred North Whitehead's classic logic treatise, *Principia Mathematica.* (Folklore has it that Russell called GPS's proof of one of the theorems "elegant"—the mathematician's highest word of praise.) One might quibble about whether the machines could actually "think," but there was no quibbling about the fact that they were performing tasks of substantial intellectual complexity—tasks that many humans could not perform.

On the one hand, the computer programs met all the conditions for empirical research laid down by the behaviorists. Every single action taken by GPS is objectively observable and describable—GPS is, after all, a computer program. On the other hand, the route to the development of GPS and other such programs was decidedly mentalist. The computers did not solve the problems they were given by "brute force" computations, for they did not have anywhere near the computational power that would be necessary to work their way through all the possible combinations faced by players in a chess game. The program for GPS was developed by making systematic observations of people engaged in problem solving (e.g., chess playing, puzzle working, and theorem proving), looking for consistencies in their problem-solving behaviors, and codifying those behaviors as computer programs. That is, GPS was derived from the systematic description of human problem-solving strategies. (Thus the title of Allen Newell and Herbert A. Simon's classic book describing the origins of GPS: *Human Problem Solving.*[58]) To put this slightly differently, GPS and other successful AI programs were based on the codification of ascribed human thought processes. This kind of work is focused on cognitive strategies and is thus fundamentally mentalist, but it beats the behaviorists at their own game. It provides complete traces of all problem-solving decisions. AI programs are successful problem solvers whose strategies are objectively defined. The door to mentalism is thus thrown wide open. Indeed, the research methods behind AI—making systematic observations of people engaged in problem solving—became central methods of information processing psychology.[59]

But the door is thrown open in a different way from before. Along with the legitimization of mind as an object of study came an obligation to describe the workings of mind with a sense of *mechanism*—to say how things work, at a very fine level of detail. In studies of learning or problem solving, for example, one could no longer simply say, "This person has this knowledge." One had to address questions such as, How is knowledge represented? How is it organized? How is it accessed during problem solving? Moreover, the answers to such questions, and models of various cognitive processes, were to be held accountable to data. The result within AI and information processing psychology was the evolution of scientifically defensible theories of the structure of memory, knowledge organization, and the like.

Information processing, however, was only one of many perspectives on human thinking, learning, and action. The perspective "from within" was necessarily limited—as were the perspectives from within fields such as anthropology, education, linguistics, philosophy, sociology, and others with long traditions of studying human behavior. Over a period of years, the interdisciplinary field of cognitive science emerged.[60] With it, much broader conceptions of mathematical thinking and problem solving evolved.[61]

There is now (at least within the cognitive camp; situated cognition will be discussed below) a general consensus that a comprehensive description of mathematical behavior must address the following: domain-specific knowledge; heuristic methods (problem-solving strategies); metacognitive knowledge and skills; beliefs; and practices. What follows describes main findings with regard to each of these aspects of mathematical behavior. Examples relate both to the learning and the teaching of mathematics. Finally, the discussion turns to issues of culture.

DOMAIN-SPECIFIC KNOWLEDGE

It might appear that issues of mathematical knowledge are straightforward, but that is hardly the case. As indicated above, a careful description of mathematical knowledge must be much more than a mere inventory: Issues of knowledge organization and access must be dealt with. But inventories are not so simple. What, for example, does it mean to understand rational numbers or fractions? The pure mathematics is simple: From the mathematician's perspective one can define rational numbers as equivalence classes of ordered pairs of integers, and be done with it. But the cognitive reality is anything but simple; see, for example, the summary of research on student understanding of rational number, ratio, and proportion by Merlin Behr, Guershon Harel, Thomas Post, and Richard Lesh.[62] In an early paper, Thomas Kieren pointed out that fractions have numerous interpretations, depending on context and use.[63] For example, a fraction can denote a part of a whole (three fourths of a pie), a proportion of a population (three fourths of the people polled prefer product A to product B) or a comparative ratio (the area of Lake A is three fourths of the area of Lake B). Indeed, these examples represent just the portion of what is possible: Figure 14-1 of Behr, Harel, Post, and Lesh, which describes the details of various conceptualizations of the fraction 3/4, spreads over three handbook-sized pages! Even this is only the beginning. Different conceptualizations of fractions may make it easier or harder to understand operations on fractions. For example, thinking of fractions as "parts of wholes" helps to explain the addition of fractions; one can visualize the decomposition of fractions such as 1/3 and 1/4 into pieces of common size (4/12 and 3/12 respectively), and then add those pieces. But such an interpretation is not helpful for understanding the multiplication of fractions, where the idea of comparative ratio is much more useful. And so on.

For a second set of examples, the teaching of mathematics will be explored. What kind of knowledge underlies competent teaching? For many years, the standard view was that teachers had two kinds of knowledge, namely, knowledge of content and of pedagogy. Shulman, however, pointed to a different kind of knowledge,[64] which he called "pedagogical content knowledge"—how to think about specific content for purposes of instruction. This includes a knowledge of typical student understandings and misunderstandings of particular topics, and how they might be anticipated or dealt with in instruction. (For example, all experienced mathematics teachers know that some proportion of students will write that $(a + b)^2 = a^2 + b^2$ and will be prepared with explanations and counterexamples when, as is inevitable, some students will make that mistake. Beginning teachers may be caught unaware.) Recent research indicates that the issue may be even more complex. Liping Ma showed that experienced teachers of elementary mathematics can develop a form of knowledge, which she called "profound understanding of fundamental mathematics," which differs from the knowledge of the same topic held by, say, research mathematicians.[65] Although the mathematicians may have a deep knowledge of the formal mathematical structure of the domain and of

the generalizations of the elementary topics, the teachers can, in complementary fashion, develop a deep sense of the interconnectedness of
the topics and of ways to think about that interconnectedness for pedagogical purposes. Such findings have implications for the ways people
are prepared to teach and for supporting their professional growth as
teachers.

HEURISTIC METHODS (PROBLEM-SOLVING STRATEGIES)

All researchers in mathematical problem solving stand on the
shoulders of George Pólya, whose classic 1945 book, *How to Solve It*,
introduced the idea of heuristic strategies, "rules of thumb" for making progress toward the solution of problems.[66] Pólya identified many
such strategies (e.g., "solve an easier related problem and exploit the
method or result to solve the original problem"). Unfortunately, it
turned out to be difficult to teach students to use rules of thumb.
Research in the cognitive paradigm indicated why: The descriptions
found in Pólya's writings were not given at a level of detail sufficient
for implementation. That problem has been solved, at least at the theoretical level. Methods now exist for describing heuristic strategies at
an appropriate level of detail, and there is evidence that students can
learn such strategies. The question is whether the follow-up work will
be done and whether such strategies will become embedded in curricular efforts.[67]

METACOGNITIVE KNOWLEDGE AND SKILLS

Metacognition refers to people's abilities to predict their performances on various tasks . . . and to monitor their current levels of mastery and understanding. Teaching practices congruent with a metacognitive approach to learning
include those that focus on sense-making, self-assessment, and reflection on
what worked and what needs improving. These practices have been shown to
increase the degree to which students transfer their learning to new settings
and events.[68]

The findings just cited, which are general, were contributed to and
buttressed by research within mathematics education. Frank Lester
summarized some of the main findings within mathematics education:

1. Effective metacognitive activity during problem solving requires knowing
not only what and when to monitor, but also how to monitor. Moreover,
teaching students how to monitor their behavior is a difficult task.

2. Teaching students to be more aware of their cognitions and better monitors
of their problem-solving actions should take place in the context of learning

specific mathematics concepts and techniques (general metacognitive instruction is likely to be less effective).

3. The development of healthy metacognitive skills is difficult and often requires 'unlearning' inappropriate metacognitive behaviors developed through previous experience.[69]

BELIEFS AND PRACTICES

It is now generally accepted that beliefs (about mathematics, about mathematics teaching and learning, about one's abilities in mathematics) are shaped by one's experience with mathematics and that, in turn, those beliefs shape people's mathematical behavior.

Commonly, mathematics is associated with certainty; knowing it, with being able to get the right answer, quickly. . . . These cultural assumptions are shaped by school experience, in which *doing* mathematics means following the rules laid down by the teacher; *knowing* mathematics means remembering and applying the correct rule when the teacher asks a question; and mathematical *truth is determined* when the answer is ratified by the teacher. Beliefs about how to do mathematics and what it means to know it in school are acquired through years of watching, listening, and practicing.[70]

To give just one example of the genesis and impact of such beliefs, consider the net effect of years of schooling in which the mathematics "problems" students experience are, in fact, brief exercises on which the students practice the implementation of known procedures. On the basis of this experience, students come to believe that all problems can be solved in just a few minutes. As a result they will give up working on problems after a few minutes have passed—even though they might have succeeded at solving those problems, had they persevered.[71]

Beliefs have an equally important impact on the practices of mathematics teachers. As Hersh wrote, "One's conception of what mathematics *is* affects one's conception of how it should be presented. One's manner of presenting it is an indication of what one believes to be most essential in it. . . . The issue, then, is not, What is the best way to teach? but, What is mathematics all about?"[72] Thus, for example, teachers who view mathematics as a richly connected discipline are likely to point out such connections, whereas teachers who view mathematics as a corpus of facts and procedures to be "mastered" are likely to present it in that way to their students.[73]

We shall now turn from *mind* (and *mechanism*) to *culture*. The perspective that has just been outlined, beginning with knowledge and proceeding through beliefs and practices, reflects the orientation of cognitivists—starting with knowledge "inside the head" and then looking for the origins of such knowledge in the practices in which one engages. This approach places individual cognition in the fore-ground, situating culture in the background as the "growth medium" within which the mind develops. This does not in any way imply that culture is not important, but it does indicate where the lens of inquiry has been focused.

As an alternative, one can place cultural issues in the foreground, making them a starting point of analysis. In their cross-national stud-ies of teaching, for example, James Stigler and James Hiebert made the case that there is much greater between-culture than within-cul-ture variation in teaching practices, and that teaching is best under-stood not as a collection of activities of individual teachers, but as a cultural activity.[74] From this it would follow that a starting place for the analysis of teaching is to understand the shared cultural beliefs and values that shape teaching. Once one understands those beliefs and values, one is in a position to explore how teachers act to implement them in their instruction.

One mainstream theoretical stance that places social and cultural issues at the core of the analysis of "being and acting in the world" has come to be called *situated cognition*. In a volume with that title, David Kirshner and James A. Whitson introduced the basic ideas as follows:

The shift within cognitive science to situated cognition theory . . . is at least as profound, philosophically and methodologically, as was the shift to cogni-tivism from behaviorism some 35 years earlier. . . . Community and culture can enter into cognitivist theory only insofar as they are decomposable into discrete elements that can participate in the stable, objective realm of experi-ence. Thus, the opportunity to explore learning and knowledge as processes that occur in a local, subjective, and socially constructed world is severely lim-ited. . . . What situated cognition theory promises as a next step is a model for dealing with knowledge and learning as fundamentally social and cultural, rather than as artifacts of an individual's journey through an impersonal and objective world.[75]

Within this perspective, the cultural and the social take the fore-ground and the individual/cognitive the background. *Communities of practice* and *participatory structures* become primary foci of analysis, and issues of individual competence and identity are characterized in terms of such structures. Thus, for example, "being a research mathemati-cian" would not be specified in terms of one's degree or one's objective knowledge per se—having a Ph.D. in mathematics or expertise in topology and measure theory. Rather, a person would be characterized as a research mathematician if that person does the things that mathematicians do (publish papers, attend meetings, interact with other mathematicians) and is accepted by other mathematicians as a member of their intellectual community. *Learning* is also redefined from within this situated cognition perspective: Learning is no longer the acquisition or development of knowledge but increased centrality of participation in a community of practice. Indeed, the very nature of knowledge is redefined, for it becomes knowledge-acting-in-the-world. Jean Lave, Michael Murtaugh, and Olivia de la Rocha offered this well-known example of mathematical thinking done in dialectic with real-world objects, as opposed to "done in the head" and applied to those objects:

> Research on the acquisition of arithmetic skills by new members of Weight Watchers posed the following problem of food portion control: "Suppose your allotment of cottage cheese for the meal is three-quarters of the two-thirds cup the program allows?" The problem solver . . . filled a measuring cup two-thirds full of cottage cheese, dumped it out on a cutting board, patted it into a circle, marked a cross on it, scooped away one quadrant, and served the rest. . . . Since the environment was used as a calculating device, the solution was simply the problem statement, enacted. At no time did the weight watcher check his procedure against a paper and pencil algorithm.[76]

Recent discussions of framing assumptions regarding situative theory and its applications may be found in two papers by James G. Greeno and the Middle-school Mathematics through Applications Project and in work of E. Wenger.[77]

At this point, the status of the cognitive and situated perspectives vis-à-vis each other is in question. Some argue that the two are fundamentally incommensurate; others claim that they reflect consistent perspectives on the same set of phenomena, but that they differ in where they place their attention. Either way, exploring the dialectic of the individual and the social is one of the key issues for mathematics education in the new century. Such issues are explored in the concluding section.

And Next?

Predicting the future is a dangerous game, as *The Experts Speak: The Definitive Compendium of Authoritative Misinformation* reminds us.[78] Within its pages, for example, one finds the following comment attributed to Thomas J. Watson, Chairman of the Board of IBM in 1943: "I think there is a world market for about five computers." Watson was not alone in the inaccuracy of his prognostications. Ken Olson, President of Digital Equipment Corporation, made the following pronouncement at the 1977 convention of the World Future society: "There is no reason for any individual to have a computer in their home." Nonetheless, part of my task here is to peer into the future . . .

In what follows I shall focus on a small set of issues that I think need attention, and on which I believe progress can be made. The issues are derived from the key words in the preceding discussion: *mind, mechanism,* and *culture.*[79]

As indicated above, a major theoretical issue that needs to be addressed is the dialectic between mind and culture, between the individual and the collective. Consider a classroom. One "lens" on the activities is that of the teacher—one can then view the interactions taking place through the eyes of the teacher, modeling the teacher's perceptions and decisions during instruction. This kind of model exists.[80] Another set of lenses consists of the views of and from individual students. But then there is the classroom as a whole, considered as an organic entity. How does it function as an entity with "distributed intelligence"?[81] How does it function as a discourse community? What are the relationships between individuals as entities-within-themselves and as constituent members of the classroom community? Can all these be described in such a way that individual and community are seen as mutually constitutive?

A related issue is the creation of "theories of competence," or theories of acting-and-being-in-the-world. What does it take to be good at mathematics, including being able to use it effectively in a wide range of contexts? What does it take to be an effective teacher? It should be noted that what makes these issues difficult is the level of precision (i.e., mechanism) required to describe them adequately, in the light of redefinitions of competence (including redefinitions of knowledge) suggested above. The goal is to specify, in very fine-grained ways, what a person would know and how the person would act in order to be seen as "being good at X."

Educational research has matured at a phenomenal pace over the past few decades. As recently as a few decades ago, researchers exploring mathematical thinking and learning had scant understanding of the dimensions of mathematical competence, as well as a corresponding paucity of methodological tools with which they could be explored. Through the 1980s and into the 1990s, much of the research on understanding people's mathematical performance had to be done in the research laboratory; the phenomena were not well enough understood to be studied, at an appropriate level of detail, amid the complexity of educational settings such as classrooms. Studies of teaching and of schools as organizations had little overlap in content, location, or theoretical perspective with studies of thinking and learning. The research community had little understanding of the individual pieces of the puzzle, much less how to put them together. What progress has been made! Researchers now have the capacity to study mathematical teaching and learning where they take place and to untangle their complexities. This can—resources permitting—allow for significant progress. Practical issues of curriculum development and assessment are within reach, if approached with the care they deserve. Issues of professional development are likewise within theoretical reach: Within the next few decades we will be able to understand not only the bases of teacher competence, but teachers' "developmental trajectories" and the kinds of support that will enable them to develop as professionals.

The issue, then, is resources. That, however, is an arena in which no sane person would try to make predictions. To put it mildly, the current context for educational research and development is problematic. Educational issues became increasingly politicized toward the end of the twentieth century, with a concomitant lessening, at least in the short term, of the potential for rational discourse and long-term progress. The "math wars," for example, have been front-page news; columnists, politicians, and others with no first-hand knowledge of the issues have not hesitated to join combat regarding mathematics curriculum and instruction.

In the political arena, "standards" may be evolving from a progressive to a conservative force. The move toward standards catalyzed by the National Council of Teachers of Mathematics was designed to focus on mathematical understanding.[82] However, in the very recent past "standards" have been adopted as rhetorical banners for programs of testing and accountability. Many states have instituted strict testing regimens, threatening to retain students in grade if they fail the tests despite a large body of evidence showing that retention has a negligible impact on academic performance, but that it does cause a significant increase in drop-out rates. These accountability tests tend to focus on the mastery of facts and procedures, because that is what can be tested cheaply and easily. (They are also comprehensible to those who received their mathematical education in a very different time, when mastery of facts and procedures was the focus of school mathematics.) Because the accountability measures are "high stakes," teachers feel compelled to focus on them, with a corresponding de-emphasis on the aspects of mathematics learning (reasoning, representation, problem solving, communication, making connections) that are not tested.

In a similar way, research on the nature of teaching is being undermined. The research community has begun to unpack the underpinnings of teacher competence and to describe the kinds of support structures that would develop and nurture that competence. However, until teaching is recognized in the political arena as a profession and is treated accordingly, the opportunities to employ such knowledge to good effect are minimal.

All this might be cause for depression, if one did not have the long view provided by the opportunity to reflect on a century of progress. Progress is not linear and, caught up in the moment, one can find as many reasons for pessimism as for optimism. Consider, for example, the wild curricular swings that have taken place since the 1960s. Or consider the fact that after the National Science Foundation had carefully developed a "ten-year plan" for research and development in science and mathematics education in the late 1970s, one of newly elected President Ronald Reagan's first actions was to declare NSF out of the education business! Nonetheless, the long view is comforting. Educational practice has improved; the research base is expanded and much more robust; and research in mathematics education, which was a fledgling field in the latter part of the twentieth century, has grown and matured at a phenomenal rate. It is hard to imagine what an NSSE yearbook on mathematics education at the quarter-mark of the twenty-first century might contain, much less the 200th Yearbook of the Society.

The author wishes to thank Hilda Borko and members of the Functions Group at Berkeley—Julia Aguirre, Ilana Horn, Cathy Kessel, Sue Magidson, Manya Raman, Ann Ryu, Natasha Speer, and Joe Wagner—for helpful comments on a draft of this manuscript. Special thanks go to Cathy Kessel for her help on this and many other projects.

NOTES

1. Douglas A. Grouws, ed. *Handbook of Research on Mathematics Teaching and Learning* (New York: Macmillan, 1992); *Journal for Research in Mathematics Education*, Twenty-fifth Anniversary Special Issue 25, no. 6 (1994); David C. Berliner and Robert C. Calfee, eds., *Handbook of Educational Psychology* (New York: MacMillan, 1996).

2. See, e.g. David Tall, "The Transition to Advanced Mathematical Thinking: Functions, Limits, Infinity, and Proof," *Handbook of Research on Mathematics Teaching and Learning*, ed. D. Grouws (New York: MacMillan, 1992), pp. 495-514.

3. George M. A. Stanic, "Mathematics Education in the United States at the Beginning of the Twentieth Century," *The Formation of School Subjects: The Struggle for Creating an American Institution*, ed. Thomas S. Popkewitz (New York: Falmer Press, 1987), p. 150.

4. See the NCTM's 1943 report, "Essential Mathematics for Minimum Army Needs," *Mathematics Teacher* 6 (1943), pp. 243-282.

5. See, e.g., the National Commission on Excellence in Education's 1983 report, *A Nation at Risk* (Washington, DC: U. S. Government Printing Office, 1983).

6. National Council of Teachers of Mathematics (NCTM), *Curriculum and Evaluation Standards for School Mathematics* (Reston, VA: NCTM, 1989; *Professional Standards for Teaching Mathematics* (Reston, VA: NCTM, 1991); *Assessment Standards for School Mathematics* (Reston, VA: NCTM, 1995).

7. Philip S. Jones and Arthur F. Coxford, Jr., "Mathematics in the Evolving Schools." *A History of Mathematics Education* (Washington, DC: NCTM, 1970), pp. 11-92.

8. Guy M. Whipple, ed., *Report of the Society's Committee on Arithmetic*, Twenty-ninth Yearbook of the National Society for the Study of Education (Bloomington, IL: Public School Publishing Company, 1930).

9. Stanic, "Mathematics Education," p. 152.

10. F. B. Knight, "Introduction," *Report of the Society's Committee on Arithmetic*, p. 2.

11. B. R. Buckingham, "The Social Value of Arithmetic," *Report of the Society's Committee on Arithmetic*, p. 15.

12. Ibid.

13. Nelson B. Henry, ed., *The Teaching of Arithmetic*, Fiftieth Yearbook of the National Society for the Study of Education, Part II (Chicago: National Society for the Study of Education, 1951).

14. Jones and Coxford, "Mathematics in the Evolving Schools," p. 53.

15. H. Van Engen, "Arithmetic in the Junior-Senior High School," *The Teaching of Arithmetic*, p. 103.

16. Edward G. Begle, ed., *Mathematics Education*, Sixty-ninth Yearbook of the National Society for the Study of Education, Part I (Chicago: National Society for the Study of Education, 1970).

17. Ibid., p. 1.

18. National Research Council, *Everybody Counts: A Report to the Nation on the Future of Mathematics Education* (Washington, DC: National Academy Press, 1989).

19. See, e.g., F. Joe Crosswhite, John A. Dossey, Thomas J. Cooney, Floyd L. Downs, Douglas A. Grouws, Curtis C. McKnight, Jane O. Swafford, and A. Israel Weinzweig, *Second International Mathematics Study: Detailed Report for the United States* (Champaign, IL: Stipes, 1986).

20. NCTM, 1989; 1991; 1995.

21. NCTM, 1989, p. 3.

22. NCTM, 1991, p. 3.

23. William H. Schmidt, Curtis C. McKnight, and Senta A. Raizen, *A Splintered Vision: An Investigation of U.S. Science and Mathematics Education* (Boston/Dordrecht/London: Kluwer Academic Press, 1997); William H. Schmidt, Curtis C. McKnight, Gilbert A. Valverde, Richard T. Houang, and David E. Wiley, *Many Visions, Many Aims: A Cross-national Investigation of Curricular Intentions in School Mathematics* (Boston/Dordrecht/London: Kluwer Academic Press, 1997); James Stigler, and James Hiebert, *The Teaching Gap* (New York: The Free Press, 1999).

24. *Principles and Standards for School Mathematics* (Reston, VA: NCTM, 2000).

25. Ronald Douglas, ed., *Toward a Lean and Lively Calculus* (Washington, DC: Mathematical Association of America, 1986).

26. Alan Tucker and James Leitzel, *Assessing Calculus Reform Efforts* (Washington, DC: Mathematical Association of America, 1995), p. 1.

27. F. B. Knight, "Some Considerations of Method," *Report of the Society's Committee on Arithmetic*, p. 5.

28. Ibid., p. 6.

29. Ibid., pp. 262-266.

30. B. R. Buckingham and Josephine MacLatchy, "The Number Abilities of Children When They Enter Grade One," *Report of the Society's Committee on Arithmetic*, pp. 473-525.

31. G. M. Norem and F. B. Knight, "The Learning of the One Hundred Multiplication Combinations," *Report of the Society's Committee on Arithmetic*, pp. 551-568; L. J. Brueckner, and Fred Kelley, "A Critical Evaluation of Methods of Analyzing Practice in Fractions," *Report of the Society's Committee on Arithmetic*, pp. 525-534; Austin C. Repp, "Mixed Versus Isolated Drill Organization," *Report of the Society's Committee on Arithmetic*, pp. 535-550.

32. Norem and Knight, "One Hundred Multiplication Combinations," *Report of the Society's Committee on Arithmetic*, pp. 551-568.

33. Lee S. Shulman, "Those Who Understand: Knowledge Growth in Teaching," *Educational Researcher* 17, no. 1 (1986), pp. 4-14.

34. Knight, "Some Considerations of Method," pp. 161-162. Emphasis in original.

35. C. E. Greene and Guy Buswell, "Testing, Diagnosis, and Remedial Work in Arithmetic," *Report of the Society's Committee on Arithmetic*, pp. 274-275.

36. Guy Buswell, "Introduction," *The Teaching of Arithmetic*, p. 2.

37. Van Engen, "Arithmetic in the Junior-Senior High School," p. 103.

38. Buswell, "The Psychology of Learning in Relation to the Teaching of Arithmetic," *The Teaching of Arithmetic*, p. 146.

39. Max Wertheimer, *Productive Thinking* (New York: Harper & Row, 1945).

40. Ibid., pp. 130-131.

41. Buswell, "The Psychology of Learning in Relation to the Teaching of Arithmetic," pp. 143-154.

42. Ibid., p. 144.

43. Harold P. Fawcett, "Proposal for research on problems of teaching and learning arithmetic." *The Teaching of Arithmetic*, p. 285.

44. Lee S. Shulman, "Psychology and Mathematics Education," *Mathematics Education*, p. 60.

45. Ibid., p. 71.

46. L. J. Cronbach and R. E. Snow. *Aptitudes and instructional methods* (New York: Irvington, 1977), p. 501. For an historical view of the limitations of such approaches and a description of the challenges of describing complex educational interventions, see Ann Brown, "Design Experiments: Theoretical and Methodological Challenges in Creating Complex Interventions in Classroom Settings," *Journal of the Learning Sciences* 2, no. 2 (1992), pp. 141-178.

47. V. A. Krutetskii, *The Psychology of Mathematical Abilities in School Children*. Translated by Joan Teller (Chicago: University of Chicago Press, 1976).

48. Jeremy Kilpatrick, "Variables and Methodologies in Research on Problem Solving," *Mathematical Problem Solving*, ed. L. L. Hatfield (Columbus, OH: ERIC, 1978), pp. 7-20; Shulman, "Psychology and Mathematics Education," *Mathematics Education*, p. 60.

49. Alan H. Schoenfeld, "Review of John G. Harvey and Thomas A. Romberg's *Problem-Solving Studies in Mathematics*." *Journal for Research in Mathematics Education* 12 (1981), pp. 386-390.

50. See, e.g., Krutetskii, *The Psychology of Mathematical Abilities*.

51. David C. Johnson, Thomas A. Romberg, and Joseph M. Scandura, "The Origins of the *JRME*: A Retrospective Account," *Journal for Research in Mathematics Education* 25, no. 6 (1994), pp. 561-582.

52. R. Shumway, ed., *Research in Mathematics Education* (Reston, VA: NCTM, 1980); Grouws, *Handbook of Research on Mathematics Teaching and Learning*.

53 David C. Johnson, "Types of Research," *Research in Mathematics Education*, pp. 21-24.

54. Johnson, "The Research Process," *Research in Mathematics Education*, pp. 29-46.

55. Thomas Kuhn, *The Structure of Scientific Revolutions* (Chicago: The University of Chicago Press, 1970).

56. Margaret LeCompte, Wendy Millroy, and Judith Preissle, eds., *Handbook of Qualitative Research in Education* (San Diego: Academic Press, 1992).

57. Burrhus F. Skinner, "The Operational Analysis of Psychological Terms," *Psychological Review* 52, no. 5 (1945), p. 270.

58. Allen Newell and Herbert A. Simon, *Human Problem Solving* (Englewood Cliffs, NJ: Prentice Hall, 1972).

59. See, e.g., Alan H. Schoenfeld, *Mathematical Problem Solving* (Orlando, FL: Academic Press, 1985).

60. For one description of the "cognitive revolution," see Howard E. Gardner, *The Mind's New Science: A History of the Cognitive Revolution* (New York: Basic Books, 1985).

61. See, e.g., Erik de Corte, Leuven Verschaffel, and Brian Greer, "Mathematics Teaching and Learning," *Handbook of Educational Psychology*, pp. 491-549; Frank Lester, "Musings about Mathematical Problem-solving Research: 1970-1994," *Journal for Research in Mathematics Education* 25, no. 6 (1994), pp. 660-675; Alan H. Schoenfeld, *Mathematical Problem Solving*; Alan H. Schoenfeld, "Learning to Think Mathematically: Problem Solving, Metacognition, and Sense-making in Mathematics," *Handbook of Research on Mathematics Teaching and Learning*, edited by D. Grouws, pp. 334-370.

62. Merlin Behr, Guershon Harel, Thomas Post, and Richard Lesh, "Rational Number, Ratio, and Proportion," *Handbook of Research on Mathematics Teaching and Learning*, pp. 296-333.

63. Thomas Kieren, "On the Mathematical, Cognitive, and Instructional Foundations of Rational Numbers," *Number and Measurement: Papers from a Research Workshop*, ed. Richard Lesh (Columbus, OH: ERIC/SMEAC, 1976), pp. 101-144.

64. Shulman, "Those Who Understand: Knowledge Growth in Teaching."

65. Liping Ma, *Knowing and Teaching Elementary Mathematics: Teachers' Understanding of Fundamental Mathematics in China and the United States* (Mahwah, NJ: Erlbaum, 1999).

66. George Pólya, *How to Solve It* (Princeton, NJ: Princeton University Press, 1945).

67. See Lester, "Musings about Mathematical Problem-solving Research," pp. 660-675; Schoenfeld, *Mathematical Problem Solving*.

68. John Bransford, Ann Brown, and Rodney Cocking, eds., *How People Learn: Brain, Mind, Experience, and School* (Washington, DC: National Academy Press, 1999), p. 12.

69. Lester, "Musings about Mathematical Problem-solving Research," pp. 666-667.

70. Magdalene Lampert, "When the Problem Is Not the Question and the Solution Is Not the Answer: Mathematical Knowing and Teaching," *American Educational Research Journal* 27 (1990), p. 31.

71. Schoenfeld, *Mathematical Problem Solving*.

72. Reuben Hersh, 1986, p. 13, cited in Alba Thompson, "Teachers' Beliefs and Conceptions: A Synthesis of the Research," *Handbook of Research on Mathematics Teaching and Learning*, p. 127.

73. For a review see Thompson, 1992.

74. James Stigler and James Hiebert, *The Teaching Gap*.

75. David Kirshner and James A. Whitson, eds., *Situated Cognition: Social Semiotic, and Psychological Perspectives* (Mahwah, NJ: Erlbaum, 1997), pp. vii-viii.

76. Jean Lave, Michael Murtaugh, and Olivia de la Rocha, "The Dialectic of Arithmetic in Grocery Shopping," *Everyday Cognition: Its Development in Social Context*, eds. Barbara Rogoff and Jean Lave (Cambridge, MA: Harvard University Press, 1984), p. 89.

77. J. G. Greeno and the Middle-School Mathematics through Applications Project Group, "Theories and Practices of Thinking and Learning to Think," *American Journal of Education* 106 (1997), pp. 85-126; J. G. Greeno and the Middle-School Mathematics through Applications Project Group, "The Situativity of Cognition, Learning, and Research," *American Psychologist* 53 (1998), pp. 5-26; E. Wenger, *Communities of Practice: Learning, Meaning, and Identity* (Cambridge, England: Cambridge University Press, 1998).

78. Christopher Cerf and Victor Navasky, *The Experts Speak: The Definitive Compendium of Authoritative Misinformation* (New York: Pantheon Books, 1984).

79. For more detail than can be offered here, see Alan H. Schoenfeld, "Looking Toward the 21st Century: Challenges of Educational Theory and Practice," *Educational Researcher* 28, no. 7 (1999), pp. 4-14.

80. For a model at a fine-grained level of mechanism, see Alan H. Schoenfeld, "Toward a Theory of Teaching-in-Context," *Issues in Education* 4, no. 1 (1998), pp. 1-94.

81. For a fine-grained discussion of how the functioning of a community transcends the capacities of its individual members, see Edwin Hutchins, *Cognition in the Wild* (Cambridge, MA: MIT Press, 1995).

82. NCTM, 1989; 1991; 1995; 2000.

CHAPTER X

The Social Foundations of Education:
School and Society in a Century of NSSE

STEVE TOZER with the assistance of ILHAN AVCIOGLU

The field of social foundations of education has changed significantly throughout the twentieth century. This chapter examines what NSSE yearbooks reveal about those changes.

It is instructive to begin by looking at two yearbooks published over 80 years apart. The Eighth NSSE Yearbook, authored by Charles Richmond Henderson, devoted both Parts I and II to *Education with Reference to Sex: Pathological and Economic and Social Aspects*. The orientation of these 1909 volumes announced itself in the first sentence of the Preface: "No apologies are made for urging upon teachers, the moral guides of the nation, the duty of helping in the cause of fighting, the black plague of the world."[1] This perspective was developed in Chapter 1, "Social Loss from Sexual Vice: Economic Aspects."

The notorious indifference and neglect of this subject by otherwise earnest and thoughtful people who desire the common welfare must be largely due to the general ignorance of the damage which the nation suffers from the various forms of sexual vice. The attitude of the unclean is easily explained; they are ready to sacrifice others and themselves to appetite and lust, and they become deaf to argument and appeal in consequence of the debasing influence of immoral indulgence and corrupting companionships.[2]

This yearbook thus attributed the perceived negative social consequences of sex among youth to ignorance and immorality, and, secondly, recommended ways in which sex education could become a part of the school curriculum.

The sensibilities reflected in this early NSSE Yearbook are telling, not just for their perspective on sexuality, but also for their perspectives on race. The author approvingly quoted the *American Breeders*

Steve Tozer is Professor in Philosophy of Education in Policy Studies at the University of Illinois at Chicago and Ilhan Avcioglu is a doctoral student in Curriculum and Instruction at the University of Illinois at Chicago.

Association Journal, which printed a report from the Committee on Eugenics chaired by President D. S. Jordan of Stanford University. The recommended passage was this:

It is a pressing problem to know what to do to increase the birthrate of the superior stocks and keep proportionate at least the contribution of the inferior stocks. One of the most promising influences is the Eugenic movement, started in England by Galton and Pearson to make proper procreation a part of religion and ethics, rather than a matter of whim only.[3]

This passage was quoted in support of a remark that "artificial avoidance of the responsibilities of having children in many well-situated families is often due to the fact that considerations of selfish comfort and ease determine the conduct and men and women ignore their obligations to the race."[4] These observations were offered as part of a sex education approach asserting that "education must aim to furnish discipline for rational community life; and the most important part of that life is the production, maintenance, and proper education of children and youth."[5]

In the last decade of the twentieth century, a volume that invites comparison to the Eighth Yearbook is the Ninety-second Yearbook, Part I, *Gender and Education*, edited by Sari Knopp Biklen and Diane Pollard.[6] Both yearbooks address the social contexts of schooling and education, but the differences between them are striking. The yearbook on *Gender and Education* sets a contrasting tone in the first pages. Chapter 1 begins:

Put very simply, we might say that one's sex is involved in every activity connected to education. Since every interaction involves a male or a female, sex is everywhere. We must take it into account. When to take it into account looms as a big question because it may be central even when it seems to have no relation to what is going on. But being male or female carries few meanings in and of itself. Its most potent meanings come from the social and cultural meanings attributed to it. These meanings we call gender, the social construction of sex. . . . Gender as a category of analysis suggests that to understand female- or male-experience each must be analyzed in relationship to the other in order to see how each is shaped by the other. Patriarchy, for example, is a central part of women's lives even when men are not around. That is why this book, even though it is mostly about women, focuses on gender.[7]

This volume does not, in any traditional sense, treat the topic of sex education. "Sex education" is not a heading nor a subheading in any of the fourteen chapters; and it does not appear as a term in the index. On the other hand, the ways in which sex and gender are constructed among children, adolescents and adults are a constant source of attention throughout the book, from Elizabeth Hansot's chapter, "Historical and Contemporary Views of Gender and Education," through various sections of the book titled, "Gender and Research," "Achievement and Technology," "Gender at Work among Adolescents and Adults," "Gender and Classroom in School Policy," or "Power, Multiplicity, and Voice."

An adequate comparison of these two yearbooks, one from the first decade of the twentieth century and one from the last, would require at least a chapter-length analysis, which is not possible here. The point of this introductory comparison is to illustrate something about how the field of social foundations has changed in the pages of NSSE during the twentieth century.

First, for example, is the matter of who has controlled and produced the scholarship of NSSE. The authorship, editorship, and executive committee for *Education With Reference to Sex* differ dramatically from the later yearbook on *Gender and Education*. The Eighth Yearbook was written and edited by Charles Richmond Henderson, a professor of sociology at the University of Chicago. Henderson wrote and edited the entire piece from his perspective as the President of the Chicago Society of Social Hygiene and an associate member of the American Academy of Medicine. The officers on the NSSE Executive Committee at that time were, like the author, all white males, from Charles McKenny of the State Normal School at Milwaukee to secretary-treasurer Manfred Holmes from the Illinois State Normal University in Normal, Illinois. In addition, Henderson wrote all of both volumes, with one invited paper by Helen Putnam, President of the American Academy of Medicine and Chairman of the Standing Committee on Teaching Hygiene. In contrast, the composition of the Board of Directors for NSSE in 1993 was equally divided between men and women, and all the contributors to the Yearbook, from co-editors Sari Knopp Biklen and Diane Pollard to the authors, were women, including women of color. Their perspectives reflect a wide range of disciplinary lenses in social foundations of education scholarship, from history of education to sociology and philosophy of education to curriculum theory.

Second, as a consequence of these differences and the evolution of research on the social contexts of education, the selection and treatment of topics differs dramatically in the two volumes. Unlike the Eighth Yearbook, the Ninety-second Yearbook examines the ways in which gender interacts with race, ethnicity, and class in the construction of adult and youth understandings of gender, sexuality, and education. The later yearbook, unlike the earlier, does not take dominant social values as unproblematic, nor does it take the responsibility of the school to be the socialization of children and youth into those dominant values. Rather, the Ninety-second Yearbook critically examines the ways in which power relations in the wider society are related to power relations in the school, and how youth and adults can understand these relations most productively. Unlike the earlier yearbook, which accepted the dominant social order uncritically, *Gender and Education* exemplifies a distinct tradition in social foundations of education that employs a critical, cross-disciplinary examination of social institutions, processes, and ideals in its effort to understand the social contexts of education and schooling.[8]

NSSE yearbooks throughout the twentieth century have differentially reflected the critical, cross-disciplinary tradition, showing how this tradition grew out of earlier phases of school-and-society scholarship. Evidence of this evolution can be found in social foundations scholarship in NSSE across three distinguishable periods: the Formative Period, in NSSE Yearbooks from 1902 through 1939; the First Generation of social foundations scholarship in NSSE Yearbooks, 1940 through 1969; and finally, the Second Generation treatments, from 1970 through 1999. These periods reflect not only the changing nature of how social foundations scholarship was conducted in NSSE Yearbooks, but also the changing nature of the field itself: the questions that social foundations scholarship asked, and how these questions were addressed.

Varieties of Social Foundations Treatments in NSSE

At its heart, social foundation of education is an attempt to understand the social bases of education, including schooling—so that education and schooling can be understood in their social contexts. On the one hand, social foundations of education is a distinctly modern (and lately, post-modern) professional and educational enterprise, with clearly identifiable roots in the 1930s at Teachers College, Columbia University. On the other hand, the notion that social contexts are fundamental to understanding educational processes goes back at least as far as Socrates. For Plato, Aristotle, and Rousseau, for example, one can't have a thorough conversation about educational ideals and practices without invoking *social* ideals and practices. Therefore, a search for social foundations treatments in the pages of NSSE Yearbooks cannot be restricted to the particular tradition that has emerged only since the 1930s, although that tradition has become the defining one since that time. In analyzing the social foundations presence in NSSE Yearbooks throughout the last century, it has been important to recognize distinctly different approaches to studying school-and-society.

The Formative Period, for example, has no yearbooks devoted to analysis of social conditions and phenomena per se, but it has several yearbooks that focus on one or another educational issue in social context, e.g., the Twelfth Yearbook, Part II, *The Supervision of Rural Schools*, edited by Franklin Bobbitt and others.[9] The First Generation period (1940-69) contains other such treatments, but also introduces something new to NSSE: yearbooks that focus primarily on individual "foundations disciplines," such as sociology of education or philosophy of education. This period also introduces yearbooks devoted to analysis of the *social conditions underlying* educational processes, as opposed to yearbooks that focus on education in social context—a difference in what is foreground and what is background. The Sixtieth Yearbook, Part II, *Social Conditions Influencing American Schools*, edited by Ralph Tyler and others,[10] is the best example. Taken together, these social foundations treatments average about six volumes per decade in the First Generation, in contrast to three social foundations volumes per decade in the Formative Period. Social critique, however, absent in the formative period, remains largely latent in the First Generation period.

The Second Generation (1970-99) introduces such critique, and it increases the number of social foundations yearbooks to an average of nine per decade. These include increased numbers of yearbooks focused on social forces and conditions themselves, those focused on educational phenomena in social context, and those which focus on single foundations disciplines. In all three periods of the century, social foundations perspectives were also incorporated, as a chapter or more, or a part of a chapter, into yearbooks that were otherwise not social foundations in orientation—less often early in the century, and more often later, as the importance of social contexts gained recognition.

THE FORMATIVE PERIOD: 1902-1939[11]

The Formative Period in NSSE scholarship in social foundations attended, in relatively underdeveloped ways, to the social contexts of schooling. It did so for the most part uncritically, accepting society as a given and accepting schooling as a mode of fitting people into society. "For the most part," because this period spanned nearly a forty-year era of tremendous social transformation in American culture. In 1901, the year before the first NSSE Yearbook was published, McKinley was assassinated and Theodore Roosevelt became President. By the end of the Formative Period in the 1930s, Franklin Delano Roosevelt had attained the Presidency and the Great Depression had reached its depths. The United States had begun to establish new social programs, entering the period of the welfare state. Hitler had seized power in Germany and had ignited World War II. These social transformations were to be instrumental in shaping the consciousness of those who developed a new field of educational inquiry and professional preparation at Teachers College Columbia, which they called the social foundations of education. Their first textbook was not published until 1941, after this Formative Period of social foundations in NSSE.[12]

While the formative period presents the fewest social foundations treatments of the three periods, there were still several moments of interest in this four-decade period. Three examples are instructive: one in teacher education, one in sociology of education research, and one on curriculum in social context.

The teacher education example came about early, in the second and third yearbooks, both of which treat issues of theory and practice. In the Second Yearbook, Part II, *The Relation of Theory to Practice in Education*, Levi Seeley wrote in "the Relation of Theory to Practice in the Training of Teachers," that there were two views of theory in the professional education of teachers.[13] In the Third Yearbook, in a chapter titled "The Relation of Theory to Practice in Education," John Dewey also indicated two different perspectives on teacher preparation regarding theory and practice.[14] Both treatments are interesting from a couple of perspectives. One is that at this time there was already a concern that normal schools had become too theoretical. Levi Seeley was himself a professor at the State Normal School at Trenton, New Jersey. It was thought that normal school training of teachers gave too much attention to the theoretical foundations of teaching and learning and insufficient attention to the practical side of learning how to teach.

As Ken Sirotnik would notice in the 1990s, teacher education candidates and graduates alike have historically viewed their social foundations coursework as too theoretical and not particularly valuable to their practice as teachers.[15] For Seeley, at the State Normal School in Trenton, two conceptions of what "theory" meant needed to be clarified in the pages of the NSSE Yearbook. One of these was, "that which involves the knowledge of the professional subjects necessary to the teacher," including history of education, philosophy of education, psychology of education, subject matter knowledge, and methods of teaching.[16] The other conception, which he preferred, he identified as learning "the science and art of teaching."[17]

Seeley argued, in essence, that the problem with the "professional subjects" view of educational theory was that it relied on discrete treatments of history of education, philosophy of education, psychology of education, and other "professional subjects." In contrast, he sought an approach to "the science and art of teaching" that integrated a knowledge of subject matter with pedagogical understanding and skill. One could argue that this same dispute exists among some teacher educators today who see the social and psychological foundations, as well as methods, as taught too discretely as separate bodies of knowledge to be learned. The claim often made by students, when they are taught these discrete subjects, is that they are "too theoretical," when perhaps a more accurate account might be that these bodies of knowledge and practice are not sufficiently integrated to provide coherent understanding for candidates—theoretical, practical, or otherwise.

In the Third Yearbook, in "The Relation of Theory to Practice in Education," Dewey presented the theory/practice dichotomy differently from Seeley, arguing for "the laboratory point of view" in which field experiences are used to stimulate the teacher's intellectual grasp of the relations between theory and practice.[18] Dewey argued that the laboratory point of view was essential to making the teacher a student of teaching. The fieldwork or practical work would be taken in the laboratory sense, for Dewey, in that it enabled the candidate to formulate intellectual and theoretical understandings of the nature of teaching practice that Dewey believed were essential to professional development.

This exchange of ideas across two yearbooks between Seeley and Dewey about theory and practice in the education of teachers is interesting from several perspectives. It illustrates questions of enduring import to teacher educators: what contribution educational theory in general, and social foundations knowledge in particular, have to make to the preparation of the practitioner—and how best to achieve that preparation.

Later in the Formative Period, however, the Fifteenth Yearbook, Part II, *The Relationship between Persistence in School and Home Conditions*, entirely authored by Charles Elmer Holley from Ohio Wesleyan University, presents a very different social foundations example.[19] This volume is remarkable in its attention to what George Counts would identify in 1934 as the Social Foundations of Education in the book by that name, by which he meant not primarily a field of study, but the actual social or cultural conditions that underlie educational processes. Holley, too, was concerned with these social conditions, and he began his volume with his statement of the problem: "This study is concerned primarily with the qualitative analysis of the relationships which exist between the schooling of children and their home conditions."[20] This detailed sociology of education study, Holley's Ph.D. dissertation at the University of Illinois, was conducted in the 1912-13 school year in the farm industry town of Decatur, Illinois.

The study focused on 198 families with over 600 older children, half of whom had secured a high school education. Holley addressed such topics as family occupations, incomes, rent, home-owning, home culture, clubs, organizations, and religious affiliations to which families belonged. He went on to study these and other variables in several midwestern towns for the yearbook. He looked into parent-child relationships, number of years of parents' education, number of books in the home and number of years of children's schooling, and so on. Holley's conclusions are of little surprise to us now because we are so familiar with the impact of socioeconomic status on schooling outcomes, but his conclusions are nonetheless interesting to review in the context of 1916. He wrote, for example, that "The most important conclusion supported by the study as a whole is that there is a close relationship between the advantages of a home, its educational, economic, and social stations, and the number of years of schooling which its children receive."[21] Another conclusion is that "environmental influences more often caused a child to stop attending school than did lack of ability to do the work."[22] He elaborated these ideas in his third conclusion, on the problem of school dropout, which he refers to as "early elimination." He wrote that,

early elimination is correlated with and largely due to factors outside the school. The school is only an institution of society. Society has created it and uses it as needs arise. Those who unreservedly blame the school for elimination forget that the school imparts instruction to the children alone. Their parents were educated a generation earlier and can seldom be reached by the present-day school."[23]

The emphasis Holley placed on the familiar variable of books in the home is noteworthy. "If a person wished to forecast from a single objective measure the probable educational opportunities which the children of a home have, the best measure would be the number of books in the home. The highest single correlation was shown by this index."[24] While Holley goes on to say that a more qualitative inquiry into this variable is necessary, students of sociology of education will recognize this familiar variable in sociology and sociology of education studies done later in the century. One of the most prominent was W. Lloyd Warner's *Social Class in America* (1949), which covered much of the same ground as Holley's earlier NSSE Yearbook.[25]

It is worth noting that this classic early sociology of education study falls into the formation of the social foundations of education tradition, including a "deficit-theory" perspective that takes the culture of the school as a legitimate, positive standard and measures the values and practices of the home by that standard. Holley noted, for example, "Truancy on the part of children is correlated, as a rule, with ignorance on the part of parents. In those cases where truancy occurred in the better homes, it was not followed by early elimination."[26] Despite this deficit-theory perspective, the study is notable for its contribution to the social foundations tradition. Unlike the Seeley/Dewey dialogue about social foundations in the preparation of teachers, Holley's treatment asks more fundamentally, "What are the relationships between home life and school performance?"

A third arresting instance in this formative period was the Twenty-sixth Yearbook, Part II, *The Foundations of Curriculum Making* (1927).[27] This is interesting in part because the contributors included George Counts, William H. Kilpatrick, and Harold Rugg, Chairman, all of whom became central to the development of social foundations as a field in the 1930s. The use of the term "foundations" in the yearbook title did not precisely reflect the later usage, and here meant more centrally "fundamentals," as Levi Seeley used the term in the title of his own book in 1901, rather than the sense of social *underpinnings* of educational processes.[28] Teachers College and University of Chicago faculty made up the majority of contributors to the volume, however, and reflected a social foundations orientation to curriculum. This volume pursued a social foundations question different from that pursued in the earlier volumes: What understanding of social context was fundamental to curriculum design?

Editor Guy Whipple wrote in the Preface that "The idea of attacking the problem of curriculum in a fundamental way, not trying to determine what the content of the curriculum should be, but trying to determine how that content should be selected and assembled, was broached by Dr. Harold Rugg, the chairman of the Society's committee responsible for this Twenty-sixth Yearbook more than two years ago."[29] In his Foreword, Rugg indicated his concern for the social context of curriculum making:

It is most important that those who are constructing our school curriculum shall maintain an overview of the total situation. Lacking that, their orientation will be biased, their emphases misplaced. . . . Synthesis is needed especially because of the gap between school and society and between curriculum and child growth. Life on the American continent has moved in two parallel but rarely merging currents. One has been the dynamic rush of land settlement, industry, and politics—exploitive, mercenary, and unmeditative. The other— the academic stream of letters, art, and education—has lagged sluggishly behind. . . . Curriculum making must become comprehensive, all embracing, and continuous, not partial and intermittent, as it has been during a century of national development.[30]

These three examples—one in teacher education, one in sociology of education research, and the third an example of curriculum in social context—illustrate three kinds of social foundations of education inquiry in the Formative Period. As the field would soon become defined by Counts's work at University of Chicago and by the Foundations Division at Teachers College, these early examples were not, strictly speaking, social foundations of education, but they nevertheless show important early efforts at reckoning with the social contexts of educational phenomena.

SOCIAL FOUNDATIONS IN HISTORICAL PERSPECTIVE

The social foundations approach that was self-consciously developed at Teachers College in the 1930s was committed to a critical, cross-disciplinary analysis of the relations between schools and their social contexts. Kenneth Benne, R. Freeman Butts, and Harold Rugg, three of the co-founders of the social foundations curriculum at Teachers College, have each written separate accounts of the faculty group representing various different "foundational disciplines" that met for over a decade to discuss how the relationships between schools, education, and the wider culture should be taught to educators. (Rugg had already edited two NSSE Yearbooks by that time, and Benne would do one later.) Of the Teachers College study group, Benne wrote:

They came to believe that all teachers should become students of the issues of contemporary society and culture and of the relations of these issues to questions of educational aims, methods, and programs. They also believed that a cross-disciplinary approach was conducive to adequate treatment of these issues. In keeping with this thinking, they brought the psychological, sociological, economic, historical, and philosophical perspectives together into a division of educational foundations.[31]

Before the 1930s, if teacher and administrator candidates took foundations courses, they tended to be of two kinds. One was single-discipline coursework such as philosophy of education, history of education, or sociology of education. Scholars like R.M. MacIver in sociology, Elwood Cubberly in history and W. H. Kilpatrick in philosophy used the lenses of the social sciences and humanities to study and teach about education in cultural context. The other kind of foundations course at the turn of the century used a different meaning of foundations: more akin to "fundamentals" or "basics." Thus, New Jersey State Normal School Professor Levi Seeley's 1901 book, *The Foundations of Education*, was really an introduction to teaching practice, rather than an effort to use foundational disciplines to study school and society.[32]

In 1934, however, near the nadir of the Depression, George S. Counts published *The Social Foundations of Education*,[33] which focused not on teaching or schools at all, but on the cultural context in which education in the U.S. takes place. A few years earlier, the multidisciplinary faculty group at Teachers College had begun meeting regularly to devise a two-semester curriculum, culminating in *Readings in the Foundations of Education* (1941).[34] These two efforts shared a common approach to foundational study in professional preparation: they sought to provide a critical, cross-disciplinary study of the social institutions, processes and ideals that underlie educational processes, including schooling.

The metaphor "foundations," then, was not intended by Counts, Rugg, and others to represent the "fundamentals" of education or the "basic" component of teacher preparation programs. Rather, "foundations" referred to the two fundamental *bases* on which all teaching and learning must rest. One of these two bases was the human learning organism, and the other was some cultural context in which that organism must reside. The first of these emerged in professional study as the *psychological foundations* of education, and the second as the *cultural or social foundations* of education. It was the critical, cross-disciplinary view of social foundations of education, not the "introduction to teaching" approach, nor the single-discipline study of history or philosophy of education, that marked the development of the field from the 1940s onward—and that led to the founding of the American Educational Studies Association (AESA) in the late 1960s, near the end of this First Generation of social foundations scholarship in NSSE yearbooks.

THE FIRST GENERATION OF SOCIAL FOUNDATIONS OF EDUCATION IN NSSE: 1940-69

The next period of social foundations scholarship in NSSE yearbooks, following the Formative Period, might be called the First Generation of social foundations as a self-conscious field of scholarship and professional preparation. This thirty-year period spanned the United States involvement in World War II, followed by the beginning and the maturing of the Cold War, Cold War mentality, and social conservatism of the 1950s. This conservative mood was soon disrupted. Betty Friedan published *The Feminine Mystique* in 1963; the National Organization of Women was founded in 1966; and *Roe v. Wade* was decided in 1973. In civil rights and race relations, Dr. King marched on Washington in 1963 and was assassinated in 1968, the same year Malcolm X and Robert Kennedy were assassinated and the Civil Rights Act of 1968 was passed. In 1969, the Stonewall Riot began the Gay Pride movement, youth culture reached new expression at Woodstock, and the economic class implications of the Vietnam War were beginning to be expressed. In short, the First Generation was a period of tremendous change in terms of social consciousness. By the end of this period, NSSE scholarship began to reflect a new emphasis on understanding social contexts in educational analysis.

The First Generation marked a sharp increase in the number of social foundations treatments in NSSE yearbooks. Instead of approximately three Yearbooks per decade addressing school and society relationships (only twelve throughout the first four decades), the First Generation era produced an average of at least six such yearbooks per decade in the 1940s, 50s and 60s. More importantly, the content of these treatments changed. In the twelve social foundations volumes that spanned the Formative Period, there had been none focusing centrally on social influences nor any devoted to a single foundational discipline such as philosophy or sociology of education. Instead, as noted above, the social foundations presence in the Formative Period NSSE volumes was restricted primarily to treatments of selected educational issues in social context (e.g., *The Supervision of Rural Schools*, Twelfth Yearbook, Part II).[35] This contribution was, of course, important. It reflected the groundwork being laid for the emergence of social foundations of education as an identifiable field of study after 1940.

In the First Generation era, however, such treatments were joined by volumes that focused entirely on social contexts or that dedicated a volume to a single foundational discipline. It would be expected that the volumes of the 1940s-60s would also demonstrate a more critical perspective than in the formative period, given that the Social Foundations division at Teachers College had begun to shape the field toward "interpretive, normative, and critical" perspectives, and what the Council of Learned Societies in Education *Standards* would later say.[36] Rugg's own social studies textbook series, while hugely successful at first, was eventually squeezed out of production because its socialist leanings were too critical for some influential constituencies.[37] Ironically, the First Generation work came at a historical moment when social critique was approaching an all-time low in the United States. While there had been a growing critique of American society and of capitalism in particular in the 1930s, reflected in Rugg's textbook series and in the educational journal *The Social Frontier* (critique that led directly to the formation of the TC discussion group), this would quickly change.[38] By 1940, with the rise of fascism in Europe and the impending involvement of the United States in WWII, critique of American domestic culture took a distant second seat to concern about the threat of totalitarianism from abroad. Following WWII, the rapid development of the Cold War continued to forestall social and educational critique from the left because the enemy to freedom was perceived not as internal but external to the body politic. Not until the social upheavals of the 1960s would gender discrimination, racial inequity, and protests against the Vietnam War begin to fuel a visible social critique in the U.S. Surprisingly, almost none of this critical climate was reflected in the NSSE yearbooks of the 1960s, though it would appear soon thereafter.

Following the formative decades, then, which were characterized by comparatively little attention to the social contexts of education, and by even less critical perspective, a great deal of attention to social contexts appeared in the 1940s-60s. This attention to social context, however, was also largely uncritical of anti-democratic impulses in American society and schooling. These First Generation treatments essentially affirmed the structure and values of the culture, and they affirmed the school as an agent of democracy and social mobility, as examples will illustrate. While there was substantial attention to foundations disciplines such as philosophy or comparative education, the critique one might expect as the result of the Teachers College work in the depression-era 1930s was largely absent. That critical dimension, that would emerge prominently in the 1970s and 1980s, was latent in the First Generation period.

LATENT CRITIQUE IN THE FIRST GENERATION

This non-critical foundations of education presence in NSSE yearbooks is evident from the beginning to the end of the 1940s. Important examples of yearbooks devoted to foundations disciplines were the Fortieth Yearbook, *Art in American Life and Education*, edited by Thomas Munro,[39] and the Forty-first Yearbook, Part I, *Philosophies of Education*, edited by John S. Brubacher.[40] Neither of these was critical, however, in the sense of examining, for example, the relations of knowledge and power in education, or in questioning the social order and its inequities.

The Fortieth Yearbook, *Art in American Life and Education* (only one volume appeared that year because of its 800-page length), was a tour de force of cataloging art in American life: in public architecture, in landscape design, in industry, in clothing and apparel, in commerce, in motion pictures, in dancing, even in television at that early time. It remains an extraordinary look at art in popular culture, thus foreshadowing, in some ways, the cultural studies movement in the humanities, social sciences, and education beginning in the 1970s and 1980s. It also looked at art in education, education in the arts, education of artists, preparation of art teachers, and it introduced an important critical note: the accusation that arts were badly neglected in schools at that time. This was a special volume in scale and approach. It was clearly a social foundations treatment in that (a) it stood in an aesthetics of education tradition and (b) it addressed the question: What is the nature of the arts in society, and what significance does this account have for arts in education?

The volume on *Philosophies of Education* was one of several throughout the century devoted to philosophy of education. This one represented a traditional *–isms* approach, with chapters by such familiar philosophers as W. H. Kilpatrick and W. C. Bagley of Teachers College and Mortimer Adler of the University of Chicago. There was a chapter on experimentalism, one on realism, one on idealism, and so on. This volume might serve to illustrate why students in teacher and administrator education programs have historically found their philosophy of education courses of questionable application to their professional work. Adler wrote a chapter "In Defense of the Philosophy of Education," but it is a defense that few students would find comprehensible or applicable to professional practice. Adler took the position that the ends of education are "absolute and universal"[41] and provided a definition of education that is most notable for its obscurity. He later apologized: "I regret that this essay may be unsatisfactory to many who are genuinely seeking enlightenment about the philosophy of education."[42] For the modern reader, that apology may well apply to the entire volume. It is of considerable interest to those in the field of philosophy of education, but the treatment of philosophical discourse as inert schools of thought is typically of little value to any but a few with distinctively philosophical interests. This would have concerned the founders of the social foundations tradition such as Counts, Rugg, Butts, Benne and others who believed that social foundations of education should make an important contribution to professional preparation.

In 1945 the Forty-fourth Yearbook was published in two volumes. The first was *American Education in the Post-War Period: Curriculum Reconstruction*, edited by Ralph W. Tyler. The second was *American Education in the Post-War Period: Structural Reorganization*, edited by Bess Goodykoontz.[43] Both were school-and-society volumes in that they sought understanding of educational phenomena in the social context of a particular moment in history, but again they were missing a critical perspective. The aims of schooling, like the aims of the social order, were affirmed as unproblematic. In his introduction to the first volume, Tyler described in some detail how much we had learned about education from "war training experiences themselves." These included new insights about motivation that had been achieved via the training of soldiers, the importance of clear-cut objectives, and the use of such training aids as "motion pictures, records, models and the like."[44] Tyler also indicated that the war had given us new insight into educational responsibilities such as cultivating international understanding among students. The treatments throughout both volumes had little or nothing to do with critique and a great deal to do with reintegration of American soldiers, workers, and students into a post-war society. The driving question of these volumes was how to make American schools and society work more efficiently together in service of putatively unproblematic goals of democratic social structures and social mobility through education.

This general orientation toward understanding the relations between American schools and society continues throughout the 1950s. The yearbooks on *General Education* (Fifty-one, Part I), on *Education in Rural Communities* (Fifty-one, Part II), on *Adapting the Secondary School Program to the Needs of Youth* (Fifty-two, Part I), on *Citizen Cooperation for Better Public Schools* (Fifty-three, Part I) and so on, were efforts at articulating a more harmonious relationship between schools and society.[45] The working assumption was still that the society itself was structured on democratic ideals and that schools were a vehicle for upward mobility within that society. This continued throughout the 1960s, with two particularly good examples of yearbooks that examine the wider social context without a critical bent.

The first of these was the Sixtieth Yearbook, Part II, *Social Forces Influencing American Education*, edited by Ralph W. Tyler. One of the yearbook's contributors and editors, Robert Havighurst, had in 1957 co-authored *Society and Education* with Bernice Neugarten, and their book soon became the leading text in social foundations of education instruction.[46] That their book presented virtually no critical social perspective stood in contrast to other social foundations textbooks of its era, such as the popular *Social Foundations of Education* by Smith, Stanley, Benne and Anderson (1956), or Rugg and Withers's book by the very same title from the year before.[47] *Social Forces Influencing American Education* was virtually without a critical voice, though social foundations categories of analysis abounded in such chapters as "Educational Politics," "Education and Economics," "Demographic Factors," a historical chapter on "Traditional Values in the Shaping of American Education," and Havighurst's chapter on "Social Class Influences on American Education."[48] The foundations disciplines were well represented, but the critical perspective central to the founding tradition was lost.

Still, there are a number of interesting features to the Sixtieth Yearbook. Havighurst's chapter on social class features a qualitative analysis that includes an interview with "a girl from a lower class family."[49] The interview is intended to illustrate "class consciousness in America," including "a considerable degree of hostility towards the middle class by some of the lower class who are unsuccessful by middle class standards."[50] Here then is at least limited recognition of class tension in the U.S. as well as an interesting demonstration of the use of qualitative method, where a young women tells her own story of her working class experiences and her sense of second-class citizenship in a middle class school. However, Havighurst doesn't grab the ring, here or elsewhere. His apologist perspective is demonstrated at the end of this chapter when he acknowledges that "The educational system is run by middle class people with middle class standards," then goes on to present a class-centered view:

[These middle class standards are] tempered by some understanding of the fact that working class values and aspirations as well as habits are enough different from those of the middle class to make educational adaptations desirable. These adaptations take the form on the one hand of encouraging and motivating the brighter lower class students to aspire to middle class status by means of education and on the other hand of recognizing that many lower class students will not profit from such academic fare and should be treated differently in school, with more emphasis on getting them through school and into a job or into marriage with or without high school graduation. Thus, the schools give educational and thereby economic and cultural opportunity to large numbers of people and play an essential part in keeping the social structure fluid.[51]

Although Havighurst warned that there may be "tendencies toward hardening of the social structure and toward more rigid stratification" in metropolitan areas, he concludes on a bright note:

Under present conditions of economic growth and population expansion, it appears likely that the class structure will remain open and fluid and the tendencies toward stratification and rigidity can be successfully controlled if educators understand the social forces which are influencing the society and act wisely with respect to them.[52]

Despite the fact that Havighurst and the NSSE committee did a good job selecting the disciplinary lenses through which to examine the social contexts of schooling, the apologist discourse pervades the volume. A final example from the First Generation period was Havighurst's 1968 volume on *Metropolitanism: Its Challenge to Education* (Sixty-seventh Yearbook, Part I), by which time one would expect to see considerable evidence of urban and civil rights unrest, though this was a bit early (given publication schedules) to expect to see any evidence of student protest against the Vietnam War. At this point, significant white flight was affecting urban schools, poverty was becoming concentrated in African American urban neighborhoods and highrises, and Havighurst introduced the book as follows:

The metropolitan area is taking the place of the city as the most useful geographic unit for thinking about the coordination and the organization of educational, governmental, and other social systems. Educators, governmental officials, and businessmen are developing a theory and a practice of the relations of the physical environment to human satisfactions in the metropolitan area. The attention of educators will be increasingly fixed on the metropolitan area rather than on the growth or decline of the city or on the proliferation of suburbs.[53]

In the context of what was taking place in the cities by this point, this reads almost like a willful disregard for urban problems. Although this volume was an outstanding representative of attention to social context as presented in First Generation NSSE yearbooks, there was no critical examination in this volume of the nature of oppression, how power and economics serve some people at the expense of others, how education reflects those power and economic differences, and so on. Such discussions remain absent until the Second Generation of Social Foundations work, beginning in the 1970s. Instead, insofar as the First Generation increased its attention to the social contexts of education and schooling, the driving questions had more to do with making educational systems function more effectively than with questioning the legitimacy or value of those systems.

THE SECOND GENERATION

The next thirty-year period, the 1970s through the '90s, introduced the post-modern period in social foundations of education, as well as in educational scholarship more broadly. The growing post-modern perspective that knowledge is intimately related with power, and that knowledge and power are social constructions, helped to stimulate attention to the cultural bases, or the social foundations, of educational phenomena. As a consequence, the number of NSSE volumes that could be called social foundations escalated dramatically in the 1970s and 1980s, until by the 1990s, nearly every year finds at least one NSSE volume that one could say is an education-and-society treatment. The prominence of social critique as a component of social foundations increased throughout this time. Finally, late-century NSSE yearbooks featured a greater prominence of people who are distinctly social foundations of education scholars, from philosophy of education, history and sociology of education.

By 1968, as the First Generation drew to a close, the American Educational Studies Association was founded as an organization to support social foundations of education scholarship in the cross-disciplinary, critical tradition; and it would soon launch publication of *Educational Studies* and later, *Educational Foundations*. By the early 1970s an umbrella organization for such professional societies as History of Education, Philosophy of Education, Comparative and International Education, and other foundations associations was formed as the Council of Learned Societies of Education (CLSE). By the end of the 1970s, CLSE had produced the *Standards for Academic and Professional Instruction in Foundations of Education, Educational Studies, and Educational Policy Studies* that, with one revision in the 1990s, would serve the foundations disciplines until the present day.[54] What began as a distinctly *pedagogical* scholarly enterprise at Teachers College—the formation of a social foundations faculty and the founding of a social foundations curriculum for the preparation of teachers and administrators—has developed over the last sixty years into new organizational forms to sustain and ultimately transform the original pedagogical and professional vision developed by Counts, Kilpatrick, Benne, Rugg, Butts, and others. The CLSE *Standards* have for over twenty years presented an explicit rationale for the role of social foundations of education in the professional preparation of educators: that social foundations uses the lenses of the social sciences and humanities to help teacher candidates develop "interpretive, normative, and critical perspectives on education" and that such perspectives are important to interpreting educational practice in cultural context. The knowledge, skills, and dispositions indicated in the standards were (and are) explicitly intended to help teachers develop the socio-cultural understandings, critical skills, and habits of mind to interpret and evaluate educational aims, practices, and problems in their institutional and cultural contexts.[55]

The Second Generation of social foundations scholarship had effectively begun by the 1970s, in the field itself and in NSSE yearbooks. Whereas in the Formative Period relatively few yearbooks could be identified as social foundations in orientation, by the Second Generation an average of nine yearbook volumes per decade were readily identifiable as relying on the social contexts of schooling for their analysis. Not only were there many more foundations-oriented treatments in the last three decades, but there were more that stood firmly in the critical, cross-disciplinary tradition that emerged in the 1930s from Teachers College—or they represented a single foundations discipline as the focus of the volume. In the 1970s alone, for example, individual volumes appeared on philosophical, legal, sociological, and political foundations of education. Also significant from a foundations perspective were those cases in which a yearbook theme was not particularly foundations-oriented, but in which the social context of that educational issue received much more attention than it had in the past. One example is the Seventieth Yearbook, Part I, *The Curriculum: Retrospect and Prospect*, edited by Robert M. McClure. Instead of a portion of an introductory chapter devoted to a brief historical overview as we might have seen earlier in NSSE yearbooks, this volume begins with three full chapters on the history of curriculum development. Following that, two more chapters are dedicated to the social contexts of curriculum development, one focusing on "Curriculum Development in Relation to Social and Educational Systems," and the other (by philosopher Harry Broudy) on "Democratic Values and Educational Goals."[56]

Similarly, another example of a volume that is not centrally social foundations in its topic is the Seventy-second Yearbook, Part II, *Elementary Schooling in the United States*.[57] It relies much more heavily on social analysis than similar yearbooks in the first two NSSE periods. This yearbook, edited by John Goodlad and Harold Shane, begins with Goodlad's chapter, "The Elementary School as a Social Institution," in which the author looks at how social policy shapes the elementary school. Another foundations treatment immediately follows Goodlad's: "Historical Roots of Contemporary Elementary Education," by Henry J. Otto. This is followed by a historical and sociological chapter by Sol Cohen, "The Elementary School in the Twentieth Century: A Social Context." Chapter 5 in this volume is "The Philosophical Context," by philosopher of education Philip Smith. In the concluding section of the yearbook, "The Urban Elementary School Today," Scribner and Knox examine "socio-political forces" affecting the contemporary urban elementary school.[58] Even in volumes that are not on their face social foundations yearbooks, the social context is raised to a new level of attention in the Second Generation treatments.

Another volume of interest in the 1970s is the Seventy-third Yearbook, Part I, *Media and Symbols: the Forms of Expression, Communication, and Education*, edited by David R. Olson.[59] This fascinating yearbook examines media, symbol systems, mass communications, sign theory, visual imagery, uses of film, and so on. It is a thorough and provocative treatment, in 500 pages, of the educative and mis-educative significance of various media in society. It is something of a forerunner to the Cultural Studies in Education scholarship that would begin to appear in the 1980s. The concept of ideology is treated in this volume, for example, but the volume in general does not address how power is embedded in symbol systems as later cultural studies work would—and is thus not particularly critical in orientation.[60]

Another illustrative Second Generation volume is the Seventy-third Yearbook, Part II, *Uses of the Sociology of Education*, edited by C. Wayne Gordon.[61] Unlike yearbooks of the 1960s that did not seem to reflect the social unrest of the period, this volume certainly does. The first chapter is "The Psychology of Student Protest" by Joseph Katz, in which the author tried to provide an analysis of the origins of student protest in terms of the social conditions of the student movement, the political and economic conditions of the wider culture, and what Katz called "the life space of the adolescent."[62] The Ralph W. Larkin chapter takes up the issue of the counterculture with "Protest and Counterculture: Disaffection among Affluent Youth."[63] His conception relies heavily on analysis of the economic system and its relationship to the counterculture. Several other chapters in this volume address youth culture in the United States at that time, including Thomas A. LaBelle's "Youth as Sociocultural Systems in American Society."[64]

In the first seven chapters of the volume, we see that one primary use of sociology of education at that time was to try to understand the nature of youth in American culture. A second section of the book examines equality and inequality of educational attainment, raising questions about the effectiveness and equity of the system as well as about the discipline of sociology of education itself—and the extent to which it can provide adequate explanations for equality and inequality. Another section of the volume addresses segregation and desegregation along racial and ethnic lines, in which a series of chapters examines public school desegregation as well as desegregation in the community. The volume's final section deals with the role of the federal government in education, with particular attention to the federal role in poverty in cities, racial unrest in the cities, and modes of government intervention—all themes that were skirted in the First Generation yearbooks.

Because of the nature of the conflicts under examination in this volume, a form of "ideologically complex discourse" is used.[65] Instead of only one ideological perspective being represented, as was true of volumes in the first six decades of the century, we see a portrayal of competing perspectives, for example between youth and "the establishment," or between civil rights workers and proponents of Jim Crow South. In those treatments of conflicts, even treatments of violence (as in Smith and Grigg's treatment of public school desegregation in the South), a much more critical perspective is presented in the effort to represent the source of the conflict in the perspectives of those seeking change vs. those seeking to protect the status quo.[66]

In the 1980s, the number of yearbook themes that rely on social context analysis to understand educational phenomena increases. Examples are the Eighty-first Yearbook, Part II, *Education and Work* (edited by Harry F. Silberman); the Eighty-third Yearbook, Part I, *Becoming Readers in a Complex Society* (Alan C. Purves and Olive S. Niles, editors); the Eighty-fourth Yearbook, Part I, *Education in School and Non-School Settings* (edited by Mario d. Fantini and Robert Sinclair); the Eighty-seventh Yearbook, Part II, *Cultural Literacy and the Idea of a General Education* (Ian Westbury and Alan C. Purves, editors); and the Eighty-eighth Yearbook, Part I, *From Socrates to Software: The Teacher as Text and the Text as Teacher* (edited by Philip W. Jackson and Sophie Haroutunian-Gordon).[67]

The 1980s also present volumes that represent a single foundations discipline, such as the Eightieth Yearbook, Part I, *Philosophy and Education*.[68] Edited by Teacher College philosopher Jonas Soltis, the volume is a who's who of philosophy of education for its time. Unlike earlier yearbooks in philosophy of education, in 1943 and 1955, which were all male volumes, the 1981 yearbook features chapters by Donna Kerr, Jane Roland Martin, and Maxine Greene (the volume features only white authors, however). This volume was a rejection of the world-views or -isms approach of the 1940s and 1950 volumes and was also a return to the social foundations tradition in the sense that it explicitly addressed itself to the needs of pre-service and practicing teachers in an effort to connect philosophy of education to the world of educational practice. Martin's chapter on liberal education, or Kerr's chapter on the structure of equality in teaching, or Greene's piece on aesthetic literacy in education—all sought connections to the world of practice. Similarly, Robert Ennis's chapter on "Rational Thinking and Educational Practice" was explicit about connections to practice.[69] The volume is not organized by world views or –isms, like idealism or progressivism, but rather by philosophical categories such as epistemology, aesthetics, logic, ethics, social philosophy, and even metaphysics, all explored for their educational import. Two specific categories of educational theory are also explored: curriculum theory and theory of teaching.

Given that Education Policy Studies has become one of the theoretical perspectives of social foundations identified in the *CLSE Standards*, it is useful to note the Eighty-first Yearbook, Part I, *Policy Making in Education*, edited by Ann Lieberman and Milbrey W. McLaughlin.[70] The Eighty-fourth Yearbook, Part II, *Learning and Teaching the Ways of Knowing*, edited by Elliot Eisner, is also very much a foundations approach, addressing epistemological perspectives in education and society.[71]

A yearbook from the 1980s that was prepared consciously in the tradition of the Teachers College approach to social foundations of education was the Eighty-sixth Yearbook, Part II, *Society as Educator in an Age of Transition*, edited by Ken Benne and Steve Tozer.[72] Benne was a member of the Teachers College study group in the 1930s and a contributor to their first volume of *Readings*. The flavor of this yearbook can best be captured by looking at two components: the section organization and philosopher Harry Broudy's concluding chapter. The three-section organization of the yearbook begins with Section One, Technology and Democratic Society; Section Two addresses Social Heterogeneity and Power; and Section Three addresses School and Society. Critical perspectives pervade the volume, and the relations between power, economics, education, and democratic ideals are addressed in different contexts. The critical thread is visible in Broudy's retrospective chapter, "Becoming Educated in Contemporary Society."

Broudy summarizes each of the preceding chapters in a sentence or two, providing insight into the critique each chapter offers. Some examples from his summary:

- Chapter 1 (Benne): Despite an expressed social commitment to democracy, there is no social consensus on what democracy means, in theory or in practice.
- Chapter 3 (Wirth): The workplace is at once inconsistent with democratic ideals, inimical to intellectual challenge and growth for most people, and diminishing in its ability to promise employment *at all* for many people in the future.
- Chapter 7 (Tozer): The hierarchy of power in the U.S. is not consistent with democratic ideals, and the stability of this condition rests, in part, upon the power of ideology over critical thought; this is in part sustained by media and schools that consistently miseducate the populace with regard to its own interests.
- Chapter 8 (Greene, Raywid): Neither the schools nor other educative institutions in society hold promise of social mobility nor personal fulfillment, and it is not clear where else to place hope for one's self and one's children. [73]

This volume is similar to only a handful of NSSE volumes in that its primary focus is the society in which educational processes and institutions are grounded. Moreover, the volume is intentionally, like few other volumes in the NSSE series, a critical, cross-disciplinary examination of social institutions, processes, and ideals. That intent could have been better achieved, in retrospect, with a greater diversity of authors, of whom only three were women and none were people of color.

By the 1990s, the prominence of the social had been clearly established in educational analysis. In sharp contrast to the Formative Period and the First Generation era, by the last decade of the century, nearly every year had at least one volume that made social context explicit in its approach. In 1990 it was *Educational Leadership and Changing Contexts of Families, Communities, and Schools*, edited by Brad Mitchell and Luvern L. Cunningham (Eighty-ninth Yearbook, Part II). In 1991 it was *The Care and Education of America's Young Children*, edited by Sharon L. Kagan (Ninetieth Yearbook, Part I). In 1992, both volumes were foundations-oriented: *The Changing Contexts of Teaching*, edited by Ann Lieberman; and *The Arts, Education and Aesthetic Knowing*, edited by Bennett Reimer and Ralph A. Smith (the Ninety-first Yearbook, Parts I and II).[74] And so on, culminating in the year 2000 yearbooks *Constructivism in Education*, edited by D. C. Phillips, and *American Education: Yesterday, Today, and Tomorrow*, edited by Thomas Good (Ninety-ninth Yearbook, Parts I and II).[75] While neither of these is an example of a yearbook fully devoted to examining the social contexts of education, the social foundations perspectives are evident in both: primarily philosophical in the first, with a strong historical perspective in the second.

Further, the 1990s, unlike any other decade, had at least two year-books that clearly focused first on social phenomena themselves, not primarily on educational phenomena in social or philosophical or historical context. These were the *Gender and Education* yearbook mentioned at the beginning of this chapter, and *The Adolescent Years: Social Influences and Educational Challenges*, edited by sociologists Kathryn Borman and Barbara Schneider. In the Formative Period, adolescence was treated as centrally, almost purely, a psychological category. In the Second Generation treatment, adolescence is fundamentally a social construct. The fundamental question asked by social foundations scholars had shifted from, in the early part of the century, "What do we need to know about the social contexts of schools to make schools more effective at fitting people into that social context?" to the late-century question, "How are we to interpret the socially constructed nature of power and knowledge in human relations, including relations of domination and subordination, and what significance does such interpretation have for theory and practice in education?"

Conclusion: New Directions in the Social Foundations

The twentieth century was marked by a dramatic increase in the use of social analysis to interpret the meanings of education and schooling in American society. In NSSE treatments of social foundations, this increase can be understood as developing across three identifiable periods in the twentieth century: the Formative Period (through 1939), the First Generation (through 1969), and the Second Generation (through 1999). These periods are defined partly by changes evident in social foundations analysis in the NSSE yearbooks themselves, and partly by events in the field of social foundations external to NSSE.

While the critical interpretive potential of social foundations of education was articulated as early as the 1930s, it lay latent in NSSE until the 1970s and developed further throughout the Second Generation. Here, in the period during which the CLSE *Standards* defined the social foundations in terms of "interpretive, normative, and critical perspectives" on the social contexts of schooling, the critical component of social foundations found a firmer footing in NSSE volumes. In this second generation, critical social analysis became a more pervasive dimension of NSSE efforts to represent research on education and schooling in contemporary society—and in teacher education.

The questions pursued by social foundations scholars changed, reflecting in part the experiences of women and people of color, who had not participated in early NSSE volumes to the extent that they did in later decades. The new questions also reflected the strengthening of cultural critique in education, in social sciences and the humanities more generally.

In fact, social foundations critique has been influenced by a recent element that is to date only barely visible in the pages of NSSE yearbooks: the advent of cultural studies in education. In his Introduction to *The Cultural Studies Reader*, editor Simon During wrote in 1999, "Since the early 1990s, there has been a cultural studies boom, especially in anglophone universities. . . . most, maybe all, humanities and social science disciplines have increasingly emphasized culture over the past decade or so."[76] During, like other cultural studies scholars, is worried that the boom in cultural studies will serve to water it down so that it loses its critical agenda, which During describes as "engaged cultural studies":

[E]ngaged cultural studies is academic work (teaching, research, dissemination, etc.) on contemporary culture from non-elite or counter hegemonic perspectives ("from below") with an openness to the culture's reception and production in everyday life, or, more generally, its impact on life trajectories . . . it aims to produce knowledge from perspectives lost to and in dominant public culture, and to listen to far-off or marginalized voices.[77]

Similarly, Henry Giroux and Peter McLaren begin their book, *Between Borders: Pedagogy and the Politics of Cultural Studies*, as follows:

During the last decade, the fields of cultural studies and critical pedagogy have been expanding within the United States and abroad. Within the University, both fields are developing in a diverse number of disciplines and are generating a boom industry in undergraduate and graduate courses. . . . Of course, the proliferation of these two fields has not gone on unproblematically. There is an enormous debate over the central categories, premises, and practices that are being legitimated within various discourses that address these fields.[78]

Part of that debate is familiar to social foundations scholars who, following the field's founders, wish to see their social and educational critique make a difference in practice. Influential cultural studies scholar Stuart Hall points out a problem inherent in the recent growth of the cultural studies project in the United States: that it is becoming institutionalized in ways that may blunt its power to effect change. He writes:

I come back to the difficulty of instituting a genuine cultural and critical practice, which is intended to produce some kind of organic intellectual political work, which does not try to inscribe itself in the overarching meta-narrative of achieved knowledges, within the institutions. I come back to theory and politics, the politics of theory. Not theory as the will to truth, but theory as a set of contested, localized, conjunctural knowledges, which have to be debated in a dialogical way. But also as a practice which always thinks about its intervention in a world in which it would make some difference, in which it would have some effect. Finally, a practice which understands the need for intellectual modesty. I do think there is all the difference in the world between understanding the politics of intellectual work and substituting intellectual work for politics.[79]

Through the lens of cultural studies, Hall serves to remind the social foundations scholar of the difficulty of making critical educational analysis matter in the world of practice.

Throughout the twentieth century, NSSE yearbooks have lagged somewhat behind the field of social foundations of education in terms of social and critical analysis. NSSE yearbooks have yet to take up the field of cultural studies in education in a purposeful way, though the 1993 volume on *Gender and Education* certainly reflects the gender studies component of the wider agenda of cultural studies in education. As the annual conferences of American Educational Studies demonstrate, the future of social foundations of education is already intertwined with cultural studies in education. The two have very different histories, but their critical social and educational projects intersect. The difficulty of making those critical projects matter in practice is one that NSSE yearbooks in the future will do well to address.

Notes

1. Charles Richmond Henderson, "Preface," *Education with Reference to Sex: Pathological and Economic and Social Aspects*, Eighth Yearbook of the National Society for the Study of Education, Part I, ed. Charles Richmond Henderson (Bloomington, IL: Public School Publishing Co., 1909), p. 7.

2. Charles Richmond Henderson, "Social Loss from Sexual Vice: Economic Aspects," *Education with Reference to Sex: Pathological and Economic and Social Aspects*, Eighth Yearbook

of the National Society for the Study of Education, Parts I and II, eds. Charles Richmond Henderson and Helena C. Putnam (Bloomington, IL: Public School Publishing Co., 1909), p. 21.

3. Charles Richmond Henderson, "Introduction: Education in Relation to the Sexual Life," *Education with Reference to Sex: Pathological and Economic and Social Aspects*, Eighth Yearbook of the National Society for the Study of Education, Part II, eds. Charles Richmond Henderson and Helena C. Putnam (Bloomington, IL: Public School Publishing Co., 1909), p. 11.

4. *Ibid.*, p. 11.

5. *Ibid.*, p. 11.

6. Sari Knopp Biklen and Diane Pollard, eds., *Gender and Education*, Ninety-second Yearbook of the National Society for the Study of Education, Part I (Chicago: National Society for the Study of Education, 1993).

7. Sari Knopp Biklen and Diane Pollard, "Sex, Gender, Feminism, and Education," *Gender and Education*, Ninety-second Yearbook of the National Society for the Study of Education, Part I, eds. Sari Knopp Biklen and Diane Pollard (Chicago: National Society for the Study of Education, 1993), p. 1.

8. The history of that tradition is detailed in Steve Tozer and Stuart McAninch, "Social Foundations of Education in Historical Perspective," *Educational Foundations* 1 (Fall, 1986), pp. 5-32.

9. Franklin Bobbitt, J. W. Hall, and J. D. Wolcott, eds., *The Supervision of Rural Schools*, Twelfth Yearbook of the National Society for the Study of Education, Part II (Bloomington, IL: Public School Publishing Co., 1913).

10. Ralph W. Tyler, Merle L. Borrowman, Robert J. Havighurst, and Vincent Ostrom, eds., *Social Conditions Influencing American Schools*, Sixtieth Yearbook of the National Society for the Study of Education, Part II (Chicago: National Society for the Study of Education, 1961). Harold Rugg used the term "foundations disciplines" in Rugg, *The Teacher of Teachers* (New York: Harper and Brothers, 1952), p. 22.

11. While social foundations of education was given clear shape as a field of study and practice in the 1930s, concerns about relationships between education and society had started centuries earlier. One could write a separate essay, for example, on the Herbartian antecedents of NSSE yearbooks with respect to social foundations of education. Although notions of culture and society are mentioned repeatedly in the five volumes of the National Herbart Society, this early approach to notions of culture and society is very different from that which would emerge three decades later. For example, the Herbart Society Yearbooks 1 and 2 pay a great deal of attention to the *cultural epochs* theory of education. However, the cultural epochs theory is a distinctly psychological concept, one that essentially embraces a Herbartian or a G. Stanley Hall notion of the recapitulation of phylogeny—the idea that each individual's development recapitulates the development of the human species through various stages, or cultural epochs, of civilization. When the concept "social" appears, as in DeGarmo's piece in the Third Yearbook on social aspects of moral education, we don't find a study of the social or the cultural context of schooling or of moral education, but rather a notion of the social basis of morality that requires that the individual assimilate to the dominant social order. DeGarmo posits "social versus non-social" individuality, and he claims in the Third Yearbook that only the former is moral from the social standpoint. At least some attention to social context appears here, as DeGarmo attends to the disappearance of the frontier and the growth of the cities as creating a new social context for thinking about moral education.

The author in the Herbart Society who most foreshadows the social foundations of education as it would later emerge is John Dewey. In the Third Yearbook, Dewey contributed a chapter called, "Ethical Principles: Education." He writes, "All ethical theory is two-faced. It requires to be considered from two different points of view and stated in two different sets of terms. These are the social and the psychological. We do not have here a division, however, but simply a distinction." But in the Herbart society yearbooks there was a division; these volumes clearly emphasized the psychological as the basis of the scientific study of education, and social analysis, apart from Dewey's work, was pretty thoroughly neglected.

12. Division I, Foundations of Education, Teachers College, Columbia University, *Readings in the Foundations of Education*, General Editor, Harold Rugg (New York: Bureau of Publications, Teachers College, Columbia University, 1941). Two volumes.

13. Levi Seeley, "The Relation of Theory to Practice in the Training of Teachers," *The Relation of Theory to Practice in Education*, Second Yearbook of the National Society for the Study of Education, Part II, eds. M. J. Holmes, J. A. Keith, and Levi Seeley (Bloomington, IL: Public School Publishing Co., 1903), p. 39.

14. John Dewey, "The Relation of Theory to Practice in Education," *The Relation of Theory to Practice in the Education of Teachers*, Third Yearbook of the National Society for the Study of Education, Part I, eds. John Dewey, Sarah C. Brooks, F. M. McMurray, T. D. Wood, D. E. Smith, C. H. Farnsworth, G. R Richards (Bloomington, IL: Public School Publishing Co., 1904), p. 9.

15. Kenneth A. Sirotnik, "On the Eroding Foundations of Teacher Education," *Phi Delta Kappan* 71:9 (May 1990), pp. 710-716.

16. Levi Seeley, "The Relation of Theory to Practice in the Training of Teachers," p. 39.

17. *Ibid.*, p. 40.

18. John Dewey, "The Relation of Theory to Practice in Education," p. 9.

19. Charles E. Holley, ed., *The Relationship between Persistence in School and Home Conditions*, Fifteenth Yearbook of the National Society for the Study of Education, Part II (Bloomington, IL: Public School Publishing Co., 1916).

20. Charles E. Holley, "Introductory Statement," *The Relationship between Persistence in School and Home Conditions*, Fifteenth Yearbook of the National Society for the Study of Education, Part II, ed. Charles E. Holley (Bloomington, IL: Public School Publishing Co., 1916), p. 9.

21. Holley, "General Summary and Conclusions," in *Ibid.*, p. 96.

22. *Ibid.*, p. 97.

23. *Ibid.*, p. 99.

24. *Ibid.*, p. 100.

25. W. Lloyd Warner, *Social Class in America: A Manual of Procedure for the Measurement of Social Status* (New York: Harper & Brothers, 1949).

26. Holley, "General Summary and Conclusions," p. 101.

27. Harold Rugg, ed., *The Foundations of Curriculum Making*, Twenty-sixth Yearbook of the National Society for the Study of Education, Part II (Bloomington, IL: Public School Publishing Co., 1927).

28. Levi Seeley, *The Foundations of Education* (New York: Hinds and Noble 1901).

29. Guy Whipple, "Preface," *The Foundations of Curriculum Making*, Twenty-sixth Yearbook of the National Society for the Study of Education, Part II, ed. Harold Rugg (Bloomington, IL: Public School Publishing Co., 1927), p. vi.

30. Harold Rugg, "Foreword," in *Ibid.*, vii.

31. Tozer and McAninch, op. cit., page 9. See also the indispensable account of these origins in R. Freeman Butts, *In the First Person Singular: The Social Foundations of Education* (San Francisco, Caddo Gap Press, 1993).

32. Levi Seeley, *The Foundations of Education* (New York: Hinds and Noble 1901).

33. George S. Counts, *The Social Foundations of Education, Report of the Commission on the Social Studies*, Part IX (New York: Charles Scribner's Sons, 1934).

34. Division I, Foundations of Education, Teachers College, Columbia University, *Readings in the Foundations of Education*, General Editor, Harold Rugg (New York: Bureau of Publications, Teachers College, Columbia University, 1941). Two volumes.

35. A. C. Monahan, L. J. Hanifan, J. E. Warren, Wallace Lund, U. J. Hoffman, A. S. Cook, E. M. Rapp, Jackson David, and J. D. Wolcott, eds., *The Supervision of Rural Schools*, Twelfth Yearbook of the National Society for the Study of Education, Part II (Bloomington, IL: Public School Publishing Co., 1913).

36. Council of Learned Societies in Education. (1996). *Standards for Academic and Professional Instruction in Foundations of Education, Educational Studies, and Educational Policy Studies*. Second edition. (San Francisco: Caddo Gap Press).

37. Herbert Kliebard, "What Happened to American Schooling in the First Part of the Twentieth Century?" *Learning and Teaching the Ways of Knowing*, Eighty-fourth Yearbook of the National Society for the Study of Education, Part II, ed. Elliot Eisner (Chicago: National Society for the Study of Education, 1985), pp. 16-17.

38. Ibid., p. 16. Also, Tozer and McAninch, pp. 15-17.

39. Thomas Munro, ed., *Art in American Life and Education*, Fortieth Yearbook of the National Society for the Study of Education (Chicago: National Society for the Study of Education, 1941).

40. John S. Brubacher, ed., *Philosophies of Education*, Forty-first Yearbook of the National Society for the Study of Education, Part I (Chicago: National Society for the Study of Education, 1942).

41. Mortimer Adler, "In Defense of the Philosophy of Education," *Philosophies of Education*, Forty-first Yearbook of the National Society for the Study of Education, Part I, ed. John S. Brubacher (Chicago: National Society for the Study of Education, 1942), p. 246.

42. *Ibid.*, p. 247.

43. Ralph W. Tyler, ed., *American Education in the Post-War Period: Curriculum Reconstruction*, Forty-fourth Yearbook of the National Society for the Study of Education, Part I (Chicago: National Society for the Study of Education, 1945). Bess Goodykoontz, ed., *American Education in the Post-War Period: Structural Reorganization*, Forty-fourth Yearbook of the National Society for the Study of Education, Part II (Chicago: National Society for the Study of Education, 1945).

44. R. W. Tyler, in *American Education in the Post-War Period: Curriculum Reconstruction*, pp. 1-2.

45. T. R. McConnell, ed., *General Education*, Fifty-first Yearbook of the National Society for the Study of Education, Part I (Chicago: National Society for the Study of Education, 1952). Ruth Strang, ed., *Education in Rural Communities*, Fifty-first Yearbook of the National Society for the Study of Education, Part II (Chicago: National Society for the Study of Education, 1952). William G. Brink, ed., *Adapting the Secondary School Program to the Needs of Youth*, Fifty-second Yearbook of the National Society for the Study of Education, Part I (Chicago: National Society for the Study of Education, 1953). Edgar L. Morphet, ed., *Citizen Cooperation for Better Public Schools*, Fifty-third Yearbook of the National Society for the Study of Education, Part I (Chicago: National Society for the Study of Education, 1954).

46. Robert J. Havighurst and Bernice L. Neugarten, *Society and Education* (Boston: Allyn and Bacon, 1957). Also see Tozer and McAninch, p. 31.

47. B. O. Smith, W. O. Stanley, K. D. Benne and A. W. Anderson, *Social Foundations of Education* (New York: Holt, Rinehart, and Winston 1956). Harold Rugg and William Withers, *Social Foundations of Education* (New York: Prentice-Hall, Inc. 1955).

48. Ralph W. Tyler, ed., *Social Forces Influencing American Education*, Sixtieth Yearbook of the National Society for the Study of Education, Part II (Chicago: National Society for the Study of Education, 1953).

49. Robert J. Havighurst, "Social Class Influences on American Education," *Social Forces Influencing American Education*, Sixtieth Yearbook of the National Society for the Study of Education, Part II, ed. Ralph W. Tyler (Chicago: National Society for the Study of Education, 1953), pp. 120-142.

50. *Ibid.*, p. 127.

51. *Ibid.*, p. 143.

52. *Ibid.*, p. 143.

53. Robert J. Havighurst, "Introduction," *Metropolitanism: Its Challenge to Education*, Sixty-seventh Yearbook of the National Society for the Study of Education, Part II, ed. Robert J. Havighurst (Chicago: National Society for the Study of Education, 1953), p. 4.

54. Today, CLSE has changed its name to the more straightforward Council for Social Foundations of Education and is the official voice of other foundational organizations (e.g., History of Education Society, Philosophy of Education Society, AESA) in the governing structure of the National Council for Accreditation of Teacher Education.

55. Steve Tozer, "Toward a New Consensus among Social Foundations Educators: Draft Position Paper of the American Educational Studies Association Committee on Academic Standards and Accreditation." *Educational Foundations* 6:4 (1993), pp. 5-22.

56. Robert M. McClure, ed., *The Curriculum: Retrospect and Prospect*, Seventieth Yearbook of the National Society for the Study of Education, Part I (Chicago: National Society for the Study of Education, 1971).

57. John I. Goodlad and Harold G. Shane, eds., *Elementary Schooling in the United States*, Seventy-second Yearbook of the National Society for the Study of Education, Part II (Chicago: National Society for the Study of Education, 1973).

58. Jay D. Scribner and Owen Knox, "The Urban Elementary School Today," *Elementary Schooling in the United States*, Seventy-second Yearbook of the National Society for the Study of Education, Part II, p. 327.

59. David R. Olson, ed., *Media and Symbols: the Forms of Expression, Communication, and Education*, Seventy-third Yearbook of the National Society for the Study of Education, Part I (Chicago: National Society for the Study of Education, 1974).

60. Kathy Hytten, "Cultural Studies in Education: Mapping the Terrain." *Educational Foundations* (Fall 1997), pp. 39-60; and Kathy Hytten, "The Promise of Cultural Studies of Education," *Educational Theory* 49:4 (Fall 1999), pp. 527-43.

61. C. Wayne Gordon, ed., *Uses of Sociology of Education*, Seventy-third Yearbook of the National Society for the Study of Education, Part II (Chicago: National Society for the Study of Education, 1974).

62. Joseph Katz, "The Psychology of Student Protest," *Uses of Sociology of Education*, Seventy-third Yearbook of the National Society for the Study of Education, Part II (Chicago: National Society for the Study of Education, 1974), pp. 3-16.

63. Ralph W. Larkin, "Protest and Counterculture: Disaffection Among Affluent Youth," *Uses of Sociology of Education*, Seventy-third Yearbook of the National Society for the Study of Education, Part II, ed. C. Wayne Gordon (Chicago: National Society for the Study of Education, 1974), pp. 17-35.

64. Thomas A. LaBelle, "Youth as Sociocultural Systems in American Society," *Uses of Sociology of Education*, Seventy-third Yearbook of the National Society for the Study of Education, Part II, ed. C. Wayne Gordon (Chicago: National Society for the Study of Education, 1974), pp. 78-99.

65. Tozer and McAninch, "Four Texts in Social Foundations of Education in Historical Perspective," *Educational Studies* 18:1 (Spring 1987), p. 21.

66. Charles U. Smith and Charles M. Grigg, "Public School Desegregation in the South," *Uses of Sociology of Education*, Seventy-third Yearbook of the National Society of the Study of Education, Part II, ed. C. Wayne Gordon (Chicago: National Society for the Study of Education, 1974), pp. 330-379.

67. Harry F. Silberman, ed., *Education and Work*, Eighty-first Yearbook of the National Society for the Study of Education, Part II (Chicago: National Society for the Study of Education, 1982). Alan C. Purves and Olive S. Niles, eds., *Becoming Readers in a Complex Society*, Eighty-third Yearbook of the National Society for the Study of Education, Part I (Chicago: National Society for the Study of Education, 1984). Mario d. Fantini and Robert Sinclair, eds., *Education in School and Non-School Settings*, Eighty-fourth Yearbook of the National Society for the Study of Education, Part I (Chicago: National Society for the Study of Education, 1985). Ian Westbury and Alan C. Purves, eds., *Cultural Literacy and the Idea of a General Education*, Eighty-seventh Yearbook of the National Society for the Study of Education, Part II (Chicago: National Society for the Study of Education, 1988). Philip W. Jackson and Sophie Haroutunian-Gordon, eds., *From Socrates to Software: The Teacher as Text and the Text as Teacher*, Eighty-eighth Yearbook of the National Society for the Study of Education, Part I (Chicago: National Society for the Study of Education, 1989).

68. Jonas Soltis, ed., *Philosophy and Education*, Eightieth Yearbook of the National Society for the Study of Education, Part I (Chicago: National Society for the Study of Education, 1981).

69. Jane Roland Martin, "Needed: A Paradigm for Liberal Education," *Ibid.*, pp. 37-59. Donna Kerr, "The Structure of Quality in Teaching," *Ibid.*, pp. 61-93. Maxine Greene, "Aesthetic Literacy in General Education," *Ibid.*, pp. 115-41. Robert H. Ennis, "Rational Thinking and Educational Practice," *Ibid.*, pp. 143-83.

70. Ann Lieberman and Milbrey W. McLaughlin, eds., *Policy Making in Education*, Eighty-first Yearbook of the National Society for the Study of Education, Part I (Chicago: National Society for the Study of Education, 1982).

71. Elliot Eisner, ed., *Learning and Teaching the Ways of Knowing*, Eighty-fourth Yearbook of the National Society for the Study of Education, Part I (Chicago: National Society for the Study of Education, 1985).

72. Kenneth D. Benne and Steve Tozer, eds., *Society as Educator in an Age of Transition*, Eighty-sixth Yearbook of the National Society for the Study of Education, Part II (Chicago: National Society for the Study of Education, 1988).

73. Harry Broudy, "Becoming Educated in Contemporary Society," *Society as Educator in an Age of Transition*, Eighty-sixth Yearbook of the National Society for the Study of Education, Part II, eds. Kenneth D. Benne and Steve Tozer (Chicago: National Society for the Study of Education, 1988), pp. 264-265.

74. Brad Mitchell and Luvern L. Cunningham, eds., *Educational Leadership and Changing Contexts of Families, Communities, and Schools*, Eighty-ninth Yearbook of the National Society for the Study of Education, Part II (Chicago: National Society for the Study of Education, 1990). Sharon L. Kagan, ed., *The Care and Education of America's Young Children: Obstacles and Opportunities*, Ninetieth Yearbook of the National Society for the Study of Education, Part II (Chicago: National Society for the Study of Education, 1991). Ann Lieberman, ed., *The Changing Contexts of Teaching*, Ninety-first Yearbook of the National Society for the Study of Education, Part I (Chicago: National Society for the Study of Education, 1992). Bennett Reimer and Ralph A. Smith, eds., *The Arts, Education and Aesthetic Knowing*, Ninety-first Yearbook of the National Society for the Study of Education, Part II (Chicago: National Society for the Study of Education, 1992).

75. D. C. Phillips, ed., *Constructivism in Education*, Ninety-Ninth Yearbook of the National Society for the Study of Education, Part I (Chicago: National Society for the Study of Education, 2000). Thomas Good, ed., *American Education: Yesterday, Today, and Tomorrow*, Ninety-ninth Yearbook of the National Society for the Study of Education, Part II (Chicago: National Society for the Study of Education, 2000).

76. Simon During, "Introduction," *The Cultural Studies Reader*, Second Edition, ed. Simon During (London: Routledge, 1999), p. 24.

77. *Ibid.*, p. 25.

78. Henry Giroux and Peter McLaren, "Acknowledgements," *Between Borders: Pedagogy and the Politics of Cultural Studies*, eds. Henry Giroux and Peter McLaren (London: Routledge, 1994), p. ix. For two recent analyses of the growth of cultural studies on educational theorizing, see Kathy Hytten, "Cultural Studies in Education: Mapping the Terrain," op. cit.

79. Stuart Hall, "Cultural Studies and its Theoretical Legacies," *The Cultural Studies Reader*, Second Edition, ed. Simon During (London: Routledge, 1999), pp. 108-9.

Name Index

N.B. The Notes at the end of each chapter have not been indexed.

Subject Index

N.B. The Notes at the end of each chapter have not been indexed.

RECENT PUBLICATIONS OF THE SOCIETY

1. The Yearbooks

100:1 (2001) *Education Across a Century: The Centennial Volume.* Lyn Corno, editor. Cloth.

100:2 (2001) *From Capitol to the Cloakroom: Standards-based Reform in the States.* Susan H. Fuhrman, editor. Cloth.

99:1 (2000) *Constructivism in Education.* D. C. Phillips, editor. Cloth.

99:2 (2000) *American Education: Yesterday, Today, and Tomorrow.* Thomas L. Good, editor. Cloth.

98:1 (1999) *The Education of Teachers*, Gary A. Griffin, editor. Cloth.

98:2 (1999) *Issues in Curriculum*, Margaret J. Early and Kenneth J. Rehage, editors. Cloth.

97:1 (1998) *The Adolescent Years: Social Influences and Educational Challenges.* Kathryn Borman and Barbara Schneider, editors. Cloth.

97:2 (1998) *The Reading-Writing Connection.* Nancy Nelson and Robert C. Calfee, editors. Cloth.

96:1 (1997) *Service Learning.* Joan Schine, editor. Cloth.

96:2 (1997) *The Construction of Children's Character.* Alex Molnar, editor. Cloth.

95:1 (1996) *Performance-Based Student Assessment: Challenges and Possibilities.* Joan B. Baron and Dennie P. Wolf, editors. Cloth.

95:2 (1996) *Technology and the Future of Schooling.* Stephen T. Kerr, editor. Cloth.

94:1 (1995) *Creating New Educational Communities.* Jeannie Oakes and Karen Hunter Quartz, editors. Cloth.

94:2 (1995) *Changing Populations/Changing Schools.* Erwin Flaxman and A. Harry Passow, editors. Cloth.

93:1 (1994) *Teacher Research and Educational Reform.* Sandra Hollingsworth and Hugh Sockett, editors. Cloth.

93:2 (1994) *Bloom's Taxonomy: A Forty-year Retrospective.* Lorin W. Anderson and Lauren A. Sosniak, editors. Cloth.

92:1 (1993) *Gender and Education.* Sari Knopp Biklen and Diane Pollard, editors. Cloth.

92:2 (1993) *Bilingual Education: Politics, Practice, and Research.* M. Beatriz Arias and Ursula Casanova, editors. Cloth.

91:1 (1992) *The Changing Contexts of Teaching.* Ann Lieberman, editor. Cloth.

91:2 (1992) *The Arts, Education, and Aesthetic Knowing.* Bennett Reimer and Ralph A. Smith, editors. Cloth.

89:1 (1990) *From Socrates to Software: The Teacher as Text and the Text as Teacher.* Philip W. Jackson and Sophie Haroutunian-Gordon, editors. Cloth.

89:2 (1990) *Educational Leadership and Changing Contexts of Families, Communities, and Schools.* Brad Mitchell and Luvern L. Cunningham, editors. Paper.

Order the above titles from the University of Chicago Press, 11030 S. Langley Ave., Chicago, IL 60628. For a list of earlier Yearbooks still available, write to the Secretary, NSSE, University of Illinois at Chicago, College of Education, MC 147, 1040 W. Harrison, Chicago, IL 60607.

2. The Series on Contemporary Educational Issues

This series has been discontinued.

The following volumes in the series may be ordered from the McCutchan Publishing Corporation, P.O. Box 774, Berkeley, CA 94702-0774. Phone: 510-841-8616; Fax: 510-841-7787.

Academic Work and Educational Excellence: Raising Student Productivity (1986). Edited by Tommy M. Tomlinson and Herbert J. Walberg.
Adapting Instruction to Student Differences (1985). Edited by Margaret C. Wang and Herbert J. Walberg.
Choice in Education (1990). Edited by William Lowe Boyd and Herbert J. Walberg.
Colleges of Education: Perspectives on Their Future (1985). Edited by Charles W. Case and William A. Matthes.
Contributing to Educational Change: Perspectives on Research and Practice (1988). Edited by Philip W. Jackson.
Effective Teaching: Current Research (1991). Edited by Hersholt C. Waxman and Herbert J. Walberg.
Moral Development and Character Education (1989). Edited by Larry P. Nucci.
Motivating Students to Learn: Overcoming Barriers to High Achievement (1993). Edited by Tommy M. Tomlinson.
Radical Proposals for Educational Change (1994). Edited by Chester E. Finn, Jr. and Herbert J. Walberg.
Reaching Marginal Students: A Prime Concern for School Renewal (1987). Edited by Robert L. Sinclair and Ward Ghory.
Restructuring the Schools: Problems and Prospects (1992). Edited by John J. Lane and Edgar G. Epps.
Rethinking Policy for At-risk Students (1994). Edited by Kenneth K. Wong and Margaret C. Wang.
School Boards: Changing Local Control (1992). Edited by Patricia F. First and Herbert J. Walberg.

The two final volumes in this series were:

Improving Science Education (1995). Edited by Barry J. Fraser and Herbert J. Walberg.
Ferment in Education: A Look Abroad (1995). Edited by John J. Lane.

These two volumes may be ordered from the Book Order Department, University of Chicago Press, 11030 S. Langley Ave., Chicago, IL 60628. Phone: 312-669-2215; Fax: 312-660-2235.